Singing for the Dead

D1649012

Singing for the Dead

THE

POLITICS OF

INDIGENOUS

REVIVAL

IN MEXICO

Paja Faudree

DUKE UNIVERSITY PRESS

Durham and London   2013

Designed by Amy Ruth Buchanan
Typeset in Quadraat and Quadraat
Sans by Tseng Information Systems, Inc.

Duke University Press gratefully acknowledges
the support of the Faculty Development Fund
at Brown University, which provided funds
toward the publication of the book.

Library of Congress Cataloging-in-
Publication Data
Faudree, Paja.
Singing for the dead : the politics of indigenous
revival in Mexico / Paja Faudree.
pages cm
Includes bibliographical references and index.
ISBN 978-0-8223-5416-1 (cloth : alk. paper)
ISBN 978-0-8223-5431-4 (pbk. : alk. paper)
1. Mazatec Indians—Songs and music.
2. Mazatec Indians—Political activity.
3. Mazatec Indians—Ethnic identity.
4. All Souls' Day—Mexico. I. Title.
F1221.M35F38 2013
305.897′6—dc23 2013003136

TO MICAH AND DAHLIA

I hope you will sing for me

once I, too, am living in

the land of the dead.

Contents

Acknowledgments

This book is at least in part about the repayment of debts—above all, those the living owe the dead. Although I am fortunate that most of those who helped me the most have not yet "shed their bodies" (a literal translation of a Mazatec expression for dying), I nevertheless incurred enormous debts in writing this book. Beginning with the most recent, I thank Brown University, and especially the Department of Anthropology, for their support as I was revising the book and seeking a publisher. Special thanks go to Jen Ashley, Marcy Brink-Danan, Deborah Cohen, Bianca Dahl, Lina Fruzzetti, Matt Gutmann, Susan Ellison, Sherine Hamdy, Marida Hollos, Steve Houston, Karl Jacoby, David Kertzer, Yukiko Koga, Marie Lee, Jessaca Leinaweaver, Cathy Lutz, Kiri Miller, Kathleen Millar, Rhacel Parreñas, Marc Perlman, Pat Rubertone, Vanessa Ryan, Wendy Schiller, Bill Simmons, Dan Smith, Michael Steinberg, Pat Symonds, Joshua Tucker, and Kay Warren for commenting on drafts and sharing their knowledge of the publication process. I also thank Shay O'Brien, who at each stage of preparing this book proved herself the most competent, intelligent assistant I could have asked for. And I am extremely grateful to Matilde Andrade, Kathy Grimaldi, and Margie Sugrue, who on a daily basis helped make my job and my life easier.

I was also very fortunate in having supportive mentors and peers at two other institutions: the University of Chicago, where I spent a marvelous year as a Harper-Schmidt postdoctoral fellow before coming to Brown and where I also spent considerable time as a doctoral student, and the University of Pennsylvania, where I completed my doctorate. I have no doubt that, whatever its flaws, this book is immeasurably better for the time I spent immersed in the intellectual lives of both universities. Special thanks go to Asif Agha, Deborah Augsburger, Amahl Bishara, Summerson Carr, Jessica Cattelino, Mike Cepek, John and Jean Comaroff, Cherai Cotton, Hilary Dick, Nancy Farriss, Sue Gal, Rob Hamrick, Wendi Haugh, Reha Kadakal, Webb Keane, Paul Kockelman, John Lucy, Tanya Luhrmann, Paul Manning, Alex Mawyer,

Sevda Numanbayraktoroglu, Brian and Tara Schweger, Stephen Scott, Olga Sezneva, Robin Shoaps, Michael Silverstein, Dan Suslak, Tanya Taylor, Gary Tomlinson, Joshua Tucker, Greg Urban, Bob Vitalis, Hylton White, and Karin Zitzewitz. Some of these were participants in the "Colonial Dialogues" seminar, which has profoundly affected my thinking; other people from that group to whom I am indebted include Charles Briggs, Tom Cummins, Bill Hanks, and Joanne Rappaport. I also thank two scholars associated with Penn, Chicago, and "Colonial Dialogues" whose work and personal friendship influenced me more than either will ever know, in part because both passed away before their time: Luis Castro Leiva and Michel-Rolph Trouillot.

I was fortunate that the research on which this book is based was generously funded. Initial research consisted of thirty-six months of field research conducted in Oaxaca, Mexico. I thank the organizations that made this research possible financially: the Social Science Research Council; the U.S. Department of Education, which awarded me a Fulbright-Hays fellowship; the Wenner Gren Foundation; the University of Pennsylvania, which awarded me summer and year-long fieldwork grants and fellowship support for the entirety of my doctorate; and the Ford Foundation. Follow-up research was funded by a Fulbright Senior Scholar Research grant and a Salomon Research Grant from Brown University.

My experience with Duke University Press and its staff has been consistently delightful. I am especially grateful to have had such a wonderful pair of editors, Valerie Millholland and Gisela Fosado. I am also grateful to Lynn Stephen and Yanna Yannakakis, who were anonymous reviewers until after the review process ran its course. Their extensive, generous, detailed comments on the book have made it immeasurably better.

I am also profoundly indebted to the many people in Mexico who helped make this book a reality. In Yalálag, I thank Joel Aquino, the extended Aquino family, the late Mario Molina Cruz, and members of Uken Ke Uken. I thank in particular Juana Vazquez and the entire Vazquez family, who took me in with such hospitality when I first decided to work in Oaxaca and have treated me with love ever since. In the Sierra Mazateca, I thank Edward Abse, who first directed me to Florencio Carrera; Maestro Florencio, who directed me to Nda Xo; and various other people from the Mazatec region at large who helped me along the way, including Juan Garcia Carrera, Juan Casimiro Nava, and Juan Gregorio Regino. In Nda Xo, I thank the authorities for their support; beyond that, there are far more people to thank than I could recognize here, and as most are not public figures, I will not name them to protect their anonymity. Special thanks to my *compadres* and their extended family in Naxrin

Ča, the people of Amatlán and Nangui Ni (particularly the families in each community who invited me to live with them), and the entire extended Prado family in the Nda Xo *cabecera*—especially, of course, Alberto Prado and Heriberto Prado and their immediate families, who are all now close friends. They have made not only my work but my life incalculably richer. In Oaxaca (city), I thank the Centro de Investigaciones y Estudios Superiores en Antropología Social (CIESAS)–Pacifo Sur, the Instituto Nacional de Antropología e Historia (INAH), and the Centro Académico y Cultural San Pablo, which at various times supported me as a visiting researcher.

Other people in the city who were especially helpful to me include Juan Carlos Acuña; Ramiz Adeeb Azar; Flor Cervantes; Diana Fasen; Derek Frazier; Gaby García García; Aracely Gil; Lourdes Gutierrez; Xilonen Luna; Tere Pardo; Zenon Ramírez and his wife, Yolanda; Noemi Sánchez; Ben Smith; Michael and Ingrid Swanton; Lucero Topete; and Bas Van Doesburg. I am especially indebted to Manuel Esparza and Angeles Romero, who from my first days in Oaxaca not only have offered intellectual support and companionship but have been unfailingly generous in their emotional and logistic support, as well—a *convivia* of the highest order that only deepened once their daughter Angela and her husband, Mark Dillon, become close friends and sources of support for my family. Finally, everywhere I have lived in Oaxaca, I have been fortunate to be surrounded by wonderful kids, some of whom are now adults. Their playfulness and relentless questions have saved me from the worst excesses of my personality while teaching me to see the world around me in new ways: Aby, Aldair, Alma, Arturo, Beto, Bety, Camilo, Chucho, Emilia, Emilio, Esteban, Fidencio, Kian, Jose Luis, Misael, Nayeli, Neyla, Omar, Oziel, Rocío, Sawyer, Valentina, and Yunitza.

Most of all, I thank my family and close friends, among whom I include many of those thanked earlier. Those not already mentioned include Rui Da Silva, Josh and Jocelyn Kreiss, Kanthi Krishnamurthy, Paul Magwene, Rosemary Masters, Melissa Murphy, Beatriz Reifkohl, and Rachel Snyder. And, of course, members of my family deserve special mention because they had no choice but to put up with me, however insufferable I became while writing this book: my parents, Ralph and Pat; my sister, Jill; my brother-in-law, Ed; my niece and nephew, Thomas and Vera; my in-laws, the extended Woodward family; and above all, *mi hombre*, Daniel, and our two kids, Micah and Dahlia. I would never have been able to write this book without your support and love.

Thank you so much, all of you, for everything you did to make this book possible.

Note on Orthographic
and Linguistic Conventions

An argument I make in this book is that one of the revival movements discussed, the Day of the Dead Song Contest, has broad popular appeal in part because it embraces orthographic heterodoxy. In contradistinction to many other movements promoting vernacular literacy, this project promotes the idea that people should be allowed to write their languages using whatever alphabetic conventions suited them best. This move implicitly disentangles two aspects of vernacular writing that are often treated as coextensive: orthographic standardization and orthographic consistency. Taking my cue from the song contest's approach to writing Mazatec, I stress internal consistency in how I write the language while insisting that the orthographic conventions I have chosen are necessarily arbitrary and not inherently superior to others. Those I use in this book are based largely on the standard orthographic conventions of Latin American Spanish. (See tables Note.1 and Note.2 for the alphabet used in this book.) These conventions are also based on those widely used by indigenous writers—though, as I describe in this book, there is no universally accepted alphabet for writing Mazatec and native writers' orthographies often conflict.

The symbols in parentheses represent sounds that occur only in Spanish loan words commonly used in Mazatec speech. The symbol *x* is used here as it is often used in indigenous Mesoamerican languages: to refer to the sound that in English would be represented by *sh*. When an *x* appears before a vowel, its pronunciation is very retroflexed and sounds almost like *xr* (or *shr* in English); before a consonant, the retroflexion is more subtle. The symbol *č* indicates the retroflexed form of *ch*; the retroflexion causes it to sound somewhat like *chr*, a sound Mazatec speakers refer to as "almost whistled." The symbol *j* represents a sound like *h* in English—softer than the sound represented by a Spanish *j*. The symbol *ñ* is used, as in Spanish, to refer to the sound that in English might be represented by *ny*.

Mazatec has four vowels, all of which are voiced. Each also exists in nasal-

TABLE NOTE.1. Mazatec consonants

	Labial	Alveolar	Alveolar Palatal	Retroflexed Alveolar-palatal	Palatal	Velar	Glottal
Stops							
voiceless	(p)	t				k	'
voiced	(b)	(d)					
Affricates							
voiceless		ts	ch	č			
Fricatives							
voiceless	f	s		x			j
voiced	v						
Nasals							
voiced	m	n			ñ		
Lateral		l					
Flap		r					
Trill		(rr)					
Glide			y				

ized form, indicated by adding the symbol n after the vowel. The nonnasal-ized forms mirror the corresponding vowels in Spanish — that is, i represents what to English speakers sounds like a long e (as in me). The symbols o and on vary freely from high back rounded to low back rounded without contrasting.

Finally, Mazatec is a tonal language, with four distinct pitch levels. The tonality of the language has facilitated the development of a whistled regis-ter, well-known among linguists, in which people whistle utterances to each other using tonal patterns whose contours follow the tones of the spoken language. The levels are numbered 1–4, with 1 being the highest in pitch and 4 the lowest. Note that while Mazatec intellectuals who mark for tone often use this convention, as does the Summer Institute of Linguistics (SIL), this diverges from conventions that academic linguists often use. Tone levels are represented by numeric superscripts following a syllable, a convention that is used not only by the SIL, which has published much basic linguistic research on indigenous languages, but also by indigenous authors. Combinations of numbers on a single syllable represent glides in which the tone shifts from one level to another. The actual pitch of any given tone depends in part on the tones that precede and follow it. Tone is extremely important in Mazatec and

TABLE NOTE.2. Mazatec vowels

	Front unrounded	Central unrounded	Back rounded
High	i, in		
Mid	e, en		o, on
Low		a, an	

serves to make lexical, grammatical, and syntactic distinctions. In the text, I give tones at the first instance of a given word or phrase and omit them thereafter, unless tone is directly relevant to the matter discussed. This is similar to what most native speakers do when writing Mazatec: they rarely indicate tone except when failing to do so is likely to produce confusion. In most cases, they leave the reader to resolve ambiguities by context.

When excerpting indigenous authors' work, unless noted otherwise, I have preserved their orthographic decisions. If I give the Spanish version of an indigenous language text, it is the author's own. All translations into English, unless noted otherwise, are mine.

Introduction

LEAVING THE PUEBLO

Years ago, when I left the pueblo, . . . the senior elder, charged with offering wisdom, spoke: . . .

> "When you come back, my son, perhaps we will no longer be alive. . . .
> Probably by then you will not be the same, you will have distanced your-
> self from us, you will not continue with our way of life. I hope that you
> are never embarrassed of our pueblo or of your people. . . . Leave us to
> go on here, where our ancestors are. We will suffer the rest of our lives
> for failing to keep you here with us."

—Mario Molina Cruz, poet from Yalálag, from the poem "The Tortilla
Tastes Bitter (Leaving the Pueblo)," in *El Volcan de Petalos/Ya 'byalhje xtak yeje*

A Tale of Two Pueblos: Toward a New View of Political Violence

Two months after I began research for this book in the Zapotec town of Yalálag, in Mexico's Oaxaca State, a man named Roberto Limeta Mestas was
killed.[1] According to half of the town, he was murdered by his political enemies. According to the other half, he was the victim of so-called friendly
fire, killed not by those he was fighting against but by his own compatriots,
who shot him by accident. He and others on the same side of the town's
longstanding political divide were indeed carrying firearms that day: they
were guarding the town hall against their enemies on the town's "other side."
Since the beginning of the year 2000, when the new authorities should have
been sworn in, the town had been in the midst of a tense standoff tied to
the annual elections. All municipal offices, from the president to the police
officers, had been vehemently contested along a political fault line that has
divided the town for more than a century. A couple of months into the new
year, despite frequent appeals to state officials for intervention, the problem
remained unresolved.

The group that Limeta Mestas belonged to, claiming to be the rightful winners of the election, held the municipal buildings by force. The opposing group included the family I lived with and everyone else I knew in town, among them leaders well known nationally for their work in defense of indigenous rights. They continued to call the possession of the municipal buildings illegitimate. One day in March 2000, in the dark hours of the morning, men from the group that opposed Limeta Mestas's faction became fed up with the stalemate. They decided to take back the town hall. Just before dawn, they staged an attack on the men guarding it—armed, according to them, with sticks but no guns.

A violent struggle followed. Several people from both sides were hurt, but Limeta Mestas was the only one who died. In the aftermath, the town filled with state troops and lived under martial law; for months afterward, the political crisis in Yalálag made state and national news. Dozens of suspects spent more than a month languishing in jail, then months more trying to exit the judicial quagmire into which they had fallen. People on both sides were afraid of reprisals and left town to live with relatives; many stayed away for the rest of the year.

Yalálag's political divisions are longstanding and deep. Of the numerous scholars who have conducted research on the town, all comment on Yalálag's entrenched factionalism. Works on the town include Julio de la Fuente's classic ethnography documenting both internal and intervillage conflicts (de la Fuente 1949); Lourdes Gutiérrez Najera's more recent ethnography, in which her informants repeatedly told her, "Yalálag's history is a history of conflict" (Gutiérrez Najera 2007: 16); and Peter Guardino's history of political culture in Oaxaca, in which his periodic mentions of Yalálag describe more than a century of disputes and conflicts (Guardino 2005: 227, 243, 245, 248). Nonetheless, after this particular event, the hostility in town was more open and bitter than it had been in decades. This reinscription of longstanding factionalism had a profound and pervasive impact on how people lived their daily lives: which stores they visited, which telephone kiosks they used, which paths they took through town, whom they spoke to and whom they refused to greet, what they discussed, and whom they sat next to and—conversely—avoided on the buses in and out of town.

I never met the man who died. Even if I had, he probably would have refused to speak to me, writing me off as a committed partisan biased by my close friendships with people from the opposing faction. Nevertheless, his death and the political crisis surrounding it affected me directly: my plans to conduct research in Yalálag on revival activities tied to the Zapotec language ultimately became impossible to pursue. More important, though, Limeta Mestas's death contains a powerful lesson about how political violence is routinely conceptualized: what typical accounts of ethnic conflict stress and, just as crucial, what they often elide and render invisible.

From a statistical point of view, Limeta Mestas's death was but one of hundreds of politically motivated deaths that occur each year in indigenous communities in Oaxaca alone. There is no official accounting of the phenomenon, but incidents of lethal violence in indigenous settlements appear nearly daily in the state newspaper. Anthropological depictions of the region frequently have stressed its endemic violence; proportionate to the overall population, the murder rate in many indigenous communities exceeds homicide levels in some of America's most violent inner cities (see Greenberg 1989).[2] Yet it is precisely because this single death forms part of a larger pattern of violence that it is of broader significance. Furthermore, its importance goes beyond the most commonly proposed reasons for such violence: centuries of institutionalized exploitation, structural poverty, and new social and economic pressures linked to globalization and neoliberal land reforms, among others. Rather, the issues at stake that day when the two groups fought each other in the dark in front of the town hall included many aspects of social life that rarely appear in accounts explaining the occurrence of violence.

One of the least publicized casualties of the conflict was a cultural revitalization movement then taking place in Yalálag. It unfolded under the auspices of an organization called Uken Ke Uken, or the Center for the Study and Development of the Zapotec Language and Tradition. The projects introduced by this relatively recent addition to Yalálag's cultural landscape included a language workshop promoting Zapotec literacy and producing Zapotec texts, a municipal brass and wind band that performed for town fiestas, a cultural center promoting a variety of activities that included instruction for children and adults in how to read and play music, and a municipal radio station with Zapotec-language programming.[3] Until the political crisis attached to the municipal elections, all of the activities had been housed at the town hall. The center's leaders claimed that holding its activities in the town hall allowed them to be fully communitarian, open to participation by any and all. Given the town's entrenched political divisions, however, it is not surprising that this view was not universally held. Members of Limeta Mestas's group opposed the activities as partisan and shut them down once they took control of the town hall at the beginning of the year.

This attempt at cultural revival, then, was directly involved in the violent altercation that took place at the town hall. Several of Uken Ke Uken's leaders were among the lead suspects in Limeta Mestas's death. The legal and financial hardships they faced after the attack meant that for the rest of that year, and for much of the year that followed, they were unable to even begin seriously discussing, let alone acting on, plans to continue with the center's activities. Not until years had passed was Uken Ke Uken as a group able to tackle its internal disagreements about how best to realize the center's vision. It took years before they were able to resolve the problem of whether or not to go on with the center's plans, even if they could not do so as part of the official local government. Once the group made the difficult decision to proceed outside formal municipal support, it faced the long process of acquiring the necessary resources to support the center's activities and build a new structure to house it.

As the political crisis in Yalálag wore on, I began looking for a new site where I could research linguistic revival. I focused on other communities in Oaxaca State, one of the world's most culturally diverse regions. Officially, Oaxaca has sixteen distinct indigenous groups living in an area roughly the size of Indiana.[4] Most of the groups speak languages with multiple mutually unintelligible variants, a level of internal variation that is dramatically greater than that found in some other Mexican indigenous languages.[5] For example, the Instituto Nacional de Lenguas Indígenas (National Institute of Indigenous Languages; INALI) claims that the two largest Oaxacan language groups each have more than sixty variants (sixty-two for Zapotec and eighty-one for Mixtec) and lists sixteen variants for Mazatec, the third-largest linguistic group. By contrast, Yucatec Maya, the country's second-largest group, has only one variant (INALI 2008a).

Eventually, I found my way to Nda Xo, a small town perched on the edge of a deep canyon in the Sierra Mazateca.[6] Like Yalálag, it is home to various local projects aimed at cultural and linguistic revival. While the projects in the two towns are similar—and somewhat unusual nationally—in being linked to music, on this point they also differ in one significant way: Yalálag's communal music program is directed at instrumental music played by the town's wind bands, tied, in turn, to literacy in Western musical notation. Thus, this aspect of the initiative is not an indigenous revival project (although it is institutionally and practically enmeshed with many activities that are), nor does it directly support the indigenous language. Given that the medium of instruction and much of the communication for the band's activities take place in Spanish, such musical practices arguably operate at the *expense* of the indigenous language. By contrast, Nda Xo's revival projects are based on singing in the indigenous language, Mazatec, rather than in Spanish. These musical practices not only bolster the use of Mazatec, but they also expand its use into new realms while recruiting new speakers: young people who grow up hearing Mazatec but do not speak it. Yet a result of the revival projects I describe here, they are now beginning to sing in the language. As I discuss further, the broad—and in many ways, remarkable—success of these Mazatec revival projects is also intimately bound to the strategic use of singing across a range of contexts.

In other respects, though, Yalálag and Nda Xo are remarkably alike. Both towns are deeply divided politically, and competing ideas about indigenous language and culture are thoroughly implicated in longstanding political tensions. The two towns are also similar to each other—and unlike many other indigenous communities—in that the revival initiatives are widely popular. In my hunt for a new field site, I was surprised to learn that communities where revival movements have substantial appeal beyond the indigenous leaders spearheading them are relatively rare. Instead, revival initiatives often remain the pursuit of educated elites. I will have more to say in due course about why this is so, but what I repeatedly encountered at that time was the tendency for indigenous writers and activists who promote revival projects to live in regional cities rather than in the indigenous communities from which they hail—driven there, ironically, by the same economic forces that cause the cultural erosion against which revival movements fight.

Such forces touch ground in indigenous communities across Mexico, nowhere more so than in Oaxaca, Mexico's poorest state and, not coincidentally, its most indigenous (see map I.1; see table I.1).[7] Oaxaca is filled with the kind of communities that have been hit hardest by the negative effects of globalization and the neoliberal restructuring measures of the 1980s and 1990s. With few exceptions, the cornerstone of rural Mexico's economy until that time was overwhelmingly agricultural; maize was far and away the most important crop. With the elimination of farm subsidies and the reversal of postrevolutionary measures aimed at protecting—and co-opting—the rural peasantry, indigenous farmers were forced to compete on the free market as never before. Once the North American Free Trade Agreement (NAFTA) passed, the fate of Oaxaca's farmers became increasingly linked to U.S. markets, where corn remains heavily subsidized by the federal government.

As a result, the small-scale agriculture pursued by indigenous communities has become dramatically less viable since the economic crisis of the 1980s. Out-migration, now spanning generations, has been a widespread response, as people leave the pueblo in search of work elsewhere. Oaxaca has been at the leading edge of this trend, with one of the highest rates of domes-

MAP I.1. The country of Mexico (officially, the United States of Mexico), showing Oaxaca State and the major regional cities discussed in the book.

tic and international migration in the country.[8] Although Yalálag is a small town by American standards, it is the largest in the Sierra Norte; only half of its 5,000 citizens are permanent residents — roughly 2,500 live in Yalálag permanently, while roughly 2,500 live in the United States, mostly in Los Angeles. According to locals interviewed by journalists following the confrontation at the town hall, 80 percent of young men leave the community, primarily for economic reasons, although also to pursue educational opportunities.[9]

These migration patterns have material effects, no less for indigenous writers than for indigenous farmers. One effect is that language revival movements in Mexico frequently play out in regional and national urban centers and, ironically, unfold less frequently in the rural, indigenous communities where indigenous languages remain the primary medium of communication. In communities where such movements do become part of quotidian life, they become enmeshed with other communitarian issues and invariably are implicated in political divisions. Certainly this was true of the confrontation taking place in Yalálag. As the two groups fought each other that morning in front of the town hall, their bloodied hands dragged Yalálag's divisive past

TABLE I.1. States in Mexico with the highest percentage
of speakers of indigenous languages

State	Number of speakers older than five who speak at least one indigenous language	Percentage of indigenous language speakers relative to total state population	Number of indigenous language speakers older than five who do not speak Spanish	Percentage of indigenous language speakers who do not speak Spanish relative to total population of indigenous language speakers
Oaxaca	1,165,186	34.2	188,230	16.2
Yucatán	537,516	30.3	40,273	7.5
Chiapas	1,141,499	27.2	371,315	32.5
Quintana Roo	196,060	16.7	8,867	4.5
Guerrero	456,774	15.1	134,797	29.5
Hidalgo	359,972	15.1	43,991	12.2
Campeche	91,094	12.3	2,926	3.2
Puebla	601,680	11.7	57,649	9.6
San Luis Potosí	248,196	10.7	19,439	7.8
Veracruz	644,559	9.4	66,646	10.3
United States of Mexico	6,695,228	6.7	980,894	14.7

Source: INEGI 2010.

into the new millennium, reinscribing it at the same time with present conflicts. Among them are opposing views about local language and culture, the
meaning of modernity, and the town's relationship to the nation. The fight to
preserve and promote particular ideas about indigenous language and culture
is not only figurative but also literal. Although it may be rare for people to
kill or be killed for those ideas, people are nevertheless willing to make great
sacrifices to defend them.

Nationalism and Its Discontents:
The Modern Renaissance in Indigenous Literatures

This book offers a different perspective on ethnic politics from the one that
scholarly accounts generally consider, a perspective whose insights about the
lived stakes of political difference are grounded in concerns that are not explicitly political.[10] I argue that the meaning of one of the most distinctive hallmarks of the present era—that globalization and the assertion of local ethnic
identities are advancing hand in hand across the globe—can be interpreted
only by looking beyond the narrowly political.[11] Understanding the political
dynamics of modern—and postmodern—entities such as the nation requires
ethnographically examining how people experience activities that are only
sometimes read in political terms, and that relate to ideas about the nation
not directly but in oblique and hidden ways.[12]

I take up these issues of broad social and scholarly import by using
Mexico's contemporary indigenous revival movements as a case study. One
of the leading forces in the growing ascendance of the global South, Mexico
exhibits characteristics of many postnational states: it remains at once one
of the most powerful and cohesive nation-states in Latin America and yet
recently has begun to be spoken of as a "failed" state. While the spectacular narcotrafficking violence has been instrumental in eliciting such discourses, drug violence is not the only threat to Mexican national cohesion.
Nor is it the only force eroding the importance of national boundaries while
strengthening the power of both international influences and local ties in
the everyday reality of many Mexicans. Other forces include the development
of a truly multiparty democracy, as the power of the Partido Revolucionario
Institucional (Institutional Revolutionary Party; PRI) has waned and that of
other parties has increased.[13] Oaxaca's elections of 2010, for example, mark
a watershed event in state politics while also fitting into a broad national
trend—the PRI lost its first gubernatorial election in the state when parties
from opposing ends of the political spectrum formed a coalition to defeat the

ruling party. Other forces, too, have played a role: the ever changing face of migration to the United States in the wake of NAFTA, the various attempts at so-called immigration reform in the United States and their attendant backlash, and, of course, mounting drug violence and shifting government policies toward the illegal drug trade.

This book engages with all of these forces but focuses on another still: escalating demands for indigenous autonomy and recognition, which have led to broad-based social movements and internal political conflict. Revival movements are a particularly fruitful place to examine how assertions of ethnic difference and their challenges to national belonging are worked out in practice. In particular, viewing such politically charged issues through the lens of the not explicitly political—by looking at art and culture as rich sources of information about political conflict—yields new perspectives on the dynamics of political difference. Furthermore, in the case of a particular revival movement I document, the ostensibly apolitical character of its artistic and cultural activities is precisely what allows it to create specific political effects. In other words, the political success of this revival movement is possible only because of how it draws on realms of life that are valenced as apolitical and free of economic interest.

This book thus tells the story of an astonishingly successful cultural revival. People from the Sierra Mazateca have managed to reverse decades of cultural and linguistic erosion to revive and reinvent lost customs. The center of this renaissance is a fierce vindication of the indigenous language spoken—and sung—throughout the region. Not only is Mazatec the shared medium of daily life for most people, but some of its specific qualities foreground its relationship to music. Mazatec is a tonal language with a whistled register. In this "whistle speech" so famous among linguists, people communicate by whistling the tonal contours of spoken language. These features are among those that support the linguistic ideology, commonly expressed in the Sierra, that "our language is like singing."[14]

Renewed attachment to the Mazatec language is promoting powerful new ideas about community by tying people not only to others living across the region but also to the dead who share their language. Through communion with the dead, the living are linked to history, to the land, and to utopian visions of the past that are transforming the present. The key sites for this transformation are the region's most distinctive customs: rituals held annually during Day of the Dead and the religious use of hallucinogenic plants to heal the sick and divine the future. More importantly, the revival of indigenous-language singing in such settings has been tied innovatively to the introduction of writing, making literacy in the indigenous language a potent political catalyst promoting broad unity across the region. This newfound linguistic and ethnic solidarity has in turn become a powerful new political reality. By collectively singing in a shared, stigmatized language, people forge new ideas about community that bind the living with the dead and the old with the young, balance the pull of past traditions against the pressures of modernization, and demand recognition within the national imagination while claiming distinctive ethnic identities at odds with standing models of Mexican citizenship.

This case, in other words, offers an alternative model of national plurality and ethnic politics in which revival practices presented and perceived as apolitical can produce powerful political results. The political success of this case suggests why ethnic revival has had such prevalence worldwide: revival promises—and in some cases, delivers—a resolution between the often untenable costs of national belonging for ethnic minorities and the often unacceptable threat to national unity posed by minorities' assertions of difference. In describing why I think that this case was popularly successful where others like it have not found similar popular appeal, I identify two interrelated tensions—two sets of opposing forces—that haunt all revival movements. The first of these polarities I have already touched on: the tension between the overtly political agenda of revival projects—their goal of restructuring relations between ethnic groups and the state—and the need to position them as rising above political factions in order to acquire broad appeal. The second polarity is related to the first and concerns those who lead revival movements. They face the structural paradox that their authority and legitimacy are based on their "representativeness" with respect to the community at large. Yet the practical demands of leading revival movements requires them to have skills, take part in activities, and indeed live lives that set them apart as unique. This pair of interrelated tensions is manifested in the Sierra Mazateca in the lives of people—mushroom shamans, coffee farmers, indigenous authors, village schoolteachers, local shopkeepers, political activists—who are affected by the revival projects I document. The methods used in these revival projects— methods tied to the indigenous language and even more specifically to singing—have been critical to the movements' success, opening new possibilities for reconciling the tensions raised by revival.

Both of these tensions are related, furthermore, to the temporal aspect of social movements, which require particular relationships to the past and to its lived realities in the present. Human beings have long viewed the past as a resource, an ark housing cultural treasures that can be recovered and given new flesh in the present. Thus, histories across the globe are marked by periods of renaissance, when people renew and reinvent something from the past that was literally or metaphorically lost.[15] The present is no exception: the widespread emergence of indigenous and ethnic revival movements worldwide attests to as much. Postcolonial and postnational in nature, these projects ostensibly aim to rescue extinct past practices and endangered present ones from the eroding, marginalizing legacies of colonial and national domination. At the heart of such projects, however, lies a paradoxical tension between departure from the past and allegiance to it. For in reviving the past, people necessarily also rely, deliberately or not, on innovation and creativity. Sometimes the newness deployed in revival is explicitly admitted and sometimes it is deliberately denied, but adapting the past to the present always involves a generative friction between the two when perceptions of the past—often incomplete and selective—knock against the needs and norms of the present.

Thus, revival projects by definition are counterhegemonic and by disposition are ethnically purist; nativism and revival are two sides of the same coin. Among the critical tropes on which both notions turn—for intellectuals driving revival projects as well as their audiences—are two closely related concepts: authenticity and tradition. Both, in turn, are tied—particularly in the context of indigenous revival and identity politics—to ideas about authority. In promoting conceptions of the past as prescriptive guides for the present, indigenous intellectuals must adopt views of the past that emphasize above all their link to tradition as representative of essentialized indigenous identities, codified as the authentic "us" as a people.

At the same time, such intellectuals must make explicit how the practices they promote differ from present ones, for their prescriptive value—their ability to shape and change current practices—lies in such distinctiveness. However, this recontextualization introduces resistance between the original context and the new one, which turns around precisely the concepts of authenticity and tradition. Although the dynamic interplay of the old and the new is evoked by the labels (renaissance, revival) for such movements, the ideology that intellectuals use to promote them is explicitly retro-normative, locating the rules for proper behavior in an idealized past. Such agendas center on notions of tradition embodied in ostensibly authentic past practices that simultaneously exclude and seek to replace corresponding practices in the present. Yet tradition represents not only a timeless past that no longer exists, but also its persistence in the present as collective norms. The slippage between the two lends an inherent instability to what individuals mean by the terms *authenticity* and *tradition*—slippage that leads to shifting understandings about the authority on which indigenous representatives draw. Thus, the essentialized collective identity promoted by indigenous intellectuals, pitched against at least some present norms, is often at odds with the lived reality of many members of their audiences.

The ambiguity produced by this semantic instability places both indigenous intellectuals and their revival efforts in an inherently paradoxical position. Although such leaders must appeal to authenticity and tradition, their interpretations of these terms often conflict with the norms of other community members. This is arguably a particularly acute tension for indigenous peoples and their representatives, as some recent scholarship suggests (e.g., de la Cadena and Starn 2007) and as is underscored by ongoing popular discussions of indigenous leaders such as Evo Morales of Bolivia. Furthermore, many of the very qualities that allow indigenous individuals to lead revival projects—that they are highly literate, bilingual, and relatively cosmopolitan—make them further subject to claims of inauthenticity by the very people for whom they purport to speak. To put the issue another way, the abilities and ideological dispositions that authorize indigenous intellectuals to participate in national and even international debates about indigenous rights are often the very same ones that, from a local perspective, may delegitimize them as authoritative representatives of indigenous communities.

The negotiation of such disparities, the social conflicts they engender, and the challenges they can pose to large-scale unifying entities such as nations have, of course, been a central concern in the social sciences since their inauguration. From the founding fathers of the discipline through leading theorists of the present, social scientists have been deeply interested in how complex social collectivities endure despite profound internal differences. One of the most important lines of inquiry has addressed the construction of the modern nation-state, whose rise as a dominant global paradigm is closely linked historically to the scholarly ethos out of which the modern disciplines themselves were born. Yet recent social science research has also grappled with threats to this paradigm, such as increasing globalization and the emergence of various transnational and subnational ethnic and indigenous movements.

In Mexico, the interaction between indigenous people and the state as it continues to incorporate them has been of special interest because, unlike many other Latin American countries, the Mexican state is relatively strong. Thanks to the Revolution, the state has engaged directly and actively with its indigenous populations rather than, for example, treating them with benign (or not so benign) neglect. However, the Zapatista uprising of 1994 in Chiapas—a state that, like Oaxaca, is both ethnically diverse and heavily indigenous—made only too clear the limits of state power and relevance. Often called the first "postmodern rebellion," the armed conflict itself was extremely short and a farce, militarily speaking: some of the ski-masked indigenous insurgents gracing the covers of newspapers across the world carried not actual guns but slabs of wood painted to resemble them. Rather, the power of the rebels was almost entirely moral and political as they leveraged media coverage of the uprising into international pressure on the Mexican government to listen to their demands. Through both explicit rhetoric and strategic use of Revolutionary symbols, the Zapatistas demonstrated how completely the Mexican government had failed to deliver on the Revolution's promise to redress the chronic social inequality and marginalization experienced over centuries by the nation's poor and indigenous populations. The leaders of the Ejército Zapatista de Liberación Nacional, especially the media darling Subcomandante Marcos, were extremely savvy in their use of press coverage. Their power within Mexico owes as much to the pressure their international support brought to bear on the government as it does to pressure from "below"—that is, from the millions of indigenous people in Mexico who to this day are living in conditions of abject poverty.

The ethnic diversity that such indigenous peoples represent—and the challenge it has posed for the modern Mexican state's attempt to form a unified national identity—are not new. Long before Columbus's first voyage, the portion of North America that became Mexico was a region of overwhelming linguistic and cultural diversity. In the centuries before the Spanish Crown made Mexico a center of its colonial enterprise as New Spain, rulers of several successive Mesoamerican empires faced, in the diversity of the populations they subjugated, similar threats to large-scale cohesion. The area's immense linguistic diversity has been particularly problematic for pre-Columbian imperial, European colonial, and nationalistic projects. Today, sixty-eight officially recognized languages are spoken in Mexico, a number much diminished from pre-Contact levels due to the deaths of massive numbers of indigenous people during the conquest and colonization. Further, the number of indigenous languages currently spoken in Mexico would expand exponentially if the languages were divided into units that reflect mutual intelligibility.[16] At the same time, language use has been one of the key sites of resistance to and critique of imperialist projects. In Mexico—unlike in neighboring Guatemala, for example—the primary marker of indigenous identity is language use.[17] The valorization of indigenous languages has played a critical role in countering the state's efforts aimed at assimilating indigenous people and erasing ethnic difference. Furthermore, many indigenous groups have specifically focused such efforts at bolstering indigenous languages on their poetic and literary uses.

Such projects are precisely what a narrowly political view of ethnic difference tends to ignore. Particularly in social contexts of extreme power imbalance, the importance played by poetic concerns often becomes relegated to the margins as interethnic relations are read primarily in economic or political terms. Yet ethnic conflicts often center on the right to control which cultural narratives matter and will become emblematic of the core beliefs and values that define, unite, and position a group within larger collectives such as nation-states. The worldwide emergence of cultural and linguistic revival is one of the most important indicators of the vital role played in social life by the ability to control poetic expression.[18]

Revival takes a variety of forms, but one of the most common concerns writing: the creation of written literatures in minority languages. Literary creation also requires a secondary process of producing audiences with the skills — such as literacy in indigenous languages — needed to use such texts. Like other indigenous peoples worldwide, Zapotecs and Mazatecs who can read and write are overwhelmingly literate exclusively in the national language. Though a large corpus of pre-Columbian and colonial texts in Mexican indigenous languages exists, this indigenous literary tradition is discontinuous. Writing in indigenous languages was largely abandoned early in the national period once bilingualism and literacy in Spanish became sufficiently widespread.[19] Thus, modern literatures in indigenous languages date almost entirely from the last few decades.[20] During this period, indigenous peoples across Mexico have witnessed an impressive renaissance in indigenous writing. Almost all languages still spoken have at least one indigenous author and various books published in the language; the larger languages have many of both. Because indigenous languages circulate almost exclusively orally, literacy movements have emerged alongside the literary ones, aimed at teaching indigenous peoples how to read and write in their native languages.

These indigenous texts include older as well as more innovative forms in various media, whose central unifying characteristic is the poetic use of language: oral narratives, written poems and novels, song performances, recorded songs, and written lyrics. An enduring question raised by revival concerns how continuity with tradition and the generative potential of creativity are negotiated in practice — on poetic and cultural terms, as well as political ones. The tension between maintaining stasis and introducing change also involves how indigenous writers navigate the inherent contradictions entailed by adapting traditional expressive forms to new (Western) genres and media.

These matters are of particular interest here because they are live concerns for indigenous Mexican writers. But they have also been of enduring consequence to scholars working on themes of broad and enduring relevance such as literature and nationalism, the social meaning of literacy, the politics of artistic representation and value, the social importance of differences across genres and media, and the role of art in promoting social change. The case I discuss and the approach I take to it address a need in existing work on literatures and literacy while also posing a challenge to the corpus in important ways. I thus turn briefly to this research, demonstrating from another angle why the case study at the center of this book is illustrative beyond its immediate context.

On Great Divides: Toward a New Methodology

In this book I focus on social movements tied to indigenous literatures and literacy. I examine the activities of intellectuals who lead revival movements, as well as responses others have to their revival initiatives. By providing a holistic ethnography of indigenous texts—coupling textual history and analysis with the community-based study of textual production and reception—I offer a new perspective on ethnic politics in Mexico.

Little has been written about modern indigenous literatures and literacy in Mexico, despite their broad significance. Efforts to promote indigenous literatures and literacy affect every indigenous community in Mexico and constitute a highly visible portion of Mexico's national commitment to ethnic plurality. My contribution to our understanding of indigenous language literatures and literacy is methodological as well as substantive. I approach this field of inquiry by addressing a conceptual problem running beneath the scholarly and applied work that analyzes ethnic revival and indigenous writing. Namely, both bodies of work often share the underlying assumption that text and context are separable. I argue that text and context, production and reception, cannot be separated in practice. Furthermore, understanding the nature of their interconnections—how text and context co-construct each other, how creation and reception are dialectically intertwined—is essential to understanding why people alternately embrace and resist revival movements.

The key to understanding how text and context, reception and production combine in this case is to focus on language use in its totality. This means attention not just to the "total linguistic fact"—linguistic form, ideology, and use (Silverstein 1985)—but also the related triad of writing, speaking, and, crucially, *singing*. By studying revival movements in this way, I illuminate the practical challenges people face in balancing political agendas against apolitical inclusiveness, present innovations against fidelity to the past. The case study I present sheds light on the paradoxical position that indigenous intellectuals—and, perhaps, minority representatives generally—must navigate in stabilizing such tensions. Their predicament, furthermore, mirrors parallel constraints haunting Western scholarship.

ON ORALITY AND LITERACY: THE MISSING THIRD TERM

Any discussion of the impact of literacy and the creation of new writing traditions invokes by design or by accident the old debate about the social implications of oral versus written communication. This question, of course, has been the target of intense theorization across the humanities and social sciences. Although positions on the matter do come in shades of gray, those taken by leading figures in the debate cluster around two poles. Some theorists have claimed that the introduction of systems of writing into oral cultures—whether historical or contemporary—leads to generalized, universal transformations in cognition and social complexity. Such proponents of the autonomous model of literacy tie the advent of writing to the development of law, democracy, individualism, Protestantism (and therefore, capitalism), science, and even rational thought.[21] Theorists who support the opposing view, known as the ideological model, have challenged both the monolithic Great Divide that the opposing theorists posit between orality and literacy and the linkage they presume between large-scale social change and literacy per se (see Besnier 1995; Clanchy 1990; Finnegan 1988; Street 1993, 2003).[22] Linguistic anthropologists in particular have stressed that viewing orality and literacy as separable or uniform across cultures is inherently untenable. They argue that the preoccupation with the transformation from oral to written expression is predicated on Western, logocentric views of communication.[23]

The debate has been going on long enough within scholarly circles that it sometimes ceases to be very productive, with those on opposing sides speaking past each other. Nevertheless, the debate does have ongoing practical relevance: social programs espoused by entities ranging from federal governments to ethnic organizations to individual actors engage variously with the issues it raises. Literacy policies and initiatives rely on a range of claims about the social transformations that literacy and the promotion of new writing practices will or will not produce. They make a variety of assumptions about the modularity of literacy, about how permeable or impervious it may be to local contexts. For this reason, it is worth discussing the debate not with the aim of settling it but, rather, with the intention of understanding the salience of its competing claims in the world of literacy and writing as practice. Tools from linguistic anthropology have a contribution to make here. By looking at literacy ethnographically, in specific social contexts in which literacy practices come into contact with ideologies about texts and the people who use and produce them, we can understand the concrete effects that literacy does—and does not—have. By looking at language in practice, we can see how literacy policies and the claims and assumptions on which they are predicated touch ground and come to have specific material expressions.

One important strain of linguistic anthropological research—though it does not consider the literacy debate per se—examines the practical dynamics and political import of social engagement with texts. This work focuses on the processes by which texts of various sorts are produced, disseminated, interpreted, used, and placed in productive intertextual and interdiscursive relations to other texts and discourses.[24] This literature foregrounds how practice and ideology shape text creation, creating a space for examining the role of innovation in "the social life of texts"—even in revival movements where the past and tradition are explicitly invoked. The ethnographic focus of this work has allowed for a humanistic, cross-cultural approach to textuality in which individuals in social context interact in specific ways with texts.

However, largely missing from this literature is the consideration, alongside speaking and writing, of a third linguistic mode: singing. Leading theorists have consistently cast the literacy debate as a question about the relationship between orality and literacy. In addition, influential theorists primarily pursuing other scholarly agendas—for example, Jacques Derrida in *Of Grammatology* (1998 [1976])—merely reinforce the discursive grooves that confine discussions of language to speech and writing.[25] Even otherwise careful analyses do not consider singing—for example, Benjamin Lee's analysis of Habermas's ideas on textuality: "the textuality of language raises questions about the relations between oral and written communication" (Lee 1992: 416). What about singing? Should not discussions of genre—which follow in Lee's discussion—consider how song would expand the taxonomy? Lee's characterization is symptomatic of a pervasive bias in discussions about relations among modes of communication, in which singing is relatively rarely considered in its own right alongside writing and speaking.

Yet singing is often critically involved in the processes by which texts are created, circulated, and transformed. In other words, singing is as central to the processes by which "culture moves through the world" (Urban 2001) as is speaking or writing. While an argument about the importance of song as a vital human communicative activity is hardly new, the consideration of singing in studies of literacy is almost entirely absent.[26] Despite extensive literature on relations between music and language, discussions about writing, speech, and music (or song) remain rare.[27] Song has fared better in discussions about literature, especially poetry; as I discuss later, the famous Mazatec shaman María Sabina, who never became literate, was hailed by leaders of the Ethnopoetics movement as a "true poet" for the songs and chants she used in curing rituals.[28] However, such discussions treat songs as a unique kind of written literature or a special form of oral communication. In other words, singing is rarely considered a communicative category unto itself—one that may interact with and mediate between speaking and writing in distinctive ways.

In this book, I consider how song's unique expressive qualities and cultural loadings allow people to create texts of enduring social resonance. I argue that a key attribute of song is its performative flexibility. Coupling revival movements to song practices allows a more fluid interface with new types of technology than is possible when relying on written texts alone; my analysis centers on cassette tapes, compact discs, and video recordings that might lend themselves to popular commodification and popular markets more easily than books.[29] However, my more immediate concern is that the strategic use of song has played a critical role in the success of the revival projects I describe. For reasons I discuss later, in the Sierra Mazateca song has become an effective cultural and political tool that plays a pivotal role in reconciling customary practice with the innovations necessary for any revitalization project to thrive. Inasmuch as successfully balancing tradition with creativity is a perennial problem in revival movements, the success of this particular case—and my claim that song has been a critical element of that outcome—has relevance beyond Mexico. At the least, the case study at the heart of this book demonstrates how incomplete a social portrait of literatures and literacy is without considering the vital role played by singing.

ON TEXT AND CONTEXT:
BELLETRISTIC VERSUS SOCIOLOGICAL APPROACHES

Shortly after the collapse in the sixteenth century of the Aztec capital, on whose razed remains Mexico City was built, indigenous authors began writing texts in indigenous languages using the Western alphabetic script.[30]

Scholars have been enormously interested in these texts, particularly those relating to the conquest and its aftermath. Research on these texts has typically taken a belletristic approach.[31] Grounded in theories from literary criticism, such scholarship views indigenous texts as belles lettres in nature, valuable for their aesthetic properties. Within such an approach, indigenous texts are treated as relatively independent of context, analyzable in terms of content and form (genre, poetic structure, language use, rhetorical strategies, authorial style) to the near exclusion of social contexts of production and use.[32] Much of this work examines indigenous texts for the light they shed on ancient Mesoamerican societies.[33] Even recent work on modern indigenous writers, although it demonstrates a more present-centered approach, has nevertheless been driven by the same underlying concerns.[34] Such research may take great interest in the personal history of indigenous writers and how they draw on cultural knowledge, particularly oral literatures. Nevertheless, the texts themselves are squarely at the center of the analysis. As a result, we learn little about either the social worlds in which indigenous authors live or the social lives of the texts themselves: how other people, particularly people who are not indigenous authors, read the texts, talk about them, speak them, sing them, understand them.

Belletristic approaches have been prevalent for numerous reasons, including pragmatic ones. For historical texts, the relative dearth of documents in indigenous languages poses challenges to contextualizing them.[35] For modern texts, the sheer diversity of indigenous languages and the numerous obstacles to learning them makes textual analysis the most feasible approach.[36] Because modern literary texts almost always appear in bilingual editions, many scholars of indigenous literatures operate entirely in Spanish. Thus, scholars who are able to work with the texts in indigenous-language versions have valuable insight to offer even when they focus narrowly on textual exegesis.

In addition, scholarship on indigenous texts has been tied to a political agenda: to valorize native cultures and languages, including texts produced in them.[37] This is especially true of indigenous literary texts, in which the poetic aspects of language use are critical to expressive labor. Thus, belletristic research has stressed the artistic sophistication of Amerindian texts, raising them from documents of purely ethnohistorical interest toward texts worthy of inclusion in the canons of Literature proper. Such research illuminates how the distinctive resources of Amerindian languages provide a rich expressive array, simultaneously complicating their translations into majority languages and deepening the terms on which they can be read.

Yet in attempting to elevate the value of these texts above the merely socio-logical and historical, this scholarship weakens the links between indigenous texts and their contexts of production and use, which are equally critical to their value and meaning. In evaluating a work of art, the tension between privileging the object unto itself and stressing its ties to context is, of course, as old as critique: the history of literary criticism has been driven by com-peting urges to view a work's significance in contextual terms and to assess it through internal qualities alone. As I discuss later, this tension animates modern indigenous revival movements, as well, figuring the divergent atti-tudes indigenous writers and activists take toward their audiences.

Another scholarly trend that runs counter to the belletristic tradition, however, takes a more sociological approach to indigenous language texts, particularly written ones.[38] This research tends to be framed as the investiga-tion of nationalism and focuses on literacy rather than literature (Heath 1972; King 1994).[39] Such work emphasizes the social factors that motivate literacy movements and examines how social agendas condition practical outcomes. Within this approach, researchers generally work entirely in Spanish, paying little attention to how indigenous languages and language ideologies are im-plicated in the relative success of literacy and literary movements. As with the belletristic approach, this body of scholarship reflects, though from an opposing angle, the same tensions surrounding the relations between text and context. The elitist agenda underlying much of the belletristic research weds it, in its decontextualizing tendencies, to insensitivity to practice, and the populist orientation undergirding a sociological approach to literacy im-ports difficulties in considering local variables such as interactions with in-digenous languages. As with the belletristic literature, the benefits and short-comings of the sociology of literacies scholarship are echoed in tensions that animate indigenous literary and literacy movements themselves.

Little has been written about modern indigenous writing and ethnic revi-val in the Americas.[40] Yet to a greater or smaller extent, such movements have an impact across Mexico on indigenous people and communities. Funding for indigenous writing and literacy constitutes a small but highly visible por-tion of Mexico's national commitment to education, culture, and ethnic di-versity. Nearly every language currently spoken in Mexico has authors writing in it, and most are involved to some extent in teaching indigenous literacy. Throughout the country, organizations dedicated to the defense and valoriza-tion of native cultures promote literacy in indigenous languages and publish literary books and magazines in them. Through its bilingual and adult edu-cation programs, the federal government spends considerable sums annually on literacy programs in indigenous languages. It produces textbooks in all of the officially recognized languages, including numerous versions in languages with multiple variants; it supports thousands of administrators and teachers who deliver its bilingual education programs for children and its adult literacy programs. The government spends hundreds of thousands of dollars each year supporting indigenous language literature, from annual grants to indigenous writers to publication series for indigenous literatures. Examples of these bilingual texts are found in most research libraries in Mexico and the United States.

Yet these books are rarely found in indigenous households. Unless they have considerable experience reading in their languages — and note that this often requires reading across variants — people who own such books rarely read them. When they do, it is generally with great difficulty, relying on the Spanish translation as much as the indigenous "original."[41] The sheer dearth of texts in indigenous languages is a critical factor. This situation both limits opportunities for practice and makes indigenous language texts a relatively tiny portion of the reading diet of those — that is, regular readers — inclined to read the texts in the first place.

This situation — in which indigenous texts are rarely read by indigenous speakers — reflects a deeper reality about ethnic revival movements. The belletrist scholars of indigenous literature and the sociologists of indigenous literacy choose their approaches to the relationship between text and context in conscious dialogue with their audiences; indigenous writers do so, as well. The difficulty for indigenous writers, however, is that they have two audiences, with widely divergent, if not mutually exclusive, expectations. They have their peers — other indigenous authors and intellectuals, such as Miguel León-Portilla and Carlos Montemayor, who are sympathetic to indigenous causes and champion indigenous literature. This audience is made up of highly literate people with well-developed understandings about literature and explicit discourses for expressing those views. While its members are often bilingual, this audience rarely reads the indigenous language in which the author writes. These readers rely heavily or exclusively on Spanish versions. But indigenous intellectuals also have a second audience of peers: people who speak their indigenous language. Members of this audience have a much wider range of educational experiences and literary skills. While some will have as much formal schooling as, if not more schooling than, the authors, the majority will have less extensive educational experience. Thus, most members of indigenous audiences will be less likely to engage regularly in reading literary texts and will rarely have well-developed, explicit views about literature. To the extent that such audience members can read in the indigenous language, they do so with difficulty, relying on both versions of the text and often more heavily on the Spanish.

At the level of language alone, the author's priorities are divided. Ironically, the indigenous language version—on which the author's legitimacy as an indigenous author rests—is the least subject to heavy use or thoughtful criticism. On ideological matters, the author often has other difficult choices to make. Concerning the crucial matter of indigenous identity, for example, other intellectuals—indigenous or not—are much more likely than are other natives of indigenous communities to have been regularly exposed to national and international discourses about indigenous rights and indigenous identity. Such discourses often rely on ideas about what it means to be indigenous that turn on notions of faithfulness to tradition and an idealized past. Yet the majority of speakers of a given indigenous language on the whole are less likely to have serial experiences of such ideas about indigeneity. Works trading on such tropes thus may be less likely to be popularly compelling and often are rejected outright as old-fashioned or irrelevant.

Thus, for an indigenous intellectual to attend to text as context independent—to become an ethno-belletrist—is to turn toward the audience of fellow intellectuals and often away from fellow indigenous language speakers. As I discuss further, this is the path most indigenous authors follow, by deliberate choice or in response to external pressures (or both). They focus on producing autonomous texts—works of art whose aesthetic value is internal to the text and whose political value derives from what they represent: that indigenous languages are not mere dialects spoken by peasants and peons but are worthy of sonnets, plays, liturgical hymns. The many authors who have followed this path and achieved national and even international recognition have begun not only to raise the stature of indigenous languages and their speakers but have had a demonstrable effect on national indigenous policy.

Almost all authors who follow this approach to creating indigenous literatures speak of the project as proceeding hand in hand with promoting indigenous literacy and creating reading publics. Thus, they acknowledge the importance of becoming essentially sociologists of literacy for their own speech communities. Yet this is a path few indigenous intellectuals take, and those who do rarely rise to regional or national prominence. Such work requires focusing not primarily on the texts themselves but on their social contexts of use by promoting the range of skills needed to "read" them. While promoting these abilities begins with literacy, it rarely ends there; it also involves passing on particular skills required not only to literally read texts but also to understand their meaning and significance, skills that include knowledge of wider discourses about indigenous identity and solidarity and ideas about "good" literature. By taking this approach, however, indigenous writers largely guarantee that their work will have little relevance beyond speakers of their native languages. While they may gain a local audience, they are likely to limit or lose altogether the national one. And although most writers try to blend the two approaches, it remains a difficult balancing act that few have pulled off.

This predicament is gracefully invoked in an article—written, significantly, in Spanish—by the Mazatec author Heriberto Prado Pereda. It appeared in *La Faena*, a cultural magazine published in the Sierra Mazateca:

> Of those involved in redeeming indigenous culture, there are two attitudes:
>
> 1. There are those who do so from above and outside. They are like spectators. They narrate what indigenous people do, as if they weren't themselves indigenous. They talk about dances, communal labor, stories, the language, wakes for the dead . . . and yet never participate. They want to set the indigenous person free but depend on the outside. They speak the language only for their personal use.
> 2. Those who live, share, work, and spend their lives in the service of their pueblo, of their culture; they participate in everything and are self-directed. They aim to liberate their pueblo and their culture from below and inside. This is the best posture to have. I invite all those who love their pueblo to fight for the fundamental vindication of our values. (Prado Pereda 2001: 15)

I agree with this assessment that indigenous authors and activists tend to fall into two groups that differ in important ways. However, I characterize the sets differently and provide an analysis of the differences between them that is based as much on systemic constraints as on individual motivation and orientation. Furthermore, I claim that both groups have critical roles to play in the broad project of indigenous revival. And their differences, while in some ways opposing, are in other ways complementary as they work in tandem to forge new possibilities of inclusion for indigenous peoples in modern Mexico.

Singing for the Dead: An Overview

This book depicts that rarest of beasts: a success story. It tells how a group of authors, composers, and activists launched a wildly popular revival movement: by inventing a new yet old form of singing, they transformed their social world. While this initiative shares characteristics with other ethnic revivals in Mexico and beyond, its value derives primarily from the ways that it is extraordinary—and yet at the same time offers a model for other revival projects, suggesting terms on which others might likewise navigate the tension between courting popular appeal and promoting the creative departure from received norms. As the political fallout from the confrontation in Yalálag illustrates, social movements are often fragile and fail at great cost. The politics of ethnicity requires engaging in a discursive field that is fraught with inherent contradictions. As the Yalálag incident also demonstrates, the ethnic solidarity required to make claims against the state can itself be internally elusive. Yet even when it is not so fleeting, the assertion of distinctive ethnic identities on which such claims rest routinely collides with the universalizing impulses of liberal regimes of governance. This book illuminates both the difficulty of successfully balancing such tensions and the social payoff that is possible when the competing forces at play in indigenous revival are brought into a state of harmony.

However, before turning to the case at the heart of the book, I first sketch the context from which it arose. Chapter 1 gives an ethnographic and historical overview of the relevant cultural politics in Mexico. I discuss the antecedents of modern efforts at ethnic revival, focusing on recent histories of writing and singing in indigenous communities. Chronicling relations between indigenous populations and the state from the Mexican Revolution to the present, I analyze how this history colors the contemporary landscape of identity politics in Mexico. I pay special attention to the relationship between political representation and linguistic affiliation, as this link has special salience and political power for indigenous Mexicans. I locate the social movement at the heart of this study within the constellation of indigenous social movements in Mexico and Latin America, outlining the general historical and cultural trends that have shaped language politics and conceptions of ethnic identity across the region.

In chapter 2 I focus on key recent historical events in the Sierra Mazateca. Two events in particular have strongly influenced the region's revival movements, shaping popular ideas about representing Mazatec ethnic identity in written texts, songs, and other public performances. The first concerns a singular yet pivotal historical event through which national and international discourses about indigenous identity were first encountered on a massive scale by people living in the Sierra Mazateca. The Sierra was a rugged and still relatively isolated region until the 1960s, when the region's psychedelic mushrooms were "discovered" by outsiders. Almost overnight the plants were converted into a commodity as the area was flooded by mushroom-seeking hippie mycotourists (a play on the term *ecotourists* that I use to describe tourists seeking "mycological" experiences). Previously, the plants had been seen as the bedrock of "Mazatec tradition," doorways through which local people gained access to the most intimate and distinctive aspects of social life in the Sierra. Furthermore, singing in Mazatec played a critical role in the *veladas* (mushroom ceremonies), making them key sites where singing was coupled to ethnic distinction through the Mazatec language. I offer a detailed discussion of veladas on which I draw later in the book to show how mushrooms, veladas, and talk about both are implicated in the Sierra's revival projects. Once the mushrooms and veladas became the focus of outsiders, they were placed squarely in the path of forces that would sustain their use through veneration while fundamentally altering them through appropriation. This unique encounter with globalizing forces nevertheless reveals globalization's most fundamental tensions, which are refracted in various ways through the region's revival projects. The friction in this case between local and global discourses about indigenous identity illuminates the alternately liberating and limiting features of the politics of ethnicity.

The second event began a few years later, with the rise of Catholic Church's prominence in the Sierra. Crucially pegged to the founding in 1972 of the Prelature of Huautla, which housed the Sierra's first resident bishop, the church's increasing local presence coincided with the rise of Liberation Theology as the dominant ideological paradigm in the church throughout Mexico but especially in the country's poor and indigenous south. The introduction of liberationist thought had a profound effect on daily life and laid the groundwork for new singing practices and written text production in Mazatec, tied to liberationists' interest in increasing the church's local permeability. Combined, these two events—the influx of mycotourists and the rise of the liberationist church—importantly prefigured the Sierra's revival movements, providing infrastructural support for writing and singing in Mazatec while introducing a new and highly ambivalent symbolic lexicon for representing "Mazatec tradition." By way of introducing the contested and historically specific understandings people have of that symbolic repertoire, I close the chapter by discussing the term *indigenous*, considering how it is—and is not—a useful category of analysis and how its use relates to revival in the Sierra.

I then lay out the ethnographic material at the book's core. In presenting support for my claims about the grassroots uptake of indigenous revival I work through two levels of analysis and comparison. I first present in detail two different revival initiatives from within the Sierra, analyzing them alongside each other and offering an explanation for why one project was widely popular while the other was less successful at gaining grassroots support. Then I compare these Mazatec revival movements with others occurring in Oaxaca and beyond. While many indigenous communities have produced nationally prominent authors successful in affecting national discourses and policies about indigenous people, few have produced vibrant local revival movements where literacy and writing have extended beyond well-educated, bilingual elites. Essentially no communities have produced both, and in comparing revival movements across the country, I present an argument for why this is so.

I begin my discussion, though, in the Sierra Mazateca. Chapter 3 focuses on a revival project that is both wildly popular and politically effective: the annual Day of the Dead Song Contest. The Day of the Dead is an important holiday throughout Mexico but nowhere more so than in Oaxaca. In the Sierra, Day of the Dead festivities are marked by culturally distinctive forms of singing. Musicians and dancers disguised to embody the dead roam nightly from house to house, singing to the dead as they symbolically give them flesh, bringing them to be with the living. A song contest founded some thirty years ago is now held annually at the start of the holiday. It draws on highly salient cultural practices, striking a balance between tradition and innovation, history and modernity, in the process recruiting an intergenerational audience and synthesizing a complex matrix of Mexican national emblems and symbols of ethnic distinction.

I argue that the contest's flexible relationship to such boundaries is the key to its grassroots appeal and social impact. The contest has become the engine driving a widespread, multifaceted cultural revival. It has produced a dramatic increase in Mazatec literacy; it founded a new tradition of Mazatec authorship and new forms of intellectual ownership as for the first time people across the Sierra now create new, individually authored works in their language. The contest has also led to new forms of performance and entrepreneurship, not only in the contest but also through a burgeoning popular market in Mazatec musical recordings. The contest's popular success stems from how it draws on cultural practices that are highly salient markers of ethnic cohesion, apolitical unity, and adherence to tradition. Such practices involve, above all, honoring the ancestors and unseen deities through speech and song. These strategic linkages allow the contest to be embraced as an intensification of standard practice, despite its obvious innovations, rather than rejected as inauthentic or false, as are so many projects aimed at social change. I also discuss the wider social implications of the song contest, as the entire revival movement that it spearheads has been linked to the rise of newly politicized ideas about regional interdependence and solidarity. At the same time, the contest has been instrumental in recruiting the most linguistically vulnerable young people to participate in these activities and, through them, to ideas about being Mazatec.

Chapter 4 presents an opposing case: a revival project with more limited popular appeal. I tell the story of one of the most contentious events in the region's recent history: the birth of the Mazatec Indigenous Church. This nativist religious movement aims to cleanse the Catholic faith of non-native, contaminating influences. Its most central and controversial practice involves replacing the Eucharist with the region's hallucinogenic mushrooms, which are traditionally used in veladas. Although the movement has attracted ardent followers, it remains very small, and many people remain openly hostile to its ideas. I discuss the textual and singing practices of members of the Mazatec Indigenous Church and how they relate to veladas before exploring how the similarities and differences condition arguments local people have about the Mazatec church. Furthermore, in analyzing criticisms of the Mazatec church, I discuss how they relate to the region's longstanding political and religious factions and to competing ideas about ethnic identity and moral personhood. I suggest that the ways the movement positioned itself with respect to these divisions was directly tied to its limited popular uptake.

Chapter 5 discusses what these two social movements—the nativist religious movement and the song contest, along with its penumbra of associated activities—tell us about the politics of indigenous revival when examined on an intimate scale. My discussion is grounded in the story of two half-brothers who have been centrally involved in the development of the two movements. I document how the brothers have taken positions about the nature of community that are in some ways complementary and conciliatory—symbolically represented by their annual, amicable gathering at their father's grave during the Day of the Dead—yet in other ways are violently opposed. Their differing positions on a host of religious and political issues are tied to social fault lines running through their community and the region, divisions that often haunt minority groups. This pair of cases reveals the double constraints placed on ethnic social movements as they balance the demands of internal regional audiences against those of national and international institutions and discourses. Yet the contrast between the two brothers' ideas about what it means to be Mazatec—and the different orientations the Mazatec church and the song contest bear toward being indigenous—is ultimately symbiotic rather than opposing. In chapter 5, I discuss some of the ways that the two brothers and two movements, despite their at times pointed differences, are mutually supportive and reinforce each other.

Chapter 6 is the last ethnographic chapter. It embeds the two revival projects discussed earlier in both Mexican and Latin American contexts by locating them within the broad, hemispherewide movement to create indigenous literatures. I discuss nationally and internationally known authors who are creating poetry, novels, and other works in indigenous languages—authors whose work has had substantial impact nationally but who have been largely ineffective at stimulating grassroots support and interest. The literary movements these authors promote have the explicit political goal of valorizing indigenous languages and rejecting the stigma of inferiority to which they have been subjected in comparison with so-called superior languages such as Spanish, Portuguese, French, and English. Yet in Mexico, as elsewhere, indigenous authors publish their work almost entirely in bilingual editions, featuring indigenous-language texts alongside versions in the national language. Songs, which are often printed solely in the indigenous language, are the notable exception to this convention. However, songs are a genre rarely used by indigenous authors outside the Sierra Mazateca—a situation that further contributes to the bifurcation I discuss throughout the book between the two sets of indigenous authors and their correspondingly distinct audiences.

In turning from the lives of indigenous authors to how people read the books they write, I discuss why the convention of producing bilingual texts turns indigenous writing, at the level of practice, into a double entity whose meaning resides not in one language alone but, rather, in a coupling of the two. This renders indigenous literatures semantically fluid in ways that majority literatures are not. Such instability in turn has substantial practical ramifications: reading bilingual texts becomes inherently difficult for all but an elite, well-educated few with specialized literary skills. These difficulties mirror the higher-level structural paradox that indigenous authors are forced to confront. Namely, they must simultaneously address two audiences—one local and one national—whose expectations and demands are often mutually exclusive. I suggest that this dilemma is one that routinely haunts political representatives of many minority groups.

The concluding chapter returns to a reconsideration of the Sierra's revival projects—the Day of the Dead Song Contest and the Mazatec Indigenous Church—as they compare to the national landscape of indigenous writing laid out in chapter 6. I compare the local case against the national context, exploring persistent tensions between national hegemonic discourses and local attempts to subvert them. While one of the darkest legacies of the post-modern celebration of diversity is the worldwide eruption of ethnic violence, this book shows that a brighter side is the global emergence of ethnic revival as a political tool. Although it is less bloody, this side of political conflict is likewise fraught with risks. Cross-cultural interaction requires an accommodation to the terms on which the interaction rests, even if those terms are themselves subject to debate. I argue that claims to rights within polyethnic, postcolonial nation-states such as Mexico become necessarily linked to a peculiar form of cultural violence, in which notions of culture and tradition must be codified and thereby fundamentally altered in the process of presenting them to national audiences. Thus, the vehicles by which ethnic minorities make such claims on the state may become locally suspect, violations of the very norms they seek to promote. However, it is as a response to this dilemma that the revival movements examined here offer their greatest rays of hope. This case suggests that one solution to such structural paradoxes is a culturally sensitive synthesis of the global and the local, a revival that is both innovation and restoration, a critique of the nation that preserves the possibility of national imagining.

FROM REVOLUTION TO RENAISSANCE

A Political Geography and History of "Deep Mexico"

The grandfathers would tell this legend:

> "When the god of places distributed the lands of the universe . . . only the Mazatecs, who wanted to live free from everyone, accepted these far and inhospitable parts that no one else wanted, . . . [choosing] to dwell, with Chikon Tokoxo as guide, in the lands of the huge carnivorous eagles. . . .
>
> The eagles hunted the new inhabitants, . . . and fed them to their babies. But the Mazatecs found a way to fool the eagles by wearing *chiquihuites* [tortilla baskets] on their heads. Thus when they passed by the eagles' lair, the birds carried the baskets away instead, and as they did, the Mazatecs hunted the eagles in return, killing them."

The old people say that is why we wear our *mecapales* [tumplines] in front and always carry our heads erectly and with pride because the eagles could never carry away our heads. We are not like those Indians of other tribes who wear their *mecapales* on their chests because the eagles took off their ancestors' heads.

—Renato García Dorantes, indigenous intellectual from Huautla, from "Se acaba este año: Je tifeta no jebi" ("The Year Comes to an End")

Mapping Ethnic Landscapes

As some Mazatecs would have people believe, they are the only Indians left in Mexico yet to lose their heads.[1] Yet whatever it is that unites people as Mazatecs—setting them apart from other groups while creating a place for them in the national imagination—is not nearly as heroic and primordial as the story suggests. Nevertheless, the attempt to draw such boundaries is itself illuminating, bringing to the fore contradictions born of adhering to political geographies in which such moves are meaningful. Delimiting cultural territory within such a national landscape—whose basic units are ethnic enclaves within a liberal and democratic but selectively heterogeneous collective—is fraught with ambivalence. It involves the simultaneous insistence on difference and belonging, on an identity at once dependent on the nation and yet distinct from it. Notwithstanding the assumptions made by Renato García Dorantes, quoted in the epigraph, his story raises questions about whether people labeled Mazatecs—or Zapotecs or other indigenous groups—are aligned behind so bright and binding a line. For Mazatecs also act as their neighbors do: they use mecapales and chiquihuites, they eat tortillas, they celebrate Day of the Dead. Yet many Mazatecs—writers like García Dorantes and other indigenous authors and activists hailing from across Mexico—insist on their difference, on their unique indigenous identities that simultaneously distinguish them from the unmarked Mexican citizenry and from other indigenous peoples. Their desire to carve out a place for themselves within such a geography, thus eliciting allegiance to its underlying logic, raises questions about why such a pursuit is valid and what consequences are entailed by doing so.

Of course, indigenous people have little choice about participating in the work of ethnic cartographies. García Dorantes and millions like him are routinely assigned to ethnic categories regardless of whether they find value in such taxonomic systems. Like blotches of color on linguistic maps, ethnic categorizations make some things visible while obscuring others, all the while creating new realities. Certain forms, performances, and scales of identity formation "are 'called out' by hegemonic structures of managed multiculturalism," yet at the same time these relatively new structures of identification "transform and translate . . . local roots" (Clifford 2007: 211). Once indigenous intellectuals participate in ethnic identification terms that the state stipulates through its policies of "managed multiculturalism," they are constrained by those available forms yet participate in their destabilization once the officially licensed forms interact with local, unofficial forms of identification. In retelling a well-known story circulating throughout the Sierra, García Dorantes positions his category of "the Mazatecs" as an alternative to and critique of other versions. The view of Mazatec ethnicity he expresses contrasts sharply with other widely circulating representations of Mazatecs, turning them on their heads by making virtues of purported Mazatec vices.

Even relative to the various indigenous populations surrounding them,

Mazatecs are frequently represented as difficult, stubborn, and extremely hostile to outsiders. Such popular characterizations include reports written by spelunkers. For more than thirty years—it is probably not coincidental that spelunking in the region began when hippies first arrived in search of "magic mushrooms"—cavers have come to northern Oaxaca to investigate its vast systems of caves, among the deepest and most extensive in the world. The caves lie under the mountains on both sides of the massive Santo Domingo Canyon, which, at more than six thousand feet deep, is deeper than the Grand Canyon. The northern cave, Sistema Huautla, extends underneath most of the Sierra Mazateca, while the other, Sistema Cheve, lies in an adjacent area to the south inhabited by Cuicatec speakers. As told by the well-known caver Bill Stone, who has led numerous explorations of both systems, "the difference between the north and the south sides are [sic] momentous in terms of the politics." He and others report that Mazatecs were (and are) openly hostile to the cavers, constituting a human obstacle the explorers must surmount alongside floods, cave-ins, falls, hypothermia, and oxygen depletion. Stone claims that Mazatecs view caves as "portals to the underworld," and, labeling the spelunkers brujos, claimed the explorers "had come to their land for the purpose of communing with the devil."[2] Stone continues, "It was not uncommon for us to have our ropes cut by machetes."[3] Such actions at least once nearly killed a caver, an event that continues to figure in stories about caving that circulate internationally as well as in regional Serrano discourse.[4] The human terrain of the southern cave system, however, is characterized quite differently: "On the other side of the Santo Domingo canyon is the Cuicatec Indian tribe, and that particular group was less hostile [historically] to outsiders than were the Mazatecs. . . . Because of that, number one, they all speak very good Spanish, the amount of Cuicatec that is spoken indigenously today is much, much less than is spoken on the Mazatec side, and as such [the Cuicatecs] don't have the mysticism associated with caves that they do on the northern side."[5]

Such ideas are by no means limited to cavers. Ben Feinberg (2003: 192) quotes a Mexico City resident who had visited Huautla: "'The people are just creepy,' he said. 'I mean, they're real Indians, scary ones. Not your happy, smiling Maya Indians in Yucatán but real Indians who just don't like you!'" I heard similar statements—often from other indigenous people—whenever I mentioned my research in the region. In the early days of my work there, when I solicited advice from knowledgeable outsiders about working in the Sierra, people often spoke of Mazatecs as "cerrado (closed)"—that is, difficult to work with and not welcoming to outsiders.

In the story about the man-eating eagles, however, echoes of these negative characteristics are transformed into evidence of valor: Mazatecs alone display the wisdom and courage that status as "real" Indians would demand. A broadly symbolic reading of the story, which the author seems to invite, would equate the eagle—a common symbol for both the Aztec Empire and the postrevolutionary Mexican nation—with state domination, suggesting not only that the powerful survive by devouring the weak but also that Mazatecs are unrivaled in their ability to resist, to fight back against "the great eagles, symbol of Mexico power" (Neiburg 1988: 14). While all of this could be chalked up to a common rhetorical move within the paradigm of identity politics, it also has a parallel in the Sierra's paradoxical location at Mexico's geographic heart and yet at its psychic and material periphery. Such a situation is not atypical of indigenous Mexican communities, but it means that a place like Nda Xo is both similar to indigenous and other rural communities throughout the region and yet also singular.

A tension between centrality and marginality, between what is locally distinct and what is typical nationally, animates myriad aspects of daily life in Nda Xo, including the dynamics of indigenous revival movements. While heavily in dialogue with regional, national, even international social movements, the Sierra's revival movements are also unique, above all in how literacy is tied to singing. In this chapter, I tie that tension between the Sierra's national centrality and its marginality to a history of Mexico's ethnic politics, viewed through the prism of language and literacy policies as they have shaped relations between indigenous groups and the state. These include antecedents of modern indigenous revival, which prefigure recent indigenous writing. State educational and language policies have shifted dramatically over Mexican history, changes that color the contemporary landscape of national identity politics. This gives linkages between political representation and linguistic affiliation special salience for indigenous Mexicans, residents of that submerged country within a country that the anthropologist Guillermo Bonfil Batalla described as "Deep Mexico" in his groundbreaking but controversial book (Bonfil Batalla 1987). I locate the social movements from Nda Xo within the constellation of indigenous social movements in Mexico and beyond by outlining the general historical and cultural trends that shape language and ethnic politics across the region. I further contextualize the Sierra's social movements within the region's particular historical, ethnographic, and scholarly context, outlining how the region is both nationally representative and yet distinct—an ambivalence echoed in the nature of the Sierra's revival movements.

The Birth of the "Indian Problem":
A History of Language and Literacy in Mexico

Mesoamerica was the seat of many mutually influencing societies prior to the conquest. Some civilizations exhibited social stratification and centralization that rivaled the leading cities of Europe and, indeed, the globe. However, one quality that distinguished Mesoamerica from the rest of the New World—and that has attracted centuries of academic and popular attention, from Spanish colonizers through present-day scholars—was the existence of indigenous writing systems.[6]

These writing systems—from Mayan and Zapotec glyphic writing to Mixtec and Nahua pictography and painted codices—differed. Each had ethnically, linguistically, and historically unique characteristics. Yet they were united in their great social importance, being fully infused with cultural meaning and value (Boone and Urton 2011). Pre-Columbian writing was heavily aligned with elite and noble classes (Monaghan 2002; Urcid 2005). As Stephen Houston (2011: 21, 23) writes of the Maya case, while the sculptors and scribes who produced glyphic texts were mostly nonroyal, "the practice of glyphic writing" was a tradition deployed "as a diglossic device for consolidating elite bonds across a conflictive political landscape." Furthermore, the differences among Mesoamerican scripts pale compared with their collective variance from European alphabetic writing. The phonetic basis of Old World literacy was markedly different from the pictorial basis of New World literacy, as was the centrality of oral performance to the process of gaining access to meanings encoded in Mesoamerican writings.[7]

Differences between Old World and New World writing had far-reaching implications for European colonization and indigenous responses to it. Spanish colonizers were keenly aware of the existence of Mesoamerican writing and the power of controlling written expression; the political potential and apparently idolatrous content of pre-Columbian texts often led the Spanish to view them with deep ambivalence. Thus, colonizers often responded to Mesoamerican texts by destroying them, razing existing urban centers—including their glyphic texts—and burning Mesoamerican codices while torturing those who harbored them. The famous idolatry trials of 1562 overseen by Fray Diego de Landa involved "the wholesale destruction of Maya codices . . . [resulting in] the gradual extinction of a priestly class who could interpret them, and the general decline in literacy after the Conquest (including a total loss of the ability to decipher the pre-Columbian glyphs)" (Farriss 1984: 291, 313). While that particular reaction to indigenous writing was especially severe, it represents an established response to indigenous writing.

However, colonizers also reacted in opposite fashion, with respect for Mesoamerican literacy and its potential utility for evangelization and secular rule. Among the first Europeans to live for extended periods in the Americas, colonial priests were the first Westerners with deep knowledge of indigenous languages, social practices, and cultural knowledge. The first efforts to record native languages and native literatures in Western alphabetic scripts stemmed from the evangelization mission, as Spanish priests educated themselves about the customs and languages of the native peoples whose souls they were charged with saving. The prior existence of writing systems in Mesoamerica was of great interest as a potential evangelization tool. Beginning in the 1520s, friars in Central Mexico began rendering Nahuatl in alphabetic script alongside pictographic writing; by the 1540s, documents in various styles were being produced (Restall et al. 2005: 12–13). While pictorial literacy was eventually replaced with alphabetic literacy, there was significant regional variation in friars' early responses to native pictography. In places such as Oaxaca's Mixtec region, pictorial traditions persisted well into the colonial era, even meriting use in court cases (Boone 2007; Monaghan 2002). Nevertheless, it "proved difficult to reconcile the primarily pictorial writing with the exacting requirements of the Spanish legal system," so that eventually, as stated by leading ethnohistorians of Mesoamerica, "alphabetic literacy in Nahuatl . . . [became] the dominant form of expression" across the Americas (Restall et al. 2005: 12–14). Today "the vast majority of native-language manuscripts and imprints are in Nahuatl" (Restall et al. 2005: 14), notwithstanding thousands of documents in other languages. The larger corpuses have been of special scholarly interest and include those in Yucatec Maya (Chuchiak 2010; Hanks 2010; Restall 1997b), Mixtec (Romero Frizzi 2003a; Terraciano 2004), and Zapotec (Chance 2001; Farriss, personal communication, 2012; Romero Frizzi 2003b; Távarez 2010).[8]

Friars initially passed the technology of alphabetic literacy in indigenous languages to indigenous elites. As they developed orthographies, vocabularies, and grammars in indigenous languages, friars also collected native texts and elicited linguistic and cultural information from native informants. While such work was always linked to "the extirpation of idolatry" (Chuchiak 2005), the priests' desire to understand and document such practices stimulated the production of a range of native-language texts through extensive collaboration with native speakers. Though not so credited, these indigenous elites "were at least contributing authors, usually produced the final versions of texts, and often participated in every level of production and printing" (Restall et al. 2005: 14). This process imparted literacy skills to key indigenous people. Indigenous scribes became critically important to the colonial bureaucracy, producing the official documents on which local administration depended—and on which the entire structure of colonial rule rested, given that indigenous people heavily outnumbered European colonizers.

The wealth of indigenous-language documents in colonial Mesoamerica has facilitated vibrant research into what light they shed on indigenous perspectives of colonial rule. Scholars generally classify these documents into two types. The first are those James Lockhart terms "mundane," which include official notarial texts of indigenous community *cabildos* (town councils); they make up "the vast majority of extant documentation" (Restall et al. 2005: 15). The second type are nonnotarial documents spanning many genres that are sometimes termed "Classical Nahuatl texts" (when they come from central Mexico) and have been the primary focus of belletristic approaches. Examples include descriptive linguistic materials (dictionaries, grammars, pedagogical materials); religious texts (confessional manuals, *doctrinas* [catechisms]); historical accounts (*annales* organized around the Mesoamerican calendar);[9] ethnographic compilations such as the massive Florentine Codex;[10] literary texts such as songs, speeches, and plays;[11] and heterogeneous texts that are "virtually unclassifiable" within Western genres (Farriss 1984: 247), such as the Books of Chilam Balam, the *titulos primordiales* (primordial titles), and the Popol Vuh (Durston 2008: 42–43; Restall et al. 2005: 13–15; see also Edmonson 1982, 1986; D. Tedlock 1985). The abundance of resources in indigenous languages in Mesoamerica has given rise to the New Philology, an approach to ethnohistorical research that advocates privileging indigenous-language resources.[12]

Here, too, Mesoamerica is unique in that no other part of the Americas has a remotely comparable corpus of colonial indigenous-language materials. As on so many matters of Latin American history, the Andes region is an important point of comparison, by turns foil and mirror. Differences and similarities across the two regions illuminate not only the shifting dynamics of colonial rule but also the nature of scholarship produced in each area. As Alan Durston (2008: 41) writes, "While abundant and diverse records are available in a number of Mesoamerican languages, texts of native Andean authorship are rare even in Quechua, today the most widely spoken indigenous language family of the Americas," a language with six or seven times the population of modern Nahuatl, the most widely spoken Mesoamerican language.[13] By contrast, colonial Quechua texts are dominated by pastoral literature produced by nonindigenous priests (see Durston 2007). Although the church's standardized form of written Quechua was used widely by indigenous elites, in the Andes indigenous-language literacy did not become the instrument of empire — a critical medium for keeping local records — as it did in Mesoamerica (Durston 2008). The celebrated chronicles of the Andes by the indigenous Peruvian Guaman Poma de Ayala and the mestizo El Inca Garcilaso de la Vega, despite some use of Quechua, were written mostly in Spanish (Adorno 1982; Salomon 1982). The famous Quechua-language Huarochirí manuscript, covering religious life in the Peruvian province of the title, "is entirely unique in the Andean context" (Durston 2008: 42; see also Salomon and Urioste 1991).

The relative paucity of indigenous-language documents in the Andes and their abundance in Mesoamerica has had ramifications for scholarship in both regions. Pioneering work in the Andes on colonial language use — Bruce Mannheim's work on the history of Quechua (Mannheim 1991; see also Mannheim and Van Vleet 1998), or Frank Salomon's work on the meaning of khipus (talking knots) in Andean ritual life (Salomon 2004) — has forced scholars to develop methods that rely on the "integration of Spanish and Quechua sources into a single framework of analysis" (Restall 2003: 127). By contrast, scholars of Mesoamerica have only recently begun explicitly advocating this synthetic methodological strategy. Yet the general dependence in the Andes on Spanish sources continues to impose serious limitations, given the difficulty of approaching indigenous social categories and accessing Andean "voices and social realms" (Durston 2008: 45) through non-native sources. By contrast, indigenous categories, particularly as accessed through language, remain defining foci of colonial ethnohistorical research in Mesoamerica.

For modern revival movements, this history has important legacies. First, while glyphic-pictorial literacy was definitively discontinuous among most indigenous peoples, the existence of pre-Columbian writing systems is far from irrelevant for modern indigenous writers: they frequently stress this heritage in claiming legitimacy and in furthering political agendas. Their indigenous-language literacy programs often include minor attempts to teach ancient writing. The fact that these initiatives rarely succeed in producing glyphic literacy is somewhat irrelevant. For the intellectuals promoting them, the efforts themselves are saturated with meaning. However opaque, the scripts themselves are emblems of distinctive, non-Western identities, and the reinscription of modern writers' ties to pre-Columbian writing represents continuity with ancient, illustrious, and autochthonous indigenous expression.

The second legacy concerns the descriptive linguistic work of colonial priests.[14] Initial orthographies in Western script were devised for many Mesoamerican languages.[15] Often such orthographies are deeply flawed—for example, few colonial orthographies marked for tone, a feature central to many indigenous American languages, present in all Oto-Manguean languages (including Mazatec), and, not coincidentally, absent entirely from Indo-European languages. Indigenous intellectuals often state that their literary and literacy efforts will correct such flaws, which they view as linked to the larger project of colonial domination. Nevertheless, these initial works form a critical point of departure for modern indigenous writers. As many of them assert, the early texts provide basic tools for analyzing indigenous languages. Features of many colonial orthographies are used today by indigenous writers—or form a pivotal locus animating their critiques and "corrective" orthographic choices.

Third, the corpus of colonial indigenous-language texts is critically important to indigenous authors. The birth under colonialism of indigenous literatures in the Western sense initiated a long history among indigenous elites of using written texts to negotiate the discrepancy between widely varying systems of expression and divergent schema for the ascription of social identity. This project also animates indigenous literary movements in the present. Colonial texts written by natives set the precedent for modern indigenous literary movements, constituting a longstanding tradition that can be built on and appealed to for authority. Further, the very existence of indigenous-language colonial texts has great relevance in current political debates over cultural and linguistic rights. From the first contact between the Old World and the New World, indigenous populations have been regarded with competing tendencies toward glorification and vilification, viewed alternatively as the representation of a purer human essence or as the debasement of human potential. Attitudes toward indigenous languages and their relative sophistication have followed a similar trajectory. Observers have oscillated between viewing such languages as inherently inferior and valorizing them for their richness and complexity. The prevalence of the former view during the colonial period is part of what Spanish priests involved in writing grammars and compiling native language texts were reacting against. Indigenous authors are in a structurally similar position today: the persistence of views about the relative simplicity and poverty of indigenous languages is the framework against which modern indigenous authors and language activists react. Invoking a long tradition of well-developed literatures in native languages thus becomes a key tool such intellectuals use in furthering their political, cultural, and linguistic agendas.

Nevertheless, this legacy does have at least two important limits, neither of which is widely acknowledged—for reasons I return to later—by modern indigenous authors. The first concerns the nature of pre-Columbian and colonial literacy. As before the conquest, colonial literacy was a skill available only to a small subset of the total population. Most indigenous people neither learned to speak Spanish nor became literate in Spanish or indigenous languages. For modern authors, the situation is somewhat different: most readers are at least nominally literate in Spanish. Yet most modern indigenous audiences, like the majority of pre-Columbian and colonial indigenous peoples, are not literate in indigenous languages. Indigenous authors actively lament this situation and, to varying degrees, aim to redress it by promoting indigenous-language literacy. As we will see, it is rare for indigenous authors who champion the legacy of their pre-Columbian and colonial forebears to acknowledge the elite circles in which indigenous documents circulated. Nevertheless, the legacy of this limited literacy, magnified by the inability to look to the past for models of popular indigenous-language literacy, is a situation with which indigenous authors continuously grapple.

The second important constraint attached to indigenous writing in Mesoamerica concerns how authors working in so-called minority indigenous languages interact with this history, as for them the legacy of indigenous writing is more mixed. As Matthew Restall (2003: 127) writes, "The fact remains that most native groups of colonial Latin America either did not write at all in their own languages or they left behind very few such records indeed." Authors in only a few indigenous languages can claim a long history of texts in their languages. Even during the golden age of colonial indigenous-language literacy, the hegemony of key languages such as Nahuatl meant that even in heavily indigenous regions—Oaxaca above all, with its deep linguistic diversity—the vast majority of indigenous texts were produced in "majority" indigenous languages.[16] In Oaxaca, Nahuatl was routinely used between the Spanish and smaller indigenous groups; legal proceedings were minimally bilingual, if not multilingual, crucially hinging on the services of bilingual interpreters and notaries who were fluent in Nahuatl and one or more other indigenous languages (Restall et al. 2005: 17–18). Thus, in places like Oaxaca, the institutionalization of Nahuatl literacy as the administrative medium in indigenous communities proceeded at the expense of literacy in the local language.

This has produced an ongoing disparity in scholarly research. The vast body of scholarship on Mesoamerican history has focused on a few key regions: Central Mexico, the Mayan regions of Mexico and Guatemala, and the Mixtec and Zapotec areas of Oaxaca. The vast body of work on these regions dwarfs the few historical studies of marginal areas like the Sierra Mazateca. For some Mazatec intellectuals—who claim a history of both colonial and pre-Columbian oppression by Nahuatl and Mixtec speakers—this casts the hunt for literate ancestors even further into the past, toward Olmec writing, as historically closer precursors are all tainted by having been imposed. For similar reasons, tattoos of Epi-Olmec glyphs have become something of a fad among young people from Mixe communities in Oaxaca,[17] who share a similarly ambivalent history with majority ethnic groups such as Zapotecs, Mixtecs, and Nahuas.

This history's final legacy was the demise of literacy and literatures in native languages. The clergy's efforts to create native-language materials were tied to teaching indigenous people to read liturgical works in their languages. Priests also aimed to teach at least elites to speak and write Spanish; Spanish was always the official language of the empire, despite the semiofficial status of some indigenous languages as administrative media. The overwhelming institutional weight behind Spanish, coupled with New World linguistic diversity, meant that the "transition from native-language writing to Spanish [was] almost complete by the end of the colonial period" (Restall et al. 2005: 19). Partially the result of changing linguistic demographics, this shift also stemmed from formal decrees in the late colonial period, especially those that fell under the Bourbon reforms of 1770. These new laws constituted "a new hegemonic project for the colonial state" that aimed to "modernize and acculturate New Spain's Indians" (Guardino 2005: 109, 111). Over the three centuries of colonial rule, laws were periodically issued to strengthen Spanish-language dominance, but they were rarely enforced. Despite early legislation that officially promoted indigenous languages for colonial administration, the Crown subsequently reversed those policies. Yet in practice indigenous languages were widely used in official contexts.[18] Peter Guardino's discussion of late colonial court cases in Oaxaca shows that although indigenous-language documents were rare by that period, their existence, coupled with the grammatical and spelling errors in related Spanish-language documents, suggests that "even late in the colonial period . . . [in] some villages aspiring *escribanos* [scribes] learned to read and write Zapotec before learning Spanish" (Guardino 2005: 75). Given the pervasive use of indigenous languages such as Zapotec in official contexts, the decree of 1770 amounted to "linguistic shock therapy" (O'Hara 2009: 63) in which formal law was strongly at odds with existing practice. Under the new law, indigenous languages became officially barred for notarial purposes, and a range of language policies enforced Spanish competency in official matters, in concert with which the church founded hundreds of Spanish-language schools in indigenous villages (Tanck de Estrada 1999; see also Guardino 2005: 107–11; O'Hara 2009: 60–64; Van Young 2001: 478–79; Yannakakis 2008: 169–80).[19]

As Yanna Yannakakis (2008: 177) writes, quoting from formal documentation surrounding the new laws, "Civil and ecclesiastical authorities presented a united front on the matter, stating that 'the Council of the Indies, the Crown's representatives, the Viceroy, and the Archbishop of Mexico agree on the grave necessity of abolishing the great diversity of languages spoken by the Indians of America and of making the vassals of the King of Spain of that vast dominion monolingual in Spanish.'" New Spain's linguistic diversity was deemed unacceptable by secular authorities, as well as by clergy, the sector of colonial society that earlier had been the leading force behind documenting indigenous languages and promoting indigenous-language literacy. Now, however, the church espoused the view that "the barrier of language . . . acted as a spiritual prison for the Indian faithful" (O'Hara 2009: 63). The new schools were meant to instill Spanish-language competence while also serving as "the major venue . . . for the forced enculturation of indigenous people" (Van Young 2001: 479). The language policies and their institutionalization were thus an explicit attempt both to put an end to literacy in indigenous languages and to eliminate the use of indigenous languages themselves, cast as a crucial obstacle that prevented indigenous peoples' full incorporation into the empire. Following the decline of Nahuatl as a lingua franca, many colonial officials "thought that Indian languages posed an even greater challenge to cross-cultural communication in the eighteenth century than at the time of the conquest" (O'Hara 2009: 63).

The transition in the official domain sometimes coincided with broader language shifts from indigenous languages to Spanish; by the close of the colonial period, Spanish had become common as a second language among indigenous nobility, and many indigenous people were competent enough in Spanish that they could testify in it in court (Guardino 2005: 76). However, indigenous people largely resisted the schools (Guardino 2005: 109), whose effectiveness was "always less than encouraging to royal policy-makers" and whose reality was stronger on paper than in fact (Van Young 2001: 479). Thus, in much of New Spain indigenous languages appear to have been used as vibrantly as ever.[20] However, their circulation became almost exclusively oral by the nineteenth century, when the colonial regime was replaced at independence (Cifuentes 1998). Writing became tightly associated not only with Spanish but also with nationalization. This trend found especially strong focus in the wake of the Mexican Revolution at the beginning of the twentieth century, when indigenous peoples became incorporated into the nation as never before, largely through postrevolutionary education policies (King 1994).

This dynamic is tied in turn to another crucial issue against which indigenous intellectuals are reacting: the birth of the "Indian problem." The cultural apartheid at the heart of the colonial enterprise involved separating racial castes through formal and informal mechanisms and limiting intermediaries such as literate indigenous scribes and bilingual interpreters. Obviously a tool of colonial repression, this institutionalized separation of populations nevertheless allowed for widespread persistence of indigenous languages so that in Mexico today, language use remains the single most important marker of indigeneity. Despite great losses from disease and warfare during the conquest and early colonial period, vast numbers of indigenous people survived. While cultural survival "is a considerably more debatable issue," as Nancy Farriss (1984: 86) says, the continued existence of populations categorized as indigenous in Mexico and Latin America nevertheless created what has been called the "Indian problem": the question of how the state should deal with its subject indigenous populations.

Competing answers to this question have been present since the initial encounter between Europe and the New World. They are hinted at in the two distinct goals of the colonial enterprise, succinctly captured by the soldier and chronicler of the conquest, Bernal Díaz del Castillo (1968: 366): "To bring light to those in darkness, and also to get rich, which is what all men commonly seek." The Catholic missionaries' evangelical project and the colonizers' economic one often came into violent conflict. Although the two shared a desire to assimilate natives into European civilization, the overwhelming diversity among the indigenous peoples lumped together under the colonial category *indio* and the enormous cultural and linguistic differences between them and the Spanish continually posed challenges for realizing this aspiration. For the Spanish, the problem raised a host of questions—practical, theological, ontological, moral, legal—about how to deal with indigenous peoples.

One response initiated the tradition of *indigenismo*. Although indigenismo later appeared in more codified form in the postrevolutionary policies of the Mexican state most closely associated with the term, its iterations under colonialism viewed indigenous populations as a substrate for forms of social engineering. The result has been centuries of thought about indigenous peoples in Mexico (and the Americas) that are shot through with the agendas of nonindigenous peoples rather than those of indigenous peoples themselves. The very terms under which such people have been classified betray this orientation. They were labeled "Indian" from the earliest European contact forward and subsequently relabeled "indigenous," though with the category itself remaining intact. This category foregrounded difference from European and later national culture at the expense of emphasizing diversity within the category and similarities across its boundaries. In response to this categorization and its enduring legacy, debates about social and ethnic identity consistently have been salient. Language use has played a special role in the dialogue: linguistic difference figured prominently in the conquest's initial classification process, and it has played a critical role in scholarly attempts to grapple with its consequences.[21] These different layers of writing about indigenous peoples have been a crucial point of departure for modern indigenous authors, whose attempts at revival are a response to generations of state policies designed to manage the so-called Indian problem.

The history of indigenous language writing and literacy prefigures it for a later renaissance. The precolonial and colonial eras give way to decline and disuse of those languages in public settings, setting the stage for revival in which discontinuous traditions are revitalized along contemporary concerns. The dawn of this renaissance in the twentieth century inaugurates the modern period of indigenous literary and literacy movements. Its meaning and character, however, come into focus only when viewed against the period that intervened between the golden age and its modern revival: independence and national consolidation.

INDEPENDENCE: NATIONAL UNITY AND THE HEGEMONY OF SPANISH

In general, scholars of Latin America's independence era have considered the prime factor mobilizing action against Spain to be the politicization of identity among *criollos* (American-born people of European ancestry). In New Spain, as elsewhere, the ongoing immigration of peninsular Spaniards, who entered the colonial hierarchy above criollos, caused increasing unrest (Brading 1991; Halperín Donghi 1993). Within the paradigm emphasizing how criollo identity shaped Latin America's wave of independence, Indian identity has been considered marginal; the social position and material conditions of life for most indigenous people were viewed as differing little from what they had been under the colonial regime.

According to this narrative, few indigenous people participated in the Mexican War of Independence (1810–21). Their explicit inclusion in Mexico as part of the criollo elite's nation-building project was viewed as largely symbolic: criollos drew on carefully chosen images of indigenous peoples, positioning themselves as inheritors of their glorious but inert past to distinguish themselves from their European-born counterparts (Brading 1991). This strategy denied any place within the national space for Indians living in the present, a legacy that continues to haunt national life in modern Mexico.[22] Works including Bonfil Batalla's famous treatise *México profundo* (1987) have emphasized the selective benefits of liberalism, which ushered in independence and flourished in its wake: liberalist ideals articulating attitudes about contemporary indigenous populations sought their gradual erasure through behavioral *blanqueamiento* (whitening) This narrative stresses postindependence privatization and capitalist expansion leading to massive land expropriations of the church's vast holdings but also lands of indigenous communities. Thus the nineteenth century witnessed the dramatic growth of vast haciendas in southern Mexico precisely where indigenous populations were the densest. Accounts in this vein highlight the powerful negative effect these developments had on indigenous peoples, eroding the land base that traditionally insulated them from the worst excesses of colonial rule.

This view of independence-era history is widely held by many indigenous Mexican intellectuals. Many of the country's leading indigenous authors completed their formal education when books like *México profundo*—a seminal text for many indigenous intellectuals—forcefully articulated this view of Mexican history and definitively linked it to the contemporary problems faced by indigenous Mexicans. Nonetheless, recent scholarship on Mexico's postindependence history has called this view into question.

Eric Van Young's magisterial work forcefully challenges the idea that indigenous people did not take part in the independence movement, troubling claims that its participants formed an emerging nationalistic alliance unifying masses and elites across class and ethnic lines. The book's "submerged history of Mexico's anti-colonial struggle" (Van Young 2001: 3) shows that beyond being the nineteenth century's first great war of decolonization— where criollo elites rejected the power of Spain while forging a new nation— Mexico's independence movement was also an internal struggle involving popular class and ethnic conflicts in the countryside. In this "other rebellion," the "'official' history nourished by nationalist ideology and creole triumphalism" is countered by local struggles as indigenous people and peasants fought nonindigenous elites to protect their communities from new forms of state intervention (Van Young 2001: 3). Raymond Craib (2004) accomplishes a similar feat for a slightly later period: the reform era and the Porfiriato, collectively running from the middle of the nineteenth century through the start of the Mexican Revolution in the early twentieth century. He shows that the cartographic practices that consolidated the nation, while intimately tied to liberal ideals and elite state-making agendas, took shape through complex processes playing out in so-called fugitive landscapes, where federal forces intent on "fixing" the national landscape most sought to intervene. Craib argues that these cartographic processes, far from being a simple rehearsal of hegemonic power relations, involved active participation by rural peasants coming into ideological conflict with landholders, state mapmakers, surveyors, and government officials.

Research on Oaxaca has further rethought "official" Mexican history, placing indigenous people in the role of active participants during and after independence. Researching popular political culture in Oaxaca from the late colonial period through the early national period (1750–1850), Guardino (2005) shows that the state's rural, indigenous peasants were centrally involved in the transformation from colonial rule to national independence. His research comparing the state's urban and rural politics emphasizes the dramatic difference between the two spheres yet demonstrates that Oaxaca's indigenous people, far from being alienated from popular politics, were actively involved in ideological struggles. Edward Wright-Rios (2009: 24) revises conventional understandings of the relationship between the church and indigenous parishioners in the tumultuous period from the Porfiriato through the Revolution, when "social and cultural tensions coinciding with the Bourbon reforms of the eighteenth century served as the calling card of emergent modernity." Received wisdom has held that liberalizing measures taken by the Mexican state to weaken the church disempowered indigenous people, as well, who during colonialism depended on the protection and assistance of religious authorities against secular ones. Juxtaposing elite church agendas against popular indigenous Mexican Catholicism, Wright-Rios shows that the historical reality was more complicated: the clergy's attempts to institute Vatican revitalization and reform programs met with unpredictable results when interacting with the visionary movements of Oaxaca's indigenous laity.

Beyond adding new complexity to our understanding of Mexican history, recent work offers a more nuanced picture of indigenous languages and writing in this period. None of the aforementioned works dwell on the status of indigenous languages; indeed, even in accounts focusing on indigenous literacy and literature, the nineteenth century is a largely empty middle age between the colonial period and the modern one that dates from the second half of the twentieth century.[23] Some recent anthologies of indigenous writing even make the omission explicit. In the volume *In the Language of Kings: An Anthology of Mesoamerican Literature, Pre-Columbian to the Present* (2001), edited by Miguel León-Portilla and Earl Shorris, the book's chronological order moves immediately from the "Colonial Literature of Daily Life" to "Modern Nahua Literature." Nor is the failure to take account of the nineteenth century confined to belletristic scholars such as León-Portilla. Others have stressed the decline in indigenous literatures and literacies by identifying the abolition of colonial indigenous courts as a pivotal event that meant indigenous people no longer had a special venue for pleading their claims. Such accounts stress that through this shift, indigenous languages lost their most important source of valorization and indigenous language literacy lost its primary institutional backing and the most important context where literacy skills were practiced and transmitted (King 1994).

Certainly the move toward one legal system for all Mexican citizens, regardless of linguistic background, placed indigenous people at multiple layers of disadvantage compared with their mestizo and criollo fellow citizens. This weakened position stemmed not only from differential competence in the Spanish language itself, narrowly construed, but also from limited fluency in particular legal and bureaucratic registers of Spanish and reduced familiarity with the full array of Western legal practices rooted in Enlightenment thought. The fact that Nahuatl, Maya, and other indigenous languages lost the status they held under colonialism—that of semiofficial languages routinely used in administrative and legal settings—did entail, as a blunt fact, the dramatic decline in the production of indigenous-language texts after independence. Nevertheless, recent research gives a more complete and varied picture of this decline.

The authors mentioned earlier, among others, concur that there are few indigenous-language documents produced in this period; many of those few were copied from colonial documents for use in independence-era court cases. Earlier practices—where at least some people learned to read and write an indigenous language before learning Spanish—had ended by the close of the colonial era (Guardino 2005: 15, 75). Yet the nature of the indigenous-language documents that do exist from this period is revealing, suggesting that indigenous-language writing did not vanish as fully or evenly as conventional narratives would suggest. In Oaxaca's Mixtec region, the church's declining interest in indigenous-language writing and instruction toward the end of the colonial period and early independence was countered by an uptick of interest in supporting indigenous languages beginning around 1830 (Smith 2012). Following on the heels of the local divisiveness of the war for independence (Van Young 2001), the new republic witnessed the outbreak of a succession of caste wars (O'Hara 2009; Rugeley 2009). These violent racial and class divisions led the church to attempt increasing its popular appeal by reverting to institutionalized support of indigenous languages. Hence, in the decades following independence, the church published many catechisms in indigenous languages. This enthusiasm for religious texts in indigenous languages was repeated toward the end of the nineteenth century with the creation of new dioceses and the expansion of rural clergy, including pastors with interests and abilities in indigenous languages (Smith 2012). In both periods of the nineteenth century, renewed support often involved publications in indigenous languages that previously had been ignored. Some of the first texts in Mazatec were produced beginning in 1820, possibly by indigenous priests who were native speakers, followed by another handful of publications at the end of the century.[24]

The period's secular texts suggest a similarly shifting and historically specific engagement with indigenous-language writing by state and civil society institutions. Over the nineteenth century and into the twentieth century, a variety of texts—many of them appearing relatively isolated and unique—were produced in indigenous languages. This was especially true of Nahuatl; examples include the historical and linguistic works of Faustino Galicia Chimalpopoca, translations of national and state constitutions (Cifuentes 1998; Thomson and LaFrance 2002: 241) and even Apolonio Martínez's translation in 1910 of Virgil's fourth *Eclogue* (León-Portilla and Shorris 2001: 11). In Oaxaca, a particularly interesting case was a letter published in 1832 in El *Zapoteco*, a partisan newspaper that catered primarily to urban, mestizo elites. Written in Zapotec, the letter denounced the local government for forcing villagers to work on a major road being built between the state capital and the isthmus. In mentioning the letter, Guardino (2005: 194) is doubtless right that "literacy in Zapotec was probably extremely rare by the 1830s" and that the newspaper's editors and authors "were probably trying to make a point about their openness to the problems of rural Indians." Nevertheless, the linguistic qualities of the letter suggest a more complex reading: it is written in a variant of Zapotec spoken only in one pueblo in the surrounding valley and uses loan words and other lexical items that clearly link it to local oral discourse while distancing it from the last notarial text published in Valle Zapotec just a few years earlier (in 1824).[25] The stark differences between official Zapotec writing and the vernacular version printed in the letter in *El Zapoteco* do not contradict conventional understandings that writing in indigenous languages declined after independence. However, they do suggest— perhaps precisely due to the lack of sustained, institutionalized support for indigenous writing by the state or the church—that indigenous writing in this period was more varied, contingent, and locally driven than had been the case for much of its previous history.

Nonetheless, independence introduced a new chapter in the story of the so-called Indian problem. The era turned around a rejection of colonial rule, but the driving philosophy was the political program of liberalism, which united two Enlightenment ideals: Adam Smith's free-market theories and French Enlightenment commitment to the rights of man. Throughout Latin America, liberalism formed the blueprint for early nationhood and remained the dominant ideology throughout the nineteenth century (Guardino 2005). This political ethos emphasized egalitarianism but above all citizenship— hence, private property and individualism. This, in turn, gave rise to a pervasive contradiction in the era's state-making projects: the coexistence of political equality and socioeconomic inequality. Privileging citizenship meant a radical revaluation of the Indians, at least officially, whose status as citizens was equal to that of other ethnic groups. Yet the implementation of official policies ostensibly aimed at redressing the systemic inequalities of colonialism often affected Mexico's indigenous populations negatively. Where nationalization involved linguistic homogenization through the institutionalized imposition of Spanish, indigenous languages faced greater threats than they had under colonialism, when institutionalized separation of the castes had provided protective buffers for Indians' expressions of ethnic difference, including those tied to their languages.

By the end of the national period—which coincided with the emergence of modern academic disciplines, including anthropology, and the ascendance of Social Darwinism—"the Indian" was increasingly seen as an impediment to a modern Mexican nation. Some intellectuals promoted the notion that the best solution to this problem was assimilation, a project crucially hinging on the national educational system. As expressed in 1902 by Justo Sierra, a leading intellectual who became Mexico's minister of public instruction and fine arts, indigenous languages posed "an obstacle to the complete formation of the consciousness of the motherland," and their suppression would be "the invaluable vehicle of social unification" (quoted in King 1994: 58). This characterization prefigured the indigenismo that would become so central to postrevolutionary political ideology in Mexico.

The focus on assimilation and education as its crucial vehicle played an essential role, directly and indirectly, in the formation of modern indigenous intellectuals. The assimilationist ideology of the independence era critically prefigured many postrevolutionary policies that in turn form a central background against which indigenous intellectuals are reacting, even as they have also been shaped by it. While such policies had roots in independence, they were shaped more immediately by more-recent histories of relations among indigenous peoples, the state, and the church that date from the second half of the twentieth century—that is, from the living memory of Mexico's most-prominent indigenous intellectuals. Recent work on the independence era shows that local practice was often at odds with official policy, and the fate of indigenous languages and writing in this period apparently varied widely from one region of the country to another. Yet official narratives of Mexican history have largely eclipsed this view for one in which, during independence, indigenous writing enters a state of near-moribund decline. In portraying the history of indigenous-language writing as one of dormancy and decay after independence, indigenous intellectuals participate in a complex feedback loop with academic research and popular discourse, furthering the perception that the most important fact about indigenous people in this era is their overall disenfranchisement, including the loss of indigenous-language writing, if not also the loss of the languages themselves.

FROM REVOLUTION TO RENAISSANCE: THE CHANGING FACE OF INDIGENISMO

Unlike the war for independence, the Mexican Revolution (1910–29) is a struggle in which, scholars have long claimed, indigenous people actively participated—famously, in the figure of Emiliano Zapata.[26] Nevertheless, as Alan Knight (1990: 76) claims, although it was "fought on the basis of considerable Indian participation," the war lacked "any self-consciously 'Indian' project." Van Young (2001: 521), in supportive dialogue with Knight, claims that the "forms of localist autodefense and cultural resistance within the context of ethnic conflict between indigenous and nonindigenous social sectors" that drove independence were impossible by the dawn of Revolution; by then, "the identity of many communities formerly indigenous in their primary auto-identification was reconfigured from Indianness to peasantness."

Indigenous people's active but largely nonethnicized participation in the Revolution was linked to the state's ongoing ambivalence toward indigenous people, revealed in the brand of mestizaje espoused in early postrevolutionary policies. Although this variant of indigenismo had roots in the national period, it blossomed as an institutionalized discourse with the rise of the postrevolutionary state. It took on special importance during the presidency of Lázaro Cárdenas (1934–40), whose administration aimed to realize Revolutionary goals through large-scale land redistribution and collectivization, the expropriation and nationalization of foreign-owned industries, and the syndicalization of workers and peasants.

Revolutionary indigenismo shared with its independence-era precursors the goal of integrating indigenous people into the nation. However, the two versions held different views of the state's role, which in turn were tied to contrasting attitudes toward indigenous people themselves. Rather than being indios, the "backward" peasants of the national period, indigenous people—now referred to as indígenas, an explicit attempt to subvert the pejorative connotations of the label "indio"—were seen as victims of the state's historical abuse and neglect. They were considered a segment of the Mexican population the nation had the ethical obligation to bring fully into national life, eradicating their chronic poverty and marginality. Proponents of indigenismo promoted a policy holding Indians to be distinctive recipients of a unique cultural heritage, yet recognized their ethnic difference largely as a preamble to mestizaje: in converting Indians into campesino peasants the state was simultaneously creating Mexican citizens (Bonfil Batalla 1987; Frye 1996; Jung 2008; Lomnitz 1992). Mexico's Secretary of Education José Vasconcelos articulated these ideas clearly. His seminal work La raza cósmica (The Cosmic Race) claimed that mestizos were a superior "cosmic race" who would bring about a peaceful third age while serving as canonical Mexican citizens (Vasconcelos 1997 [1925]).[27] Miscegenation and assimilation became the prime vehicles for social progress. The so-called Indian problem could be solved by making Indians more like mestizos, and cultural homogeneity became the basis of a new national unity.

Recent scholarship on the Revolution and its legacies has not so much questioned the powerful role that such official ideologies played in managing ethnic diversity as it has emphasized that the local implementation of state cultural policies often produced unpredictable results. The emphasis on nationalizing and democratizing the rural and indigenous populace necessitated local interactions that in turn forced national policy to accommodate to local terms. This work, like earlier scholarship, emphasized that indigenismo was driven by elite formulations of the so-called Indian problem. Leading national figures—from intellectuals such as Vasconcelos to artists such as Frida Kahlo and Diego Rivera—supported ethnic diversity while simultaneously promoting the transcendence of race as a crucial step in forging a unified, distinctive national identity (Dawson 2004; Vaughan and Lewis 2006). However, this work also portrays a more complex picture not only of how those ideas fared in practice but also of how these crucial national policies and symbols were brought into being. Alexander Dawson's work emphasizes that indigenismo, while driven by elites, was also mediated by popular pressures: implementation of state policies required a pact of domination between indígenas and the ruling party forged through active negotiation between the government and indigenous people. The Eagle and the Virgin: Nation and Cultural Revolution in Mexico, the collection of essays edited by Mary K. Vaughan and Stephen Lewis (2006), equally stresses the critical role played by elites, broadening their ranks from government officials, social scientists, and indigenous leaders to include muralists, musicians, architects, engineers, and entrepreneurs. The book complicates any easy narrative of top-down nationalism by emphasizing the wide range of actors and interests involved in forging national identity. As its title signals, the volume is particularly helpful in exploring tensions between two powerful symbols and, in turn, two powerful Mexican institutions. The eagle, symbol of the modern and secular state, and the Virgin of Guadalupe, symbol of the Catholic faith on which Mexican national identity has long depended, jointly contributed to forming a cohesive nation. By emphasizing both state and church, the book foregrounds the church's ongoing importance in this era, in contrast to official narratives of Mexican nationalism that stress the Revolution's success in weakening the church as a necessary step toward making Mexico a secular, modern democracy.

Relatively little research has been done on the state of indigenous languages in this period. What has been produced focuses primarily on education policies.[28] During independence, indigenous languages became closely tied to oral circulation; following the Revolution, these languages experienced renewed official interest in relation to national education programs. In keeping with the postrevolutionary focus on national identity formation, the school system was conceived as a mechanism through which to unite the country linguistically by promoting Spanish "as the only [language] capable of transmitting official knowledge" and discouraging the use of indigenous languages, mere dialectos that were inferior to so-called full languages such as Spanish (King 1994: 61). During this period, indigenous languages became oral in a new way, defined not only by their oral transmission but also through contrast with Spanish. Through the expansion of the educational system, Spanish became rooted in daily life in new ways for indigenous people as it became the language of print, learning, and the nation. Ideas that indigenous languages are just dialects and hence "cannot be written down" found increased traction in this era and to this day remain widespread, routinely expressed by indigenous people as well as by other Mexicans.

This is not to say that official aspirations met uniform success in practice as the state expanded the educational system into rural and indigenous areas. In examining the politics of schooling in the 1930s, Vaughan (1997) argues that while the state succeeded in using its education to promote a particular model of multiethnic nationalism, it did so only through intense debate with rural communities, which used negotiations about education to create an arena for protecting local identities. While Vaughan (1997: 126) says little about how indigenous languages were affected in this period, local communities' leveraging of discussions of education to preserve local power doubtless involved shoring up the autonomy of indigenous languages in some areas of social life even as it ceded ground in others. In the cases Vaughan discusses, teaching was done—in accordance with official policy—almost exclusively in Spanish, however partially students learned the language before leaving school. In other cases, education did take place in indigenous languages, if under the radar and in contradiction to official policy. This is especially well documented in Oaxaca's Sierra Juarez (Clarke 2000; Smith 2007), where students were taught in Zapotec by bilingual teachers—which is to say, teachers who were bilingual, a sort of prototype of the institutionally backed maestros bilingües who were officially trained in bilingual instruction later in the century. Beginning in the late 1970s, official language policy shifted to embrace bilingual education, setting up a system of bilingual schools—which continues today—that were a vehicle for linguistic and cultural mainstreaming and yet accorded certain respect to indigenous languages and cultural differences.

This shift was part of a series of changes in indigenous policy in the mid-twentieth century, as the indigenismo of the young Revolutionary state and Cárdenas's presidency gave way to other variants of the movement that were less concerned with unity than with progress and economic development. Following the Inter-American Indigenist Congress in Patzcuaro, Mexico, in 1940, indigenismo became "a model of state indigenous policy throughout Latin America" that "framed the 'indigenous problem' as one of development and aid. As a result, Indians themselves were located as objects of modernization, health, and education programs, rather than as political subjects" (Jung 2008: 94–95).

Beginning in the 1940s, an emphasis on modernization became the dominant paradigm for indigenista thought and policy. Founded in 1948, the Instituto Nacional Indigenista (INI) was the key government agency instituting official indigenista policy. Until the 1960s, this framework guided both national development and anthropological investigation—research with a demonstrable effect on state programs and the cultural dimensions of Mexican nationalism. Anthropologists and archaeologists in Mexico, as elsewhere in Latin America, were directly involved in applied anthropological projects that shaped and executed state policy, particularly those that concerned indigenous populations (Lomnitz 2001). The focus on modernization in this variant of indigenismo, and the collaborative work between policymakers and anthropologists, is exemplified in numerous cases but perhaps nowhere more than in the Papaloapan Commission, which led to the construction of a vast hydroelectric dam in the heart of the Mazatec lowlands. The dam's construction entailed flooding nearly fifty thousand hectares of fertile farmland and displacing some twenty thousand campesinos, mostly Mazatec speakers (Barabas and Bartolomé 1973: 4). A key figure in the commission's work was the Mexican anthropologist Alfonso Villa Rojas, who, with Robert Redfield, a leading figure in the discipline at large, wrote the pioneering ethnography *Chan Kom: A Maya Village* (Redfield and Villa Rojas 1934). Villa Rojas later wrote about the Papaloapan Project in a work that doubled as an ethnography of the affected region and a documentation of anthropologists' work interfacing with those who had been displaced (Villa Rojas 1955). Quoting from Villa Rojas, Gabriela Soto Laveaga (2009: 33) writes, "The Papaloapan Commission was the first 'tropical development scheme' in Mexico, with the modest mission of 'conquering the tropics.' . . . [The] plan's teams of engineers, anthropologists, and botanists made the Papaloapan one of the most studied regions at a time when the tropics beckoned with promises of development and prosperity."

By the 1970s, the tide had shifted once again, and indigenismo policies, as well as Mexican anthropology, became critical of modernization projects (Lomnitz 2001). This shift is reflected in different attitudes taken toward the Papaloapan Project by prominent Mexican anthropologists. Villa Rojas's collaboration with the project is reflected in his book's title, *Los mazatecos y el problema indígena de la cuenca de Papaloapan* (The Mazatecs and the indigenous problem of the Papoloapan Dam). Conversely, Alicia Barabas's and Miguel Bartolomé's fervent critique is equally reflected in their title, *Hydraulic Development and Ethnocide: The Mazatec and Chinantec People of Oaxaca, Mexico*.

A seminal moment in the shift toward greater critique of the state was the student movement of 1968, which culminated in the infamous Tlatelolco Massacre. Anthropologists were critically involved both in the protests that preceded that event and in the groundbreaking reactions to it. The period began in the early 1960s with the growth of a generational rupture in Mexican anthropology as the counterculture ethos of the decade gained momentum and Marxism gained influence in Mexican universities. At the time, "The identification of Mexican anthropology with official nationalism was at its peak" (Lomnitz 2001: 231). In response, dissident anthropologists harshly critiqued Mexican anthropology in the seminal manifesto *De eso que llaman antropología Mexicana* (That's what they call Mexican anthropology; Warman et al. 1970). Arturo Warman and other young luminaries of the age claimed that "Mexican anthropology had placed itself squarely in the service of the state, and so had abdicated both its critical vocation and its moral obligation to side with the popular classes" (Lomnitz 2001: 231). These critics, advocating distance from the state, "were interested in breaking the domination of *indigenismo* and returning to the discipline's critical engagement with the problems of poverty, hunger, and the cultural and political domination fomented by the Mexican state" (de la Peña 1997: 58).

These critics joined with others—above all, indigenous and campesino activists—to push indigenista policies in the direction of greater direct participation by indigenous people in formulating national policies that affected them. A defining event in the change toward *nuevo* (new) indigenismo occurred in 1970 when the anthropologist Gonzalo Aguirre Beltrán was named director of the INI. Although he had been "an early architect of *indigenismo*" (Jung 2008: 94), and hence had shaped indigenista ideologies for years, the evolution in his thought toward new models (as expressed in Aguirre Beltrán 1973) helped the INI take on a new character. Indigenista thought shifted from interest in assimilation and integration toward the promotion of acculturation, stressing reciprocity and respect. Aguirre Beltrán argued that indigenous communities were best viewed not as participating in a broad peasant populace but as part of "intercultural regions," or regional systems of "caste-based" domination. In these "regions of refuge," mestizo and Ladino powerbrokers controlled regional capitals, perpetuating systems of oppression and propagating the historical exploitation of indigenous people. The indigenista policies of Aguirre Beltrán's era aimed to break these power structures. The INI dramatically increased the number of regional centers and charged them with combating the intercultural power emanating from the regional capitals where the centers were located. These changes within the INI were echoed and furthered in the late 1970s when president José López Portillo instituted a new program called *indigenismo de participación* (participatory indigenism) or *etnodesarollo* (ethnic development). Under this initiative, the INI implemented programs that were "intended to stimulate and defend indigenous cultures, eventually drifting from its initial brief as a development organization and focusing more pointedly on explicitly cultural projects" (Jung 2008: 164).

According to Aguirre Beltrán (1973), education was a crucial arena in which the state should disrupt cycles of repression. While many have criticized nuevo indigenismo as primarily a cosmetic and discursive change (see, e.g., Ros 1992), "The most consequential result of the new policy was the defederalization of education and the development of bilingual education in indigenous areas" (Jung 2008: 165). The rural school system that educated most indigenous children expanded substantially as the INI took over institutions that promoted bilingual education. Previously, the Summer Institute of Linguistics (SIL) had been responsible for what in effect was bilingual education, although it was not institutionalized as such (King 1994).[29] Emphasizing so-called biculturalism, bilingual education was meant to use culturally sensitive pedagogy coupled with respect for indigenous languages. Ostensibly, teachers taught in the indigenous language until the third grade, and students learned to read and write in their native language first. Only in the fourth grade did Spanish-language instruction begin, and not until fifth grade did Spanish become the primary language of schooling (Jung 2008: 165; King 1994).

However, bilingual education often functioned quite differently and less effectively in practice: "bilingual education is judged to have been a resounding failure in Mexico" (Jung 2008: 166). In chapter 6, I consider reasons for this, and legacies of the system's failures, in discussing a pervasive if unintended consequence of the bilingual education program: its role in forming indigenous activists and intellectuals who are key figures in modern indigenous revival. The implementation of bilingual education created great demand for bilingual schoolteachers, and through the formal training program for bilingual schoolteachers, people from indigenous communities were exposed to discourses and ideologies that encouraged them to respect and preserve indigenous languages and cultural practices. At the same time, it tied them into a vast network of other indigenous people with similar backgrounds and burgeoning interest in cultural and linguistic preservation. Some underwent further education and training, through which they became even better equipped to serve as culture brokers and activists. The ethnolinguistics program was started in this period (in 1979); this program gave speakers of indigenous language specialized training in analyzing their languages and became critical in forming many of Mexico's leading indigenous authors.

Thus, nuevo indigenismo found expression not only in changing educational policies but also in the increasingly visible role indigenous intellectuals—particularly Oaxacans—played in formulating national policy. Given Oaxaca's heavily indigenous character, linguistic diversity, and administrative complexity (it houses nearly a fourth of the country's municipios [counties]), national bilingual education has long been shaped by its regional implementation in Oaxaca. Oaxaca's maestros bilingües have for decades strongly influenced national educational policy; the influence of Section 22, the Oaxaca division of the national teachers' union, was symbolized in the social movement of 2006, an event that captured ongoing national and international attention. That movement's extended disruption of "normal" life in the state, coupled with the violence with which it was repressed, have made it a particularly well-known example of political activism. The revival projects I discuss here are a less well known but no less concrete expression of the influence the bilingual education system has had in laying the groundwork for popular activism in Mexico.

One other critical development in this period has strongly influenced ongoing development of the so-called Indian problem, shaping both indigenismo and indigenous-state relations. This is the rise within the church, following Vatican II (1962–65), of Liberation Theology. The church's shifts toward greater outreach to Mexico's poor and indigenous people had a formative, if less widely acknowledged, influence on indigenous intellectuals who drive ethnic revival movements. In ways both similar to and dramatically different from the SIL, the church has been variously involved in indigenous education since the Revolution, especially in teaching indigenous-language literacy. This has meant that the church, in ways that differ dramatically from the state, has encouraged indigenous people to valorize their languages and cultures. However, the church's influence in this realm has been less consistent and uniform, less widespread, and less widely known than the state's. The majority of Mexican indigenous intellectuals were at some point bilingual schoolteachers, while far fewer indigenous activists, authors, and intellectuals trace their intellectual lineage through the church (or the SIL). Thus, the role of the state in education and indigenous literacy has been the prime focus of scholarly research, and the role of the church—and, to a lesser extent, that of the SIL—often falls out of the analysis. Because the Sierra Mazateca is one region in which the church has had clear effects in producing indigenous intellectuals, I turn to the recent history of the church's influence in the next chapter, discussing key historical events that have had an immediate impact on the region's ethnic revival movements. I thereby hope to reintroduce to scholarship a consideration of the role of the church in forming Mexico's indigenous intellectuals and in making possible the country's ongoing indigenous linguistic and cultural revivals.

LEGACIES AND LESSONS: A VIEW FROM THE MARGINS

The ambivalence with which the state has historically viewed its indigenous people continues to appear in the present as a many-faced and tenacious ghost, haunting attempts to find a new place for indigenous people in the nation. Mexico's ambiguous relation to its indigenous citizens is born of the two poles between which official attitudes about the so-called Indian problem have oscillated: the recognition of indigenous difference as an essential element in the multiethnic collective and the desire to erase such difference and replace it with cultural homogeneity. At one extreme, indigenous people and their languages, although almost always seen as inferior, are allowed to persist despite their difference; at the other end, the price for full access to society's bounty is the eradication of ethnic difference. This erasure is often exacted through the control and elimination of indigenous languages. The unresolved conflict at the heart of such a system is its fundamental inability—in practice, if not in theory—to find a space within the nation where the recognition of difference and full participation in national life can coexist.

Literacy, education, and writing have been intimately bound up in these vacillating national policies, partaking of the same ambivalence. Despite the liberal discourse that attends the promotion of literacy and universal education, the knowledge offered through such programs is never neutral. Rather, it is an extension of structures of power and domination. Such projects, intentionally or not, import the fraught issues that underlie the so-called Indian problem: who defines indigenous identity and how that formulation is used in practice. By the time the Revolution took place, indigenous languages in Mexico had become almost exclusively oral in circulation, even among elites. This meant that in contradistinction to earlier periods, practices of writing became associated with the Spanish language, and hence with nationalization. Thus, for many indigenous people, literacy, writing, and formal education have been inseparable from the "civilizing" and developmental agendas of the state. Whatever benefits might be conferred by learning to read and write are inevitably tied to the requirement of accepting, at least in part, state-promoted definitions of and attitudes toward indigenous people. Furthermore, the ambivalence with which indigenous people have viewed these projects and the skills they potentially instill can be directed toward other indigenous people: those who have benefited from the programs while others have not. Guardino touches on this in discussing the historical roots of present-day *caciquismo*: "Mexican political shorthand for situations where a powerful individual [cacique] uses patronage, friends in higher offices, and sometimes violence to dominate the politics of an area for a long period of time" (2005: 243). He goes on to state that "in Oaxacan villages today [caciquismo] is often associated with literacy, bilingualism, and corruption." I return to this theme later in the book when I discuss similar criticisms leveled at leaders of ethnic revival movements. Indigenous authors and intellectuals frequently discuss being the target of similar skepticism, viewed by other indigenous people as—in the words of one indigenous author I interviewed—cultural caciques, or literary "bosses" who profit at the expense of other indigenous people.

Finally, the fundamental ambivalence with which the state has viewed indigenous Mexicans—and its pervasive inability to grapple fully with the essential diversity among them—has created widespread mechanisms of marginalization. From the colonial period forward, the state has been highly selective in its recognition of diversity among indigenous people. Even in periods of relative acceptance of difference, the state has privileged some markers of ethnic identity over others, paying attention to some indigenous populations while ignoring others. While the effects of this marginalization have sometimes been positive—indigenous languages are often widely spoken where the apparatus of the state has been weakest—the benefits and pressures issued by the state have varied widely and are experienced differentially.

Furthermore, scholarly literature on Mexico's indigenous people falls victim to and is complicit in the ongoing marginalization of some peoples over others. Just as the Spanish focused the colonial enterprise on the centers of preconquest Mesoamerican societies, scholars have paid far greater attention to these areas of Mesoamerica and to descendants of the region's "high" civilizations. The focus on Mesoamerica's pre-Hispanic writing systems— indices of social complexity—is part of this trend. Archaeological and historical studies alike exhibit this weighted attention: the closer one is to the nuclei of empire, the greater the density of material traces serving as data. But

FIGURE 1.1. The Sierra Mazateca.

of necessity or not, the focus on particular regions—with correspondingly less attention paid to the rest—has profoundly shaped scholarly research. The interest stimulated by pre-Hispanic writing systems and, later, by colonial indigenous texts has taken a similar form. While scholarly literature on pre-Columbian and colonial texts in Nahuatl and Mayan languages is well developed, the literature on Mixtec and, particularly, Zapotec writing is far thinner, and the drop-off for other groups is exceedingly steep. Ethnographic work concerning modern populations shows a similar bias, concentrating heavily on the living descendants of Mesoamerica's so-called high civilizations, particularly those living in Mexico and Guatemala. Within those nations, anthropological research has privileged peoples linked with the Aztec and Mayan civilizations and, to a lesser extent, those tied to the Zapotec and Mixtec civilizations of Oaxaca.

Entire peoples thus become confined to the peripheries of state and scholarly projects. The Sierra Mazateca is one such periphery (see fig. 1.1). As García Dorantes (2001: 17) tells us in this chapter's opening epigraph, it is a land of "parts that no one wanted because they were inhospitable and far," a place that perhaps suffers, perhaps prospers, but in any event is characterized by this double marginalization. Historically, Mazatecs were shut out of the benefits, such as they were, of full inclusion in the empire, while the Sierra's status as a backwater insulated its inhabitants from imperial excesses. The region today remains far less nationalized than neighboring areas, a feature directly related to national administrative structures. The Sierra Mazateca is located on the edge of Oaxaca State, and the entire region has been oriented toward urban centers in other states. The state capital is—as I heard people in the Sierra frequently express—"a long way away"; few Mazatec people migrate there, and few people from the Sierra would go there at all if not for the express purpose of attending to state business. Mazatecs form the third largest ethnic group in the state, yet members of the state's smaller groups form a far greater presence in the capital. Compared with Zapotecs and Mixtecs, for whom Oaxaca is not merely an administrative center but a commercial and educational one, as well, most Mazatecs are far less familiar with the city and have less experience dealing with state bureaucracy.

What we know about the history of the Sierra Mazateca is extremely thin. With few exceptions, in-depth studies of the Sierra, particularly those by anthropologists, have almost exclusively focused on Mazatec shamanism. The weighted nature of scholarly literature is largely driven by facts on the ground rather than intellectual bias per se. The vast majority of the indigenous Mesoamerican peoples live in Guatemala and Mexico; in Mexico, the majority live in Central and Southern Mexico, and so on. But whatever the causes, the effects are clear: marginality at one level promotes marginality at others. It is arguably true that the more we know, the more we know how little we know. But the view from the margins also suggests that the less we know, the less we are equipped to learn what we do not know.

On Authenticity, Indigeneity, and Unity: An Introduction to the Sierra Mazateca

K'uakuan ninga
Kinijch-chija je ndi chjon neina jña
K'uakuan ninga
Lijme tso jmitje si ti kuan ni-i
K'uakuan ninga
Tofi-tofi kitsoba je chita
K'uakuan ninga
Sakjai sakjai kjima naxinanda.

Ali niba jon
Tjin i k'a chita xi tso nga tojobe
Nga f'i kanengui
Tojo tso'ba je
I tinjnako na

In this way
we lost the image of our saint.
In this way
the crops failed.
In this way
the people scattered.
In this way
many problems arose, my people.

But don't be sad.
Some say they see her still,
that she comes to wash her hair,
that she is still here,
she is here with us.

—Heriberto Prado Pereda, from the song "Magdalena," in Kui⁴Nndja¹le⁴
nai³na¹ nga³ en¹ na¹-cantemos a dios en nuestra lengua

A short time later, they brought the copy of Mary Magdalene's statue to Chilchotla, but it is not the original, because they left that one in Nangui Nsoba.
Then things began to change in Chilchotla. Before, the land produced *guasmole*, gourds, yellow *zapotes* [a tropical fruit], custard apples, oranges, and
bananas, and also *chile* in abundance. But these began to disappear, and now
nothing remains, only rocks, some guavas, and rain. Not a twenty-second of
July passes on which it is not raining, and one can hear the people's lamen-
tations, above all from the old people, about how they left the saint in a town
no one can locate, in the Mixteca, which in Mazatec they call Nangui Nsoba.

There are other people, though, who claim the saint never left Chilchotla and they have seen her. Many people who have taken the mushrooms say
the saint has spoken to them and counseled them about how they should
live: without envy or animosity but, rather, by pardoning, living with, and
serving one's neighbor.[30]

—Alberto Prado Pineda, from "La historia de 'María Magdalena,' la santa
que se apareció en Chilchotla" ("The history of Mary Magdalene, the saint
who appeared in Chilchotla")

Heriberto Prado Pereda and Alberto Prado Pineda have been centrally involved
in the creation of modern Mazatec literature. They are the most active and
prominent indigenous intellectuals in Nda Xo (Chilchotla); they are also half-
brothers. Embedded in their different versions of the story about the town

FIGURE 1.2. A Catholic mass held during annual feast day celebrations for Mary Magdalene, patron saint of Nda Xo, who is said to have appeared at the town spring atop which the mass is held. Women and girls participating in the ceremony wear the traditional huipil of the Sierra Mazateca. Note that two ceremonial arcs have been constructed for the event. The one on the left was made by members of the Catholic Church, and the one to the right of the priest, which had been left earlier in the day, was made by members of the Mazatec Indigenous Church (see chapter 4).

saint—who appeared long ago at the town spring (see fig. 1.2) and then turned into a statue, an enduring sign of the town's blessed status—are two quite different views of modern life in a marginal indigenous community, in a place far from centers of power like Oaxaca.[31] In both versions, the appearance of the saint coincides with an epoch of abundance as the bounty and richness of the land is matched by the harmony, piety, and fidelity of its inhabitants—features that even draw people from across the region to live there. But, as the story goes, over time the saint became covered with dust and dirt, and some people from Nda Xo took her to Oaxaca to be repaired. The sculptor they hired in Oaxaca told them their saint had not been made by men but was alive, for the moment he started working on her, she began to bleed. Fearing misfortune if they did not return her immediately, the people set out for Nda Xo. But somewhere in the Mixtec region of the state, in an unknown town, the saint began to weigh a great deal; the men, unable to carry her further, left her there. The authorities from that town whose name no one remembers promised to take good care of her and made a copy for the men to take back to Nda Xo.

What both authors agree on is that once the men returned with the copy, Nda Xo began to change and fall from its state of paradise. The return to the Sierra from the city is a tale of loss: the statue of the saint, the symbol of community itself, becomes too heavy to bear. For the men charged with such cargo, the price for going on with their lives is that they return with less. What these authors also agree on is that the future is nevertheless hopeful. The saint who watches over them has not abandoned them, even if her statue, her physical presence, is gone forever.

The authors disagree, however, on the substance and meaning of the loss. One version portrays a fractious, divided people whose problems are at least partly internal; in the other version, people must deal with their sorrow in the wake of modernity, in the midst of a world that has changed around them. These differences say a great deal about how each author feels the people from Nda Xo should react to the community's "fallen" state—and to the pressures and promises, allure and threat, of modernity. As we will see, these two versions reflect two profoundly different views about the locus of "authentic" Mazatec identity and the nature of social unity in indigenous communities such as Nda Xo. What attitudes should people take toward the past, and what actions are entailed by them? Is someone to blame for the fact that things are not as they used to be? If the present is an impoverished replica of the past, what should be done about it? Is that lost past recoverable, and if so, how?

To put these matters in terms that have relevance for both indigenous intellectuals and scholars: what role do modern life and its trappings play in being indigenous? Is modernity an inevitable reality in the lives of indigenous people, or is it lethal to so-called true indigeneity and, possibly, to social unity, too? Are the answers to these questions linked to the enduring national preoccupation with the "Indian problem" and the quest it generates to reconcile national unity and modernity with indigenous difference? How are they linked to social realities, past or present, that are distinctly Mazatec? The people who live in the Sierra Mazateca have been subject, as indigenous people, to the same ambivalence with which the Mexican state has treated all indigenous people within its borders. They have been viewed as a barrier to achieving a unified national identity and modern nation. Yet given the Sierra's historical status as a zone of marginality, the people of the Sierra have had their own, unique history of relations to the state and nationalizing, modernizing forces—and their own, distinctive reactions to such forces: culturally inflected strategies for negotiating the tension between modernization and the pull of tradition. Here, I introduce some of these strategies and the particular historical events that shape them. A brief overview of the region is in order before turning to how its particular history squares with national history. I then conclude with a discussion of the region's last century of history through an examination of its ethnographic treatment in anthropological scholarship.

TALES FROM THE LAND OF THE EAGLES:
AN OVERVIEW OF THE SIERRA MAZATECA

There are roughly 210,000 speakers of Mazatec, making Mazatec speakers one of the country's largest indigenous groups (see table 1.1).[32] Almost all live in northern Oaxaca, in a region divided into a highlands (the Sierra Mazateca) and a lowlands (the Mazateca Baja). This division reflects not only geographical differences but also historical, linguistic, and political differences dating from at least a thousand years ago (Espinosa 1910). The two regions are now even more deeply divided by the Presa Miguel Alemán, the enormous hydroelectric dam project overseen by the Papaloapan Commission between 1949 and 1955 (see fig. 1.3). The Baja lies southeast of the reservoir, while the mountainous Sierra lies to the west and includes lowland areas along the edge of the reservoir (see map 1.1). Such communities—two of which were field sites for my research—are referred to locally (and confusingly) as the *baja* (or *nangui tsje* 'hot country'), meaning the lowlands *within* the Sierra, to which they clearly belong, administratively and linguistically.

A notable difference between the regions is that, although they have dispersed settlement patterns, the Sierra is more densely populated; this density intensified once dam refugees relocated there. Land is also privatized in the Sierra while still collectively owned in parts of the Baja.[33] Two nonindigenous cities anchor each end of the Mazatec region: Teotitlán de Flores Magón (Teotitlán del Camino) in the west and Tuxtepec in the east. Both are connected by long and mountainous but paved highways to Oaxaca and other regional cities. As is the norm in Oaxaca, the neighborhood is linguistically diverse: speakers of Cuicatec, Mixtec, Chinantec, Ixcatec, and Nahuatl live in the regional vicinity.

In the Sierra, communities exist across a range of climatic zones, from altitudes near sea level to 2,500 meters above sea level and higher. The communities where I did most of my research, though all part of the municipio of Nda Xo, vary in size and climate. Nda Xo's *cabecera* (county seat) has approximately 1,600 residents and is located at 1,800 meters above sea level, while Nangui Ni (*Tierra Colorada* [Red Earth]), a *ranchería* (village) of some two hundred people, is located at approximately five hundred meters above sea level. The Sierra is rugged—full of caves, canyons, and precipitous drop-offs. The

TABLE 1.1. The most widely spoken indigenous languages in Mexico

	Linguistic grouping	Language family	Language variants	States with speaker settlements	Number of speakers[a]
1	Náhuatl	Yuto-Nahua (Uto-Aztecan)	30	Colima, Distrito Federal, Durango, Estado de México, Hidalgo, Guerrero, Jalisco, Michoacán, Morelos, Nayarit, Oaxaca, Puebla, San Luis Potosí, Tabasco, Tlaxcala, and Veracruz	1,376,026
2	Maya	Mayan	1	Campeche, Quintana Roo, and Yucatán	758,310
3	Mixtec	Oto-Manguean	81	Guerrero, Oaxaca, and Puebla	423,216
4	Zapoteco	Oto-Manguean	62	Oaxaca	410,906
5	Tseltal	Mayan	4	Chiapas and Tabasco	371,730
6	Tsotsil	Mayan	7	Chiapas	329,937
7	Otomí	Oto-Manguean	9	Estado de México, Guanajuato, Hidalgo, Michoacán, Puebla, Querétaro, Tlaxcala, and Veracruz	239,850
8	Totonac	Totonac-Tepehua	7	Puebla and Veracruz	230,930
9	Mazatec	Oto-Manguean	16	Oaxaca, Puebla, and Veracruz	206,559
10	Ch'ol	Mayan	2	Campeche, Chiapas, and Tabasco	185,299
11	Huastec	Mayan	3	San Luis Potosí and Veracruz	149,532
12	Chinantec	Oto-Manguean	11	Oaxaca and Veracruz	125,706
13	Mixe	Mixe-Zoque	6	Oaxaca	115,824
14	Mazahua	Oto-Manguean	2	Estado de México and Michoacán	111,840
15	Tarascan	Tarascan	1	Michoacán	105,556

Source: INALI 2008b.

[a] The figure in the final column for number of speakers refers to individuals age five and older.

FIGURE 1.3. The reservoir of the Presa Miguel Alemán in the Mazateca Baja, with the Sierra Mazateca in the background.

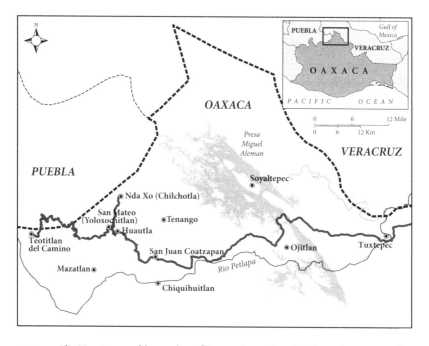

MAP 1.1. The Mazatec-speaking region of Oaxaca State, showing the major towns and cities discussed in the book.

FIGURE 1.4. Maize cooking in limewater on an outdoor fire. The resulting *nixtamal* is ground, and the *masa* (dough) is used to make tortillas, a dietary staple in the Sierra Mazateca and also throughout Mexico.

rocky land is almost never flat, making farming arduous. The main crop is maize (see fig. 1.4), followed by beans and squash, and until recently coffee was the leading cash crop. At lower altitudes, sugar cane and cattle ranching are prevalent. Most families own at least a few chickens and sometimes own pigs or goats. Although wild game is increasingly rare, people living in more isolated communities hunt and eat the animals they find in and around their jno⁴ (*milpas* or cornfields). People also eat the wide variety of fruit, vegetables, and grains that grow wild throughout the Sierra; the land is fertile, covered with lush vegetation and, at higher altitudes, cloud forests.

In the rainy season, roads wash out, isolating entire communities, and the frequent mudslides are sometimes fatal.[34] In the dry months, water becomes scarce; water rights are a constant source of dispute, and few communities have centralized water-distribution systems. Eunice Pike, a missionary with the SIL, wrote in the 1950s that women from the community outside Huautla lined up at the town spring before daybreak, spending hours waiting for their water jugs to fill, drop by drop, before lugging them home (Pike 1971). More than fifty years later, I witnessed a similar scene: for poor people in many

TABLE 1.2. Linguistic data and Spanish-language literacy rates of Mazatec-speaking municipios, as compared with all municipios in Oaxaca

Region	Percentage of population who speak only an indigenous language	Percentage of population who speak an indigenous language and Spanish	Spanish-language literacy rate for age 15 and older (%)
Chilchotla	28.82	97.60	62.29
All Mazatec-speaking municipios (average)	19.37	81.00	66.88
All municipios in Oaxaca (average)	6.32	39.55	79.76

Source: INEGI 2010.

communities, waiting in line at the spring for water and hauling it back home is still a fact of life. In Nda Xo, affluent people construct cisterns where they collect rainwater during the wet months and guard it jealously in the dry ones. People who own trucks make extra money during the dry season by driving to a spring out of town, filling up drums, and selling the water for a significant sum: one drum of water (approximately sixty gallons) costs roughly an unskilled laborer's daily wage.

The Sierra and the Baja also differ linguistically. The Baja has low levels of internal linguistic variation, but lowlands variants are unintelligible to speakers from the Sierra. Variation is higher in the Sierra, with as many as eight distinct variants (Gudschinsky 1958); however, people living in the central Sierra (including Chilchotla, Huautla, and Tenango) use the same variety, with minor variations. By national standards, most Sierra communities are linguistically conservative: in most municipios, more than 90 percent of inhabitants speak Mazatec, and more than 20 percent are monolingual Mazatec speakers, placing them near the top of the list nationally (see table 1.2).[35] Speakers of Spanish (only) or of other indigenous languages also live in the Sierra, in most cases because they have married in or because work (in schools, clinics, or government offices) brought them there.[36]

PEOPLE OF THE DEER: A SKETCH OF MAZATEC HISTORY

Little is known about Mazatec history before the Spanish arrived. The little archaeology that has been done in the region has focused mostly on caves, the sites of elite burials (Hapka and Rouvinez 1997; Steele 1987; Winter 1984). The following account—labeling the Mazateca a *tierra de brujos* (land of witches)[37]—is a not uncommon scholarly representation of the region's history. Though more tongue cheek than most—a wry critique of how indigenous peoples often have been characterized, in keeping with the critical ethos of post-1968 anthropological writings—the description nevertheless hints at widely held views of Mazatec society:

> The Mazatecs lack history. No one knows where they come from or how they traversed the first centuries of their existence. . . . People without art . . . without important ruins, without notable tombs, without codices, without jewels, [the Mazatecs] are a people, to judge by these deficits, so sufficiently weak or peaceful that they never gained, thanks to their warlike actions, an honorable place in history. Neighbors of Zapotecs, Mixtecs, and Totonacs, [the Mazatecs'] singular position in the region they occupy even now tells us that this people was a lamb in the midst of tigers, a blank space between the richly colored zones of those known as the "high cultures of Mesoamerica." (Benítez 1970: 35)

Nonetheless, we do know a little about the area's history. Most sources agree that the highlands–lowlands division reflects not only geographic and linguistic realities but also longstanding political ones. By AD 1300, the two regions existed as separate kingdoms (Espinosa 1910). Around this time, the Mazatec region came under the partial influence of Mixtecs (Gudschinsky 1958; Pearlman 1981; Villa Rojas 1955). In 1456, the Aztecs invaded Oaxaca and eventually brought the Sierra under their control, lending its residents the label "people of the deer" from the classical Nahuatl term *mazaatl*. Historians have generally claimed that little changed internally in the Mazateca during this period. New rulers extracted tribute through the Mazatec nobility, and the two kingdoms themselves remained intact (Gudschinsky 1958; Villa Rojas 1955). Presumably, during this period elite Mazatecs spoke Nahuatl. No sources discussing Mazatec history speculate on how Mazatecs participated in Mesoamerican literacy, though the three (perhaps four) known colonial Mazatec *lienzos* (cloth paintings) show stylistic conventions of pre-Columbian writing (Cline 1966; Rincón Mautner 1996). This suggests that Mazatec speakers participated, if peripherally, in Mesoamerican practices of producing and circulating written texts.

Like others subjected to Aztec rule, Mazatecs allied themselves with the Spanish during the conquest (Martínez Gracida 1883). During the early colonial period, various epidemics cut the population in half (Pearlman 1981:

65–66; Villa Rojas 1955: 71). Coupled with the region's relative isolation and lack of resources considered valuable in the colonial economy, the demographic decline meant *encomiendas* established in the sixteenth century were short-lived (Boege 1988).[38] As under the Aztecs, the Sierra remained administratively peripheral, its marginal status in the secular arena mirrored in the religious realm. Evangelization there initially failed (Weitlaner and Hoppe 1969: 516). Despite attempts by Franciscans, Dominicans, and secular clergy, the church never established a permanent presence in the Sierra during the colonial period. Likewise, no priest seems to have mounted any serious study of Mazatec, and the few Mazatec texts that were produced—a couple of *confesionarios* and *vocabularios*—are schematic and did not appear until the end of the eighteenth century, toward the close of the colonial era. By contrast, in-depth linguistic work on neighboring languages appeared some two hundred years earlier. Even Mazatecs who were exposed to church teachings, though they might have attended Mass, "continued practicing their traditional ceremonies in caves, springs, and sacred places in the mountains" (Villa Rojas 1955: 72).

Mazatecs were involved in the fight for independence and fought against the French intervention of the 1860s (Pearlman 1981: 71). This period marked the close of one form of self-rule, as the death in 1869 of the Sierra's last "king" ended hereditary leadership (Bauer 1968 [1908]: 247–48). As nationwide liberal reforms led to the expropriation of communal and church lands, Sierra land was privatized and increasingly concentrated in large holdings. The arrival of the first *finca* (coffee plantation) in 1893 marked an agricultural transformation. Soon after, coffee haciendas appeared throughout the region (Duke 1996: 60; Feinberg 2003: 44). Those who owned the fincas were primarily foreigners, many of them (as in Chiapas) Germans, although at least one landowner in Chilchotla was ostensibly Hungarian (leaving behind the name Hungaria as one of the municipio's settlements) but more likely Roma or Romanian. These European landowners were also responsible for introducing silkworm husbandry (Pearlman 1981: 72), a cash endeavor in which many Huauteco families engaged.[39] Meanwhile, in the lowlands, President Porfirio Díaz was expressing gratitude to the people of the region, who had supported him with soldiers, by modernizing the area with roads (Villa Rojas 1955: 73). These actions ultimately led to the dispossession of the very people Díaz was ostensibly helping by accelerating the arrival of cattle ranchers (Feinberg 2003: 46). The first substantial works on Mazatec language and history also date from this period (Belmar 1978 [1892]; Brinton 1892a, 1982b).

The Mexican Revolution marked a new era of nationalization for the region. Many Mazatecs who had never left the Sierra fought in the Revolution (Pearlman 1981: 73). When they returned, they brought with them stories about their experiences and new ideas about nationhood. Occasional interviews in *La Faena* with old men who were alive at the time of the Revolution reflect the effect that era had on Serranos' shifting attitudes toward the state. Also during this period, many people fled the cabeceras and formed smaller settlements on uninhabited land attached to haciendas. When the postrevolutionary state nationalized large landholdings and enforced land redistribution, the population became further dispersed, reflected in present settlement patterns. Families with means would acquire land not only in cabeceras but also outlying areas (Cowan 1954: 89). This was true of wealthy and even so-called middle-class families in Nda Xo. Today when people talk about this era—when polygamy was still common—they often claim that it was typical for prospering campesinos to keep one wife in town and another one (or more) at the rancho, a more remote settlement where the majority of the family's crops were grown.

HIPPIES, COFFEE, AND VIOLENCE: ETHNOGRAPHIC RESEARCH ABOUT MAZATEC COMMUNITIES

Shortly after the Revolution, the first articles on "Mazatec culture" were published, followed by the first full-length ethnographic works on Mazatec communities. Studies of the Mazatec region fall into two broad categories: those concerned with the impact of modernization and those that examine resistance to it through practices that represent adherence to tradition. Much of this research aims to consider both trends by exploring how the competing forces of tradition and modernity interact. Nevertheless, most works, here as elsewhere, have tended to privilege either continuity with the past or rupture from it.

Most ethnographies on Mazatec cultural stability concentrate on mushroom use, with particular attention paid to the shaman María Sabina. Other research that focuses on "traditional Mazatec culture" includes descriptive articles on Mazatec society and more analytical articles on its specific aspects, such as Mazatec witchcraft, the Mazatec calendar, and head washing in Mazatec marriage ceremonies.[40] Collectively, these studies emphasize Mazatecs' resistance to acculturation while maintaining practices and beliefs that are markedly different from those of Mexican national society. This work furthers prevailing discourses about Mazatec people as being among the few Indians in Mexico who have held fast to their traditions and resisted modernization and nationalization. Like that of the brave Mazatecs in the opening story, their uniqueness stems from refusing to be eaten alive by the forces represented by the Mexican eagles.

Studies of change in Mazatec society over the past century have focused on one or more of the major vectors of modernization in the Sierra: coffee, the dam, roads, hippies, and political parties, arriving in roughly that order. The following brief overview of these studies not only provides a sketch of the Sierra's recent history but also indicates some of the forces that have influenced the region's revival projects.

Ethnographies about coffee emphasize how its emergence as a cash crop tied the region into the market economy in new, socially transformative ways (Boege 1988; Neiburg 1988).[41] More recent work (Feinberg 2003) discusses the equally transformative effects of coffee's devaluation. Its decline as a cash crop figures prominently in Nda Xo today, in both discourse and action. People routinely bemoan the bad market for the crop, harvest their coffee only for their own use, and seek out a host of replacement crops, from vanilla beans and passion fruit to (in a particularly unusual case) the meat and feathers of ostriches.[42]

Research on large public-works projects has followed a roughly similar line of argumentation. Scholarship on the dam emphasizes the massive social upheaval it caused. Two prominent researchers call the project a "program of ethnocide" (Barabas and Bartolomé 1973: 3); they and others claim that it furthered distrust of the federal government while increasing dependence on it (Barabas and Bartolomé 1973, 1983; Partridge and Brown 1983, 1984; Villa Rojas 1955). While the dam had a less direct effect on people from the Sierra, it deepened the social distance between the highlands and the lowlands. The government's "compensatory" development programs, directed toward the people from the Baja, nationalized and urbanized the area more quickly than the Sierra. Among the most important interventions by the government was the founding of an INI center in the lowlands; the radio station attached to it, part of a national system broadcasting in local indigenous languages, became one of the most important vehicles through which indigenismo and other national policies were transmitted.[43]

Literature on the completion of the Teotitlán–Huautla road in 1963 likewise emphasizes how major infrastructural developments transform social realities.[44] Although it remained unpaved for more than two decades (until 1984), the new road further elevated Huautla's importance, making it the unparalleled economic and political capital of the Sierra. The road also brought many other things: institutions such as the INI and Inmecafe (Mexico's now defunct coffee institute), schools, medical clinics, vehicular access to the rest of the country, and new migration opportunities. As coffee once had, the transportation of people and goods represented a new cash crop, an opportunity to generate wealth. The road also accelerated the arrival of the trappings of modern life: telephones, televisions, public address systems, computers, and, recently, the Internet.

Finally, the road brought with it two additional new social forces: hippies and political parties. Both became openly tied to factionalism, even violence. I will return to hippies and political divisions in the next chapter, where I discuss the recent history of ethnic relations in the Sierra Mazateca, in which hippies played a pivotal role. In brief, hippie mycotourists, like coffee and cars, represented a novel form of economic possibility. Nonetheless, the newfound prosperity and prestige found in this area by some Mazatecs, achieved by "selling" cultural property, led to widespread conflict (and in María Sabina's case, attempts on her life). Likewise, the national rise of opposition parties placed new pressure on systems by which local authorities were selected. Once political parties began to affect local politics in the 1970s, and the party system increasingly became the paradigm, traditional leaders such as the Consejo de Ancianos (Council of Elders) found it difficult to participate without being seen as affiliated with a political party, which generally meant tied to the PRI. This, in turn, raised questions about whether leaders truly served the community rather than party interests.[45]

In sum, this second type of ethnographic research focuses on the impact of modernization on Mazatec communities. The approach taken by most of these scholars foregrounds the interplay between internal conflict and ethnic identity, whether it is political conflict born of the collision between local and national systems for creating authority (Boege 1988; Neiburg 1988) or social conflict generated by competing claims about packaging "Mazatec culture" for outsiders (Duke 1996; Feinberg 2003). In privileging cultural discontinuity in indigenous communities, such scholars tend to present modernization as inherently divisive, regardless of the particular vehicle through which modernity arrives.

Conclusion: Toward New Ethnic Cartographies

I offer a somewhat different perspective by arguing that revival constitutes a particular form of modernization. Innovation is a central feature of revival projects, and at least some forms of revival offer an important critique of the assumptions made in the aforementioned literature—and, indeed, in much ethnographic literature about modernization across the globe. In successfully balancing adaptation with allegiance to the past, effective cases of revival provide myriad ways to synthesize the traditional and the modern that allow for harmony rather than rupture in the shift between the two. A second, and related, point is that modernization in the form of revival is not inherently divisive. It can also build community and promote harmony.

Haunting the edges of these studies on Mazatec communities and the broader history sketched earlier are themes I revisit throughout this book. They include the locus of social unity; competing ideas about and attitudes toward ethnic identity generally and Mexican indigeneity in particular; and the politics and price of belonging and not belonging, whether to the nation or to an indigenous collective—or, perhaps, to both at the same time. To return to a question raised by the story about the ravenous eagles and the wily natives who outsmarted them, who are the Mazatecs, anyway? Where does authentic indigenous identity lie: in a lost but recoverable past or in the degraded but vibrant society of the present? The writings of the half-brothers Heriberto Prado Pereda and Alberto Prado Pineda raise these questions by offering answers that might clarify the nature of ethnic belonging. However, as we see in the chapters that follow, their answers differ radically, and their divergent responses have material consequences for how they and other Serranos live their lives. The answers they give—and, even more, the way they frame the questions that elicit them—play a vital role in setting the terms by which collective conversations about indigenous identity can happen in the Sierra. They are lines drawn across an ethnic landscape, mapping the territory of belonging and its limits. But they are more than that: they describe social realities but also create them. Like all cartographic gestures, such representations of territory can, and often do, take on a life of their own, becoming material realities.

This interplay between representations and their material incarnations returns in the chapters that follow, in which I discuss different revival projects from the Sierra Mazateca and the material effectiveness of their representations of "Mazatec tradition." First, though, I turn to specific recent events in the history of the Sierra—events that have had a clear impact on ethnic relations in the area and the publicly circulating discourses about them. These events, in turn, have crucially figured the region's revival projects, serving by turns as substrate and foil: laying the foundations on which living revival movements rest and yet standing as the locus of their strongest critiques.

REVIVAL IN THE "LAND OF THE MAGIC MUSHROOM"

A Recent History of Ethnic Relations in the Sierra Mazateca

Ndi xitjo tsjin,
ndi xitjo xoño.
K'uasin fáyale,
k'uasin fakole.

Mushroom of milk,
mushroom of dew,
In this way, I ask you,
in this way, I speak with you.

—Heriberto Prado Pereda, from the poem "About the Little Mushrooms,"
in "Kjuale ndi ik'ien itsan"

Outsiders and Indigeneity in the Sierra

In this chapter I focus on the social implications of two recent historical
events in the Sierra Mazateca. These events involved encounters between
cho⁴ta⁴xi¹n and cho⁴ta⁴yo⁴ma⁴—locals from the Sierra and people from outside it—and suggest how locals' understandings of indigenous identity are
at odds with those who arrive from beyond the region.[1] Although both events
began in the twentieth century, they tie directly to ongoing events that continue to shape interethnic relations between Serranos and outsiders today.
These histories have had a demonstrable effect on how people from the Sierra
represent themselves and Serrano society in a range of media, from written
texts to songs and other public performances. These representational practices are also wrapped up in a complex feedback loop with the region's revival movements.

The first historical change began in the 1950s but accelerated over the following decade as people across the Sierra began to experience national and global discourses about indigeneity through new kinds of social encounters. At that time, the Sierra remained relatively isolated, accessible primarily by mule, foot, or small airplane. In the 1960s, however, the region's psychedelic mushrooms were "discovered" by outsiders just as its first major road was completed. Almost overnight, hippie mycotourists began flocking to the Sierra in search of "magic mushrooms" and shamans who used them. *Veladas* (mushroom ceremonies) revolve around hours of prayer, chanting, and singing in Mazatec, marking the rituals as key sites where the local language, deployed across various expressive channels, is linked to practices of ethnic distinction. However, once the mushrooms and veladas were subjected to acquisitive interest from outsiders, they were exposed to new sources of support and veneration that also posed threats to their sustainability and local meanings (Abse 2007; Duke 1996; Feinberg 2003). This rather atypical history of global interaction nevertheless reveals widespread tensions in globalization processes—tensions reflected in the region's revival movements as well. This historical event illuminates ruptures between local and global discourses about indigeneity, illustrating the alternatively empowering and disenfranchising dimensions of global identity politics.

The second event began slightly later. However, as the influx of mycotourists lasted for more than a decade—and continues in different form today—the two events coincided and have been mutually influencing. The later event concerns the Catholic Church's "incursion" into the Sierra, establishing unprecedented influence over Serranos' lives. Particularly critical was the founding in 1972 of the Prelature of Huautla, the seat of the region's first resident bishop. Installing this new office and establishing resident priests across the Sierra provided the church with new visibility and power in the region. Furthermore, the creation of the prelature was motivated by the rise of Liberation Theology following Vatican II (1962–65); it became a dominant ideological paradigm in much of Mexico, especially in the poor and indigenous south. The new gospel of liberationist thought had a profound effect on the Sierra: the church related to local people with unprecedented intimacy, political engagement, and cultural sensitivity. This period laid the groundwork for new singing and writing practices in Mazatec, stemming from the church's desire to increase its popular appeal while deepening its receptiveness to local customs.

These two historical events prefigured the Sierra's Mazatec revival movements, establishing new traditions of Mazatec literacy and performance while providing institutional support for both. This support was material and financial but even more critically moral, as local practices that were ethnically marked became valorized by powerful outsiders. But these events also introduced a new and highly ambivalent lexicon for representing "Mazatec tradition," whose linkage to the historical era of its birth produces ongoing reverberations in the present.

Land of the Magic Mushroom: Shamans, Tourists, and Ethnicity for Sale

During my first day in Nda Xo, I visited the house of a $cho^4ta^4chji^4ne^4$ (sabio, shaman).[2] It happened by accident. A family I met invited me to stay with them, but I hoped first to collect my things from the hotel room I had taken in Huautla, an hour away by pickup truck. Because the family had business to take care of along the road to Huautla, they suggested we all walk together while I tried to catch a ride. But it was late afternoon, and trucks were scarce; I still had no ride to Huautla when we arrived at the family's destination—the sabio's house. Because it was getting dark, they urged me to come inside with them, return to their house to sleep, and leave for Huautla in the morning.

I discuss that ceremony in more detail later, but for present purposes, a seminal moment came at its close. The sabio closed the ritual by performing a limpia (ritual cleansing) on each of us: the parents, their two young boys, and finally me.[3] Afterward, the sabio—switching from Mazatec to Spanish—told me that if I wanted to come back for the cositas ("the little things"; i.e., mushrooms), he could do a velada with me. Open approaches by sabios to outsiders about the mushrooms are quite common and speak volumes about social changes that have taken place over recent decades in the Sierra Mazateca.

As in many indigenous communities, educational and media systems administered by the federal government have been particularly powerful agents of change in the region. Throughout Mexico, postrevolutionary indigenista policies expanded the educational system into ever more rural, indigenous areas. This is linked to the growth of the "indigenous middle class," a development that in many places—including parts of the Sierra Mazateca, especially Huautla—has emerged alongside economic shifts that include the rise of tourism economies (Babb 2011; Baud and Ypeij 2009; Brown 2004; Castañeda 2001; Colloredo-Mansfeld 1999; Hellier-Tinoco 2011; Stephen 1991, 2005). Members of this emergent class are often the first in their families, and even in their communities, to become educated through the national school system and to be fully bilingual and literate in Spanish. Like the two half-brothers who are authors discussed in the previous chapter, these people often form the first generation in their families to have formal schooling beyond elementary school. The expanding school system has also been a key vector for disseminating ideologies about indigenous identity. Mass media has also been crucial: first newspapers and, later, television and radio broadcasts, especially those offered through the Instituto Nacional Indigenista's (INI) rural radio stations.

In the Sierra Mazateca, mycotourists have constituted another critical site for the diffusion of new ideas about indigenous identity. Because mycotourists come in search of both mushrooms and "authentic" indigenous rituals, they seek not only the mushrooms themselves but also essentialized representations of indigenous culture. And like customers of other goods and services, they play a significant role in shaping the products they consume.

Conversations between Mazatecs and this unusual set of outsiders have been going on for some fifty years now. Through such cross-cultural interactions, discourses about indigenous culture and rights have touched ground in Sierra communities. Clearly, *indigenismo* and other national discourses have themselves been heavily influenced by globally circulating ideas linked to indigenous activism and human rights. These ideas have also found influence in the region through face-to-face interactions tied to institutions such as the Catholic Church and the national school system. Yet the mushroom trade in the Sierra has been a distinctive conduit for the introduction of national and international discourses about native peoples. Mycotourists include Mexican nationals—particularly from Mexico City—and foreigners from Europe and the United States. In their interactions with local people, they routinely invoke global discourses about indigenous peoples and their cultures. Furthermore, the cultural practices targeted by these views are highly marked as key loci of ethnic identification: veladas are a central site where normative ideologies about collective belonging are enacted and disseminated.

In the next chapter I discuss the Day of the Dead Song Contest, whose popular success draws from the holiday's central place in local economies of ethnic affiliation. But the contest's popularity also stems from its emphasis on singing, whose value locally is dependent on other singing practices in Mazatec, most crucially those done in veladas. The innovation at the heart of the song contest is the creation of new Mazatec songs. Yet local people view this as an extension of tradition partly because the intellectuals who promoted it "advertised" it not as an invention but, instead, as a fundamentally *restorative* project engaged in the active recovery of traditions—*singing* for the dead rather than merely dancing and playing music for them—that were nearly lost in the decades before the contest was founded. A critical component of the contest's popular success was not only its ostensibly "traditional" character but also its resonance with present practice through the multiple realms of life involving singing in Mazatec that are marked as ethnically distinct.

Veladas are a particularly important arena. Singing and chanting are its central activities and what make the ceremonies medicinally effective. These practices in turn constitute veladas as a critical forum for the institutionalization of "traditional" speech and song norms. Furthermore, many Mazatec authors and composers claim that the inspiration for particular works — or even for the more fundamental ability to be able to write texts or compose songs — was bestowed on them in mushroom ceremonies. This makes veladas an important site in which ideologies about texts, song, and creativity are formed. Yet veladas are also key loci where ideas about Mazatec identity meet a host of modernizing forces attached to commodification and ethnic tourism. Thus, mushroom ceremonies and the talk about them are sites where the tension between modernity and tradition is particularly salient. Discussions about veladas invoke many of the same conflicts that animate debates about the Sierra's revival projects and, more generally, about the meaning of community and the role within it of a distinctly Mazatec form of sociality. This same tension thoroughly permeates the opportunities and challenges of indigenous intellectuals, for whom writing about the mushrooms and Mazatec shamans not only is extremely widespread but, in some cases, is mandatory.

This chapter takes up the legacy of such external pressures for indigenous intellectuals and others living in the Sierra, particularly as they surround discourses about mushroom use and indigeneity. I recount the history of the Sierra's "discovery" by mushroom-seeking outsiders when they began visiting the region on an unprecedented scale, in the process making mushrooms and veladas commodities for the first time. This complicated their status as signifiers of Mazatec "tradition": the arrival of mycotourists subjected both the mushrooms and the veladas to new acquisitive forces, new pressures to perform "indigenous identity" for people from beyond the Sierra. This singular case of globalizing forces meeting local communities nevertheless exposes fundamental tensions raised by the global interpenetration of nations. Furthermore, these tensions are also refracted through the Sierra's revival projects. The friction between competing conceptualizations of indigenous identities reveals the simultaneously liberating and limiting dimensions of the politics of indigenous revival.

A Page from Life: Gordon Wasson, María Sabina,
and the Psychedelic Revolution

In 1953, the professional banker and amateur mycologist R. Gordon Wasson arrived for the first time in the Sierra. A vice president at J. P. Morgan Bank, Wasson had long pursued self-financed research on the global use of hallucinogenic mushrooms, especially their role in the origins of religion. This pursuit culminated in *Soma: Divine Mushroom of Immortality* (Wasson 1968), which examines cross-cultural mushroom use in support of the controversial but respected thesis that the famed ritual drink Soma, which figures prominently in Vedic scriptures, was distilled from the mushroom *Amanita muscaria* (fly agaric). Wasson's studies led him to Mexico, where Aztecs, among others, were known to have ingested hallucinogenic mushrooms. In 1955, two years after Wasson first arrived in the Sierra Mazateca, he and the photographer Allan Richardson participated in two veladas.

I will pause here to briefly describe veladas. Numerous scholars and more popular writers have described them, both before Wasson (see, e.g., Johnson 1939a, 1939b) and countless times since. Based on these experiences and on my experience as a participant and observer, there appears to be considerable flexibility and variation in how veladas are realized—differences that are clearly regional and historical; these differences may be generational and idiosyncratic as well.[4] Nevertheless—generalizing from my experience, from ethnographic interviews, and from published accounts—I offer the following description of the ritual's central characteristics.

Veladas always involve the ingestion of hallucinogenic plants. In the Sierra, mushrooms are preferred as the most potent. Especially in the dry season, when mushrooms do not grow, sabios will turn to the Sierra's other three psychotropic plants.[5] Veladas last for several hours and always take place at night in a darkened room lit by altar candles, before which the ceremony is performed, with participants sitting or kneeling.[6] It is important that the room be relatively quiet to hear received messages. I was often told, for example, that the Day of the Dead, when musicians wander from house to house, playing music throughout the night, is noisy and hence a bad time to hold veladas, even though mushrooms are often available then. Most veladas involve a small group of people: a shaman, the person in need of help, often one or two others assisting the shaman (family members or apprentices), and relatives of the person for whom the velada is held. If others are present, they may or may not take mushrooms. Mushrooms are taken in pairs; the shaman always takes them, generally in the highest dose, and often the patient does as well.[7]

The purpose of the velada is to gain access to divine spirits whose knowledge and skills can bring about changes in the world. The deities contacted include those dwelling within the plants themselves and other beings that populate the spirit world. These "earth spirits," "spirit lords," or "spirit-owners" are widely discussed in literature on Mazatec cosmology. In Mazatec they are known as chi³kon³. This lexical item is used in a variety of contexts and in conventionalized combinations with other words that suggest the beings' divine and ethereal nature, superior power, and close ties to the natural world—above all, to unique geographic features such as bodies of water, caves, and mountains.[8] Each topological feature has its own chikon; failure to treat the chikon with proper respect or the infliction of accidental offense can have negative, even disastrous, consequences.[9] The deities contacted during the ceremony guide and inform participants, helping the shaman diagnose transgressions the patient might have made—or malevolent actions taken against him by a tje³ (brujo, witch)—that require corrective intervention, such as burying sacred bundles. The spirits with whom participants communicate during the ceremony reveal knowledge and in the process bestow power, for knowledge is in itself powerful medicine, necessary for action that leads to healing—or, alternatively, to acceptance if the patient is beyond saving. A critical portion of the healing process unfolds in the ritual itself, through hours of chanting and singing in Mazatec (and sometimes in Spanish). In addition to the critical role the chants play in gathering information, they are medicinal. The language used in veladas is conventionalized and highly structured, repetitive, elevated in diction and syntax, figurative, poetic, sometimes archaic, and replete with reported speech. Transcripts of mushroom ceremonies are full of the words tso² (says) and ti¹tso² (is saying), which invoke the words of another person, a deity, or even divine vehicles such as the mushrooms. These qualities heighten the subjective experience that participants—the sabio, above all—are engaging in dialogue with deities and are receiving divine texts.[10] This is not to say that shamans are primarily passive recipients of information. Shamans are active forces whose special skills—the ability, as María Sabina memorably put it, to "translate" the words of divine sources (Estrada 1989 (1977): 94)—allow them to actively pursue knowledge imparted through words and visions that are rich beyond their occurrence in daily life.[11]

Thus, in veladas, language and visions achieve an extraordinary level of fluorescence. Conversely, the taboos tied to veladas produce a similar effect through negation: the absence of activities common to daily life marks veladas' separation from quotidian existence. People in the Sierra say that failure to observe these taboos can cause illness, insanity, even death. The most-important taboos pertain to sexual relations. Participants in veladas must refrain from sexual contact for four days each before and after the rituals take place.[12] Furthermore, the spiritual contamination from prohibited sexual relations can spread from one person to another. Nonsexual taboos (e.g., those concerning diet and gift exchange) are ultimately linked to preventing both participants and mushrooms from being tainted by association with people who have not observed the sexual taboos.[13] Ultimately, the taboos aim to render people tsje⁴³ (clean) when they are contacting divine sources.[14] Because shamans cannot know in advance when their services will be needed, most live in long-term—and public—sexual purity. If they do not maintain a state of ritual celibacy, they run the risk not only of being ineffective but also of bringing harm to their clients. Thus, ritual specialists are "culturally marked as celibate as a social category" (Duke 2001: 129). Most are unmarried or widowed—that is, individuals who are presumed not to engage in sexual intercourse. María Sabina, for example, worked as a shaman only during periods in her life when she was not married (Estrada 1989 (1977): 40, 46, 62).

Finally, although to my knowledge no author has included in these taboos the oft-remarked "euphemisms" that pervade academic and popular discussions about veladas, such speech does indeed constitute a form of verbal taboo. Talk about veladas requires unique linguistic practices whose logic of reference preserves a marked boundary between the most sacred objects and events in Mazatec communities and those that fill everyday life. Veladas are almost always referred to using indirect phrases that emphasize their nocturnal context—for example, ni⁴tje⁴n xi³ va³ca³so¹n (the night one stays awake), or the equally indirect Spanish loan word *velada* (vigil; cf. *desvelarse*, to stay awake). Referring to the mushrooms themselves also depends on verbal taboo. The most commonly used phrases include ndi¹xi³tjo³, which is usually translated as *pequeños que brotan* (little ones who spring forth); ndi¹xti³santo (saint children); ndi¹santo (little saints); and ndi¹tso³jmi² (little things). Even in Spanish, the denoting phrases are similar: *niños santos, niñitos, las cositas,* or, rarely, *honguitos*.[15] I have never heard (or seen in print) any literal, non-euphemistic references to these mushrooms. Mazatec does not appear even to have words that definitively, predictably, and exclusively denote hallucinogenic mushrooms and their attached rituals.[16]

Wasson's velada experiences purportedly made his group "the first outsiders to participate in the Mazatec Indians' sacred mushroom rituals."[17] Although other Westerners had, in fact, written about Mazatec mushroom use (and done so in English), Wasson's writings did transform Huautla's—and the entire Sierra's—"place in the symbolic economy of Mexico, Europe, and the United States" (Feinberg 2003: 51). Wasson himself made dramatic statements about the singularity of his experiences. "No . . . white men had ever partaken of the sacred mushrooms under any circumstances," he wrote, reveling in his participation in "a tradition of unfathomed age, . . . [going] back perhaps to the very dawn of man's cultural history, when he was discovering the idea of God" (Wasson and Wasson 1957: 290).

Within the Sierra, this event was earthshaking for different reasons entirely. Momentous changes took place in the Sierra in the wake of Wasson's visit that would touch Serranos' lives for generations. This transformation began modestly enough, however, with the publication in May 1957 of Wasson's short article "Seeking the Magic Mushroom." It appeared in *Life* magazine, one of the most popular and influential news outlets in the country, with a readership in the tens of millions. The sensationalistic qualities of the article, which appeared in a series titled "Great Adventures," is captured by its subtitle, "A New York banker goes to Mexico's mountains to participate in the age-old rituals of Indians who chew strange growths that produce visions." The article alluded to Wasson's velada experiences—"nine in all"—but focused on those from 1956, when he and Richardson witnessed "a strange, solemn rite and wonders in the dark."[18]

The article became a phenomenon. The accidental discovery in 1943 of lysergic acid diethylamide (LSD) by the chemist Albert Hofmann provoked scientists to search for other natural substances that produced the same psychedelic effects and that might be linked to the cause of schizophrenia. Wasson collaborated with the French mycologist Roger Heim and with Hofmann himself in identifying the mushrooms' active compounds as psilocybin and psilocin, whose chemical structures are close to LSD's (Hofmann 1990). In exposing a wide audience to the effects of the mushrooms, the *Life* article provided accidental fodder for the nascent counterculture movement. While Wasson concealed the veladas' setting and the identity of the *curandera* (healer)—he used the pseudonym "Eva Mendez" from the mythical "Mixeteco" ethnic group—those whose interest had been piqued quickly uncovered the hidden location.

The real name of the shaman was María Sabina Magdalena García. A sabia who thereafter was known simply as María Sabina, she was made famous by the *Life* article and Wasson's subsequent work. Her *huipil* (native dress), however, gave her away—the very Sierra huipil she would make instantly recognizable, as both she and it became symbols of Mazatec society. As important as the text of the article were its photographs—particularly so for a photography-driven magazine like *Life*. Wasson and Richardson wanted to photograph the ceremony; although María Sabina initially resisted, she gave in during the second velada on the condition that they "please refrain from showing [the photographs] to any but our most trusted friends," for if the images were shown widely, "it would be a betrayal" (Wasson and Wasson 1957: 304).

Wasson and Richardson published the photographs anyway. In an "absolutely breathtaking example of meta-textual double talk" (Duke 1996: 99), Wasson justified publishing the photographs by claiming, "We are doing as the Señora (María Sabina) asked us, showing these photographs only in those circles where we feel sure that she would be pleased to have them shown. . . . We have withheld the name of the village where she lives, and we have changed the names of the characters in our narrative" (Wasson and Wasson 1957: 304). In the photographs published with the article, Wasson is featured prominently. He appears as an Indiana Jones–like figure—worldly, learned, intrepid, the perfect guide to bring the story of an exotic, archaic ritual home to rest on the coffee tables of 1950s America. The ultimate token of the distance Wasson had traveled to acquire that story were the images of María Sabina herself, kneeling in her huipil with her hands pressed to the sky as she invoked the spirits in the visions Wasson described.

Within three months of the article's publication, a photographer from San Francisco, who had seen a photograph in Oaxaca city of a woman dressed identically to "Eva Mendez," learned that her huipil was from Huautla (see figs. 2.1 and 2.2). As Ben Feinberg writes, "The secret was out" (2003: 130; see also Duke 1996: 106). Of course, anyone who really wanted to learn the identity of "Eva Mendez" and find the mountains where she lived had only to get hold of another work by the Wassons: *Mushrooms, Russia, and History*, also published in 1957. María Sabina and Huautla are identified by name, alongside a detailed description of the arduous journey into the Sierra. Thereafter, Huautla saw a dramatic increase in the arrival of outsiders in search of mushrooms.

Among them was Timothy Leary. He traveled to Mexico after reading Wasson's article and tried the mushrooms, an experience that transformed his life and work. When he returned to Harvard, where he was a lecturer in psychology, Leary started the Harvard Psilocybin Project with his colleague

FIGURE 2.1. Huautla de Jiménez, with the town church, the seat of the Prelature of Huautla, in the background.

Richard Alpert, later known as Ram Dass. The project's experiments with graduate students on the effects of psilocybin and LSD ran from 1960 until 1962, when other colleagues questioned the legitimacy and safety of the research. Leary and Alpert were dismissed from Harvard after an acrimonious and highly publicized dispute with the university's administrators, parents, and state public health officials. Shortly thereafter, Leary published *The Psychedelic Experience: A Manual Based on the Tibetan Book of the Dead* (1964), an enormously popular and influential book that became a bible of the psychedelic revolution and a key text of the counterculture movement.

Such writings resonated with the antiestablishment ethos of the time and were attractive to various "seekers" in search of spiritual experiences ostensibly more profound than were those available in Western religions. Soon people began arriving in the Sierra in search of the transcendental spiritual encounters these texts claimed to find in psychedelic substances. *Jipis* (hippies) flooded Huautla, seeking the visions and communion with primordial knowledge that Wasson's article seemingly promised. The rapid influx of hippies continued throughout the 1960s, and by the end of it, they had constructed a permanent camp a few miles out of town (Feinberg 2003: 52). Most were unknown young people, but a few were famous—purportedly, the

FIGURE 2.2. The traditional huipil of Huautla and the Sierra Mazateca. The shaman María Sabina wore such a huipil throughout her life; the woman in the photograph wears the huipil only for special occasions. Here she is dressed for a wedding.

Beatles and other rock luminaries. Today, *La Faena*, the Sierra's cultural magazine, regularly features articles about that era: photographs of half-naked hippies bathing in a local waterfall, for example, or profiles of the local baker who sold bread to the Rolling Stones.[19]

Not surprisingly, this incursion of outsiders had a dramatic impact, exposing Huautla and, to a lesser extent, the entire Sierra to a host of new influences and pressures. Aside from the other disruptions their presence caused as outsiders who did not speak the language (and often did not speak Spanish, either), the hippies flagrantly disregarded the taboos associated with mushroom use. They streaked through town naked, took the mushrooms in the middle of the day, had sex in cornfields, and smoked "dangerous drugs" such as marijuana.[20] Such behavior not only desecrated the sacred mushrooms but also constituted brazen, scandalous invitations for divine retribution. In 1968, Huautla's municipal president asked the government to act, and the Mexican Army set up military roadblocks that sealed off the entire region until 1976 (Feinberg 2003: 131).

In many ways, these actions came too late to head off the social trauma hippies left in their wake. Although some people in Huautla prospered, they appear to be the minority. Even María Sabina did not fare well. By the late 1960s, she was "under near-constant harassment by the authorities, who were convinced she had been selling marijuana to foreigners" (Duke 1996: 108–9); her neighbors, growing envious, burned her house down (Estrada 1989 (1977): 74–75). She later talked about the profound changes in her spiritual life: "From the moment the foreigners arrived to search for God, the niños santos lost their purity. They lost their force; the foreigners ruined them. . . . Before Wasson, I felt the niños santos elevated me. I don't feel that way anymore. The force has diminished. If Cayetano [the town official who first brought Wasson to her] hadn't brought the foreigners . . . the niños santos would have kept their power" (quoted in Estrada 1989 (1977): 85–86)

This sentiment was echoed by another sabio from Huautla, Apolonio Terán: "What is terrible, listen, is that the divine mushroom doesn't belong to us anymore. Its sacred Language has been defiled. The Language has been spoiled and it is indecipherable for us. . . . Now the mushrooms speak nqui³le² [English]! Yes, the language the foreigners speak. . . . The mushrooms have a divine spirit; they always had it for us, but the foreigner arrived and frightened it away" (quoted in Estrada 1989 (1977): 87).

Wasson responded to such charges in characteristically self-assured fashion:

Here was a religious office . . . that had to be presented to the world in a worthy manner, not sensationalized, not cheapened and coarsened, but soberly and truthfully.

We alone could do justice to it, my wife Valentina Pavlovna and I, in the book that we were writing and in responsible magazines. But given the nether reaches of vulgarity in the journalism of our time, inevitably there would follow all kinds of debased accounts erupting into print around the world. All this we foresaw and all this took place, to a point where the "Federales" had to make a clean sweep of certain Indian villages in the highlands of Mesoamerica in the late 1960s, deporting the assortment of oddballs misbehaving there. . . .

[María Sabina's] words make me wince: I, Gordon Wasson, am held responsible for the end of a religious practice in Mesoamerica that goes back far, for a millennia [sic]. . . . A practice carried on in secret for centuries has now been aerated and aeration spells the end.

At [my first velada] I had to make a choice: suppress my experience or resolve to present it worthily to the world. There was never a doubt in my mind. The sacred mushrooms and the religious feeling concentrated in them through the Sierras of Southern Mexico had to be known to the world, and worthily so, at whatever cost to me personally. If I did not do this, "consulting the mushroom" would go on for a few years longer, but its extinction was and is inevitable. The world would know vaguely that such a thing had existed but not the importance of its role. On the other hand, worthily presented, its prestige, María Sabina's prestige, would endure. (Wasson 1981: 13–14, 20)

Wasson was right: María Sabina's prestige did endure, though not in the form he intended. His reputation, however, has met with a more ambivalent fate. For many living in the Sierra, Wasson's self-vindications in the name of "the world" and "science" are at best irrelevant. While most Serranos probably have heard of Wasson, few, if asked about his legacy, would claim with "never a doubt" that the decisions he made were the right ones.

Ethnic Revival in the Land of the Magic Mushroom:
María Sabina Studies and "Mazatec Culture"

Ambivalent or not, Wasson's legacy lives on. Debates about the mushrooms are alive and well in the Sierra, thanks not only to the historical legacy of hippie mushroom seekers of the 1960s but also the ongoing arrival of their ideological heirs: a smaller but steady stream of mycotourists going to the Sierra to take mushrooms and experience "authentic" Mazatec veladas. Religious arguments that figure prominently in everyday conversations in Nda Xo—a subject to which I turn shortly—are rarely only about religion; likewise, discussions about the mushrooms open out to embrace the full gamut of issues indigenous communities face. They include questions about the nature and locus of indigenous identity, about the attitudes toward "outsiders" dictated by different views of indigeneity, and about how societies balance tradition and modernity. In the Sierra, discussions about mushrooms are a site where ideas about ethnicity become explicit. Indigenous intellectuals who are prime movers of revival—and of the metacultural ideas and social innovations on which revival depends—are heavily involved in debates about mushrooms. Insofar as the mushrooms are key emblems of local ethnic identity, intellectuals who self-consciously codify ideas about Mazatec ethnicity must turn their essentializing gaze upon the mushrooms and the veladas in which they are used. How should indigenous authors go about representing "authentic" versions of Mazatec identity, and what role should mushrooms and veladas play in the effort? What strategy is more effective in promoting ideas about what it means to be Mazatec? What role should outsiders play in "being Mazatec"? Questions like these are raised daily by indigenous authors, as well as by people from across the Sierra as they live their daily lives.

Discussions about mushrooms and Mazatec identity continue apace partly because Wasson's writings continue to stoke popular interest. María Sabina became an icon not only of indigenous culture but also of the earthy "Neolithic" (Munn 1973) wisdom of indigenous peoples. As the longstanding narrative in the West of the Noble Savage aligned with the particular antiestablishment ethos of the 1960s, María Sabina, "High Priestess of the Magic Mushrooms," came to represent an antidote to the social ills of Western civilization. This interest has fueled a small cottage industry in work about María Sabina that circulates in discourses around the world and continues to reinscribe her as a symbol of indigeneity.[21] While much of this literature tirelessly plows the same ground that has become foundational myth of the psychedelic subculture, "María Sabina studies" also has had a lasting impact on scholarly research about the Sierra Mazateca (Duke 1996; Feinberg 1996, 2003).

There are literary legacies, too, and Mazatec writers are directly engaged with many of them. María Sabina's chants—mesmerizing cascades of esoteric, poetic words in an exotic language—were a big hit with the Beats. The post-Beat poet Anne Waldman wrote a famous extended poem, "Fast Speaking Woman," based on María Sabina's recorded veladas. The sabia became a darling of the Ethnopoetics movement, culminating in a volume of work by and about her edited by Jerome Rothenberg (2003), the movement's foremost figure. María Sabina was the subject of a play by Camilo José Cela (1970 [1967]), the Nobel Laureate in Literature in 1989, and her words were the basis of a choral work by the composer Libby Larsen (1994). Alice Walker claims that a recent book of poems (Walker 2003), a meditation on the post–9/11 world, was inspired by María Sabina's life and words. The list of texts, both musical and written, stimulated by María Sabina and her work could go on and on.

María Sabina and the mushrooms have had a vibrant afterlife as a visual and linguistic symbol in the Sierra, and in the world beyond it. In Huautla, María Sabina and the mushrooms are ubiquitous, prominently featured in the names and signs of taxi stands, hotels, restaurants, tortilla shops, and, of course, the Casa de la Cultura (House of Culture). In Oaxaca, such symbols are only slightly less prevalent, surfacing in the names of hotels and restaurants, songs by Oaxacan musicians, the names of regional rock bands, and on countless T-shirts sold in the zócalo (central square). And in Mexico City, through her chants from Wasson's recordings, María Sabina has become the voice of the "Mazatec Nation," a chanting loop of song that echoes hour after hour, day after day, in the upper hall of the National Museum of Anthropology.

This corpus of ethnic symbols is augmented by the mycotourists arriving in the Sierra each year. Unlike the earlier generation, these "neohippie" mycotourists are more explicitly interested in ethnic tourism. They seek transcendent religious experiences but also "authentic" experiences of indigenous culture; as a result, they are self-consciously more "culturally sensitive" than their hippie ancestors. They also tend to be somewhat better off financially, and by now local people who interact with mycotourists are aware that such relationships are fundamentally commercial. An ironic reality of twenty-first-century life in the Sierra is that the mushrooms that a young man once told the missionary linguist Eunice Pike (1960) were a gift to the Mazatecs because they are poor have now become a form of spiritual wealth offered to (relatively) rich "refugees" from the industrialized and alienated West.

Interviews with María Sabina and other sabios indicate the profound ambivalence many Serranos feel toward commercialization of the mushrooms. As such discourses often go, outsiders are complicit in converting mushroom use from a medicinal, spiritual activity into a recreational one. Arguments about this are more intense and frequent in Huautla than elsewhere in the

Sierra; Huautla remains the destination of the vast majority of mycotourists, the only place in the region where the volume of transactions approaches a "mushroom trade." However, even in Nda Xo, which is too remote and unknown to receive more than a handful of mycotourists each year, people have strong attitudes about the mushrooms and outsiders. Some—perhaps like the sabio I saw my first day in Nda Xo—see mycotourism as an opportunity they hope to work to their advantage. Others, however, view the *honguistas* (mushroom seekers) of Huautla with deep suspicion, if not outright disdain. When I mentioned that on trips to Huautla people would try to sell me veladas—or, even more scandalous, to sell me mushrooms directly—people from Nda Xo, while not surprised, generally responded with disgust, characterizing this as further evidence of Huautla's commercial decadence.

My point is not so much to characterize these debates; discourses about the mushrooms were not the focus of my research. On the contrary, I went to the Sierra intending to stay as far away as possible from the mushrooms. I feared that by putting myself in the well-defined category of an outsider who had come to the Sierra in search of mushrooms—either as a mycotourist or as a less common but likewise identifiable type of person, the mushroom researcher—I would typecast myself, importing ideological and ethical baggage I wanted to avoid. When asked the routine question, "You're here for the mushrooms?" I always said no and talked about my interest in Mazatec writing. But in the end, as will become clear in coming chapters, it was impossible to avoid the mushrooms; they popped up in conversation all the time anyway. On occasions when local people are called on to behave in ethnically inflected ways—such as during the Day of the Dead, and in particular during the song contest that is the subject of the next chapter—the mushrooms feature prominently in public performance.

And that is my point: attitudes and discourses about the mushrooms are everywhere, and almost no one is neutral on the subject. Veladas, mushrooms, and *chota chjine* (shamans) such as María Sabina likely were not such highly salient symbols in local talk before the age of Wasson. Now, however, they have become inseparable from representations of Mazatec society.[22] Even those who reject identification with such symbols, or refuse association with the tarnish that commodification has left on them, nevertheless take an oppositional stance because everyone is, in essence, required to "weigh in" on mushroom use, and no one is permitted the luxury of remaining indifferent. As I will show in the following chapters, indigenous intellectuals, as cultural intermediaries, are more likely than other locals to engage with discourses about indigeneity voiced by outsiders. For authors such as Heriberto Prado, taking a stand on issues about mushroom use is even more thoroughly mandatory. Thus, these authors are necessarily in dialogue, both in their work and in discussions about it, with symbols such as mushrooms, veladas, María Sabina, and chota chjine. The different approaches Mazatec authors take toward these symbols reflect their varying responses to the pressures of speaking at once to internal and external audiences—pressures that pervade indigenous revival projects, including those in the Sierra Mazateca. Their divergent lives and work are representative of similar challenges faced by indigenous authors and activists elsewhere in the Sierra—and, indeed, in the country. The competing models of authorship set forth by different Mazatec writers demonstrate the fraught nature of the issues with which they must grapple, such as how best to represent "authentic Mazatec identity," promote ethnic norms, and engage with (or reject) outsiders. Questions about how best to resolve these tensions are raised not only by indigenous authors, however, but also by others across the Sierra—perhaps especially on occasions, such as the Day of the Dead fiesta, when questions about ethnic identity are called to fore. But they are, at bottom, trick questions and unanswerable: in the post-Wasson Sierra, it is impossible to tease apart "traditional" Mazatec practice—however much it is now codified as such—from modernizing, globalizing discourses about "Mazatec culture" and "indigenous identity" that have arrived via generations of mycotourists, anthropologists, cultural journalists, documentary filmmakers, and others searching for stories about Mazatecs and their mushrooms.

Furthermore, such groups are not the only outsiders who have had formative influences on local discourses about "Mazatec culture." While many outsiders, from coffee middlemen to INI officials, have left their mark on the region, for local revival movements, clergy of the Catholic Church have been especially important. The enduring power of the church's influence in the region is best viewed by describing how the church has shaped—and in some cases, failed to shape—the lives of some of the Sierra's most-prominent indigenous intellectuals.

The Collected Works of the Brothers Prado:
Liberation Theology and the Birth of a Mazatec Literature

The single most important figure in the Sierra's revival movements—particularly those tied to songwriting—is Heriberto Prado Pereda. He is the oldest son of a relatively successful campesino from Nda Xo, whom I will call Plutarco Prado.[23] While not wealthy even by local standards, Plutarco Prado owned enough land and other resources to be able to afford two wives.[24] In 1963, he helped found Nda Xo's annual Feria del Café (Coffee Fair), an event that celebrated the importance of coffee as a lucrative cash crop. Although it was once well attended by people across the Sierra, by the time I arrived in the region, the fair had become "very sad"—a ghost of its former self, a reflection of falling coffee prices and the crop's declining local importance. Had Plutarco Prado not died relatively young, he might have reached prominence similar to that of his only brother, who had three wives and once held the highest civic post: municipal president.[25]

Plutarco Prado's fourteen surviving children by his two wives (two by the second died in early childhood) grew up in the same unusually close-knit Mazatec-speaking household. While it was not atypical for co-wives to live together, the more common situation—or the discursively normative one— would be for them to have had separate households: one "in town" run by the first (i.e., "legitimate," and in many ways favored) wife, and another at the rancho run by the second wife. A common expression in Nda Xo refers to the first wife as the "cathedral" and the second as the "chapel." (Occasionally, a married man would tease me by asking me if I wanted to be his chapel, which always elicited laughter when bystanders and eavesdroppers saw that I got the joke.) In the case of Heriberto Prado's family, the closeness among the siblings was intensified because the first wife was bedridden for many years. While some in the family joke that this did not prevent her from carrying on some "wifely duties"—she did, after all, continue to bear children—it nevertheless meant that the second wife ran the household, caring for the first wife and all the children.

From an early age, Heriberto Prado was bright and interested in religious matters, which caught the attention of the local priests. He and others sometimes speak as if the presence of the Catholic Church in the Sierra began in 1972, when the Josefino missionaries arrived.[26] Although this simplifies a more complex history of evangelization that dates back to the mid-sixteenth century, it does accurately depict the lived reality of many people in the Sierra: evangelization in the colonial period was not very successful, and there was no permanent church presence in the Sierra before the end of the nineteenth century. Thus, the arrival of the Josefinos was groundbreaking (see fig. 2.3). Heriberto Prado finished *secundaria* in Nda Xo and, under the sponsorship of Huautla's bishop, Monsignor Hermenegildo Ramírez Sánchez, left for the seminary in Tehuacán.[27] Eventually, Heriberto's half-brother Alberto Prado Pineda followed him into the seminary, and for a time they studied in Tehuacán together with the intention of becoming priests.

FIGURE 2.3. The procession for a First Holy Communion, near
Tierra Colorada, a tiny settlement in greater Nda Xo. The girl in
the photograph was seventeen when she received the sacrament—
relatively old to do so, even by local standards. This situation
suggests the extent to which even in the Sierra's large towns, the
Catholic Church was not a strong presence until recent decades,
and in small communities, its presence is still expanding.

Heriberto and Alberto Prado studied at the Seminario Regional del Sureste (Regional Seminary of the Southeast; SERESURE). The seminary, which was founded in 1969, flourished in the wake of Liberation Theology, a movement that was strongly opposed elsewhere in Mexico but was powerful in the south (Sherman 1997)—not coincidentally, the country's poorest and most heavily indigenous region. Three bishops from "Pacifico Sur" (Oaxaca and Chiapas) were crucial in making the region a liberationist stronghold and the most "radical" of Mexico's eighteen pastoral regions. Bartolomé Carrasco, archbishop of Oaxaca, and Arturo Lona Reyes, bishop of Tehuantepec, were the leading forces during the 1970s and 1980s in making the Catholic Church in Oaxaca an extremely progressive institution (Norget 1997). Don Samuel Ruiz, the famous bishop of Chiapas, was actively documenting government corruption and mistreatment of the indigenous population even before the Ejército Zapatista de Liberación Nacional (EZLN) uprising of 1994, the most notable expression of unrest in southern Mexico and a rebellion that was fueled partly by liberationist ideas. "Don Samuel," as the bishop was often called, subsequently played a critical role in mediating between the Zapatista insurgents and the government, incurring the wrath of progovernment ranchers and Ladinos in Chiapas and earning him the title "Red Bishop." These bishops and other liberationists relied on SERESURE to promote their agendas. The seminary's mission was to further the liberationist ideal of "integral evangelization" in the service of which seminarians, as part of their training, combined theological studies with practical pastoral experience. In this way, SERESURE's "priests in training" were crucial to spreading liberationist ideals while serving local needs: the rural areas where most people lived suffered a chronic shortage of priests (Norget 1997: 100).

This mission, furthermore, was compatible with that of the Sierra's Josefino priests, whose focus on indigenous communities, especially in Oaxaca, also meant that they concentrated on poor ones. Thus, the promise offered by the Prado brothers fit neatly into the goals of local and regional clergy. The enthusiasm with which their ecclesiastical aspirations were encouraged reflects the general turn the post–Vatican II church took toward greater acceptance of local customs, practices, languages—even actors. Although the Prados would not be the first Mazatec natives to become priests, very few have followed that course. When the brothers entered the seminary, no priests working in the Sierra were natives of the region and, therefore, none spoke Mazatec, a serious limitation in an area with an isolated and, at the time, largely monolingual populace. In the 1970s, when Heriberto and Albert Prado were studying at the seminary, the percentage of monolingual people would have been much higher. But even in 2010, more than 95 percent of the population of greater Nda Xo spoke Mazatec as a first language, and nearly 30 percent were monolingual Mazatec speakers.[28] Indeed, the Prelature of Huautla was founded precisely out of awareness of the Sierra's "under-evangelization," a situation underscored by the persistence of practices the church found problematic, such as polygamy and the ritual use of hallucinogenic plants.

The church authorities saw the Prados' interest in the priesthood as highly beneficial, and the bishop and others encouraged them to complete the long years of training. Even while studying at the seminary, Heriberto and Alberto Prado became important religious leaders in the Sierra. Their linguistic and cultural positioning and high level of education earned them deep respect. And SERESURE's "hands-on" approach to pastoral training meant they were involved in outreach activities aimed at increasing local participation in the church. Of these activities, the one whose legacy has been the most enduring involved the introduction of Mazatec-language songs.

The inspiration for the composition of Mazatec-language songs for the church grew out of a pair of contradictory realities that are nevertheless—paradoxically—codetermining, as well. While the church aims to incorporate "under-evangelized" indigenous peoples more completely, the very characteristics of people eliciting such an impulse are also what often frustrate it. In this case, the paradox means that fuller involvement in the church often proceeds as ethnic pride diminishes, yet the church makes itself more attractive to indigenous people as it demonstrates tolerance for indigenous difference. Certainly, Liberation Theology operates by embracing the idea that affirmation of the reality of indigenous experience is a prerequisite for deep, widespread evangelization. Or to put the issue in the movement's own language, promoting more active involvement with the church while also valorizing "Mazatec culture" falls under the rubric of *concientización* (consciousness raising) and *enculturación* (enculturation).

The term *concientización* comes from the work of the Brazilian populist educator Paolo Freire. A method of peasant education, concientización emphasized the development of critical thinking through reference to quotidian, locally salient political issues. Under Liberation Theology, the concept became an evangelization tool that involved promoting assimilation of the Gospel through everyday experience, including the lived reality of oppression and poverty. The related concept of enculturación "denotes a process wherein the priest or church agent evangelizes through the norms of the local community, using them as a sieve of interpretation, producing a kind of hybrid 'indigenous theology' (*teología indígena*)" (Norget 1997: 110).

Many of the songs Heriberto Prado began writing were heavily influenced by such liberationist ideas, beginning with the conceptualization of the project itself. With time, over his successive song collections, liberationist influence became increasingly explicit and began to affect his songs' content and aims. Heriberto Prado's first book, published in 1986, emerged in the years that Liberation Theology became increasingly influential in southern Mexico, having arrived there nearly a decade after it had reached other parts of Latin America. However, his later books, published in the 1990s, appeared after Liberation Theology fell out of favor as the conservative Pope John Paul II acted to suppress the movement. In 1990, SERESURE was "accused of being a hot-bed of radical theology," and then closed. Carrasco, the liberationist archbishop of Oaxaca, was replaced in 1993 by a conservative one, effectively neutralizing the liberationist tone of the region (Norget 1997: 100). Nevertheless, liberationist ideas survived, most publicly in Bishop Samuel Ruiz of Chiapas, and more privately in the work of people like Heriberto Prado.

Two of his published song collections contain prefaces by Bishop Ramírez. The bishop addressed the audience—explicitly categorized as speakers of Mazatec—using the second-person singular familiar form in Spanish throughout, thereby invoking the solidarity and intimacy Liberation Theology sought to promote among clergy and parishioners. "Friends and brothers," he wrote, "these songs in the Mazatec language . . . will allow you . . . to sing to God with your mouth and heart, and in this way to participate more fully in the Eucharist, in the Sacraments and on all occasions when you come together with Christian Mazatec people to praise God" (preface to Prado Pereda 1986: 3, 1991: ii). Heriberto Prado likewise drew explicitly on classic themes of Liberation Theology in his own introductions to the volumes. For him, Mazatecs are the "dignified descendants of the Olmecs [who] want to offer the world their cultural riches" (Prado Pereda 1994: v). He dedicated his songs to "my Mazatec brothers, especially the poorest ones, that they may be inspired to recover their dignity" (Prado Pereda 1986: 5). In another volume, he dedicated his songs to "all Mazatecs, especially the choirs and singers lost in the mountains who with their message and work awaken the hope of giving birth to a better community" and to "all those who put their pen, thought, and courage in the service of indigenous peoples . . . and to those writers who promote the literature of 'deep Mexico'" (Prado Pereda

1997: ii). This refers to the pathbreaking book by Guillermo Bonfil Batalla (1987), which, while not drawing on liberationist ideas per se, shared many of the same political impulses. Finally, Heriberto Prado dedicated songs to "the base groups of the Sierra" (Prado Pereda 1991: viii), a reference to Christian Base Communities, which formed the self-sufficient social "atoms" on which liberationist ideals were to be built, community by community. Heriberto Prado designated some songs specifically for base communities' celebrations and others for concientización: to educate people about problems ranging from cholera to the effects of neoliberalism (Prado Pereda 1994).

Of Heriberto Prado's work, the single most pointed demonstration of liberationist ideas is *La misa autóctona* (The autochthonous Mass), songs written for the Masses held during the Day of the Dead fiesta (Prado Pereda 1986, 1991). Heriberto explicitly drew on a stated goal of Bishop Arturo Lona Reyes of Tehuantepec to make his diocese into an *iglesia autóctona* (autochthonous church), where people could encounter Christianity "from their own [sociocultural] reality" (Lona Reyes, quoted in Norget 1997: 110). Inasmuch as the Day of the Dead is seen by Heriberto Prado, as well as by many other Mazatecs, as a foundational locus for expression of "Mazatec identity," it is also the single most important site, viewed from within liberationist thinking, at which the church should make itself permeable to local custom, maximizing local participation in the life of the church. Indeed, the music Heriberto Prado (and, later, others) wrote for religious occasions and for Masses especially—Day of the Dead Masses above all—was very popular and extremely successful in encouraging people to participate more actively in the church. As a result of his efforts, and those of his half-brother Alberto and others involved in performing and teaching the songs, the songs are now sung every week by thousands of people across the Sierra in religious ceremonies that range from the full Catholic Mass to small, familial ceremonies for the sick and the dead. Even "outsider" priests, none of whom know more than a few phrases in Mazatec, have learned many of the songs. They continue today to sing them each Sunday during Mass.

The two brothers continued to be actively involved in this project even after Alberto Prado decided not to complete his seminary studies. He left SERESURE to marry a woman from Nda Xo who, like him, was from a prominent but not especially well-off family; her father was extremely well respected and served twice as municipal president.[29] As he left, Alberto Prado assured the bishop that he would always be very involved with the church, and he went on to become Nda Xo's chief catechist. He remains heavily involved in the church's activities, serving as one of the leaders of his *kjuachikon* (prayer or rosary group), directing the music every week for Mass, regularly providing the Mazatec version of the priest's homilies, and leading various church-sponsored civic activities—most important, the Day of the Dead Song Contest. In contrast, Heriberto Prado finished the seminary and, after his long years of study, returned to the Sierra. He went on to be formally ordained as a priest in the *cabecera* (county seat) of Nda Xo. The ordination ceremony marked the culmination of his triumphant homecoming. Local church officials asked families throughout the cabecera to host visitors, and the celebrated event was one to which local people from across the Sierra traveled in droves to attend.

Heriberto Prado was ultimately appointed to serve as priest in Tenango (Ja⁴č'a¹), a nearby town in which the variant of Mazatec spoken is close to the variants spoken in Nda Xo and Huautla. He had a dramatic impact there on the involvement of local people in church activities. As will become clear from the events I discuss in following chapters, Heriberto Prado's influence on local practices and on local people's attitudes toward the church was often the subject of conversation. This influence is demonstrated, for example, by comments made by the Sierra resident María Magdalena García. She made national and international news when, dressed in a Sierra huipil (the same style María Sabina wore, which many viewers—at least, within Mexico—would have recognized instantly), she performed a limpia on Pope John Paul II during his 2002 visit to Mexico. García originally came from Jač'a but was living in Huautla, when interviewed by *La Faena* shortly after the pope's visit:

> *Juan García Carrera (editor of* La Faena*):* Where did you learn how to give limpias? Did you have family who were curanderos?
> *María Magdalena García:* I'm not a curandera, but I know how to give limpias. I gave limpias with eggs and rue to my children from the time they were little. For twelve years I have been actively participating in religious activities. The priest Heriberto Prado brought us into the religion; he organized us. (García Carrera 2002: 6)

Such comments about Heriberto Prado are common, particularly among people from Jač'a. It attests to the enormous impact that Heriberto Prado has had on local Catholic practice, increasing active involvement by many while helping to make church activities permeable to local ethnic traditions. The fact that it has become customary in the Sierra for religious officials to be given limpias in this way at the beginning of each Mass is, for example, directly linked to practices Heriberto Prado initiated and encouraged once he began officiating at Masses.

It would be difficult to overestimate the symbolic and practical importance of Heriberto Prado's presence as a priest. He represented an enormous evangelization opportunity for the church, which could finally count as one of its own someone who was culturally and linguistically conversant with local people. He was a resource people could turn to; he could understand their words and mediate as other priests could not. People could confess their sins and confide their troubles in Mazatec and, for the first time, know their speech would be understood. He translated the words of certain key prayers and activities into Mazatec—the Lord's Prayer, the Holy Rosary, and, above all, the Sign of the Cross. As a result, many people from the Sierra could utter these prayers in their own language for the first time. At the same time, Heriberto Prado's presence was critically important in making the church—if not universally, then, at least, his instantiation of it as a church official—more receptive to local realities. He performed the sacrament of marriage for second and subsequent wives and baptized babies born of such unions, something "outsider" priests rarely did. The latter service made him especially valuable to local people, given the anxiety—one I routinely heard people express—about children who had not been baptized, lest they die before receiving the sacrament. Such accommodations to local custom made him much sought after, respected, and, ultimately, beloved by local people. Precisely because he filled needs no other member of the clergy could, his influence and reputation extended well beyond Jač'a, encompassing the entire Sierra.

Meanwhile, as a priest, Heriberto Prado continued to write songs, to promote them throughout the Sierra, and to hold workshops teaching catechists and others to sing his songs and to write their own. Over time, the songs were no longer seen as his; they slowly became community property. By the time I began living in Nda Xo, most of the people younger than Alberto and him—as well as older people who did not start going to church regularly until after the songs were widely known—did not even know that the songs had an author. As indicated in a newspaper article written about Heriberto Prado, local people celebrated him for having *taught* them songs in Mazatec.[30] Yet despite the widespread amnesia about the part he has played in them, any understanding of revival projects in the Sierra would be incomplete without considering the contribution he has made through the hundreds of songs he has written and whose lyrics he has published. His work constitutes one of the most important additions to the creation of written Mazatec literature.

Revival in the Sierra Mazateca: On Indigeneity and Discursive Practices

It is obvious that . . . a person can be the author of much more than a book—
of a theory, for instance, of a tradition or a discipline within which new
books and authors can proliferate . . . [W]e might call them "initiators of
discursive practices." The distinctive contribution of these authors is that
they produced not only their own work, but the possibility and the rules of
formation of other texts.

—Michel Foucault, "What Is an Author?"

Heriberto Prado's contribution to indigenous revival in the Sierra does not
end with the texts he wrote. He and his work played a critical role in creating "authorial infrastructure" for other Mazatec writers. As a result of his
efforts to promote literacy in Mazatec and "popular authorship" in the language, there are now people throughout the Sierra who know not only how
to read Mazatec but, more important, how to *write* in it. While he did not do
so singlehandedly, Heriberto Prado played a vital part in making it possible
for other Serranos to become authors and songwriters. In addition to being
an author, Heriberto Prado has been—at least in the narrow sense—an "ini-
tiator of discursive practices." He has been instrumental in giving others not
only the tools they need to become authors in their language but also a context for using those tools by helping construct a social world in which producing texts in Mazatec has value and meaning.

An irony, however, is that some forms of authorship that Heriberto Prado
played such a seminal role in facilitating are now ones with which he deeply
disagrees. His objections are various, but one of the most pervasive differences he has with other Mazatec authors concerns their views on the crucial
category "indigenous." We have already seen, through pivotal recent events,
that competing ideas about indigenous identity—conflicting notions of
what constitutes the basis of "Mazatec culture" as a distinctive indigenous
society—are at play in the interactive field of daily life in the Sierra. The revival projects Heriberto Prado helped realize are ones that have stimulated,
and perhaps thrive on, similarly conflicting ideas about what it means to be
indigenous, to represent oneself as a Mazatec. Furthermore, such tensions
are not unique to the Sierra. The fact that the one thing all indigenous writers
have in common—that (at least officially) their *lengua materna* is an indigenous
language—means that the only language they share is Spanish. This hints at
some of the hidden contradictions in the term *indigenous*—and, hence, the
flexibility of interpretations put into motion when such a term is deployed.

It is precisely this discursive heterogeneity, and the lack of clarity and analytical purchase that categories such as "indigenous" often have, that in recent years has produced a rich and productive body of scholarly research on indigeneity, as distinct from, but in dialogue with, terms such as *indigenous*.[31] Such work commonly emphasizes the emergent, constructed, relational features of indigeneity. Viewed from this angle, what makes something "indigenous" is both historically and socially specific, dependent on particular regimes of classification and value that emerge and change over time rather than being the reflection of natural boundaries — of essential, pure, and thus corruptible categories. As Marisol de la Cadena and Orin Starn (2007: 4) put it: "indigeneity emerges only within larger social fields of difference and sameness; it acquires its own 'positive' meaning not from essential properties of its own, but through its relation to what it is not, to what it exceeds or lacks. . . . [I]ndigenous cultural practices, institutions, and politics become such in articulation with what is not considered indigenous within the particular social formation where they exist. Indigeneity, in other words, is at once historically contingent and encompassing of the nonindigenous — and thus never about untouched reality."

I agree that thinking about indigeneity as a "social formation" is the most accurate and useful analytical strategy. The forms indigeneity takes are indeed best approached by examining the histories by which specific constellations of social categories become salient. At the same time, I do not want to lose sight of the value categories such as "indigenous" have for people like Heriberto Prado. This is so, even — and, perhaps, especially — when they are contested, either by those with competing conceptions of the term or by those who reject the category altogether, despite having the characteristics (e.g., speaking Mazatec as a first language) that for others are its very hallmarks. Beyond their utility in practice, such categories capture aspects of lived experience that can be obscured by an overemphasis on their constructed and heterogeneous nature. A language is, of course, as constructed a category as is an ethnic one such as "indigenous." In places like Oaxaca, where boundaries around languages have been drawn almost exclusively by linguists and anthropologists rather than by the daily practice of speakers, the constructed nature of a category such as "Mazatec" is one that speakers experience in daily life. The constructed nature of the category "Mazatec" would be foregrounded, say, by Heriberto Prado's inability to communicate in any language other than Spanish with the author Juan Gregorio Regino, who speaks a different variant of Mazatec. Yet that experience does not make the category a fiction, either. It is a political reality, of course — meaning that independent of their own experiences, Juan Gregorio Regino and Heriberto Prado Pereda are both classified as "Mazatec authors." But it is also an experiential reality, given their ability to read—if with difficulty—each other's work in Mazatec.

While a category such as "indigenous" is clearly not unitary, it is not a discursive or political mirage, either. An important model for thinking through the utility of the category "indigenous," especially as it relates to the ostensibly more analytically versatile concept of "indigeneity," is the one Mikhail Bakhtin (1981) proposed for language. In his view, language in its natural state is heteroglossic and infinitely varied, much like indigeneity. What he calls "unitary language"—like the category "indigenous"—masquerades as a natural object when in fact it is the product of political coercion, of the constant policing of its boundaries that deny entry to the heteroglossia of everyday speech. Thus, unitary language depends on heteroglossia for its very existence: its meaning derives from that which it excludes—although this is, of course, a truth denied by supporters of the inherent validity of unitary language, who insist on its status as a real and autonomous object in the world.

What I find useful about this model is that it emphasizes the complex interdependence between categories such as "indigenous" and concepts such as indigeneity. However, in transplanting Bakhtin's ideas to a discussion of what a category such as "indigenous" means, I want to make an important amendment: that of neutralizing the polarity that infuses Bakhtin's model. In his view, unitary language is fundamentally parasitic on language in its true state; this casts unitary language in almost wholly negative light. I propose that the relationship in question is more thoroughly symbiotic. Viewing it as such emphasizes the complex, reciprocal relationship between analytical categories such as "indigeneity" and ostensibly folk ones such as "indigenous." Doing so would entail framing the relationship between the two entities—"indigenous" as an ostensibly autonomous object and "indigeneity" as designed to trouble its ontological status—as one of mutual dependence. Thus, a category such as "indigenous intellectual," while undoubtedly constructed, is also useful and, within certain parameters, analytically valid.[32] The category obviously has heuristic value, in this case by allowing me to refer collectively to a group of people who share certain characteristics— for example, that they have produced work in an indigenous language; that they have pursued education beyond the basic level; and that they spend some measure of their time on intellectual pursuits, such as writing, reading, and speaking publicly. The category has emic validity, as well; *indigenous intellectual* is a term—alongside *organic intellectual*—that I hear authors of indigenous-language texts use repeatedly to refer to themselves and one that others use regularly to refer to them. Finally, it is a category that allows analysis itself to proceed. To draw for a moment on Anna Tsing's model (Tsing 2004), the friction between categories such as "indigenous" (whose social value derives precisely from its apparent fixity and imperviousness to change) and concepts such as "indigeneity" (whose meaning stems from its emphasis on process, fluidity, and dynamism) is what produces something new in the world: creativity and productive analysis.

A similarly generative tension emerges in the context of ethnic revival in the Sierra Mazateca. There, too, one encounters not only competing understandings of what categories such as "indigenous" and "indigenous intellectual" mean but, even more profoundly, different ways of conceptualizing the broader frameworks within which such categories derive their meaning. The fervent disputes within the Sierra over the meanings of revival—over the boundaries around the social categories on which revival depends—suggest how deeply invested people are in categories such as "indigenous." Taking a broader view, the disparity between such views and the processes through which they are brought into tension can be seen as productive. As I will show, the apparently conflicting relationship between different forms of revival, and the conceptualizations of indigeneity on which they depend, are symbiotic and mutually supportive when viewed from a distance. The friction between them is necessary and generative.

SINGING FOR THE SPIRITS

The Annual Day of the Dead Song Contest

Tatsjejín nga kjabuya
isien nixtjin xi nchifu'ánijun
ngasandie.
Jé tsijemána nga k'e nchifu 'ánijun
ñanga je inimájin xi tichunjin k'e
kó xi jé inima tjíngase nixtjin. . . .
Isien nixtjin xi tjíjno inima,
isien nixtjin xi jé inimájun,
kuibi xi s'uína,
stsitsijen ngatjún ngasandiena, . . .
kui ngasandie xi tatséjibi,
kui kjabuya xi tatséjibi.

Death is not eternal,
You spirits that descend from
heaven to life.
I feel your presence among us,
where we who are alive are dead,
and you who are dead are alive. . . .
Living souls,
dead souls,
this is our fiesta.
For a moment our two worlds appear, . . .
in this life that is not eternal,
in this death that is not eternal.

—Juan Gregorio Regino, Mazatec poet, from the poem "Death
Is Not Eternal," in *Tatsjejín nga kjabuya/No es eterna la muerte*

A Popular Case of Revival

In this chapter, I consider how the histories of literacy, writing, and politics of ethnicity laid out in previous chapters condition indigenous revival in the present. While ethnic revival has taken various forms in Mexico, this book concerns a particular type centering on revitalizing and strengthening indigenous languages that are still widely spoken. Though such movements focus on language, they are ultimately aimed at broad cultural revival and political autonomy. The case of revival discussed here is one that—unlike many of its kind, in Mexico and beyond—has been wildly popular and locally effective at creating new political realities.

This revival movement has culminated in the annual Day of the Dead Song Contest. I begin with the contest's setting, including the ambivalent location that the Day of the Dead fiesta—like so many other national symbols with explicit indigenous heritage—occupies within the national imagination. I consider the contest's particular history as the offshoot of the earlier song project initiated by Heriberto Prado with support from the Catholic Church, motivated by its mission under Liberation Theology to raise its political engagement while increasing its openness to local cultural practice. The contest's background sets the stage for its present social impact. The contest has played a pivotal role in stimulating Mazatec literacy while producing a dramatic rise in popular authorship as musicians across the region now write songs in their language. The contest has also spawned an ever widening circle of innovations, all of which further ethnic revival. These include the birth of a new industry in the Sierra—the increasing popularity of the contest and its music coupled with the growing ranks of Mazatec author-composers has stimulated a popular music market in Mazatec song recordings. In aggregate, these developments are recruiting a key group of people to active participation in Mazatec speech communities: young people who speak Spanish as a first language and are at best passive speakers of Mazatec. This many-sided revival project has in turn brought with it new ideas about Mazatec tradition and ethnic belonging, notions that have political and material impact in people's daily lives.

As I discuss later, the contest, even more than the church song program that spawned it, draws on values and practices that are locally salient, highly marked emblems of "Mazatec culture." Yet the setting and symbols on which the contest draws also occupy a complex position in Mexican national iconography. Thus, the key to the contest's broad social appeal is its flexibility in dealing with the assorted boundaries in play during the Day of the Dead fiesta, including those between national and ethnic belonging, tradition and innovation, history and modernity.

On National Belonging: Day of the Dead and the "Indian Problem"

Throughout Latin America, celebration of All Saints' Day and All Souls' Day (November 1 and November 2) is referred to as the Fiesta de Todos Santos. Although Todos Santos is widely used in Mexico, as well, there it is known by a term that has become canonically Mexican: Day of the Dead (Día de los Muertos), or simply Muertos.[1] As far as the church is concerned, the official part of the fiesta centers on the celebration of special Masses on each day. However, "Most observers would agree, ironically, that mass in Mexico is the least salient part of the holiday" (Brandes 1998: 360). From local people celebrating the holiday to the tourists flocking in to film it and scholars studying it, most people emphasize "folk practices" that occur outside the church: erecting altars in homes, businesses, public places, and graveyards (see fig. 3.1); making *ofrendas* (offerings) for the deceased through candles, flowers, food, toys, and drink; holding family vigils at gravesite (see fig. 3.2). Halloween, the corresponding holiday observed in the United States, incorporates similar themes, though in a version that is so thoroughly secularized and divorced from the immediacy of death that most religious elements are absent entirely (see Brandes 1997, 1998).[2]

Day of the Dead has thus become quintessentially Mexican—Mexico's most famous holiday and a highly salient national symbol (Lomnitz 2005). It has been of special interest not only in the popular imagination, to tourists and casual Mexicanophiles, but also to scholars from various disciplines.[3] "Often cited as a manifestation of a uniquely Mexican view of death" (Brandes 1997: 273), the Mexican "cult of death" features prominently in Mexican art and literature.[4] A canonical example of such literature is Octavio Paz's influential book *The Labyrinth of Solitude*, especially the essay "Day of the Dead":

> The word death is not pronounced in New York, in Paris, in London, because it burns the lips. The Mexican, in contrast, is familiar with death, jokes about it, caresses it, sleeps with it, celebrates it; it is one of his favorite toys and his most steadfast love. True, there is perhaps as much fear in his attitude as in that of others, but at least death is not hidden away: he looks at it face to face, with impatience, disdain, or irony. . . . Our contempt for death is not at odds with the cult we have made of it. (Paz 1959 [1950]: 57–58)

FIGURE 3.1. An altar for the Day of the Dead, with a child posed in front of it dressed in *calzones* (white cotton pants) and other clothing considered traditional dress for embodying the ancestors.

While Paz's meditation on "the Mexican view of death" is remarkable for its eloquence, it is but one of a multitude professing the view that Mexicans have a unique relation to death. Although many scholars have dissented from this point of view (see, e.g., Navarrete 1982), the belief that Mexicans' unique relationship to death forms a central part of national identity continues to hold enormous popular and intellectual appeal. Day of the Dead celebrations are seen as the emblematic and most complete expression of this Mexican cult of death. As many scholars have pointed out, the mythic valorization of ancient Mesoamerican societies has played a central role in Mexican nationalism, serving to distinguish Mexico from both Spain and other Latin American nations. A uniquely Mexican view of death—as a singular legacy of preconquest civilizations—has been a special signifier in national differentiation. The religions of ancient Mesoamerica are widely known for their overwhelming obsession with death, strikingly displayed by a richly documented history of ritual human sacrifice.

FIGURE 3.2. The graveyard in Nda Xo during the Day of the Dead fiesta.

This legacy, furthermore, is seen as surviving in the modern practices of Mexico's indigenous peoples. Take, for example, the following view by two scholars of Day of the Dead: "Días de los Muertos is observed to some degree in all regions of Mexico and by all classes of society, but probably nowhere more elaborately or traditionally than in the state of Oaxaca. Away from the political and economic center of the republic, Oaxaca with its large native population of Zapotec, Mixtec, and other Indian communities has resisted cultural change and maintained a more traditional way of life" (Childs and Altman 1982: 6–7, 18).

Such attitudes about Oaxaca—which makes a cameo appearance in most books about Day of the Dead—are widespread. Yet the view is problematic, not least because existing historical evidence on the subject is contradictory (see Brandes 1997). But while studies questioning Day of the Dead's ancient roots bring welcome critical distance to nationalist dogma, they cannot fully address why viewing Day of the Dead as a primordial event continues to be so magnetic, not least for indigenous people themselves. Arguments that problematize the historical origins of the fiesta merely raise again—though now to be slaughtered rather than resurrected—the ghost of the Authentic Indian who has survived, through the magic of cultural cryogenics, from pre-Columbian days to the present.

The allure of viewing Day of the Dead as an ancient event is my point of departure. I am less interested in the debate about the origins of Day of the Dead; rather, I privilege the meaning people make of the holiday's past and the social implications of viewing the fiesta as the bastion of ancient customs. Regardless of how the present Muertos festival came into being, vast numbers of Mexicans, indigenous and not, view it as the annual instantiation of an ancient ancestral ritual. The Mazatec indigenous intellectual and author Alejandrina Pedro Castañeda expresses this view when discussing *huehuentones*, a Nahuatl word that means "old man" and that, in the Sierra, refers to the ancestors in whose honor Muertos takes place. Alluding to the fiesta's antiquity, Pedro Castañeda (2001: 10) writes, "We know, of course, that the *Huehuentones* . . . existed since centuries past, before Christ."

Such beliefs about the ancient past of Muertos are tied in complex ways to notions of indigenous peoples that date to the earliest contact between European colonizers and Amerindians. In other words, they link to the so-called Indian problem and are in dialogue with the long history of *indigenismo* that has sought to define the role of indigenous peoples in the colony or nation. *Indigenista* policies, even those formulated by Las Casas and other benign proponents, were written from the perspective of non-natives, entail a host of systemic biases, and are shot through with conflicting attitudes toward indigenous peoples. They both reflect and help create Mexico's deeply ambivalent relationship to its indigenous citizens.

Attitudes toward Day of the Dead, both official and popular, display this ambivalence. Muertos has a unique relationship to Mexican nationalism as a highly visible and canonically Mexican event. Yet it is marked as distinctly indigenous, albeit in a circumscribed sense: the inclusion of indigenous peoples in the Mexican nation often has been on symbolic—hence, stipulated and selective—terms: indigenous people are licensed to participate in larger Mexican society only under controlled conditions. These terms privilege ancient civilizations over living ones and are partial in their celebration of present indigenous societies, which are granted the space to assert difference only when doing so poses no threat to Mexican modernity. Departure from norms of national identity is confined to certain themes or certain times of the year.

Perhaps no site in Mexico displays its ambivalence toward indigenous people as concretely as the Museo Nacional de Antropología (National Museum of Anthropology), a veritable shrine to Mexican nationalism.[5] The museum's layout reflects this ambivalence, and symbols from Muertos and the Mesoamerican cult of death play key roles. The grand first floor features the history and taxonomy of Mexico's pre-Columbian civilizations, complete with exquisite artifacts and dramatic dioramas depicting images of the country's glorious past. The central exhibit focuses on Aztec society and includes the famous Aztec Stone of the Sun (the "Aztec Calendar"), longtime symbol of the Mexican nation. An enormous disc carved with elaborate figures—human hearts sacrificed to the sun god, among others—the stone occupies the museum's place of honor, the resplendent yet bloody crown jewel of Mexico's ancient wealth.

Leaving aside the "Mexico City–centered account of the history of power in Mexico" (Lomnitz 2001: 226) embodied in the ground floor's layout, the museum has an entire second floor that many visitors never see. Guidebooks barely mention it and photographs of the museum's treasures rarely include it. The second floor is dedicated to Mexico's modern indigenous populations. It is filled with dusty displays in small rooms with low ceilings, replete with all manner of "folklore" (costumes, dances, fiestas and rituals, music, oral literature). Its wealth is much diminished compared with the magnificent artifacts on the first floor. The small exhibit on Mazatec people, for example, features a female mannequin in a Sierra *huipil*, which most women wore a few decades ago. Now, however, such dress is worn daily only by a few old women and is worn by the rest only on special occasions. A recording echoes in the background, featuring the most famous woman to wear this type of huipil: María Sabina, whose disembodied voice chants away, mid-*velada*, years after her death. Her inclusion in the exhibit suggests the conflicting impulses through which people have viewed her: while some have stressed that her abilities as a *curandera* (healer) were important for their contemporary social value, for others they represented a "fundamental chapter to the cultural history of primitive man" (Wasson 1980: 10). María Sabina's presence in the exhibit thus symbolizes the broader internal contradictions and systemic ambivalence of Mexico's attempts to grapple with its "Indian problem."

Elsewhere on the second floor, many displays—particularly of Oaxacan peoples—feature Day of the Dead celebrations: the folkloric manifestation par excellence of indigeneity in Mexico. Muertos thus constitutes a special, profoundly uneasy site at which practices construed as traditionally indigenous intersect with those conceived of as typically Mexican.[6] Such representations of Day of the Dead are both a co-optation of indigenous beliefs and practices, pressing them into the service of nationalist agendas, and a successful containment of those beliefs and practices by confining them to a single time of the year and to a restricted range of licensed activities.

The notion that displays of indigenous identity are permissible only under certain circumstances promotes ideas such as those expressed by Pedro Castañeda: it is acceptable to embody the huehuentones during Day of the Dead, because in doing so, one breathes life—albeit temporarily—into an ancient Mesoamerican past that is too remote to be threatening. "Folkloric" practices such as those attached to Muertos are thus not unlike the items in the museum's second-floor gallery. They are perishable celebrations in which the community dusts off the remnants of the past, embodying them "for a moment" only, dressing itself in ancestral folklore as women would put on huipiles or men would put on *calzones* (white pants of homespun cotton): traditional attire that, once the fiesta is over, will be abandoned for the visible trappings of modernity, the factory-produced clothing of everyday life. The altars and masks and musical instruments will be consigned once again to the margins, to a fixed place in Mexican cultural history.

Yet in practice, the boundaries between past and present—folklore and folk practice—are rarely hermetically sealed. While national discourses may find recognizable echoes at the local level, they also meet unexpected fates when they leave the control of national policymakers and enter the hands of "organic intellectuals." As Antonio Gramsci (2000) reminds us, some such homegrown figures play central roles in furthering hegemonic discourses and, hence, in bolstering the status quo. But other organic intellectuals occupy an opposing position, becoming engines for discursive subversion and class-based social change. These different kinds of organic intellectuals interact in alternately predictable and unpredictable ways with discourses about national belonging, ethnic identity, and the relations of both to history. Celebrating the enactment of past tradition as more than an academic exercise—through widely embraced practices—also means importing some permeability to individual variation and present practices, including those that refuse relegation to essentialized and authorized representations of the past.

This leads to disjunctures between the ancient context in which, for example, Day of the Dead activities ostensibly unfolded and the present one in which they are reincarnated. The present is an environment full of "violations" of explicit discourses about "indigenous tradition": the Muertos fiesta in the Sierra features plastic Halloween masks alongside those carved by hand, compact discs for sale alongside the "music of the ancestors." The rupture between folklore and folk practice creates a space for innovation and creativity in which tradition can be recast in the clothing of modernity and modernity can be harnessed for the recovery of tradition. Furthermore, once entire communities are involved in celebrations and enactments of the ancient past, what constitutes "authentic" representations of that past becomes subject to debate. If at its core the so-called Indian problem turns on how the nation chooses to manage its ambivalence about indigenous people, then the matter takes on a new character when it is viewed from the perspective of indigenous communities such as Nda Xo. In Nda Xo's Day of the Dead celebrations, we see the echoes, distortions, and oppositions to national discourses about indigeneity: a novel response some indigenous people have had to the "Indian problem."

Fiesta of the Spirits, à la Mazateca: Welcoming the Cha¹jma²

Like most indigenous people in Mexico and elsewhere, Mazatecs find ways to negotiate the tensions between tradition and modernity on terms inflected by local ideas about collective belonging yet in dialogue with regional, national, and international ideas. This mirrors the situation of indigenous groups throughout the world as they navigate the conflicts between cultural continuity and innovation, both among the generations and across the geographic-discursive continuum from local to national and beyond.[7] What is unique, however, is that Mazatecs work through the relevant conflicts partly by calling on their relations to the dead and the fiesta in their honor as vital resources. The most important fiesta in the Sierra Mazateca, Day of the Dead is the single most important collective event through which people interact with the dead, with the past, and with ideas about both. In the Sierra, Mazatec is overwhelmingly the medium of daily life and Muertos festivities are no exception. During the fiesta, the Sierra's signature activity—the part of the festival that sets it apart from how it is celebrated elsewhere—consists of culturally distinctive forms of singing in Mazatec. Musicians and dancers disguised to embody the ancestors roam nightly from house to house, singing to the dead as they symbolically give them flesh once again, allowing them to commune with the living. The song contest, as one of the most recent innovations attached to the fiesta, draws directly from these practices in offering new opportunities to navigate the tensions between national belonging and ethnic distinction, allegiance to tradition and openness to social change.

I heard about the contest during my first day in Nda Xo. My initial stop had been Huautla, widely considered the Sierra's center because it is the largest town and was where María Sabina lived. As one Huautla native put it, "Huautla de Jiménez, the most important city in the Sierra Mazateca, . . . is the intellectual capital of the Mazatec world" (Pedro Castañeda 2001: 7, 23). Though Huautla's importance is universally acknowledged, other Sierra residents take issue with what they claim is Huautecos' general condescension toward other Serranos and their arrogance about their town's dominance, which obscures the importance of other regional centers, including Nda Xo. I routinely heard other Serranos complain that people in Huautla treated them like "hicks," in response to which many adopt Huautla ways of speaking.

Yet on at least two scores, Nda Xo is explicitly acknowledged to be superior to Huautla—and, indeed, to other Sierra towns. Nda Xo is often called the "most traditional," and it is known throughout the Sierra for the related distinction of having the best musicians (see fig. 3.3). While I heard both sentiments expressed repeatedly, they were voiced to me quite clearly in my first visit to the Sierra. The vast majority of the region's schoolteachers live in Huautla, as do some of its most prominent indigenous intellectuals. I sought out a couple of them, and one, the author Florencio Carrera (see Carrera González 2000a, 2000b, 2000c; Carrera González and van Doesburg 2001), told me I should pay a visit to Chilchotla (Nda Xo). He said, "It is the center, really, for songwriters in this area."[8]

A few days before we met, Carrera had been a judge in Nda Xo for the first—and, to date, only—Mother's Day Song Contest. That contest, which was also hatched in Nda Xo, was inspired by the Day of the Dead Song Contest. However, the Mother's Day contest came nowhere near to achieving the popularity of the Muertos contest, partly because Mother's Day is not an important holiday locally, but also because it is not "culturally embedded" in the way that the Day of the Dead contest is. Nevertheless, the very existence of the Mother's Day contest—as well as that of other revival initiatives that likewise have found popular success elusive—underscores the popular success of the Day of the Dead Song Contest, as well as how it continues to promote broader social innovation. The contest has set a precedent by which social creativity, within clear limits, is locally valued. Indeed, Carrera himself had been the judge many times not only for the Muertos contest in Nda Xo but also for newer, smaller spin-off contests in Huautla and other towns. The one in Nda Xo, however, remains the oldest, largest, and most important contest for the composition of Mazatec songs.

Carrera also told me he considered Nda Xo the region's most "traditional" municipio (county) not only because of its relatively high levels of "linguistic conservatism" (see table 3.1 and map 3.1) but also because of the prevalence there of practices marked as emblematic of Mazatec culture.[9] They include activities recognized as "old," with a long duration in the community, as well as those that, although they are not "new," are seen as revivals: resurgent expressions of ethnic pride. Day of the Dead festivities in Nda Xo are a mixture of the two. The song contest, a relative newcomer on the cultural scene, now

FIGURE 3.3. Musicians playing during the Day of the Dead fiesta.

TABLE 3.1. Linguistic data and Spanish-language literacy rates
for Mazatec-speaking municipios

Mazatec-speaking municipios[a]	Percentage of population who speak only an indigenous language	Percentage of population who speak an indigenous language and Spanish	Spanish-language literacy rate for age 15 and older (%)	Total population
(San Antonio) Eloxochitlán de Flores Magón	31.35	91.78	54.07	4,263
Huautla de Jiménez	26.89	87.08	63.68	30,004
Mazatlán Villa de Flores	10.75	86.93	62.06	13,435
San Bartolomé Ayautla	28.82	97.60	53.07	4,052
San Felipe Jalapa de Díaz	22.61	89.81	69.88	26,838
San Francisco Heuheutlán	25.70	92.61	55.70	1,160
San Jerónimo Tecoatl	12.91	76.90	64.48	1,606
San José Tenango	44.72	97.49	57.51	18,478
San Juan Bautista Tuxtepec	0.29	14.71	90.26	155,766
San Juan Chiquihuitlan (Chiquihuitlan de Benito Juárez)	3.78	58.72	62.23	2,458
San Juan Coatzóspam	10.73	92.02	71.64	2,535
San Juan de los Cués	1.34	33.51	83.84	2,357
San Jose Independencia	22.77	95.52	71.77	3,684
San Lorenzo Cuahnecuiltitla	21.23	93.16	68.49	771
San Lucas Ojitlan	15.72	85.64	79.34	21,514
San Lucas Zoquiapam	23.51	95.00	61.21	7,554
San Mateo Yoloxochitlan	10.73	74.14	75.25	3,475
(San Miguel) Huatepec	49.47	97.40	49.20	5,995
San Miguel Soyaltepec (Temascal)	9.00	69.94	76.98	36,564
San Pedro Ixcatlán	20.76	88.59	72.35	10,371
San Pedro Ocopetatillo	22.63	92.81	58.72	884
Santa Ana Ateixtlahuaca	25.77	95.67	60.19	510
Santa Cruz Acatepec	25.24	90.38	61.94	1,470
Santa Maria Jacatepec	5.71	61.23	78.73	9,240
Santa María Magdalena Chilchotla	28.23	94.91	62.29	20,584

TABLE 3.1. Continued

Mazatec-speaking municipios[a]	Percentage of population who speak only an indigenous language	Percentage of population who speak an indigenous language and Spanish	Spanish-language literacy rate for age 15 and older (%)	Total population
Santa Maria Teopoxco	19.52	97.66	66.00	4,651
Santiago Texcalcingo	22.04	97.70	64.79	3,076
Teotitlán de Flores Magón	0.18	19.01	88.83	8,966
Mean	19.37	81.00	66.88	14,366
Median	21.64	91.08	64.48	4,457

Source: INEGI 2010

[a] Some of the towns listed are not predominantly Mazatec speaking but are shown here either because they are located in the Sierra Mazateca or are mestizo towns with significant Mazatec populations. There are also small pockets of Mazatec speakers in other municipios, especially in the neighboring states of Veracruz and Puebla.

formally inaugurates the entire fiesta, leading off activities in which even Nda Xo's oldest residents claim they participated as children. The contest now takes up the entire first day of the fiesta. When it ends around sunset, the first night of the fiesta begins and, those in whose honor the fiesta takes place—the ancestors, the dead—arrive to share the Earth once again with the living.

In most areas, Day of the Dead is basically a two-day event, but in the Sierra Mazateca it lasts ten days and, importantly, nights. It is famous regionally even among the surrounding indigenous communities with their own Day of the Dead fiestas of which to be proud. It is also widely discussed, by both locals and outsiders, as the Sierra's most "colorful" fiesta and its most "traditional." Explicit ideology surrounding the fiesta underscores its link to the past and to dead relatives and ancestors. The various names by which the fiesta is called in Mazatec suggest as much: s'oi¹k'en⁴ (fiesta of the spirits, fiesta of the dead), s'oi¹chi⁴ta⁴jchi¹nga³ (fiesta of the ancestors), s'oi¹cha¹jma² (fiesta of the black men), s'oi¹cha¹xo³'o³ (fiesta of the umbilical-cord men—i.e., men who are tied to the land by their umbilical cords, who spring forth from the belly of the land).[10] This final name has a double sense—the *chaxo'o* (umbilical-cord men) arise from the earth and return to it, the place they "live" when they are not with the living. This sense is echoed in discursive

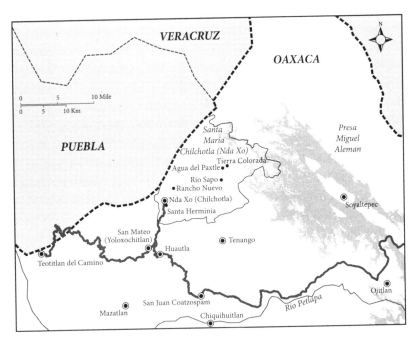

MAP 3.1. The municipio of Chilchotla (Nda Xo) in Oaxaca's Sierra Mazateca. Cabeceras, or county seats, are indicated with double circles, and smaller, dependent settlements are indicated with single circles.

conventions used to refer to the dead; one Mazatec author used this expression in his work when discussing the ancestors as "los señores que vienen del ombligo del mundo" (men who come from the navel of the Earth). The meaning also resonates with a Sierra practice now falling into disuse, in which the umbilical cord of a new baby is buried next to the house, symbolizing the child's tie to its place of birth. As one Mazatec man commented when I asked where he was from: "I'm from right here. My umbilical cord is buried here."

As is common throughout Mexican indigenous communities, the fiesta includes making altars for the dead. In fact, another way the Day of the Dead Song Contest has been linked to further social innovations is the founding in 2002 of an altar contest attached to Nda Xo's song competition. So far, the new contest has attracted only a few entries each year, but it is suggestive in its attempt to further in a different expressive medium some of the same agendas—while encountering many of the same tensions—that animate the song contest. It may eventually prove an interesting arena for increased participation by women, as they tend to be more heavily involved in altar construction than men. Women's participation in the song contest—

and in most of the practices on which it draws from the fiesta itself—has remained limited.

Alongside the construction of altars, another important Day of the Dead practice consists of long, familial visits to the graveyard to burn copal incense, make offerings, light candles, and bring flowers—above all, *naxo ngojo*, the "flower of the dead."[11] The holiday is also filled with smaller events involving family and compadres in celebrations that center on food, such as the making and serving of mole, for which family chickens are killed. This part of the fiesta is crucial in the Sierra because it is when people who have migrated out of the region are most likely to come home and visit family, both dead and living. However, the most distinctive and uniquely Mazatec part of the fiesta revolves around ritually enacting a visit from the ancestors, for whom it is said that the year between fiestas passes as just one day. The holiday is thus, in this deeper sense, the Day of the Dead, the one metaphorical "day" on which the dead will commune with the living before going away again until the following year.

In the Sierra, musical performance plays a key role in representing the ancestors. From dusk to dawn for all ten nights of the fiesta, groups of musicians and men in disguise—the *chajma* (lit., black men; see note 10) or *chaxo'o* (umbilical-cord men), the huehuentones—go from house to house, dancing and singing, symbolically embodying the arrival of the dead (see fig. 3.4).[12] The musicians and dancers from each group visit the graveyard on the fiesta's first day, disguising themselves as ancestors. When they leave the cemetery, they ring the church bell, signifying the arrival of the ancestors before singing and dancing in individual homes.[13] In return, people in the houses offer them bread, especially *pan de muertos* (bread of the dead); *xan¹* (*aguardiente*, cane liquor); beer; *ncha²¹* (*atole*, a corn drink) or *ncha²¹san³* (*atole agrio*, lightly fermented atole); *ch'oin¹* (*chayote*, a seasonal vegetable); oranges; cigarettes; firecrackers; beeswax candles; sweets; or hot cocoa. Special food and drink are also placed on the altars to the dead.[14] Most of these items must be bought and thus are luxury goods many families can afford only on special occasions.

During daylight on the fiesta's last day, groups of huehuentones return to homes where they have been welcomed more than once, singing and dancing for a final time. This time, they are given piñatas—not the papier-mâché kind sold in urban Mexican markets but homemade piñatas made from old crockery that break dramatically when hit (see fig. 3.5). After the chajma have finished visiting houses, they go to the basketball court at the center of town, between the *palacio municipal* (town hall) and the church. They string up the piñatas one by one and bring blindfolded members of the audience to swing

FIGURE 3.4. A group of chajma (or huehuentones) in Santa Herminia preparing to depart for an evening of visiting houses across the region.

at them, to the great delight of the kids who compete for the spoils. Once all of the piñatas are broken, around dusk, the chajma leave the way they came, ringing the church bell en route to the cemetery. There, after a few sad songs saying goodbye to the ancestors until the next year, they take off their disguises and leave the graveyard.[15] Then they head home as members of the living once again, and the fiesta formally ends.[16]

The sentiment that the fiesta is bedrock of old traditions is constantly expressed by Serranos, who also speak with pride about how the Sierra's fiesta is longer and more elaborate than elsewhere in Mexico. Thus, those "Indians of other tribes"—who, as Renato García Dorantes wrote, lacked the Mazatecs' bravery to outsmart man-eating eagles and live among the clouds—take less care in their veneration of the dead. Explicit discourses about the fiesta also stress it as a time during which Mazatecs are especially faithful to tradition, to ways of the past. "He who fails to do [observe Muertos] ceases to be indigenous," as Heriberto Prado Pereda (2001: 15) has written. While this ideology is particularly elaborate among educated elites who promote cultural revival, others express the idea, too, including Mazatec musicians.

FIGURE 3.5. Collecting piñatas.

In contradistinction to the backward-looking rhetoric that surrounds it, the fiesta has been a leading venue for social innovation. This stems partly from the holiday's cross-generational attraction, but especially from its appeal for young people, who play a crucial role in perpetuating (or eliminating) cultural practices. The music that features so prominently in Day of the Dead festivities has been especially central. One of the most visible—or audible—features of quotidian life in the Sierra is the nearly ubiquitous presence of Mazatec music: songs sung in Mazatec, in the general style of the music for Day of the Dead, by the same groups of musicians who perform nightly during the fiesta. Few homes are without at least a cassette or compact disc, despite their relatively high cost. The music blasts day and night from cars, shops, public buildings, and private homes. Nearly every village, even the tiny ones, has at least one group of musicians. Most chajma groups are led by a man who writes his own songs in Mazatec and aspires—if he has not already done so—to produce a recording of his music. However, these recordings are a recent phenomenon, having emerged only in the past twenty years. And although the musical tradition and the customs by which it is performed are much older, the popular composition and performance of songs in Mazatec is very recent, particularly that of songs with individual authors.

The emergence of this "new tradition" is directly tied to the founding of the annual Day of the Dead Song Contest, one of the most interesting and potent cultural innovations of recent decades in the Sierra.[17] The first contest was held almost thirty years ago in the *cabecera* (county seat) of Nda Xo. The contest is a prime example of "ethno-folklorization." A canonically Durkheimian representation of "Mazatec culture" is displayed for members of Mazatec society, on terms that are explicitly and reflexively ideologized as such. In other words, while tourists and other "outsiders" may be present, these particular displays of codified culture—"metaculture," in Greg Urban's terms, or cultural ideas about culture (Urban 2001)—are not aimed at them but, rather, at "insiders," for the very people who are the subject of the cultural metacommentary. This is not to say that the awareness of external observers does not also play a role here: these cultural displays for "internal consumption" are inflected in complex ways by contact with external representations. They are influenced by, respond to, and react against numerous external categorizations of indigenous people. They are the product of historical and more immediate experiences of ethnic categorization tied directly to colonialism and its legacies—among them, generations of indigenismo policies and other state attempts to solve the so-called Indian problem; the Catholic Church's involvement in formulating indigenista policies, most recently through variants promoted under Liberation Theology; and, of course, the Sierra's unique history of experiences with mycotourists and other visitors pursuing "ethnic tourism." Nevertheless, the immediate audience for these representations is not external but internal. The contests involve a display of "Mazatec culture" and "Mazatec tradition," aimed at an audience of local people.

The core of the contest provides a forum for celebrating Mazatec traditions and emphasizing Mazatec cultural history and social continuity. Yet the framework within which these traditions are put on display—indeed, the very acts by which "Mazatec tradition" becomes essentialized as such— are innovations in intricate dialogue with contemporary pressures and influences. Furthermore, the contest, and indeed the entire fiesta it inaugurates, are points of entry by which modern and postmodern themes and concerns brush up against an overwhelming preoccupation with the past, therein constructing a dynamic future.

The Contest and Its History: Ethno-folklore and the Beginnings of a Mazatec Literature

The contest for one of the Muertos fiestas I observed, in 2002, marked the twentieth anniversary of the first Day of the Dead Song Contest held in Nda Xo. The contest was conceived from the beginning as a vehicle for both the promotion of indigenous language literacy and the advancement of linguistic and cultural revival. Thus, its emergence is intimately tied to national and regional histories of education and ethnic relations.

Two central figures in the genesis of the contest are the half-brothers Heriberto and Alberto Prado, who wrote the texts (discussed in chapter 1) about the apparition of Mary Magdalene who appeared at the spring in Nda Xo. As discussed in chapter 2, the two brothers, with the support of the liberationist church, studied to become priests. During their training, they were active in Catholic outreach activities aimed at increasing Serranos' participation in church practices. Of those activities, the one whose legacy has been the most enduring was the first recent revival initiative to occur in Nda Xo, predating even the Day of the Dead Song Contest: the introduction of Mazatec-language songs into church services.

This development was, in many ways, an "invention": it established new practices of singing—and writing—songs in Mazatec. The limits of the existing historical record mean I cannot say how frequently or in what contexts people sang in Mazatec before this period. Many Mazatec composers claim that in the past—that is, before the Catholic Church, the national education system, and other institutions that impose competency in Spanish became locally influential—people sang in Mazatec during Day of the Dead fiestas. I have no way to evaluate this claim. However, the people I interviewed in the Sierra agreed that prior to the Catholic Church's support for Mazatec song composition, no one sang in Mazatec in church; in addition, people rarely sang in Mazatec in other contexts—although veladas are an important exception. Even during Day of the Dead festivities, in which music is so central, the songs were primarily instrumental, with minimal Mazatec lyrics. Again, whether this had been the case for many generations or was a more recently "degraded" state produced by the institutionalized ascendance of Spanish (as many indigenous intellectuals claim) is impossible to say. But it does appear that immediately before the church's promotion of Mazatec songs there was minimal Mazatec singing during Muertos. With the notable but unique exception of the song cycle "Naxo Loxa" (Orange Blossom; see note 11, p. 269), there was no previous tradition of writing songs in Mazatec, particularly as creations of individual authors.

Alberto Prado Pineda (2000: 14) has described how his half-brother Heriberto's composition of Mazatec songs for Catholic Mass led people to realize that "the most important fiesta of the Mazatecs—Todos Santos—was being lost." This "loss" was fundamentally linguistic: what little singing occurred in Mazatec consisted of repeating the names of chajma groups. This produced "an urgent need to revive our customs" by showing people that "with our mother tongue it is possible to work wonders composing songs." Left out of his account, however, is that the contest's genesis arose not only from the desire to revitalize s'oik'en, the most Mazatec of holidays, the locus of "Mazatecness." The contest also aimed to stimulate literacy in Mazatec, on which the spread of Heriberto Prado's songs for the church depended. Frustrated with existing orthographies for Sierra Mazatec, Heriberto devised his own way to write lyrics. Although somewhat idiosyncratic (e.g., it uses uppercase letters to indicate nasalization), his system was nevertheless successful as a practical orthography. Yet because the project relied on texts written in Heriberto Prado's unique alphabet, literacy was foregrounded from the beginning: in teaching his new songs, he invariably wound up teaching his alphabet at the same time. The importance of promoting Mazatec literacy was further underscored once the church began publishing the songs and disseminating them throughout the region. Their intended audience was enormous, consisting of essentially all Mazatecs, with the exception of the region's relatively few Protestants. However, the members of this vast audience, if they were literate at all, were literate only in Spanish.

The songs were intended to be sung during formal Masses, as well as during the substitute services led by catechists in rural communities that do not have resident priests. In such communities, most of the church's local operations—holding weekly services, carrying out the church's routine activities, arranging for a priest to come for special events—are left to catechists. In both formal Masses and services directed by catechists, anything in Mazatec, including the songs, has to be led by locals (i.e., the catechists), because none of the priests (except Heriberto, when he was still a priest) speaks Mazatec. Furthermore, the catechist's "job" requires basic understanding of and literacy in Spanish, as he (or she) can be called on to translate the priest's homily or to read and translate verses from the Bible. In addition, because catechists lead people in singing, they must have strong singing skills and, often, the ability to play the guitar or violin.

As a result of both their literacy and their musical skills, catechists became key intermediaries in reaching the larger audience of Mazatec speakers.[18] They also experienced increased prestige as a result: their augmented visibility in and importance to church activities was broadly empowering. Teaching literacy in Mazatec was a critical part of this process. Heriberto Prado, along with Alberto Prado and other catechists, held workshops across the region to teach the songs to people, especially to other catechists, while also teaching Mazatec literacy. The song contest was designed to advance this educational process, providing incentive to catechists (and others) to learn the new church songs while encouraging them to use the new skills to produce Mazatec songs of their own. In discussing this with me, Heriberto Prado frequently referred to the contest as "killing two birds with one stone." By this he meant that it helped people to learn his orthography while encouraging them to participate more fully in the larger project by writing their own songs. Furthermore, these twin goals were linked at a higher level to another pair of goals: promoting more active involvement with the church while also valorizing Mazatec culture.

As Heriberto Prado has written, the aim of the church song project was to "revalorize" Mazatec culture, because the area's musicians "ya no tocan canciones autóctonas" (no longer play our songs) (Prado Pereda 1993: 4–5; emphasis added). He is alluding to Liberation Theology's mission of transforming the very structures of Catholicism by remaking the church into an autochthonous church—a church that embraces rather than rejects the perspectives of the world's poor and oppressed, indigenous people, such as the Mazatecs, chief among them. Thus, Heriberto Prado is gesturing toward a vast social project in which the church helps people valorize customs they have been taught to disparage while welcoming their expressions of cultural difference as a catalyst to the church's own fundamental transformation. It is thus not surprising that the church song initiative brought about specific, demonstrable social changes: it stimulated a new, popular kind of Mazatec singing practice that to this day is pervasive in the Sierra, and it helped spread Mazatec literacy into every community in the region. But its influence did not stop there. The interest in promoting social change underpinning the church song initiative was what led Heriberto, Alberto, and the other catechists in Nda Xo to found the Day of the Dead Song Contest. That project, in turn, became the impetus for an even wider revival movement.

The Contest in Practice: Toward a Dissection of Its Popular Appeal

The contest is held every year on October 27, the first day of the Muertos fiesta. It features a main competition for adults; in 2002, a children's division was added—yet another instance in which the song contest is linked to explicit innovation. Although the contest in Nda Xo proper is still the largest by far, with more than a hundred participants and a huge crowd of spectators, "spin-offs" have appeared in communities throughout the Sierra. These contests feature groups of musicians who, along with chajma dancers, present new songs in Mazatec they hope will place among the top five entries and hence win cash prizes. Some groups enter more than one song, although they pay a separate entry fee for each.

The song itself is the core of each entry, and a written version must be submitted in advance. This text is of the words only; most composers I interviewed do not read, let alone write, musical notation. As most of the composers learned to write using Heriberto Prado's orthography, his is the most widely used. However, others are also in use, including the alphabet used in government publications for the Sierra's bilingual schools; the orthography used by Huautla intellectuals, particularly those trained in the ethnolinguistics program;[19] and alphabets devised by individual authors, which may be inconsistent with or borrow from other orthographies. Generally, one member of the group, often its leader, composes the song. In some cases, the author will be an "independent composer," a man who writes songs in Mazatec but does not have his own group of chajma.

A brief comment on the contest's orthographic heterodoxy is in order, as it is one of the central reasons the contest has been popular with such a wide range of Serranos, including those with nominal formal education. At minimum, every submission must include a written version, which enforces basic attention to writing in Mazatec and prevents the contest from centering entirely on performance. Beyond that, however, no rules are enforced concerning how the written text is produced—most critically which alphabet is used. The heterogeneity of the written versions doubtless complicates the work of the judges, who, when reading through a text for the first time, must make a series of guesses about which system is being used until the conventions that are employed become clear. Even then, though, internal inconsistencies continue to make reading the texts difficult—such inconsistency is particularly common among idiosyncratic orthographies, but even those that rely on established and relatively standardized alphabets are generally not used consistently. For most authors, even those who are active songwriters, writing in Mazatec remains an occasional activity. They do not pursue it frequently enough to weed out internal "errors"—a skill that, after all, schoolchildren in most societies spend years perfecting.

Nevertheless, I never heard the judges complain about this—even though those who serve as judges are not only proficient in at least one of the orthographies in question, but in most cases they were also critically involved in devising, standardizing, and implementing it. As I will show later, differences in opinion about orthographic choices can be highly contentious, provoking years of intense debate as people work through the politically fraught process of deciding how their language should be represented in writing. This, in turn, effectively defers writing until ostensibly more "basic" decisions about the alphabet can be resolved. Once those decisions have been made, the existence of an official alphabet—its enormous benefits notwithstanding—can be used to stifle writing that does not conform to established norms. By contrast, the song contest operates on the assumption that any text, no matter how internally "flawed," is sufficient. Participation flourishes as a result. What is all the more remarkable is that the judges—who in other contexts take the opposing view, strongly advocating standardization and *normalización*—in this context preserve open-minded acceptance of the contest's alphabetic heterodoxy.

The written text is thus crucial, but the song's performance is equally important to how it is judged. Usually there is a small group of musicians playing at least one guitar or *guitarrón* (sometimes more), a goatskin drum, a *teponaxtle*, a violin or two, and sometimes smaller instruments such as tambourines, rasps, or triangles.[20] Most musicians also sing. In addition, each

FIGURE 3.6. Two little chajma.

FIGURE 3.7. A group of musicians and dancers on the stage at the Day of the Dead Song Contest.

chajma group has its own dancers; with few exceptions, the musicians and the dancers are male. The basic dance consists of a simple, repetitive step on the downbeat from one foot to the other, a step the chajma will perform thousands of times over the evening and that children are taught from the time they can walk (see fig. 3.6). The focus — in the contest and during the regular nightly festivities of Muertos — is not on the dancing; it is on the costumes and, during the contest, on how the dancers enact themes from the song.

This enactment of the song normally involves presenting to the audience an essentialization of "Mazatec culture" (see fig. 3.7). The dances feature symbols and practices explicitly marked as traditional: shamans using mushrooms in veladas, women entering a ndo⁴ya³ (temascal, a ritual and medicinal steam bath) after childbirth, people worshipping the sun. Some of the dance presentations are elaborate; more unusual "props" used in recent years include cornstalks, *metates* (corn grinders, which are heavy), gorilla suits, piglets, and small trees. When the chajma appear, they do so as stylized representations of the dead, in clothes codified as "traditional": in calzones and homespun white shirts; in *huaraches* (sandals) or, better yet, barefoot; in handmade wooden masks rather than papier-mâché or rubber ones; and in *sombreros* (hats) woven from branches of the *jonote* (a tropical linden tree) with whimsical pointed tops that some claim are meant to evoke mushrooms.[21] Dancers often appear in drag, as well. The huipiles they wear have become a powerful, specific emblem of Mazatec tradition: Maria Sabina wore a huipil all her life, and her fame made the Sierra huipil an international symbol of "the Mazatec people." Like the mushrooms, the huipil circulates internally to signal "Mazatec tradition," but it has also been co-opted externally to signal indigeneity in general. To give but two examples: the Mexican artist Frida Kahlo frequently wore a Sierra huipil—a set piece, perhaps, but just one of her large collection of Mexican huipiles symbolizing her persona as a Mexican artist embracing her country's unique (indigenous) cultural heritage, and the Mazatec woman who blessed Pope John Paul II during his visit to Mexico wore a Sierra huipil (see chapter 2), signaling to those familiar with it that she was Mazatec but to most people, including the pope, merely that she was indigenous.

This tension between internal and external representations—how the meaning of even explicitly local symbols is inseparable from their valence beyond the Sierra—is mirrored in the reciprocal process by which explicitly external symbols take on local meaning. An important role is played here by migrants, who, if they return but once a year, will do so during the fiesta. Unlike many surrounding ethnic groups, Serranos rarely migrate to the United States, moving instead for work or education to regional cities such as Tehuacán, Córdoba, Puebla, or Mexico City. In part because young and unmarried men, many of them migrants, are among the most active participants, performances during the song contests often embrace modern themes. The contest in 2001, which took place just after September 11, included such an entry, which won third prize. It featured a song about Osama bin Laden, complete with airplanes crashing into buildings, Uzi-toting Arabs, exploding bombs, and an enraged President George Bush being consoled by Mexican President Vicente Fox.[22] The same year, another group featured an accordion player for the first time; although the accordion is a staple of Mexican folk music, it surfaces only rarely in the Sierra. Rubber masks have also become increasingly common, often depicting political figures (Fidel Castro is a perennial favorite, as are American and Mexican presidents) and ghoulish, Halloween-inspired monsters. In 2002, a man who had dressed as a mummy was the hit of the fiesta.

The introduction of modern themes does meet with resistance. The tension between innovation and tradition plays out in how the contest is judged—not only by official judges but also by "informal" ones, such as audience members and participants. The formal judging criteria have shifted across the years and from one community to another. No official contest records are kept even in Nda Xo; one year, I "rescued" the written entries from being used as toilet paper but not before some had been made into papier-mâché masks. This makes it difficult to analyze the judging process with specificity. However, the general criteria seem to be the quality of the lyrics (including the written versions), the quality of the musical performance, the quality of the dance "presentation" (especially the dancers' costumes and how the dancers enact the song), and the entire work's originality—all of which (with the possible exception of the final criterion) can be construed as implicitly tied to tradition. There is no explicit category for how traditional an entry is, and the emphasis on creativity actually pushes some in the opposite direction. Nevertheless, traditionalist ideologies pervade discourses about the contest, and people explicitly valorize entries that pay homage to "Mazatec culture," to the ways of the ancestors. An article in the state newspaper about Huautla's contest in 2005 captures the conflict between tradition and innovation well. Many locals had claimed that "the region's huehuenton contests 'have converted tradition into a show,'" reported the article's author, E. Gabino García Carrera. Lamenting the contest's commercialization, they also claimed that many groups participate only to win the cash prizes. One man—"a painting instructor in the María Sabina House of Culture"—lodged a related complaint, noting

> the particular case when "in an irresponsible manner" the panel of judges offered the first prize to the group called Cha Xohó Najjnrra (the Huehuentones of Huautla) when [their performance] "had nothing to do with the tradition of los muertos," that the only thing setting them apart was that "they play instruments well, like the violin." In addition, "They are omitting the sacred element," [the man] elaborated, suggesting that to win first place, the theme should concern the netherworld [inframundo], offerings and all that refers to this sacred day for the Mazatecs. . . . He [also] criticized the competitive nature of the contest, because, he said, "It shouldn't be a question of competing, but rather of sharing among Mazatec brothers."[23]

This situation is quite different from contests I have observed. The winning entries have been songs whose themes are in keeping with traditionalist discourse. They lament how much things have changed since the days of the ancestors or celebrate the richness of "Mazatec culture" despite the material poverty of so many Serranos (see fig. 3.8). While the more "creative" entries often place in the top five—the song about Bin Laden, for example, and a song that offered an invented "creation story" about Nda Xo's highest peak—they never win first place. A look at some titles, written by various composers, gives a sense of the prevalence of traditionalist themes:

FIGURE 3.8. The group that performed the 2008 winning entry. The man in the center is the group's leader and composer, and some of the group members are his sons.

"Enle chita jch-chinga ngas'a" (The words of the ancestors)
"Kjuan kan-ñato octubre" (The twenty-seventh of October)
—Luis Pulido and Saúl Valente

"Tsin kjua-iaxkon" (There is no respect)
—Alberto Prado Pineda

"Sole na-in jch-cha" (The grandfather's song)
"Jch-chaskon s'i je" (Let's respect this fiesta)
"Tjian chotsen s'i nanguina" (Let's go to the fiesta of our pueblo)
"Tojo jña so s'en" (Who else if not us?)
"To so k'uas'in iane jin" (This is the custom)
"Sera ni, naxo ni, sjongo ni" (Candle, flowers, and copal)
—Pedro Pineda

"Kuina nisjein f'ichotsen no jin" (In these days they come to visit us)
"Jo tsoyani nga ni'ñion" (Why do we adorn [i.e., for Muertos]?)
—Crescencio García

"T'a ts'e ya naxo tsitin" (About the arc of flowers)
"Jokuan nisjein jch-cha" (That which happened in the past)
—Modesto Espinoza

"Ts'e cha xo'o" (The song of the cha xo'o)
"Chja jch-chingana ngas'a" (Our ancestors)
—Chajma Prado

Nevertheless, the issues raised in the article about Huautla's contest demonstrate that competing forces are at play. Participants, judges, and audiences must navigate the paradox at the heart of the contest: that it employs a recent invention to promote an idealized image of "Mazatec tradition" and the Mazatec past. Furthermore, the contest relies for its popular success on being embraced by relatively young members of the community, for whom the trappings of modernity are an integral part of daily life. The prizes are a case in point. While they are smaller in Nda Xo than in Huautla (the top prize is now about 2,000 Mexican pesos, or roughly $200), they are still big enough for the money to provide a real incentive. Yet as in discourses about mushrooms, some people are very uneasy with the idea of Mazatec culture being a "business." They have a strong sense that there are right and wrong reasons for participating in the contest, reasons that are directly tied to one's relationship to the past.

Many songs use overtly political messages in an attempt to split the difference between traditionalist conventions and the pull of modernity, particularly the desire to make the songs speak to pressing current issues. Songs of this sort address life in the present by denouncing poverty and marginalization but do so by taking on an explicitly indigenous identity whose authority rests on continuity with "Mazatec tradition." Here, too, titles are revealing:

"To cho'nda kjit'ane jña" (We'll never stop being peons)
"Tofi tofi xo nča nik'ien na jña" (Little by little they're killing us)
—Heriberto Prado Pereda

"Xkon ma xone jña" (Poor us)
—Modesto Espinoza

"Kjuabale chita xa" (The sadness of the authorities)
—Silverio Pineda

"Jat'ats'e kjua imana" (That which is poverty)
"Kjua xi kjima" (Present problems)
"Katjab'eno ndiya Méjico" (Stop moving to Mexico City)
—Luis Pulido and Saúl Valente

"Kjuñ'e xi tiyojian" (Our suffering)
—Lucio Gallardo

The last title, "Kjuñ'e xi tiyojian," represents how songs of this type try to address current problems directly. But it is also informative for its explicit appeal to overcome internal divisions:

Jme kjiñ'e kjimachon ni
naxinanda jan
To kjima to kjifeni nixrjein xi tiyo jña, . . .
Tibitjoson yijeni jo tso enle, na-in na, . . .
I xo na kuan tsakin nana jña
Kuino-iani xoñui i tsakin na jña. . . .
K'uangoni kjima k'ue nga jngo
Chita xa sasenda
Ja b'exko, ja b'exko ndi miyole
Ja b'exko, ja b'exko ndi chitale. . .
Jga ñ'e kakson jña iso'nde
Jt-tin xo kuiyo jña
Kjuasi lijme chjile
Kjuajch-chan kuicho mani.

What difficulties we have in our pueblo now
What our ancestors told us would come to pass . . .
Is happening to us today . . .
Your hate will bury you, they said.
Your [in]fighting will kill you, they said. . . .
Look what happens when we elect
New authorities
Each one with his own people
Each one with his friends . . .
What can we do in this world
In this difficult situation?
Let us come together
Let us work as a group and end our fighting.

Such calls to transcend factionalism and divisiveness pervade Day of the Dead songs in the Sierra. The political songs listed here voice such concerns explicitly. Many of the traditionalist songs do as well, and all promote the message indirectly through implicit appeals to unite behind the ways of the ancestors and revere the past. The Huauteco interviewed in the article articulated essentially the same sentiment when he voiced the desire for the contest to be an occasion for sharing rather than competing. Indeed, discourses about inclusiveness are ubiquitous during the fiesta. As I will show in the next chapter, factionalism is a fact of life in Nda Xo; many people, though they may lament it, speak of internal divisions as if they are inevitable. Political divisions and politically motivated violence are chronic problems in many Sierra communities, including Nda Xo. A glance at state and national news coverage of the Sierra reveals just how prevalent such problems are. Aside from the slight but dependable attention paid to the Sierra in feature stories—highlighting the *riqueza cultural* (cultural wealth) of the Mazateca and, above all, María Sabina's legacy—the region makes the news almost entirely because of road blockages and building seizures, election disputes and political violence, and, not infrequently, assassinations.

During the Day of the Dead fiesta, however, the emphasis in conversations about internal discord shifts away from the divided reality of the present toward a more idealistic, even utopian, discussion of what the community could and should look like. In casual conversation as much as in the messages of the songs, people stress how bad it is to fight among themselves and how important it is for people—families and the entire community—to unify. This ideology of inclusion and solidarity finds expression not only in words but also in actions: extending an invitation to eat mole at one's house during Muertos is one of the most effective ways to mend frayed relationships and leave interpersonal differences behind.

"Killing Two Birds with One Stone": On the Contest and Its "Success"

The success of Day of the Dead Song Contest in promoting such communitarian ideals and erasing factionalism (however temporarily) is much harder to assess than other measures of its effectiveness. In almost every community in greater Nda Xo—if not in the entire Sierra, thanks to the spinoff contests Nda Xo's contest has produced—at least one or two men, many of them catechists, write a few new songs for Day of the Dead over the course of the year. Most write the words down while composing the songs. They then use copies of the written texts to teach the songs to the other men and boys in their groups, who, in turn, sing the words repeatedly over the course of the fiesta, taking them into homes throughout the region. People who hear the songs—including young people who are some of the weakest Mazatec speakers—learn some of their favorites. And if a group goes on to record its music, the ripples will spread even further.

In a region where thirty years ago almost no songs circulated widely in Mazatec, now songs in the native language are a central part of quotidian life.

The church songs that the contest was meant to promote (by disseminating the skills on which they depend) are sung by thousands of people each week in communities across the Sierra. For many people, the songs have become so naturalized a part of church services that they are not thought of as having authors at all. Young people continue to learn the songs by listening to them but also by consulting various published books of the words (or photocopies from the books), thus learning not only the lyrics but also how to read in Mazatec. Finally, the energy and enthusiasm with which people participate in the contest and the penumbra of practices around it suggest the extent to which the project has been embraced by Serranos. Although the allure of the prizes is certainly motivating, note that the contest merely *begins* the fiesta. The money is distributed, and the first blush of glory is gone, before the fiesta has even gotten under way. The chajma spend weeks, sometimes months, preparing their songs, and after the contest is over, the group sings its new song or songs a hundred times or more over the following week and a half in each house it enters. At that point, the contest is irrelevant for most people and pales in comparison with questions about whether the song is *nda kji* (beautiful), whether *se pegó* (it stuck), whether *je kuan nda* (it all turned out well). As people in the Sierra were constantly showing me, the fiesta is *fun*— in large measure because of the music and because of the joy of singing: old songs or new, one's own or someone else's.

This, then, is a community in which ethnic revival and indigenous literacy have had extraordinary popular success. In a comparative national study of such projects, it would constitute an interesting and unusual case, one that may contain clues about why some literacy programs, especially indigenous-language programs, are more successful than others. Certainly, some of the effectiveness of native-language literacy in the Sierra can be explained in terms of larger sociological variables that set Mazatec communities apart from other indigenous communities in Mexico—for example, low migration rates, high retention of the educated elite, low educational and (Spanish) literacy levels. However, this approach is limited in its ability to explain how this particular language-revival movement took the form it did and why it has been such a popular success—or, conversely, why other areas that have similar sociological factors have not sprouted comparable revival movements. Even taking a more standard ethnographic approach would provide an incomplete picture, for what drives the popularity of this case is the unique way that text and context intersect on culturally harmonious terms. The texts here are virtually meaningless independent of the complex of larger cultural practices, of investments in images of the community, they both refer to and embody. Even within the song contest itself, people do not consider the song alone as the "text." Rather, they view the song as the inextricable heart of a larger cultural performance. The poetic qualities of the songs resonate in highly specific, culturally salient terms, and the appeal the songs have is propagated by how they are tied into a much wider system of cultural discourses, values, and practices.

The song contest's popularity thus arises precisely because it is *not* modular along the lines of Benedict Anderson's influential argument about how national communities are imagined into being. Briefly, Anderson (1995 [1983]) argues that out of a unique confluence of historical factors, the nation emerged as a stable model, a cultural formation that could be "pirated" for export across the globe. Once it was implemented, modifications that were made to accommodate local contexts did not alter the template, leaving the model's basic structure intact. In contrast, the song contest as a revival project is "antimodular." It was specifically, carefully tailored by local intellectuals, shaped in ways that made it consciously congruent with local values and practices. Furthermore, asking why the contest has been so popular is not merely an academic question. Educational and language policy planners (perhaps development programs of all stripes) almost always have national interests at stake—or, at least, supra-local interests that encompass multiple Nda Xos. Most take some kind of modular approach, using the same type of program and following the same procedures across the country in question. Accommodations to cultural diversity often treat the "local cultural context" as if it were merely one variable in a larger equation. As a result, the local adjustments such projects pursue stop at, say, providing a set corpus of materials in local languages—or, at a more sophisticated level, local dialects or variants of those languages—without ever addressing deeper cultural differences.

By contrast, the more deeply "emic" adaptations of the Day of the Dead Song Contest take several forms. By linking the contest to practices that are highly salient emblems of ethnic identity for local people—especially those that express reverence for the dead by singing for them—the initiative was embraced as an intensification of standard practice rather than rejected as inauthentic or false, as are so many projects aimed at social change. This is particularly true of "top-down" projects—those run by the state above all—whose animating agendas, to say nothing of the methods by which they are delivered, are often profoundly at odds with the needs and concerns of local people. As Linda King (1994) points out, for literacy to take root, it needs to be surrounded by a culture in which written texts—and not just any written texts in this case, but indigenous-language texts—have practical utility and value. Teaching someone to read, even providing reading materials, is really, then, just a first step.

Another crucial aspect of the project's responsiveness to local concerns is the ease with which both the song contest and the Mazatec recording industry it has generated bridge public and private, sacred and secular spheres. That flexibility, in turn, has provided a forum for a particular kind of discourse—namely, it has created a discursive space in which people can work out ideas about politics and the meaning of community, especially ideas about "Mazatec culture," through the songs and their responses to them. Because the heart of the revival project is tied to Day of the Dead and homage to the ancestors, it is also linked to prevailing ideologies about Muertos festivities as loci of community solidarity and vehicles for mending social rifts. Singing during Muertos is singing for the dead, as well as—and, perhaps, more than—for the living. Having such an audience entails certain responsibilities, above all that the living should come together to celebrate the arrival of the dead, heightening the imperative for unity.

The passage with which this chapter opened speaks clearly to this issue. Although the author is not from the Sierra but, instead, from the Mazatec lowlands, his poem nevertheless reflects a widespread cultural motif about the immortality of death. Through such ideologies, a "community of the living and the dead" becomes possible. The political "neutrality" of the Day of the Dead practices to which the song contest was harnessed, as well as the fiesta's pervasive and often explicit ideology of inclusiveness and harmony, contribute to the creation of a special social space—a particular kind of indigenous public sphere.

Among the most important things this arena does is display and promote distinct social personae or images of persons (Agha 2007). The song contest relies on the promotion of normative, standardized images about Mazatec identity: a "virtuous Mazatec" should venerate the ancestors by singing to and for them in Mazatec, should lift up the community by celebrating the ancestors' values, should use the mushrooms as the ancestors did. At the same time, the contest is received as the articulation of what Mazatecs are. It presents a vision of Mazatec identity that is immediately recognizable to most Mazatecs by simultaneously establishing continuity with longstanding practices and leaving space for their innovative adaptation to new influences. The contest and the halo of activities that surround it thus provide the infrastructure through which Mazatecs are recruited to adopt particular social personae in the form of ethnicized identities: those that represent "good" or "traditional" or "authentic" Serranos, figures that are at the heart of the songs themselves.

Finally, by linking the new language initiative to music, the project was harnessed to essential notions of ethnic belonging that in different ways hinge on singing in Mazatec. These practices include not only the musical Day of the Dead activities discussed here but also the singing and chanting practices that occur during mushroom veladas, that central forum for the promotion of ideas about "Mazatec culture." As with most indigenous Mexicans, Serranos articulate an explicit ideology that their language is an essential part of their ethnic identity. Such beliefs are not unique, but perhaps because of the tonal nature of their language—and, perhaps, because of its whistled register, in which people communicate by whistling utterances whose tonal contours follow those of spoken language (see Cowan 1947)—local people talk about Mazatec as fundamentally "musical." I routinely hear Serranos make statements such as, "Our language is almost like singing." For all of these reasons, tying literacy and song composition to singing practices that are coupled locally to sacred, ethnically marked knowledge was an act of cultural genius. In thus embedding their revival project in local practice, the song contest's promoters found a way to introduce innovations that might otherwise be rejected as artificial on terms that cast them instead as an intensification of standard customs.

The Afterlife of Muertos: Why the Contest Is More Than an Ethnographic Postcard

For all of its popularity, the contest, like all cultural activities, is dependent on funding. Alberto Prado Pineda (2000: 14) closed his article on the genesis of the song contest with a lament about its financially precarious state. The flip side, however, is that the very lack of dedicated support purchases the contest's relative neutrality and freedom from institutionalized interest. This relates to my argument that the song contest plays a central role in negotiating social conflict. Part of the reason the contest has been embraced so widely is that the holiday to which it is tied is perceived as broadly communitarian; the apparent financial independence of the contest contributes to this perception. While many people do not consciously consider the financial status of the contest, Heriberto Prado and others are keenly aware of the "bargain with the devil" that the contest's supporters would enter if they accepted outside funds from, for example, governmental programs supporting indigenous culture.

Local people take varying attitudes toward the connection between the contest and the Catholic Church, especially its financial aspects. While some see the church as communitarian and neutral, others view it as an externally imposed institution whose interests are often at odds with local needs and customs. These differences of opinion, which on numerous occasions have led to open disputes surrounding Nda Xo's contest, also speak to the precariousness of social unity and the speed with which assumed solidarity can disintegrate.

These differences of opinion raise troubling questions about the long-term effects of the Day of Dead Song Contest's popularity. In many ways, the contest appears to transcend the merely folkloric: it bleeds visibly and audibly into the rest of the year, spilling out of the holiday box in which the Mexican state might wish to confine it. This makes it hard to argue that people who participate in the contest and its attached activities are merely "dressing themselves" temporarily in Mazatec culture solely for the sake of the fiesta. Yet when viewed alongside the Mazatec Indigenous Church (discussed in the next chapter), whose political activism is more explicit and radical, the song contest appears to be a very humble revival project. In contrast to the Mazatec Indigenous Church, the song contest appears to willfully confine its refiguration of national belonging within strict limits, accepting confinement to a kind of "designated protest area" in which expressing indigenous identity is "safe."[24]

Yet it is precisely when one places this project alongside other revival projects, such as the Mazatec Indigenous Church, that their mutually supportive nature comes into focus. When examined from another angle, their apparent opposition—which, as I will show, is how many people in Nda Xo frame the relationship—indexes their symbiosis. The two cases are contrasting yet also interdependent. As in Bakhtin's model, cleansed of its negative valence, the heteroglossia of the song contest—its willingness to embrace difference—helps define and give meaning to the Mazatec Indigenous Church. And the friction between the two revival projects—though rarely seen in this light by the participants themselves—is ultimately immensely productive. It generates a new space for innovation, for the reinscription of tradition, and for fruitful dialogue about the meaning of both as they shape the ongoing terms of indigenous and national belonging.

SCENES FROM A NATIVIST REFORMATION

The Mazatec Indigenous Church

To i sijch-cha jian nga Ñña
Śi kujajch-chan, śi kujajt-ti na Ñña. . .
Mmela śi kuan na Ñña nga kuiśkan ne Ñña
Nga to i sa n'e kjit'a Ñña ts'e naina

Here we all forget
Our anger and divisions . . .
So why do we go on fighting
If each year we perform this rite before God?

—Heriberto Prado Pereda, from the annual Day of the Dead Mass "Autochthonous
Mazatec Mass," in Kui⁴Nndja¹le⁴ nai³na¹ nga³ en¹ na¹: *Cantemos a dios en nuestra lengua*

Purism, Indigenous Revival, and the Birth of the Mazatec Indigenous Church

In chapter 3 I discussed the annual Day of the Dead Song Contest, a revival
project that has found enormous popular success.[1] I argue that the movement
has such astonishing grassroots appeal because it was tailored so carefully
to local values and norms and draws so heavily on existing, highly salient,
ethnically marked practices and discourses. In this chapter, I present a case
that appears to be the opposite: a revival project with limited popular appeal. However, its relationship to the song contest is more symbiotic than
appearances suggest, in contrast with how local people discuss the institutions in everyday talk. Although both projects emerged from an earlier revival project—the introduction of Mazatec-language songs in Catholic Church
services—their respective relationships to the church today are radically different. Furthermore, they have distinct, often competing orientations toward
Nda Xo's internal divisions, political and religious alike. Nevertheless, at a

deeper level, the two projects are reinforcing, and each defines itself against the other.

This chapter recounts one of the Sierra's most contentious recent events: the birth of the Iglesia Indígena Mazateca (Mazatec Indigenous Church). The primary aim of this nativist organization is to "cleanse" the Catholic faith of its ostensibly non-native—thus contaminating—influences. I discuss how the Mazatec church came into being, embedding it in local and national histories of institutionalized religion and indigenous politics. Returning to the Catholic Church's song initiative, which gave rise to the Day of the Dead song contest, I show how that older revival project also spawned the Mazatec church. By tying the church song initiative to recent national history, as well as to the biographies of key individuals who promoted the church song project, I set the stage for the founding of the Mazatec Indigenous Church. This narrative of the Mazatec church's past is followed by an analysis of its present: I describe the singing, writing, and reading activities of its members, some of which are tied to practices used in *veladas* (mushroom ceremonies). I focus on the Mazatec church's most central and controversial practice: replacing the Eucharist with hallucinogenic mushrooms. The reactions to this practice by Serranos who do not belong to the Mazatec Indigenous Church are revealing and feed directly into how the organization is received by other locals. The response has been largely negative: although the Mazatec church has attracted some ardent followers, it remains very small, and the majority of people in the region remain openly hostile to its ideas.

In analyzing criticisms of the Mazatec Indigenous Church movement, I discuss how they relate to competing discourses about poverty, modernity, indigenous activism, and "authentic" spirituality. These discourses have shaped the Mazatec church as an emerging institution. The Mazatec Indigenous Church is engaged in an ongoing process of positioning itself within local political and religious factions and in relation to regional and national ideas about ethnic identity and moral personhood. I suggest that the ways the Mazatec church represents itself regarding internal divisions and ideas about indigenous belonging have been closely tied to its difficulties in appealing to would-be converts.

At the same time, the Mazatec church's highly normative approach to excising some widespread local practices has actually reinforced some of those practices, particularly those linked to the song contest and the Catholic Church. By strengthening some of the very activities it seeks to "correct," the Mazatec church, when viewed alongside the song contest, demonstrates the fundamental codependence of the two institutions—local discourses to the contrary notwithstanding. Taken as a contrasting pair, these two stories constitute a pragmatic commentary on revival projects and the constraints under which they operate. When viewed as complementary rather than contrasting, they offer richer potential for theoretical insight. What are the limits on counterhegemonic action and discourse in this case, and how much can we generalize from it to others? At what point does resistance reinforce the very order it seeks to subvert? How can people involved in revival projects both participate in prevailing practices and public spheres and not place themselves at the mercy of their hegemonic force? It is a cliché that those who do not learn from history are doomed to repeat it. The experience of Nda Xo suggests instead that we are doomed to learn history and, whether we will it or not, to drag the grand narrative of the past, with all of its silencing biases, into the present.

One Day in the Sierra: Eavesdropping on a Feud

On my very first day in Nda Xo, I heard about the song contest—even though it was March, many months before the Day of the Dead fiesta would begin. I was also introduced to an equally important social matter in town: religious divisions. I experienced them initially through my encounters with members of the Sierra's prominent and widely respected Prado family, including Heriberto Prado Pereda and Alberto Prado Pineda, as well as others who, as catechists, were involved in promoting church songs in Mazatec. The outward signs of these Sierra-wide religious differences surrounded me on that initial visit, and a brief description of that day hints at some forms the schisms take. However, I did not understand until much later the magnitude of the religious differences I had stumbled upon that first day, how profoundly they divided not only the Prado family but also the entire town and others across the Sierra. Only later did I understand how Nda Xo's religious factions are linked, as are Day of the Dead and its song contest, to tensions between "traditional" Mazatec practices and cultural innovation and change. These, in turn, are tied to deep cultural cleavages in the Sierra, as well as to their annual cessation during Day of the Dead celebrations.

Alberto Prado was the first person I spoke to on my initial visit to Nda Xo. Maestro Florencio Carrera, the intellectual I met in Huautla, sent me in his direction, saying that Alberto was a leading figure in Nda Xo's revival efforts and *un hombre muy amable* (a very kind man). I explained to Alberto that I had come to Nda Xo—which receives few outside visitors and almost no foreigners—because I was interested in indigenous writers and writing.

He showed me various things he had written in Mazatec, especially songs for the Day of the Dead contest. He pointed to an illustration of the Mazatec calendar with the names of the twenty-day months written in Mazatec, as well as articles he had written for La Faena. After about three hours, he told me he was very sorry, but he had to go to the weekly meeting of his kjuachikon (rosary group). I later learned such groups had been in decline but were revived in reaction to the founding of the Mazatec Indigenous Church.[2] He also told me that I should really speak to his brother Heriberto, the real Mazatec author. Later, when I knew him better, Alberto would compare his standing as a Mazatec writer to his brother's by saying, "Me, I'm nothing next to him."

I would later see that Maestro Carrera's sending me to Alberto could be read as an implicit comment on Heriberto. As Alberto suggested, and as commentary by others echoed, Heriberto Prado is the single most important figure in the emergence of song composition in Mazatec, not only in Nda Xo, but throughout the Sierra. But he is also known (in that expression so ubiquitous in Mexico) as muy especial (difficult). The fraught nature of the relationship between Heriberto and Florencio (and, indeed, between Heriberto and other Huautla intellectuals) is based not only on the ambivalence that Florencio, like many, has about Heriberto as a religious figure. It also stems from differences among various types of indigenous intellectuals, a topic I discuss later in the book. Heriberto Prado differs in several important ways from Florencio and the other Mazatec intellectuals trained through national ethnolinguistics and other programs that target indigenous intellectuals. Florencio and Heriberto sometimes have competing intellectual stakes in promoting indigenous writing and literacy, differences manifested on such fronts as the ever contentious issue of orthography.

The difficult nature of the relationship between Heriberto and Florencio was made clear to me one afternoon a week or two after I arrived in Nda Xo. I was living with Heriberto and his family, and we were eating lunch in the back room of their store, which was divided from the front part by a sheet blocking us from view without preventing us from seeing who stopped by. Florencio then appeared. He and Heriberto spoke in Spanish rather than Mazatec, and it became clear from the behavior of Heriberto's compañera, and from their subsequent comments, that they did not want Florencio to know I was there.[3] I have often had similar experiences in which people draw lines around relationships in ways that surprised me; over time, I began to view them as related to the sharp internal divisions discussed in this chapter.

After our first meeting, Alberto took me to see Heriberto, who, as it turned out, had gone to Huautla that day. Until he returned, I waited in his store with his compañera, whom I will call Ana. After meeting me, she invited me to stay, and I lived with the family for nearly a year. Heriberto returned in the afternoon, and we talked while he showed me the books of his songs. They had been published locally under the auspices, and at the encouragement, of Hermenegildo Ramírez Sánchez, who served as the regional bishop for more than thirty years. Heriberto and I talked until late in the afternoon. At that point, the family invited me along for their visit to the *sabio* (sage, wise man; discussed in chapter 2), who introduced me not only to the prevalence of talk about mushrooms in the Sierra, but also to the strong discursive conventions for doing so.

At the time, transportation within the region was almost exclusively by foot or by *camioneta* (pickup truck). Since then, the road between Nda Xo and Huautla has been paved, and *colectivos* (collective taxis) run regularly along the route. Both pickup trucks and taxis are privately owned and, as has been discussed about other areas of Mexico (see, e.g., Cancian 1992), ownership both indicates the acquisition of wealth and is an important means for generating it. In Nda Xo, the family widely considered the richest—the Bravos, who, significantly, are Protestant—has a number of grown sons who run camionetas, one of which I rode in that first day. So on that day I was also introduced to the infamous Mazatec machismo, which some people I spoke to in Oaxaca claimed stems from the region's long tradition of polygamy. (Mazatercos, one Zapotec friend called them, playing on the Spanish word *terco* [stubborn].) When he heard I was interested in learning Mazatec, the driver—seeing that the only other person in the cab was a middle-aged woman who spoke only Mazatec—said in Spanish that in that case I should marry him and learn the language "in bed, through [his] kisses."

I did not get a ride, so I stayed with Heriberto and his family for the visit to the chota chjine, who—as is typical and indicative of the ambivalence with which people regard sabios—lived on the edge of town. The family was making an addition to their store and home by carving out the rock behind it, and they felt the man they had hired was making little progress (the fact that he had only one arm might have had something to do with this, but they did not seem concerned about that). So they went to see the sabio to find out whether they had somehow offended a *chikon* (earth spirit) and if they had, how they should make amends. The sabio chanted several prayers while consecrating tobacco and cacao seeds, folding them into little packets Heriberto later buried at their building's four corners. The sabio then performed the *limpias* (ritual cleansings), closing the ritual. As we walked home in the dark, with the boys kicking rocks in the moonlight down the stony road, a surprising level of intimacy and warmth arose among us. At the time, I thought it stemmed from the ritual experience we had just shared. Now I think it also had to do with their perception of factions and solidarity: I had, without knowing it, chosen sides in an unfolding ideological conflict that had been tearing the Prado family, and Nda Xo, apart.

Religious and Political Differences in Nda Xo:
The Background for Mazatec Revival

Indigenous Mexican communities like Nda Xo are, of course, far from alone in having deep religious divisions that can give rise to extreme actions. In the past two decades alone, religious differences have played a critical role in many of the world's bloodiest conflicts.[4] This is not to obscure the fact that such conflicts arise from diverse causes or that some are only secondarily related to religious difference. Rather, in the Sierra, as elsewhere in the world, violence is often linked to religious difference. As has been widely noted in literature about indigenous communities in Mexico, feuding is a common occurrence, and the threat of internal violence is one backdrop against which social exchanges take place.[5] Such interactions include both the religious disputes in Nda Xo I describe here and revival projects intended, in part, to transcend and mend them.

Many of these disagreements are not cast in explicitly religious terms. Not all or even most internal violence in indigenous communities is explicitly motivated by religious differences. Land disputes and political conflicts are also a major cause. In June 2002, for example, a massacre in Oaxaca made the front page of the *New York Times*: twenty-six people from the southern Sierra Zapotec town of Santiago Xochiltepec were killed by members of the same town in a longstanding land dispute.[6] In Yalálag, the divisions, and the violence they have produced, have been primarily political, as has much recent internal violence elsewhere in the Sierra Mazateca. In Huautla, political violence between members of different political parties led to the unusual—and violence-perpetuating—situation that for a while meant that the town had three presidents, to whom locals referred derisively as "the three wise men" (Feinberg 2003: 54). Mazatlán is widely considered the most violent town in the Sierra, and its inhabitants are known as "the worst in the entire Mazatec region" and "rebellious bastards [*cabrones*]."[7] There, the recent decline of the Partido Revolucionario Institucional (Institutional Revolutionary Party; PRI) has spawned a paramilitary group responsible for lethal violence at elections in 1995 and 1998. In the intervening three years, until the state governor finally interceded, thirty people were assassinated and many more were wounded and tortured.[8]

In Nda Xo, differences do not always take the explicit form of religious disputes. Although elections officially take place under the system of Usos y Costumbres—through "traditional" political mechanisms rather than national political parties—the rise nationally of opposition, non-PRI political parties has led to an increase in official political organizations. There are now five recognized political organizations in the municipio (county). Even by regional standards, this is excessive, especially for a community of Nda Xo's size. People often lament this situation as a sign of deep discord and as a radical departure from the past, when the community was (ostensibly) more united. In other words, they read the present political moment, with its visible and tangible signs of factionalism, as a falling away from the ways of the ancestors, of the dead. They view the rise of political parties and other emblems of political discord through the same prism that makes visible the communitarian ethos of Day of the Dead, of which the song contest and its penumbra of revival activities take part.

Unlike some other Sierra towns, Nda Xo does not have a history of election violence. Nevertheless, even deliberate attempts to create political unity often fail. In the elections of 2004, the various opposition parties—in other words, all but the local Organización Regional Indígena Emiliano Zapata (ORIEZA), a PRI affiliate that has won all of the elections since the rise of opposition parties—attempted to run a single candidate. The negotiations involved some 2,500 people and took place on the municipal basketball court—which is to say, directly in front of the town hall, where the current officials, all from ORIEZA, could observe the discussions from the second-floor gallery. The initiative failed, however, because of accusations that one group, in violation of prior agreements, had brought in seventeen truckloads of acarreados (people who are trucked in) from the ranchos to unfairly favor its candidate. That candidate, as claimed by coffee farmers from one of the other organizations, "has become an eternal opposition candidate in this town. Including this one, he's been a presidential candidate in Chilchotla three times, and that's why the opposition never wins" (García Carrera 2004: C4).

However, in Nda Xo, divisions explicitly viewed as religious are arguably the most salient. In daily life, they affect and involve people of both genders more directly than the explicitly political divisions, which are dominated by men. In addition, religious divisions, even when explicitly framed in religious terms, are also intimately linked to many other social differences. Although it has been several years since religious differences have been blamed for bloodshed in Nda Xo, arguments about religion nevertheless occur frequently and are often contentious. Although these arguments first erupted before I arrived, they coincidentally took on urgency around the time I began my fieldwork, which not so accidentally was roughly when the Mazatec Indigenous Church began to take shape.

In Nda Xo, as in much of Mexico, Protestant evangelization was initially highly controversial. Protestant evangelization in the Sierra began in the 1930s under the auspices of the Summer Institute of Linguistics (SIL), whose activities were greeted with suspicion, hostility, and even violence. One infamous incident in July 1961 involved a large extended family of recent Protestant converts, all of whom, including babies and children, were hacked apart by machetes while they slept. This event was attributed locally and in the national press to religious feuding (Pike 1971: 164). However, although "defection" of community members from the default religion of syncretic Catholicism is ongoing, Protestantism now represents a fairly stable variable in the overall configuration of religious affiliation. In contrast, the arguments I discuss here, rather than taking the more typical form of disputes between Protestants and Catholics, concern a more unusual and localized rift between Catholics and nativist former Catholics, adherents of the recently founded Mazatec Indigenous Church.

Before I discuss the Mazatec church's founding, though, I will return to the era that directly preceded it. As discussed in chapter 2, Heriberto Prado Pereda began writing Mazatec-language songs for the church while he was studying at the seminary. This activity was actively encouraged by his superiors as part of the church's post–Vatican II ministerial outreach; in particular, the songs were designed to further Liberation Theology's efforts to remake the Catholic Church into a church of the poor and oppressed that is responsive to local traditions and languages. Once Heriberto became a priest, he also began publishing his songs through the church. Because the Mazatec Indigenous Church positions itself against that earlier work, I take up those texts as crucial precursors to the Mazatec church's emergence as a revival movement.

Kui⁴Nndja¹le⁴ nai³na¹ nga³ en¹ na¹ *(Let Us Sing to God in Our Language)*

The title of Heriberto's first book of songs was Kui⁴Nndja¹le⁴ nai³na¹ nga³ en¹ na¹ (*Cantemos a dios en nuestra lengua* [Let us sing to god in our language]) (Prado Pereda 1986; see fig. 4.1).[9] It was also the first book of modern literature written in Mazatec. Perhaps the best-known work to date in Mazatec is *Tatsje-*

FIGURE 4.1. The cover of Kui⁴Nndja¹le⁴ nai³na¹ nga³ en¹ na¹, Heriberto Prado Pereda's first book of songs.

jín nga kjabuya: No es eterna la muerte (Death is not eternal). Written by Juan Gregorio Regino, the country's leading Mazatec author, it was not published until 1992. The title of Heriberto's book emphasizes that the importance of the collection resided less in the music than in the lyrics—the fact that the songs were written to be sung in Mazatec. Although the songs were published in Mazatec and Spanish, most were sung—and are sung to this day—only in Mazatec. A handful appeared in Spanish only, a choice Heriberto did not repeat in later collections and that, I believe, reflects the novelty of the endeavor. When people later reproduced the texts, they did so only in Mazatec, omitting the Spanish translation. This stands in contrast to the bilingual books I discuss later: printing work in bilingual editions is the overwhelming norm for Mexico's indigenous authors. In contrast, in both church songs and Day of the Dead songs, the Mazatec language text is clearly primary. Sung performance, the target of embodied learning, is the central vehicle through which meaning is conveyed. The initial work of reading the songs, before they are memorized or familiar enough to be "decoded," does require reading practices similar to those for other bilingual texts: people rely on both versions to understand how the written texts represent speech. But even then, the Mazatec version is foregrounded because the end goal is the text's *performance*—the act of singing it in Mazatec.

In the songs Heriberto wrote for the church, the music is fairly simple, both instrumentally and compositionally, and is reminiscent of music played for the Day of the Dead fiesta. It relies on the same narrow range of instruments: a guitar or two, a violin or two, a drum, a teponaxtle, a tambourine, and perhaps a bass violin.[10] The music centers on the voices. People sing in unison and break into harmony only on the occasional climactic note. The instrumental accompaniment involves three or four measures of introduction, at most, then music arranged around basic guitar chords. It is heavily influenced by such vernacular Mexican music as rancheros, corridos, and ballads. Each song lists the general category of its rhythm—*balada lenta*, *balada moderna*, *ranchero*, *huapango*, *saya*, *corrido*—and its key in the solfège (do-re-mi) scale. The text's correspondence to guitar chords is also indicated, using a numbering system linked to charts for each key that are given in the back of the book. None of this musical information was repeated in Heriberto's subsequent volumes of songs, which featured only lyrics. Heriberto explained that it had become clear that people can learn the music without the paramusical aids. This situation was doubtless enhanced by the context: people learned the music not as isolated songs but as part of a longer unit, the entire Mass. However, the musicians leading the music often do continue to note the key for each of the songs.

At least in Heriberto's first volume, the message, in its relative novelty, was secondary to the importance of the medium. In other words, most songs contained boilerplate messages about Catholic belief. This was so for at least two reasons. The first was functional. Most of Heriberto's initial book was dedicated to the first of several Mazatec Masses he wrote. The collection also featured a few other songs for special occasions, but they have never been as widely used or known as the songs for the Masses.[11] Heriberto and, later, others aimed to supply choral music for formal Catholic Mass, thereby entering a centuries-long tradition of Western composers to do so. In the words of Bishop Ramírez, the assembled songs "seek to fill the role of liturgical texts of the Ordinary of the Mass or of the respective moments of the Eucharistic celebration" (preface to Prado Pereda 1986: 3). Thus, the songs fell into a set sequence reflecting the order of the Mass: an entrance song (Introit); the Kyrie; the Gloria; a "meditational song" (Gradual); a song for the Gospel Acclamation; the Credo; an Offertory; the Sanctus and Benedictus; the Lord's Prayer; the Agnus Dei; a communion song; and a recessional song.[12] As the songs for the Ordinary are settings of specific, fixed texts, authors have relatively little textual freedom.[13] The settings of those texts involve inexact, approximate translations into Mazatec (from Spanish) and vary some from

Mass to Mass. The imprecise, variable nature of the translations is part of why the bishop conceded that the texts cannot be considered fully liturgical, despite their social utility (Prado Pereda 1986: 3). Reading between the lines of the translations, one can also see evidence of the difficulties that translation caused for Heriberto, which eventually led him to write new texts for his songs. Furthermore, even the songs for the Proper of the Mass—which either do not involve settings of particular texts or are free translations chosen from among the hundreds of Proper prayers—place strong constraints on the author's creativity, given that each must perform a specific function within the context of the Mass.

The other reason that the earlier songbooks—the first one in particular—relied on such canonical Catholic content is historical. These songs, and the project by which they were disseminated, needed to be "religiously correct" in message precisely because they were an experiment. They represented a new tool to be used in the ongoing project of evangelizing the people of the Sierra. The emphasis, however inexplicit, was on minimizing the disruptions in existing practice that this new instrument might produce. Acceptance of the songs hinged on continuity with preceding musical and linguistic practice. From the perspective of the audience—Mazatec speakers—the instrumental music and, of course, the language in which the songs were written were very familiar, and the content of the songs, if novel, was only mildly so. The innovation of these songs thus resided not in any of those aspects but, rather, in how they introduced into the church ethnically marked practices common in the community that previously had been excluded from church activities. The songs made it possible for local people to use their lengua materna in the church in new ways. They also allowed Mazatecs to use traditional music not to welcome the return of the dead but, instead, to spread the Gospel and glorify God. From the perspective of the church, however, support for the project required that the songs remain faithful to Catholic doctrine. For local church officials, who did not speak the language and had only passing familiarity with Muertos music, the novelty arose from the use of a new language, Mazatec, to impart canonical messages about Christianity.

Nevertheless, the songs do have some distinctive qualities, some of which turn on aspects of the Mazatec language itself. In general, the lyrics are organized into quatrains and couplets, often alternating between the two. This structure lends itself particularly well to reliance on common poetic tropes, perhaps particularly prevalent in sung poetry, such as repetition and parallelism. Certain aspects of Mazatec further heighten this by providing abundant opportunities for internal and terminal rhymes. The Mazatec language is composed of short words and a relatively small phonemic repertoire, partly because of its tonal richness. Furthermore, Mazatec tends to place demonstratives, pronouns, and various affixes and clitics at the end of utterances (and, therefore, the ends of lines of text). This fairly small set of lexemes further enhances the musical possibilities of Mazatec text composition, since it includes near rhymes, true rhymes, and tonemic minimal pairs. Here are a few examples taken from some of Heriberto's songs:

jña^1: us (i.e., second-person plural, inclusive)
jña^2: them (i.e., third-person plural)

ji^3: you (i.e., second-person singular)
jin^4: us (i.e., second-person plural, exclusive)

ts'an^4: mine (i.e., first-person singular possessive)
tsan^{42}: ours (i.e., second-person plural inclusive)

-li^{23}: yours (i.e., second-person singular possessive; at end of utterance)
-le^{31}: his/hers/its/theirs (i.e., third-person singular possessive at end of verb)
–le^4: his/hers/its/theirs (i.e., third-person singular possessive at end of other morpheme):

je kuan ts'ja^{3}kie^4: I have loved
je kuan ts'ja^{3}kie^3: he has loved

si^{1}je^1: he asks (requests)
si^{1}je^{13}: I ask

si^{1}ca^{3}sen^1: he sends
si^{3}ca^{3}sen^{13}: I send

b'e^{3}jo^{2}an^3: I clean
b'e^{2}jon^{32}: we clean (inclusive)

tsjoa^3-le^4: I give him
tsjoa^2-le^{23}: I give you (singular)

In addition, the lexical repertoire is primarily confined to words in common colloquial though not overly informal use. Heriberto chose an everyday register of Mazatec rather than an exalted or archaic one. Common loan words are used—*hostia* (host) and *café* (coffee)—rather than the "purifying" neologisms Heriberto would later embrace. Because of the religious context and lack of equivalent expressions in Mazatec for some Christian speech common in Spanish, this places unique pressure on some Mazatec words. For example, there is obviously no traditional expression in Mazatec for taking Communion; the author uses expressions that would seem unorthodox in Spanish but align the act with quotidian practice. The following illustrates this, as well as some of the qualities of the Mazatec language discussed earlier:

> je naxinandali naina
> kaf'i sixat'ali nd'ei nd'ei
> je xo ngañ'ionli machjenle
> kui skine nili

> your people, God,
> came to greet you today
> for they need your support
> therefore [lit.] they are going to eat you
> ("Second Mass," in Prado Pereda 1986: 31)

In a similar vein, some words are pressed into service for an extremely wide semantic field, drawing on their daily usage while also expanding it. Nowhere is this more the case than with the word *kjuanda* (*kjua* [substantive] plus *nda³* [good]).[14] *Kjuanda* has a variety of common uses, indicating good fortune, goodness, a thing of beauty, and, most striking, the often accidental discovery of hallucinogenic mushrooms that spring up across the Sierra during the rainy season. In the songs, its semantic field is widened even further:[15]

> tjian k'ile **kjuanda**   ·
> we'll give him [God] **the best** we have
>   [as an offering; also, to give glory to; to praise]
> (Prado Pereda 1986: XX)

> je **kjuanda** xi kj'as'insijele xi sitjoson
> is the **gift** that I ask of you
> (Prado Pereda 1986: 11)

> kitse **kjuanda** le jisond'e joni ng'ajmi
> joni ng'ajmi
> the world is full of your **glory** on earth
> as it is in heaven
> (Prado Pereda 1986: 17, 41, 53)

kataf'i na jin **kjuanda** li ji
that your **kingdom** come to us
(Prado Pereda 1986: 29, 41)

kjuanda katatsjali je naxinanda
that your people[16] give **thanks** to you
(Prado Pereda 1986: 43)

kjuanda chitsele naina xanyale jña chita ima
the **Good** News of God I will teach to the poor
(Prado Pereda 1986: 58)

kjua tsjana **kjuanda** le nga kjit'a, nga kjit'a
always give me your **grace**, always
(Prado Pereda 1986: 134)

to tsin ni kjuas'in **kjuanda**
nga kuas'in tiyo xkuaya
there is no **agreement** this way
we exchange insults instead
(Prado Pereda 1991: 20)

k'ue nga sak'ua biyojt-tin jña
nga bijnčia jña jngo **kjuanda**
when we come together
to seek **unity**
(Prado Pereda 1994: 53)

Such features are rooted in the unique qualities of the Mazatec language. But some of the more original aspects of the songs rely on adding local details or attempting to present messages in local terms. In other words, they follow the localist bent at the heart of Liberation Theology without adopting its more controversial, overtly political agenda. Some songs rely on explicit agrarian imagery, for example, as in this song spoken in the voice of God:

joni s'i nangui xi kixind'e
jmeni nga ndani nanda machjenle
kju'ati s'in machjenle t'a ts'an chita
jmeni nga kju'ejnakon ni

like the dry land
needs water to be fertile

men too need me
in order to live
("Second Mass," in Prado Pereda 1986: 21)

Even the few early songs that touch on social themes are only weakly political:

[mele Jesukristo]
katafet'a chita xi tsinle
tsojmi tje, katafet'a
ngats'i jixti nd'i
xi ch'in tjinle

katafet'a chita xi nitojme jin
xi tjinle, ngoson kji katas'ena
ngats'ine i jisond'e

katafe xi kjuaton in
kjuanda in xi katas'e
katafet'a chita i kjinejin
kjit'a xikjin
je xi kjuatjochia in katas'e
jo tso kjuatexomale je naina
tonga li kjin kjuini je xi kju'as'in
to jña xo s'en ku'a ko naina

[Christ longs]
for there to be none who lack
for the harvest, that
all the children
be free from sickness

that there be no one in need
that we all be equal
here in the world

that there be an end to exploitation
that there be goodness
that there be no ill will
between one another
that there be love
as God himself brought
but those who bring this change won't come from outside

only from us, helped by God
("Third Mass," in Prado Pereda 1986: 45)

One of the few incidental songs at the back of the first book, "Je ya kafé" (The coffee tree), is particularly inventive. It uses a coffee tree that does not bear fruit as an analogy for service to God and community. Rather than being about poverty as a product of exploitation, the song extols the virtues of hard work that might enable the worshipper to honor God's commandment to help the poor:

tonga tsa kju'ati ima tiyo jña,
tme xi ku'iletsa iani xi tsinle

but if we, too, are poor
how can we give to those in need?
(Prado Pereda 1986: 135)

Heriberto Prado's later songs, in contrast, are more overtly political, and the attempt to make the texts locally relevant intensifies. So does the message about the importance of unity, which emerges on gentler and less strident terms than in these excerpts. Note, for example, that the passage at the beginning of the chapter that criticizes local people's persistent feuding comes from one of the author's later Masses. The explicit yearning for a unified community takes on growing urgency over time as the songs increasingly embrace the more provocative teachings of liberationist thought. They also draw a clearer line around the limits of community, defining in ever more politicized terms the division between "outsiders" and "insiders." As in many Muertos songs, solidarity is defined not only in terms of internal cohesion but also by preserving a clear separation between "us" and "not us."

The songs, and the collaborative efforts aimed at promoting them, were conceived as a new, activist form of community building. Heriberto, Alberto, and other family members and friends who formed the Committee for the Revival of Mazatec Culture (CIPRECMA) actively promoted the songs throughout the Sierra.[17] They went to communities across the region to teach the songs, and every Sunday, the group performed the songs during Mass. Throughout the year, they led people in singing the songs for a variety of religious events outside the church. These include Christmas *posadas* (lit., "the inns"; a Mexican holiday event celebrating hospitality), celebrations of saints' days, weddings and wakes. They recorded cassettes so people could play the music at home as both entertainment and learning aids (see fig. 4.2). These first cassettes of Mazatec-language music established a trend that

FIGURE 4.2. The cover for the first cassette of Mazatec music for the Catholic Church.

would go on to become much more widespread and popular than any of the performers could possibly have imagined, kicking off a cottage industry in the production of Mazatec-language sound recordings.

The cover of the one commercial cassette made by the group contains a photograph of its members. They are standing in a field, smiling, and in the background behind them rises Nda Xo's highest mountain, visible from across the greater municipio. In the photograph, the group members physically inhabit the act of addressing—singing to, teaching, reaching out to, including—the audience: members of the community, consisting of all the people who live, work, and die in the Sierra. It is thus ironic that the community division that led to the birth of the Mazatec Indigenous Church sprang from the perception that Heriberto Prado and his followers were more like foreigners than locals, more like betrayers of the community than promoters of it. It is a poignant commentary on the events that followed the cassette's release that this group, which traveled across the Sierra singing songs that extol the importance of unity, would be split in two by the founding of the Mazatec church. And Heriberto, its author and leader, would become one of Nda Xo's most divisive figures.

The Mazatec Martin Luther: Textual Practices, Singing, and Mushroom Ceremonies in the Mazatec Indigenous Church

During the period in which Mazatec songs were being written for the church and disseminated across the Sierra, Heriberto and Alberto Prado lived collaborative and closely parallel lives. Their very names mirror this intimacy: their full names—Heriberto Prado Pereda and Alberto Prado Pineda—are so similar that local people who do not know them well get them confused. Several times I have had the experience of talking with someone about one brother and then learning in the course of conversation that my interlocutor thought I meant the other brother. Even their own brothers refer to them as a unit—as in, "my brothers who have done so much for our culture."

This long period of symbiosis came to a dramatic end when, after twelve years of service, Heriberto Prado was forced to leave the priesthood. While serving in Tenango, Heriberto met Ana. At the time, she was in her mid-twenties and legally married, with three children on the verge of adolescence, having begun "unofficial" married life (as was customary until very recently) in her early teens.[18] Accounts vary about the circumstances under which the relationship between Ana and Heriberto deepened. According to Ana, she left her husband before she became involved with Heriberto because her husband wanted to take her half-sister as his second wife. She would not accept that and defended her decision even when the municipal authorities brought her before the *ayuntamiento* (town council) and tried to persuade her to remain in the marriage.

According to others in Nda Xo, however, Ana left her husband for Heriberto. In this version, people hold her actions in particular disdain because she was the legitimate wife—that is, married not only legally but also in the eyes of the church—of another man. As one man told me, "If she hadn't already been married, I think the people would have accepted it." This remark indicates that it is not uncommon for priests to have illicit relationships. In fact, there is a widespread expression for it: the hypocritical *padre gallo* (lit., rooster priest) who "preaches morality in the pulpit and fathers illegitimate children on the side" (Loewe and Hoffman 2002: 1144).[19] The comment also indicates that such relationships are acceptable, provided they do not become too public or socially disruptive. During my initial research in Yalálag, one of the priests—coincidentally or not, he, like Heriberto, was local—had a relationship with a girl who became pregnant. At the time, I was struck by how people, while not condoning the situation, seemed not at all surprised by it. "You know how priests are" was a comment I heard repeatedly. Rather, what angered them was that the priest initially refused to take responsibility for the young woman's situation. When I told this story to people in Nda Xo, they had much the same reaction.[20]

The union between Heriberto and Ana was kept quiet for some years. Ana had a son by Heriberto and lived in a house some distance away from Nda Xo's *cabecera* (county seat), on land Heriberto had inherited from his father. Eventually, though, the bishop learned that Heriberto had in effect taken a common-law wife. Regardless of the circumstances under which they became involved, the situation was difficult for Ana. Almost no one viewed her favorably, including members of Heriberto's and her own family. Ana is strong and willful, with a tough public persona that stands in marked contrast to that of most local women. She demonstrated this, as well as her abundant sense of humor, when I asked not long after meeting her whether she and Heriberto were married. "We got married in *union libre*," she answered, meaning they were not legally married. I confused "union libre" with Union Hidalgo, a rancho in Tenango near the one on which she was born. She still teases me about that.

Accounts of how the bishop and other church officials reacted when they found out about the relationship between Ana and Heriberto also vary. According to some people in town, Heriberto willingly chose to leave the priesthood. The bishop gave him a year to consider his options and decide which vocation he wanted to pursue: father of the church or father of a family. At the end of the year, Heriberto insisted that he be allowed to do both, forcing the bishop to act.

According to Heriberto, he was kicked out of the priesthood. He claims he was pressured unfairly to leave by the bishop and singled out precisely because he was local and, more to the point, indigenous. In conversations with me he never went so far as to claim that the bishop's actions were motivated by racism per se, but he clearly felt he had been the victim of a double standard. Although he freely admitted his behavior was problematic, even putting the sentiment in writing—"I know very well that I am a great sinner" (Prado

Pereda, n.d.: 1)—he also claimed that it was not so out of line with the actions of other priests as to warrant the punishment he received.

In any event, Heriberto fought the measure and left the church deeply embittered. Furthermore, the animosity was personal. His experience of the church—and, as he saw it, the experience of all people from the Sierra—had been heavily mediated by the Prelature of Huautla and Bishop Ramírez, the man who had headed the prelature from its founding. Many people in the community interpreted the event as deeply personal, as well, and were scandalized by these events. This was a reflection of how adored and revered Heriberto had become as the Sierra's only native priest—and of how deeply ironic it is that his subsequent actions cast him, in the eyes of many local people, as increasingly foreign and under the sway of alien ideas. At the time, though, his departure from the priesthood constituted an unwelcome return to a church whose officials all came from outside and whom many saw as out of touch with their needs and realities. Furthermore, the circumstances of Heriberto's new union were particularly offensive by local norms. Ana was seen as having abandoned not only a legal husband but also children who were not yet grown up and thus innocent victims of the scandal. Many people I interviewed expressed the idea that Ana's choice to leave her first family for a man who not only had taken a vow of celibacy but whose allegiance was ostensibly to God and community cast the virtuousness of both into serious doubt.

Nevertheless, the outrage the scandal provoked might have blown over had Heriberto not formalized his rift with the Catholic Church by founding the Mazatec Indigenous Church. The Mazatec church grew out of several contentious events involving local people and church authorities that began after Heriberto officially left his post as Catholic priest on August 1, 1997.[21] The following year, as many people adjusted to his new public persona as a family man, they also began talking to him about problems between their communities and church authorities. On September 15, 1998, Heriberto Prado held a meeting with representatives of several Sierra communities during which they aired assorted grievances with the church. Regardless of the details, almost all of the problems were an expression, as the representatives saw it, of a lack of respect by church authorities, a failure to care about the needs and concerns of the people they ostensibly were there to serve.

A little more than two months later, the municipal authorities of the municipio of San Miguel Huautepec met with Heriberto about problems they had with the parish priest, who resided in Santa María Asunción, an adjoining and much larger municipio. According to the authorities, the priest belonged to the Partido de la Revolución Democrática (Democratic Revolution

Party; PRD) and only attended to people with the same party affiliation.[22] Because San Miguel's authorities were allied with the PRI, the priest "mistreated" the parishioners of San Miguel in various ways, treating them with "superiority and despotism" and providing many "pretexts and excuses" for not performing Masses. The priest arrived very late or very early for baptisms and weddings he agreed to perform, then proceeded with the rites regardless of whether people were present. Sometimes he did not arrive at all.[23] Most "absurd and cruel" of all, he insisted that people from San Miguel bring those who were dying to visit him in the parish seat rather than traveling to them to offer extreme unction. He reportedly said to the people, "Just put them in the car, and I'll attend to the matter here."[24]

As a result, in late November 1998, members of San Miguel's ayuntamiento asked Heriberto to perform Masses for them. Heriberto explained that he no longer had any official authority in the church. However, they argued that "it was no problem, for when a government employee retired from his work, he subsequently performed services privately, so in the same manner [Heriberto] could attend to them since he knew the trade."[25] After meeting with them once more, and receiving a formal request for his services from the municipal president, Heriberto agreed to perform assorted Masses in December: for the Virgin of Juquila, for the Virgin of Guadalupe, for Christmas, and for New Year's (Prado Pereda, n.d.: 4). Later, when he was interviewed by regional newspapers, Heriberto claimed that he had had no choice but to do as the community asked, because it would have been impossible to remain silent in the face of such humiliation and abuse directed at indigenous people.[26] During the same period, he also began to perform baptisms, for which he issued baptismal certificates. Other communities that were having conflicts with the church began to petition him for his services. In late January 1999, he celebrated Masses in an *agencia* (agency) of Huautla, the seat of the prelature in which the bishop was resident. These services were held for two reasons: to perform baptisms and to honor municipal authorities who had recently been elected there.[27] I suspect that Heriberto's willingness to perform baptisms made his visit especially well attended by people who, because he had long been the only priest willing to make exceptions, viewed this as perhaps their last chance to receive baptisms for children by unions that were not recognized by the church.

This event, which took place in the bishop's own backyard, so to speak, provoked an extremely angry response. In February 1999, Bishop Ramírez called a meeting of the parish catechists. He explained Heriberto's situation and declared the sacraments he had administered invalid. Subsequently,

Heriberto and the authorities from San Miguel met with the bishop and, later, with other priests, including the one from Asunción. These meetings ended without resolution, and afterward the battle lines were drawn more sharply than ever. Heriberto and his supporters insisted that his actions were virtuous, while church authorities continued to condemn them. The bishop issued a pastoral letter directed to priests and catechists, as well as to the public, that was distributed throughout the prelature. It declared that Heriberto had no authority to administer sacraments of the Catholic Church because he had "voluntarily retired from the Catholic priesthood and had freely decided to live with a woman in concubinage."[28] The bishop and other priests also publicly denounced Heriberto from the pulpit.

Members of communities seeking Heriberto's help became bitterly divided over how to proceed. Some continued to support him while others opposed him. Authorities from a few other communities invited him to celebrate Masses, even after being told not to do so by church officials. Heriberto continued to honor these requests, claiming, "The more forcefully the Church discredits me, the more [the people] invite me" (Prado Pereda, n.d.: 5).

As in many internal disputes, these divisions were neither reducible to nor distinct from other axes of social difference; such divisions were closely related, for example, to positions local people take on a variety of national issues. One article about these events that was published in the state newspaper claimed that in San Miguel the division reflected party affiliations: supporters of the PRI worshipped with Heriberto in a chapel in the town center while supporters of the PRD worshipped in a separate chapel in one of the town's barrios.[29] The article also noted that in San Miguel, as in most Sierra communities, the introduction of party politics initiated a "new era" in which municipal power was highly disputed. Thus, religious rifts might prove especially explosive if coupled with political divisions. This is not a claim I heard others make, however, about either San Miguel or other communities in the Sierra, including Nda Xo. Whatever Heriberto's party affiliation might be, he is not public about it. On the contrary, he has explicitly presented the Mazatec church's stance as nonpartisan: "we are at the service of all without distinction. We aren't at the service of one party or of the caciques" (Prado Pereda, n.d.: 9).

While people across the Sierra were working out their own positions on the evolving scandal, various factions from Heriberto's hometown began supporting him increasingly publicly, including some of the most prominent participants in local church activities. In December 1998, on the feast day for the Virgin of Guadalupe, three women from the Sierra were consecrated as

Misioneras Indígenas de Nuestra Señora de Guadalupe (Indigenous Missionaries of Our Lady of Guadalupe). Bishop Ramírez officiated at the ceremony, which took place in Nda Xo and prominently featured Heriberto's songs. The Misioneras were founded in 1992 in La Providencia, Huautla, with the "unique goal of working as needed with the people of . . . indigenous communities."[30] They follow six stages of deepening commitment that culminates in a lifelong pledge; at each stage, they take vows of chastity, poverty, and obedience. The Misioneras had official standing with the church, which, as with priests, provided them with housing and sustenance. Two of the Misioneras consecrated in 1998 took two-year vows (the fourth stage), and the third took a five-year vow (the penultimate stage). But two months later, the conflict between Heriberto and the bishop came to a head, and ultimately all of the Misioneras declared their solidarity with Heriberto. Within the next year, others from the community did so, as well, including some of Nda Xo's most senior catechists, most of whom were also members of Heriberto's extended family.

The social effects of these defections were numerous and sharply felt. Because the Catholic Church plays such a central role in social life and civic administration, departure from the church carries widespread ramifications not unlike those experienced elsewhere in Mexico by converts to Protestant Christianity. At the extreme end, such converts risk being murdered, as has happened even recently in Chiapas. Residents of the Nda Xo *congregación* of Amatlán who joined the Mazatec church received death threats from the neighboring community of La Luz, through which they have to walk daily to reach their village. Even in less extreme form, such social rifts cause severe disruptions in relations with people faithful to the church. For the Misioneras, the price was even higher: supporting Heriberto ultimately meant leaving their position with the church, which, in turn, meant a change in their social standing and in their material conditions because they could no longer depend on the church for food and housing. At the same time, those who did not ally themselves with Heriberto were frightened by the departures of those who had been among the church's strongest supporters. In response to this perceived threat to the church, the rosary groups, which had been in decline, were enthusiastically revived. Especially in their revived incarnation, however, the rosary groups focus primarily on religious themes and discussion of the Bible rather than the political issues championed by Liberation Theology. Thus, they are in harmony with the church's conservative ethos under Pope John Paul II and Pope Benedict XVI.

These assorted events prefigured and catalyzed the formation of the Mazatec Indigenous Church. After the conflict with the bishop, Heriberto and his supporters met in San Miguel and then in the agencia in Huautla in March 1999; at this second meeting, they adopted the name "Iglesia Indígena Mazateca." By the time I arrived in the Sierra for the first time, in mid-2000, the group existed as a clear entity, even though many of its policies and practices had yet to be formalized.

Actual membership in the church is small. In Nda Xo proper, it is made up primarily of members of Heriberto's family, including one of his first cousins (an older, unmarried woman), his mother (i.e., the woman who gave birth to him; his father's first wife), and his full sisters and their families, although the husbands are less enthusiastic and more sporadic participants. Neither his father's second wife nor any of his half-siblings participate; his full brothers do not belong to the church, either, although the one who lives in Nda Xo flirted with the idea for a while, attending its services over many weeks before returning to participation in Catholic Mass. That brother lives next door to his mother and directly across the street from Heriberto, providing a level of daily intimacy that underscores the rift within the family.

Some other families in Nda Xo also belong to the Mazatec church (or did; one has since left), and there are some small groups scattered across the greater municipios of Nda Xo, Tenango, and Huautla. The Misioneras, for example, now live in Huautla, having opened a small store to support themselves. The other groups each have perhaps ten adults, and sometimes fewer, usually from a single extended family. All told, the church claims fewer than one hundred adult members from across the Sierra, whose full population is roughly 100,000. Even in Nda Xo, where the group in the cabecera is the strongest and most committed, fewer than 2 percent of the population (perhaps 25 out of 1,500) have joined the Mazatec church. The fluctuating nature of the membership makes exact figures impossible; as with Heriberto's brother, the status of many individuals remains liminal for some time before their allegiance becomes clear or is forced. In all cases, however, the nature of the church's membership indicates the social costs of joining it—or, perhaps, for people such as those who are closest to Heriberto, the costs of refusing to do so. Because joining in most cases means doing so as a family, almost all of those who participate have extended families that also belong to the church. Alternatively, there are some individual members who do not have their own "nuclear families," such as widows and single adults.

The high social costs stem from the Mazatec church's explicit policy toward the Catholic Church. In the first years after the Mazatec church was born, its members were very preoccupied with managing their relationship with the official church. This was particularly true of Heriberto and the Misioneras, whose affiliation with the church had been formal and institutionalized. Although from the beginning members stopped attending regular Mass, for a while they continued to attend Masses for special occasions such as weddings, baptisms, and funerals, especially when the events involved family members and compadres. Eventually, though, Mazatec church members settled on a more hardline policy. Today, the Mazatec church's opposition to the Catholic Church is pointed. Its members are prohibited from having any association with the institutionalized church. They never enter its buildings or use its trappings in family events. They do not contribute to its annual "dues" or collections for saints' days and other fiestas. Many people take issue with this position because the division it assumes between religious and civic activities, in Nda Xo as elsewhere in Mexico, is rarely clear-cut.

Precisely because this distinction is so hard to make in practice, it forces a normative approach to the separation between civil and religious ("private") spheres. In other words, the Mazatec church devises explicit rules about behavior that then become a means for structuring practice—rather than, for example, making explicit a code of conduct derived from existing practice. Where the group draws the line between civil and religious activities is a function of stipulated definitions of their difference, which have emerged over time. Thus, in practice the group segregates itself in ways that go well beyond their aversion to the church.

For example, Mazatec church members hold their own *faenas* (communal work days) on Mondays that are separate from the general ("public") ones. Each Sierra town holds its own faena every Monday, and large, municipio-wide faenas are held on the first Monday of every year. These faenas are especially well attended every three years when new authorities are inaugurated; men travel from ranchos across greater Nda Xo, and the dark morning hours are filled with the sound of blowing conch shells, the afternoon with drunks passed out in the grass. In one large faena, the entire floor of the church in the Nda Xo cabecera was replaced, as was the broken concrete around its front, part of which abuts and "bleeds into" the municipal basketball court in front of the town hall. This is but one case—an especially literal one—where there is no clear division between "religious" and "civic" domains.

For their faena, the Mazatec church members in Nda Xo generally go to the town spring and clean the surrounding area (see fig. 1.2). They present this as part of their agenda to create (or restore) a more authentically Mazatec religion that venerates uniquely local, Mazatec expressions of spirituality such as those attached to the specific spirit that resides in the spring. Tension surrounding this practice has escalated in recent years during the celebration of Saint Mary Magdalene, whose apparition is said to have appeared at the spring (two versions of this story were excerpted in chapter 1). Mazatec church members claim the saint is a misrecognized earth spirit, the female chikon who "owns" it. They arrive early in the morning, before the official town procession and Catholic Mass, leaving their own altars and adornments in advance of the more recognizably Catholic objects—crosses in particular—that adherents and authorities of the Catholic Church will leave later in the day. This action produces new waves of critique each year, as people disparage the Mazatec church for continuing to pursue overtly divisive practices that ruin the spirit of an event meant to celebrate the source of water, or life, on which they all depend. As one woman said, as we walked together on the long procession following the Mass held at the spring, "They just want to get there first and claim it for themselves."

A particularly fateful instance of the Mazatec church's self-segregation involved one member, a woman in her early forties, who was pregnant. She already had one child, whose birth had been difficult, and she had trouble conceiving a second. Mazatec church members decided to guide her through childbirth when the time came, although none had experience delivering babies. (One member's experience as a pharmacist was the closest they came.) The baby girl died at birth, and after many hours, the mother was finally sent to the hospital in Huautla. The narrative of the event told by group members emphasized divine intervention: God had called the baby back to his side to prevent her further suffering. Many others in town, however, felt that the mother—and, indeed, the entire group—had taken an unnecessary, prideful risk. They further claimed their view was vindicated when, in the following year, the woman gave birth in the Huautla hospital to a healthy baby boy.

In general, however, the most pervasive way Mazatec church members segregate themselves is in how they live their daily lives. They maintain a new, highly marked level of social distance; in this, as in their financial abstention (i.e., their refusal to contribute money to any collective events involving the Catholic Church), Mazatec church members behave much like Protestants. As during Protestantism's foundational moment, the "Mazatec Reformation" pitches itself full tilt against the enormous power of the Catholic Church.[31] But the Mazatec church members' ideologies go beyond mere opposition, as did those of the early Protestants, by calling for purifying revisions of theology and religious practice, which in turn have profound political and social implications. On his old typewriter (and, more recently, a second-hand computer), Heriberto pounds out his equivalent of Martin Luther's Ninety-Five Theses: enraged writings crying out for sweeping changes and touching on myriad aspects of social life. Mazatec church members, however, consider themselves Catholic and adamantly reject categorization as Protestants.[32] Rather than harking back to the Reformation as a historical point of reference, members look to the life of Jesus Christ himself. They argue that much as Jesus fought the power and corruption of the Sanhedrin, they, too, are defenders of the true faith. They claim to champion the poor and oppressed who are Christianity's true targets, rescuing it from institutionalized powers that would discredit and even assassinate them, much as the Sanhedrin did Jesus: "Our concerns are like those Jesus had, to defend the authenticity of Christianity" (Prado Pereda, n.d.: 18).

Although the actual congregation of the Mazatec Indigenous Church is tiny, its aims are exceedingly ambitious. The target of its endeavors is the entire Mazatec population, the goal being "to convince everyone (people and catechists) about this project" (Prado Pereda, n.d.: 7). Despite having relatively few followers to date, Heriberto makes frequent appeals to "having an entire people behind me" whose cultural and spiritual interests he is charged with defending. Furthermore, although the most explicitly acknowledged target of the Mazatec church's ire—the enemy with which it is engaged in ideological combat—is the Catholic Church, it opposes more indirectly five hundred years of *indigenismo* believed to have been initiated by the Spanish colonial empire and perpetuated by the Mexican state. The Mazatec church's animating ideology is heavily influenced by discourses about indigenous resistance that are taken from Liberation Theology, as well as from secular critiques of Mexico's *indigenista* policies (see, e.g., Bonfil Batalla 1987).

The resulting ideology is heavily inflected by liberationist ideas, emphasizing such concepts as "assimilating the worldview" of the people and carrying on Christ's work of "bringing the Good News to the poor, liberty to the enslaved, light to the blind, and liberation to the oppressed . . . [so] that poverty, captivity, and oppression [will] be overcome and Justice [will] reign" (Prado Pereda, n.d.: 8, 18). However, the Mazatec church members' reading of Liberation Theology is one with which many liberationists would have been uncomfortable, as it has been radicalized by passage through the discourse of indigenous rights that has become increasingly pervasive in post–Zapatista Mexico. The ultimate aim of the Mazatec church is to accomplish what the Catholic Church, even the liberationist church, has not done and, because of its institutional commitments, will never choose to do. That is, the Mazatec church aims to bring a true autochthonous church into being, one in which local indigenous people are in control of its very character and workings:

> The Church as administered from Huautla has not been in its plans indigenous but rather indigenista, exactly as has been the government. Much is said of us in their projects, but we are not the protagonists and now we want to be. . . . If the Catholic Church truly wants to serve it must take on indigenous projects and renounce its indigenista project. . . . It must leave the coordination to the indigenous people. . . . The role of the official Catholic Church is to be supportive, leaving in the hands of indigenous people the formation . . . of an autochthonous church. But they want to bring about the autochthonous church without us, without taking into account our values, customs, and traditions. (Prado Pereda, n.d.: 3–4)

The programmatic ideology expressed in this passage is reflected in various practices of the Mazatec Indigenous Church, especially those by which its members try aligning daily practice with explicit ideological agendas.[33] Perhaps nowhere is the strain to make ideology and practice coincide sharper than on the issue of language use. Especially where language is concerned, the antichurch purism so important to the Mazatec church's normative agenda takes a proindigenous, anti-institutional form.

Catholic services in the Sierra are thoroughly bilingual. Even in communities where people are largely monolingual and services are officiated by native catechists who may be only nominal speakers of Spanish, services take place in both languages. In contrast, services in the Mazatec church are rigorously monolingual. Mazatec use is assumed and encouraged in church activities, while the use of Spanish—or, rather, the purging of it—is carefully policed.[34] Canonical texts such as the Lord's Prayer are recited only in Mazatec. The songs composed by Heriberto Prado are sung in Mazatec, as they would be in Catholic church services; however, rather than using the bilingual versions circulated by the Catholic church, the Mazatec church prints the songs only in Mazatec. This makes the reading of new or unfamiliar songs difficult for many people, who are accustomed to reading Mazatec in bilingual editions, where they can use the Spanish to help "decipher" the Mazatec. Even for Heriberto, the complete exclusion of Spanish from Mazatec church dealings is impossible to maintain; like everyone else, Spanish is his preferred language for most types of writing, and he uses that language for his writings about the Mazatec church. Like many other Mazatec church members, and all of those from Nda Xo proper, his children are passive speakers of Mazatec: they understand the language but rarely speak it. He and other members recognize that a critical aspect of the Mazatec church's mission is not only to educate other adults but also to indoctrinate their own children. Thus, they attempt to encourage or even force their children to speak Mazatec, although even within the Mazatec church's ceremonies these efforts are rarely wholly successful.

Studied egalitarianism and communitarianism are further implications of Mazatec church ideology. Like language use, these agendas run into conflicts in practice. The case of the pregnant woman and the group's Monday faenas illustrate how the Mazatec church aims to make itself a "full service" institution, coextensive with the community and capable of ministering to church members' every needs. The ideological building block on which this utopia rests is a reconceptualization of the Christian Trinity: "The Trinity (Father, Mother, and Child) is the first and best generator of communities. Our God is community" (Prado Pereda, n.d.: 8). In practice, however, many, even most, Mazatec church members do not belong to such families. Many are widowed or unmarried, and even in the families that resemble a Trinity-like unit, the fathers' participation in the Mazatec church is weak or nonexistent. Furthermore, the community Heriberto and his followers envision is one in which figures like Heriberto and the Misioneras, who held positions of authority in the Catholic Church, act merely as advisers. They "do not make themselves indispensable" (Prado Pereda, n.d.: 5), but rather support the work of the church and the direction it takes so that such decisions can become responsibilities assumed by all. Yet here, too, practice is sharply at odds with ideology. Heriberto is necessary and irreplaceable, as his vision is the engine driving the Mazatec church's prescriptive project. These discrepancies between ideology and practice place severe limits on the church's transformative, corrective agenda: its attempt to build a brighter future by aligning present activities with an essentialized past.

In practice, Heriberto's standing is not that of a first among equals but, rather, that of the very Weberian charismatic leader he claims to eschew. This was demonstrated especially clearly by his demand that the group take a hard, separatist line toward the Catholic Church. He stipulates that members adopt an evolving set of practices that oppose Catholic practices while recovering ostensibly lost, traditional ones. These "recovered" practices emphasize the sacredness of nature and are either opposed by the Catholic Church outright or are extensions of customs the church classifies as being of questionable Catholic orthodoxy. Practices in the former category include offering the first bite of every meal to the land, kissing the earth every time one concludes a prayer, and building the same kind of arc of flowers and leaves over a corpse that typically crowns altars, especially those for Day of the Dead festivities.[35] In the latter category, during religious ceremonies Mazatec church members spend a much longer time kneeling than is typical in Catholic Mass or other routine religious events. In some cases, they literally spend hours on their knees. The ability to withstand this discomfort has become an index of religious piety, of the authenticity of members' position as "defenders of the faith."

Also in the latter category are now formalized practices that in their enactment, if not in their genesis, foreground and instantiate the competing ideology: that the hierarchy of the Catholic Church should be leveled and replaced by a more egalitarian model. These pertain in particular to the church's formal Sunday services. In the Mazatec Indigenous Church, limpias are performed not only on the priest, as is typical now for Masses in the Sierra, but on everyone attending a service, with people "cleansing" each other until all have been purified. This occurs not at the beginning of the service, as would be the case with priests during Catholic Mass, but toward the end, after a number of songs have been sung that largely mirror the order of songs for Mass: the entrance procession, the Kyrie, the Gloria, the opening prayer, the profession of faith, and so on. After Heriberto gives his "homily"—a practice that again moves the Mazatec church away from an egalitarian model by reinscribing him as the uncontested leader—everyone kneels. Then each participant utters, individually and aloud, his or her prayer. Once everyone has spoken, people perform limpias on each other. Then people join hands and with a slight dancing motion—stepping alternately toward and away from the altar—sing the short offertory *Nguixkuin Nguindso'bai* (lit., Before your eyes, before your mouth), originally written for Mass. The final stanza evokes the communitarian reverence and solidarity to which the service has been building:

> *nanda tjijinli jos'in tiyo jin*
> *jokji kjuañ'ini nča bitjatojin*
> *tisenko na jin naxinandali*
> *me bisitjen jin*

> you well know how we live
> that we live in hard times
> we help each other, your people
> we want to rise up

While most of these practices stem from Heriberto's normative agenda, they nevertheless have become accepted by other members of the group as standard procedure, in concert with how they conceptualize their own spirituality and with the group's larger purpose.

Surely the most dramatic and controversial practice through which Mazatec church members pursue an ethnically distinct, civil-religious nonhierarchy is their use of hallucinogenic mushrooms. They consider the mushrooms to be the Mazatecs' indigenous host, thus replacing the Catholic communion wafer as the prime vehicle for divine purification and transformation. In his writings, Heriberto expresses this idea explicitly. He reminds us that when Roman soldiers stabbed Jesus on the cross, water and blood—which became the sacraments of baptism and the Eucharist—fell from his side. But the drops of water and blood not only hit the ground where he died but, "like a great arrow of God," permeated all the corners of the earth, including the Mazateca:[36]

> For this reason, in every place Christ has made it possible to know him through different media, according to the culture of every human group. Here the blood of Christ came forth in the form of the mushroom. . . . By this good fortune Christ has been present with us since his death. . . . [T]he mushrooms—the blood of Christ—is [sic] also like a Bible, because every time we take them Christ appears to us through his spirit . . . The mushrooms are God's medicine, they are advisers, they are light, they are life . . . He who takes them can find a way to resolve all his problems and receive light for his future life. . . . But he who truly wants to be instructed and wants to be a sabio.[37] . . . to have access to the celestial table[38] . . . has to seek his formation as "seminarian" by ingesting the mushrooms as many times as needed to arrive at this goal. . . . The son of God, Jesus Christ, [is] represented in the hallucinogenic mushrooms. The "Blood of Christ" instructs, gives counsel, gives life, heals, guides. From there our ancestors learned to work and to live together in harmony. (Prado Pereda, n.d.: 14–15, 20)

Of the many ideologies at work in this passage, two are especially relevant to how other people perceive Mazatec church members: Mazatecs' status as Christians and the role mushroom use plays in that status. Heriberto claims that Mazatecs were Christians prior to the arrival of the Spanish, an argument about indigenous people made in similar form by such distinguished clergy as Bartolomé de las Casas and Fray Servando Teresa de Mier. Furthermore, members of the Mazatec church are depicted as superior Christians even to those who claim to have brought them the Gospel, a quality directly tied to their use of mushrooms. "The host is the same as our hallucinogenic mushrooms. For us they are more sacred because we were born with them and they are our advisers and guides. . . . We believe our faith is more profound and refined than the faith of Westerners. . . . When we do veladas with our mushrooms, God speaks to us directly. . . . He is our teacher, prophet, doctor, comforter, priest, artist, sabio" (Prado Pereda, n.d.: 21–22). In this telling, Mazatecs are not dependent on outsiders nor on the institutionalized Catholic Church for their faith and never have been. The very nature of "authentic Mazatec Christianity," as practiced by Mazatec church members, gives them special status. They actively evangelize to people throughout the Sierra, visiting houses of those who have asked about "the project" or those they seek out. They consider themselves missionaries to all those who, like them, speak Mazatec. They discuss the church and its nativist agendas as the birthright of "the people," offering an ethnically authentic yet Christian religious experience to the entire Mazatec population.

The key to Mazatec church members' elevated Christian stature is the mushrooms—and more specifically how they use them. Mazatec church members believe that through the mushrooms they can communicate with God and Jesus and receive sacred texts that guide future actions. While that much is in keeping with views widely articulated in the Sierra, Mazatec church members also believe—departing sharply from the views expressed by many people I interviewed—that these divine messages not only cure maladies of the physical body. They also, as it were, heal the "body politic," curing communal conflicts and the even more common affliction of lack of personal direction. Indeed, the mushrooms are seen as central to Mazatec community itself, teaching people how to live in concert with each other and with the ways of the ancestors. In keeping with this ideology, Mazatec church members hold veladas in which they take mushrooms as a group, rarely to heal a sickness but, instead, to resolve problems and discord. By consulting with God, they believe, they can come to a consensus about how to proceed.

Yet here, too, the explicit, normative ideas the group espouses—the metacultural beliefs they have adopted—are at odds with their behavior in practice. Very few members of the Mazatec church act individually in accordance with the explicit ideologies about mushrooms. No one but Heriberto takes them with anything approaching the frequency he prescribes, and many of the most dedicated members—including Ana—have never taken them at all.

Conclusion: Competing Models of "Authenticity"

Of course, members of the Mazatec Indigenous Church are hardly alone in acting one way and talking another—in displaying a prominent gap between ideology and practice. However, what is illuminating about this case is how that very disparity became the target of criticism for others in Nda Xo. The perceived inconsistency of the Mazatec Indigenous Church on certain key issues seen as closely linked to "authentic" Mazatec identity—mushroom use above all—opens its members to critique and, ultimately, widespread rejection of their revival project. In the next chapter, I discuss these arguments about the Mazatec church in more detail. I do so in part by viewing them alongside popular perceptions of the competing notions of authenticity embedded in Nda Xo's other major revival project, the Day of the Dead Song Contest.

MEETING AT THE FAMILY CRYPT

Social Fault Lines and the Fragility of Community

The church is his bin Laden.

—Alberto Prado speaking about his brother Heriberto Prado

Two Brothers, Two Projects, and the Politics of Revival

This chapter considers what the Sierra's two revival projects—the Mazatec Indigenous Church and the Day of the Dead Song Contest (and its associated activities)—can tell us about the politics of ethnic revival when viewed on an intimate scale. I first discuss the contentious position the Mazatec Indigenous Church occupies in the Sierra. Objections other people have launched against the Mazatec church demonstrate how its practices and ideologies commit its members to waging war not only against the Catholic Church but also against local society more generally. These high social costs are, in turn, directly related to the project's limited popular appeal. When examined alongside the popular success of the Day of the Dead Song Contest, the Mazatec church throws into relief certain aspects of the song contest. The reverse is also true. Viewed in tandem, however, the complementarity and mutuality of the two movements come to the fore. Furthermore, reading these two revival projects as symbiotic rather than opposed—despite the ways they are constructed by local people as conflicting—provides insight into the potential revival projects have to create social change while illuminating the substantial limitations revival projects face in realizing social transformations.

While my analysis is grounded in community-wide arguments about the Mazatec church, I also maintain focus on the two Prado brothers who have been so centrally involved in the development of these two revival projects. I discuss the positions the brothers have taken on the nature of community and the "authentic" Mazatec person who makes community possible. While the brothers' positions are in some ways diametrically opposed, in other ways they are reciprocally reinforcing. Their differing attitudes toward a range of religious and political issues link them to social fault lines that cut across the Sierra, factionalism that in various forms haunts minority groups throughout Mexico and other countries around the world.

This pair of cases reveals the constraints under which revival movements labor in balancing local expectations against engagement with national institutions and discourses. Showing how such disputes ricochet within families sheds light on their lived stakes. The focus on key individuals in this case shows how people live their daily lives in the shadow of deep social rifts while also searching for ways to transcend them—through, for example, enacting such moments of détente as occur annually during Day of the Dead celebrations, when even feuding members of families meet in the cemetery and set aside their differences, if only for the day, to honor the dead.

"Ska-le" (He's Crazy): Religious Divisions and the Stakes in Arguments about Them

The Mazatec Indigenous Church emerged from some of the most shocking recent events in the social life of the Sierra Mazateca, and its founding constituted a pivotal moment in the history of the large extended family, the Prados, at the epicenter of those events. Within the family, as within the region as a whole, the often bitter arguments surrounding the emergence of the Mazatec church explicitly concerned religious difference. However, as the arguments unfolded, they pulled into their wake a number of other hotly contested issues: competing ideas about tradition, modernity, authenticity, language use, indigenous identity, and even the meaning of community itself. Thus, arguments about religion were almost never only about religion. While they often expressed localized concerns and differences, they also came to both condition and exemplify a broad range of pressing social issues with which Sierra residents grapple, as do indigenous people throughout the hemisphere. Religious affiliation in Nda Xo has become a symbol of difference as well as its substance. The different forms of religious allegiance at issue in this case entail adherence to divergent views about social solidarity, indigenous belonging, and modern life in Mexico. Furthermore, such views are linked to conflicting ways of acting on those ideas, through practices that recursively inscribe difference in the activities of everyday life.

As we have seen, what members of the Mazatec Indigenous Church claim they do (or should do) and what they do in daily life are often at odds: the gap between stated ideology and quotidian practice can be considerable. The resistance church members encounter in trying to narrow this divide is tied, in turn, to limits on the Mazatec church's popular appeal. The normative ideologies that animate the church's agenda depart enough from practices other local people consider standard that they are seen as wrong, strange, or even unrecognizable. People from Nda Xo who do not belong to the Mazatec church engage in heated disputes about the new church and its adherents; criticizing Heriberto above all, their arguments represent a continuing referendum on the project's tenability. Furthermore, their critiques often seize on precisely the rift between ideology and practice: on Mazatec church members' perceived failure to live up to their own stated goals and embody the models of "authentic" Mazatec personhood they claim to valorize.

These ongoing debates constitute a different facet of the Sierra's "public sphere" (see Habermas 1991) from that constructed by the Day of the Dead Song Contest. Whereas the contest revolves around ideas about what Mazatecs *are*, disputes about the Mazatec church focus on what Mazatecs *are not*. Of the two revival projects, the Mazatec church is the more explicit in articulating what "Mazatec identity" is. Yet it nevertheless elicits, ironically and largely by accident, explicit statements by others about what Mazatecs are not. For many Sierra residents who do not belong to the Mazatec church, "authentic" Mazatec personhood does not look like the model of Mazatec identity that Heriberto Prado and his followers extol. The perceived artificiality of practices advocated by the Mazatec church throws into relief widespread, assumed customs and the often implicit ideologies that motivate them. The image of "being Mazatec" held up by the Mazatec church violates enough of these norms that the majority of local people have rejected it.

The arguments that reject the view of Mazatec subjectivity on which the Mazatec Indigenous Church rests focus primarily on conceptions of community. What kind of collective do people feel, or want to feel, they belong to? The arguments also concern competing notions of authenticity and tradition. In what practices does true "Mazatecness" reside? What are the semantic and practical boundaries around "us" and "them"? These and related questions are raised in the three sets of arguments about the Mazatec church that I discuss here and that have arisen since the church's founding. They are also emblematic of the broader rift between its members and other locals.

The first concerns the relationship of indigenous people to the Catholic Church, in the Sierra and beyond. This set of arguments focuses not only on the church's role in the present but also on its historical legacies as a major institution interfacing with Mexico's indigenous peoples and hence grappling with the so-called Indian problem. The second set of arguments takes up the issue of how members of the Mazatec Indigenous Church should relate to people who do not belong to it, given that they share daily life and major lifecycle events with Catholics, Protestants, and others. This cluster of disputes is heavily preoccupied with boundaries of various sorts, not only those surrounding people based on religious affiliation, but also those delimiting other crucial categories — such as what constitutes "tradition." That question raises many others, such as what role innovation and present practices play in fidelity to tradition. Finally, the third set of arguments considers what it means to be "authentically" Mazatec. This issue involves not only how one relates to one's family and community but also, at a symbolic level, how one uses mushrooms to enact particular visions of "being Mazatec."

Uniting all three sets of arguments are various questions routinely raised by revival. What is the nature of "authentic indigenous identity"? Where is the locus of community solidarity? How can collective unity best be leveraged to subvert hegemonic powers that historically have oppressed indigenous people? People in Nda Xo have had very different ways to answer these questions; the lived stakes of these differences have been considerable. Although the various factions in Nda Xo, in contrast to those in Yalálag, have not resorted to physical violence, serious consequences nevertheless have resulted from the town's internal disputes.

Debating Legacies of the "Indian Problem": The Place of the Past and National Institutions in "Authentic Indigenous Identity"

The first set of arguments began with a specific dispute between the Bishop Hermenegildo Ramírez Sánchez and Heriberto Prado Pereda as the Mazatec church was taking shape. In response to Bishop Ramírez's position that Heriberto had no authority to perform Catholic sacraments, Heriberto argued he was attending the communities in question "not with official sacraments but, rather, according to rites that are from within my culture" (Prado Pereda, n.d.: 5).[1] The bishop reacted by stating that the sacraments celebrated by Heriberto were valid neither within the Catholic Church nor within Mazatec culture because within "traditional Mazatec culture" there is no Christ. In his later writings, Heriberto took pains to answer this criticism and did so with difficulty. He, like the bishop, locates "authentic Mazatec culture" in the preconquest past.

As we have seen, Heriberto argues that the Mazatecs were Christians long before the Spanish arrived, and so they are dependent neither on the church nor on outsiders for their faith. This commits him to the view that the institutionalized church is the enemy, while Christianity itself remains unscathed. It commits him, as well, to the view that his group's faith is superior to that of those who have the power of the institutionalized church behind them. This lends his followers a deeper moral force from that of those who "siempre llevan la batuta" (merely carry the staff of office) (Prado Pereda, n.d.: 23).[2] From this perspective, members of the Mazatec church are the oppressed but true defenders of the faith. The repression of Mazatec believers and other indigenous faithful occurs when the church adopts the same assimilationist, indigenista policies that have haunted indigenous–state relations for the whole of Mexican history:

> The bishop has signed many documents in which he speaks of encultura-tion. It is said the autochthonous church will not come to be unless it can depend on having its own priests, bishops, liturgies: the culture of revival. Then what . . . is the distrust about what we are doing; why isn't it accepted? We come back to the same question: the Church thinks but does not say openly that indigenous priests are witches or better, servants of the devil. To participate in their ceremonies and offer holy communion with the mushrooms is to lend oneself to evil. . . . [Like] indigenous people [who condemn us], . . . the institutional Church also acts as if it were crucial to recover indigenous culture and indigenous religion, when in reality they aim to finish it off. . . . At bottom, what the Church wants is to gain indigenous people for Christ. And if the Church gains their souls, indigenous people will leave their religion behind. (Prado Pereda, n.d.: 13, 15–16)

Arguments such as these make it hard to write off the Mazatec Indigenous Church as motivated by a mere vendetta. The personal aspects of the rift are certainly obvious. From both sides, the argument has the character of a love affair gone awry and reads like the aftermath of a betrayal, where the severity of the anger and hurt is directly proportional to the intensity of the prior attachment. Not only the bishop but also others from Nda Xo—particularly those like Alberto who have close ties to Mazatec church members—speak of the Mazatec church members' departure from the church in strongly emotional terms. Despite their declaration that "we aren't a closed group" (Prado Pereda, n.d.: 9), the Mazatec church members, in practice, act like separatists. A common lament by those outside the Mazatec church is that, as a result of its members' decision to leave the Catholic Church, "Now we are more divided." Meanwhile, Heriberto and his followers speak of the entire situation—even now, years after leaving the church—in equally emotional terms. They wait, so far in vain, for acknowledgment from the Catholic Church. As Heriberto writes, "Since we set ourselves apart . . . neither the bishop nor the priests have sought dialogue with us. They have been even less interested in resolving this matter. Rather, they further turn the people against us and our project . . . [and] no other institution will endorse our documents" (Prado Pereda, n.d.: 23).

Yet for all of the personal feelings involved, the criticisms Heriberto makes, and the eloquence with which he makes them, elevate the argument above the level of a personal feud. His condemnation of the Catholic Church in the name of indigenous rights is in keeping with—and strongly influenced by—widespread critiques of *indigenismo*. However, his denouncement of the church is somewhat novel, a departure from most criticisms voiced in the vast corpus of attacks on indigenismo and institutionalized solutions to the so-called Indian problem. Modern, post-Revolutionary criticisms of indigenismo generally target the Mexican state; they far less commonly take aim at the church. It is more uncommon still for an indigenous intellectual to mount such a critique. This is due in part to the church's historical standing as protector of indigenous interests against the abuses of power to which indigenous people were periodically subjected by secular authorities. In addition, few indigenous intellectuals achieve such status through credentialing by the Catholic Church. Heriberto's critique is relatively rare because he knows the church from inside, through years of training and service, at a level few indigenous people in Mexico achieve.

Heriberto acknowledges that the church has "given more space to indigenous people for the support of their culture. . . . [W]e can sing [and] pray in our language, we can introduce some of our cultural symbols." However, he claims, the church's support for indigenous autonomy and indigenous culture has been only superficial. Equating the church with a building, Heriberto explains that only the external veneer—the "paint" on the house of God—is indigenous. The inside remains as true as ever to old-style Catholicism, to the ways of the church before Vatican II and Liberation Theology opened the space for indigenous people to celebrate their languages and cultures. Thus, although the church's new structure looks entirely indigenous from the outside, the indigenous trappings are in fact only "a shell," a display of "that which is [merely] folkloric" (Prado Pereda, n.d.: 13).

In writing in this way, Heriberto aligns himself with a widespread critique of the direction the church took under Pope John Paul II. In his view, John Paul took the church many steps backward, reversing gains achieved during the liberal-leaning decades when Heriberto became priest. Although neither Heriberto nor other members of the Mazatec church explicitly acknowledge it, they treat the church under liberation as its moment of authenticity and the move away from it during John Paul II's tenure as a betrayal of its true mission. This shift put people like Bishop Ramírez in the difficult position of having to accommodate both the official church position opposing liberationist ideas and those parishioners and priests—of whom Heriberto could have been the poster child—who had been encouraged by those now disfavored ideas to radically rethink the role of the church in daily life.

Less directly, Heriberto also positions himself inside a rich history of critiques launched against the postindigenista Mexican nation-state. That body of criticism aims to question a move that nationalist projects routinely make: valorizing nonthreatening aspects of minority groups' cultures while denying all others. A strategy that nations frequently deploy is incorporating while simultaneously circumscribing diverse internal populations by championing their "folklore"—the very tactic that is on glorious display at Mexico's preeminent site of cultural codification and legitimation, the National Museum of Anthropology.

Heriberto's criticism against the Catholic Church resonates with this view. He claims that while indigenous people are not excluded from the church per se—he was ordained, after all—fundamentally indigenous *perspectives* nevertheless are excluded from all positions of power. He argues that indigenous people *as* indigenous people are prohibited from taking meaningful control of the direction of the church and are disqualified from serving the church as true indigenous representatives. Instead, indigenous people are permitted to participate only as mere tokens of ethnic inclusion—a rebuke that, for all of its obvious personal implications, also transcends them.

Debating the Locus of "Tradition":
Present Practice and the Innovation of Revival

The second specific argument about the Mazatec church likewise highlights the larger issues it raises about the nature of community, ethnic identity, and the place of indigenous people in modern Mexico. It concerns the death of a woman who lived in Amatlán, a small rancho in greater Nda Xo and where I was living at the time she passed away.

Before I turn to that argument, however, I want to stress that this event illustrates how the Mazatec church was still "feeling its way" with each new lifecycle event. Through Heriberto's leadership, its members were constantly seeking the "authentically indigenous" actions they should take for each new social occasion. Heriberto, in turn, was guided by the messages the group received during collective *veladas* (mushroom ceremonies), held to gain insight into particular problems. For such events, Mazatec church members were very explicit about the emergent nature of their practices. For example, the group's first baptism was held for the youngest child of a widow whose husband had been murdered in retaliation for a murder he had himself allegedly committed. When the baptism was held, there was a great deal of discussion among Mazatec church members about who should perform which part of the ceremony, the relevant social categories being parents, compadres, *sabios* (shaman; Heriberto, in this case), and elders (Heriberto's mother). This process of working collaboratively to reach a consensus about what should become codified practice for key ceremonies was common in the Mazatec church rituals I observed.

As a side commentary, the ambivalent position the Mazatec church occupies in Nda Xo is indicated by the limited terms on which the widow and her children participated in the church. After her husband's death in one of the *municipio*'s (county) distant settlements, the widow had returned to the *cabecera* (county seat), which is where her parents lived. However, her family was one of Nda Xo's poorest: her mother owned two dresses and no shoes. So initially, the widow and her children lived in part of Heriberto's house, making her more or less obliged to participate in Mazatec church activities. As soon as she established her own home—friends and relatives built a tiny shack for her from scrap wood and sheets of tin—she moved out of Heriberto's home. Although her house was on land just below Heriberto's, and she walked by his house daily on the way into town, she and her children stopped attending Mazatec church services.

Deep ambivalence also played out during the death in Amatlán, especially in the arguments that followed it. Most of Amatlán's inhabitants—basically, one extended family—had joined the Mazatec church and nominally cut ties with the Catholic Church. Two middle-aged women from the family were suffering from undiagnosed illnesses when I arrived to live at the rancho; about two months later, one of the women died. Heriberto and other Mazatec church members arrived the following day. "The first death in our little group," he said to me, articulating the challenge the group had already begun to face: here was yet another new life event, and "authentic Mazatec ceremonies" would be called for. It was incumbent upon the group to uncover the true, traditional manner for conducting these rituals, in keeping with their mission to remake their faith through fidelity to indigenous "tradition." Before coming to Amatlán, Heriberto and the group held a velada to "talk to God" about how to deal in an "authentically indigenous" way with the group's first death. Several months later, they held similar knowledge-seeking veladas during and after the aforementioned event involving the ill-fated birth.

For the death, Heriberto led primarily by example. He and the group did not call attention to the emergent and collaborative process by which they shaped their response to the event. Rather, Heriberto led the group by enacting directly the speech and actions he wanted others to mirror instead of explicitly commenting on them. I think he took that approach because he had a "mixed audience": people who were members of the Mazatec church and others who were not. The latter group of people constituted an ambivalent group for Heriberto and his followers. Those others might well be hostile to his ideas, making it less likely that he would openly discuss his views with them. Yet at the same time, given the Mazatec church's overtly evangelical stance, those people also represented an opportunity to win over new converts.

On the day Heriberto and his group arrived in Amatlán, other family members and compadres of the woman who died began arriving from neighboring ranchos. Amid all of the activity, Heriberto began composing a song especially for the occasion. He taught the song to various people present but in particular to a brother of the deceased woman. He was the most dedicated of the Mazatec church members who lived in Amatlán—indeed, he was the Sierra's strongest adherent outside the core followers in the cabecera. He went to Heriberto's house once or twice a month to conduct veladas with the group and to participate in their ceremonies, even though it meant walking about six hours each way. He was also an aspiring musician learning to compose songs; he hoped to write enough Muertos songs in Mazatec to fill a CD. He was in his late thirties and, unhappily, a bachelor; a few years later, he finally married a woman who, like him, was in her thirties and unhappily single. But because his new wife is a Protestant and her father is strongly opposed to Heriberto and his project, the man left the Mazatec church soon after, much to the consternation of its other members. This situation indicates yet again the high social costs attached to belonging to the Mazatec church—costs that even those who are attracted to aspects of the revival project often find are too high to sustain.

While Heriberto and others were working on the song, other men began building the casket, painting it a vibrant sky blue. Meanwhile, the women prepared the food—beginning, as was customary, with the sacrifice of a

FIGURE 5.1. The arc made by members of the Mazatec Indigenous Church for a church member who died in Amatlán, a village in greater Nda Xo.

spotted chicken that was first offered to the corpse. After the women made the offering, Heriberto told the people to construct an arc of flowers and branches, the kind usually made for Day of the Dead altars (see fig. 5.1). This one, however, was for displaying around the corpse—an innovation, several people commented, that surprised them because they had never seen an arc used in that way before.

That evening, Heriberto led the wake. It included prayers and songs in Mazatec, among them the new song he had written for the occasion. He spent much of the evening kneeling, as did other Mazatec church members. People who were not from the group tried to follow suit, although they were visibly uncomfortable spending so much time on their knees; they got up every few minutes to walk around or sit in the chairs arranged around the perimeter of the room. Although Heriberto led the services all through the night, the next day, one of the woman's compadres—a catechist from a nearby rancho—

took command of the procession as it left the house for the graveyard. He sprinkled holy water liberally along the way. Upon arriving at the little church, he entered. As commonly occurs during funerals, the people—led by the catechist—held a short service there before proceeding to the graveyard.

This infuriated Heriberto. He and his group stood angrily outside the church and kept their distance from the other mourners once the procession arrived at the cemetery. Discarding their original plan to stay in Amatlán for a week or more, he and the group left immediately after the woman had been interred. "They deceived me," he said later. "They missed their chance to see a real indigenous funeral." He was not particularly angry with the Catholics who did not belong to the Mazatec church, but he was extremely upset with the Mazatec church members from Amatlán. They had failed, he felt, to prevent those who still worshipped with the Catholic Church from taking charge of the ceremony. Furthermore, his criticism did not stop with the woman's family; the woman herself was to blame. If she had prayed more, he said, she would have lived.[3] He cited as proof the fact that the other sick woman—who was more involved with Heriberto's group than the one who died—had survived.

This event and the disagreements at its heart demonstrate concrete social difficulties Heriberto's followers face because of the hard line they take toward the Catholic Church. Even if their closest family members have likewise joined the Mazatec Indigenous Church and left the Catholic Church, they live in a world where most others have not and where many of those adamantly oppose the entire Mazatec church revival project. "What is it he calls his group? An indigenous church?" one of Heriberto's cousins once asked me, with palpable disdain, as she headed to Catholic Mass with her family, walking right in front of Heriberto's store as she spoke. Contempt is an extremely widespread attitude toward the Mazatec church. As Ana once commented to me, "They don't want to hear anything about anything 'indigenous.'" Heriberto and his group have come to embody, essentially, the particular class of "organic intellectuals" identified by Antonio Gramsci who are in the business of exposing the hegemonic tyranny of dominant—and dominating—ideologies. However, as many locals see it, in this very act, Heriberto and his followers cede the right to speak as authentic local authorities and representatives.

Ultimately, the rift with the people from Amatlán was not repaired until after a velada could be held. During that velada, the group came to an understanding about what had happened at the burial and how, in the future, they should handle relations with people who do not belong to the Mazatec church. The consensus—conceived, as always, as a message received from God—seems to have been that, in keeping with the group's earlier decisions, the best policy was to continue to separate themselves, both from people who attend the Catholic Church and from all other events involving contact with the Catholic Church. It is significant that the only person from Amatlán who participated in the velada was the bachelor songwriter. Perhaps because only he participated in it, or perhaps because of the more general social strain surrounding the burial itself, the group in Amatlán became divided after that, and only the most ardent supporters continued to be affiliated with the Mazatec church.

Debating the Nature of Community: Hegemony and Its Subversion

Veladas also played an important role in a conflict between Heriberto and Alberto, the third disagreement I discuss. Their argument came to a head over the administration of the 2001 Day of the Dead Song Contest. At the time, I was still living in Heriberto's house. I did not yet speak Mazatec very well, so although I was present at the relevant veladas, I did not understand their full import until later. Ultimately, I came to understand that Heriberto held veladas to seek council about the initial disagreement with his brother, as well as about the deeper familial rift the conflict caused. I believe that for Heriberto, the veladas represented an opportunity to understand what was at stake in his argument with Alberto, to make a decision about how to respond, and to reassure himself, through consultation with God, that his views and actions were correct.

The disagreement erupted when Heriberto refused to continue serving on the song contest's administrative commission, as he had done for several years. He argued that because the contest relied for its administration on committees affiliated with the Catholic Church, as had been the case since its founding, he would not participate. On a deeper level, however, family and community unity were at stake: each brother expected family and religious affiliations to coincide and religious and civic boundaries to be identical. Thus, Heriberto lamented on the morning after a velada that Alberto "did not want to have a truly profound religious faith." For his part, around the same time Alberto said, sadly, "The church is [Heriberto's] bin Laden," his number-one enemy.[4] These views, while fundamentally opposed on the surface, carry the same frustration: each felt the other was disrupting community and family unity. Furthermore, underlying their disagreement were shared preoccupations about normative local practice, about what it means to act like a (good) Prado and like a "real" Mazatec.

I did not fully understand the implications of their disagreement, however, until after another argument emerged. Veladas played a central role in this event, too, but there I was involved directly, not as incidental observer but active participant. After the initial novelty of having me live with them wore off, some members of Heriberto's group, including Heriberto himself, began viewing me with some suspicion.

There were obvious reasons I might be suspect: I was unmarried and childless; I was an outsider and an American; my interest in their language was at best bizarre if benign, and at worst a front for more sinister motives. I was a social risk, hard to explain and a highly marked locus for envy. Closeness to me meant (perceived) access to items such as my laptop, my camera, and my recorder, as well as to people and resources in Mexico and the United States. All such linkages would have been problematic to negotiate for anyone in a town as small and relatively unaccustomed to outsiders as Nda Xo. But such associations were particularly difficult to navigate for an organization and group of people who ostensibly were aiming to revive a "pure" and "authentically Mazatec" way of living.

But beyond these qualities that might raise people's suspicion under ordinary circumstances, I also became increasingly suspect as the Mazatec church hardened its position vis-à-vis the Catholic Church. Like many people in Nda Xo, I attended Mass at least for special occasions. As Mazatec church members grew increasingly purist with respect to external, "non-Mazatec" influences, their suspicions about me came to a head. One night, after I had returned to Nda Xo from a brief visit to Oaxaca city, Heriberto and other church members held a velada. Although I was staying in Heriberto's house, they made a point of excluding me. The next morning, they informed me that the mushrooms had told them that I should not spend another night under Heriberto's roof. "You see, Paja, our God is a jealous God," one of Heriberto's cousins told me when she stopped by.

I scrambled to find another place to live by nightfall. Beginning that evening, I stayed with a Mazatec church family who was not related to the Prados and who lived in a humble rented house in Santa Herminia, a little way out of town. After that, I bounced from house to house for a while before I finally wound up staying permanently with Alberto's family. For several months thereafter, Heriberto and the members of his family who belonged to the Mazatec church — at the time, the people I knew best in Nda Xo — barely acknowledged me when our paths crossed. Sometimes they avoided me altogether. It was many months before I was invited into their homes again—homes that until then I had visited daily. These invitations were issued, not coincidentally, during Day of the Dead festivities.

Although this was a difficult experience at the time, it gave me access to a wealth of commentary and critique about Heriberto and his group from which I had previously been excluded. Furthermore, the social aftermath yielded a more complete picture of the nature of Nda Xo's religious divisions, its dominant discourses, and the types of actors involved in them. That event also underscored how deep and socially significant such rifts are. Because I had in effect "switched sides," people now talked to me freely, with little or no encouragement, about all the reasons they disagreed with what Heriberto and his group were doing.

These criticisms concerned a range of issues, but many focused explicitly on religious practice, ideology, and the perceived disparity between the two in the actions of Heriberto and his followers. Other local people—particularly those who were closely tied to the Catholic Church, but many others, as well, including "casual Catholics" and Protestants—took exception to Mazatec church members' contentions that the Catholic Church is an organ of repression and that the Mazatec church's religious practices are recuperative acts of resistance. For them, the Catholic Church, rather than suppressing "authentic Mazatec identity," is central to its expression. They emphasized in particular that the church plays an integral role in civic matters and in every major community ritual and life event, from birth to death. Some of the most culturally salient representatives of "traditional" Mazatec practice—the *chota chjine* (shamans)—are also among the most active Catholics in Sierra communities.

No less a representative of Mazatec culture than María Sabina was herself an active member of the Catholic Church, belonging to the Sisterhood of the Sacred Heart of Jesus. As a local priest commented, "The Wise Ones and Curers don't compete with our religion; . . . All of them are very religious and come to mass" (quoted in Estrada 1981: 203). Many local people and church officials see shamans—those emblematic representatives of "traditional Mazatec culture"—not as "pagan" or somehow opposed to the church but, rather, as complementary to it. Furthermore, they view opposition to the church as a rejection not only of community unity but of the very basis for sociality. The practices Mazatec church members ideologize as lost cultural rituals rescued from the past are seen by other local people as bizarre innovations that violate "tradition" rather than uphold it. Other locals see these activities not as a means for returning to the ways of the ancestors but as evidence that Mazatec church members have yielded to foreign, corrupting ideas imported from outside the Sierra.

The practices particularly subject to claims of inauthenticity and even downright abuse are those involving hallucinogenic mushrooms. The serial use of mushrooms by Heriberto and his group for visionary and divinatory—rather than medicinal—purposes is viewed by many people not only as sacrilegious but as proof of mental unsoundness. Serranos presumably have used hallucinogenic mushrooms for centuries in healing rituals. Of the various taboos attached to their use, the most important is sexual abstinence: as discussed earlier, failure to observe the taboos is said to cause madness. So when people say about Heriberto and others from his group, "Ska-le" (He's crazy), they mean that he is crazy in a very specific sense—from "traveling too much," or, in other words, from taking mushrooms too often and using them improperly.[5]

The way Heriberto and his group use the mushrooms stands in marked contrast to how they are used by local chota chjine. Most shamans are widowed or have never married. Thus, they are "publicly celibate": because of this social profile, other people can assume they observe a continuous state of sexual abstinence and are ritually "clean" for contacting divine sources. Because of his history, however, Heriberto's social profile as a sexual being is radically different. The "crime" at the heart of his rift with the church was of an explicitly sexual nature. According to many of the people in Nda Xo whom I interviewed, by continuing to live with his common-law wife and their two children, he displays evidence of his presumed sexual activity and thus presumed ritual impurity.

Such assumptions about his sexuality contribute mightily toward the ambivalence with which many people in Nda Xo regard him. While the status of most shamans is also ambivalent, the caution with which they are regarded derives from a different source. People regard shamans with ambivalence less because sabios are tainted by some kind of moral stain—like the one attached to Heriberto's public persona—than because of their power to contact the spirit world. This power is shot through with risk and promise, because it can be exploited for both good and ill. While most shamans literally inhabit a marginal place in the community, living at its geographical edges, Heriberto lives, at numerous levels, "in the center of town"—or, as I often heard him describe it, "right at the first speed bump coming into town." Thus, not only is he figuratively central to the community by virtue of birth and vocation, but he also physically lives in a central location on the main road into Nda Xo from the Sierra's principal highway.

Heriberto clearly emulates sabios, and he sees his "calling" as structurally similar to theirs. In the veladas I attended with them, Heriberto and other Mazatec church members often explicitly sought to position themselves as healers.[6] In the first such velada that I witnessed, which took place not long after the Misioneras separated from the church, they and Heriberto were overwhelmingly preoccupied with economic resources and how they might make their dream of becoming healers a reality. They were particularly interested in pursuing alternative medicine as a new source of income. Interest in alternative medicine continued to be a concern in veladas (and, strategically, in discussions with me as someone they felt might know about things like external funding), not only with the Misioneras, but also with various other women in the Mazatec church, a couple of whom had experience as pharmacists.[7] A case of mistaken identity involving Alberto and Heriberto was particularly telling in this respect: a family from out of town showed up by mistake at Alberto's store, asking him to heal their gravely ill son, having heard that he was very gifted in using the mushrooms.

Although Heriberto and his group see their mission as like that of shamans, they also claim they have been called to do an even more profound kind of work. Heriberto sees the role of his church and his followers as healers of the entire community, the "body politic." Although he blames Catholic Church authorities in particular for what he claims is systematic oppression, he also holds secular authorities responsible for preventing indigenous people from living and expressing their cultures. The Mazatec church, as he sees it, is the antidote for the multiple maladies stemming from far-reaching social repression. He therefore sees himself as a healer in the broadest possible sense: a healer not only of the physical body but also of the spirit, specifically the indigenous spirit to which the institution of the Catholic Church has falsely laid claim. Thus, many of the veladas I attended were concerned not with specific instances of healing but with creating the very conditions of possibility for healing. The group was trying, through veladas, to learn how to be healers, to collectively take on the vocation of chota chjine—but not the vocation of healer as instantiated by the sabios working and living in the Sierra. Rather, the group was in search of a "truer" calling, a more profound type of shamanistic work, the vocation of wise ones who could live up to the meaning of the name in Mazatec and become truly masters of masters, chief experts in society's most profound form of knowledge.

Nevertheless, despite their shared reverence for the mushrooms, shamans are among Heriberto's strongest critics. Mazatec church members use the mushrooms monthly, if not weekly, especially in the middle of the rainy season when the mushrooms are plentiful. By contrast, for most Mazatecs, taking the mushrooms is a seminal but relatively rare event, occurring a handful of times across an entire life.[8] Shamans, of course, use mushrooms with frequency similar to that of Heriberto and his group, but they do so for dramatically different reasons: local shamans employ the mushrooms solely for curing, whereas Mazatec church members, as we have seen, use them primarily to attain divine guidance and foresight.

The Mazatec church's motives and methods in using the mushrooms—which is to say, with frequency and not medicinally—were ironically presented to me by local people as approximating the behavior of a particularly salient group of outsiders: mycotourists. Though these tourists almost never find their way to Nda Xo, everyone in the Sierra Mazateca is well aware of them, and they figure prominently in local conversations. Like the mycotourists, Mazatec church members' reasons for taking the mushrooms have less to do with curing than with the desire for guidance and foresight. In the words of María Sabina, speaking of the time before hippies began appearing in the Sierra, "Before Wasson nobody took the mushrooms only to find God. They were always taken for the sick to get well" (quoted in Estrada 1981: 73).

Mazatec church followers fall much more clearly, as others discussed the matter with me, into the first of these two categories: they appear to take the mushrooms primarily to seek God. In fact, Mazatec church members themselves reinforce this impression by referring to the ceremonies in which mushrooms will be taken as ones in which they will "speak to God." That phrase, similar to those I discussed in chapter 2, is an indirect, idiomatic expression that refers to veladas. However, it is dramatically different from phrases that chota chjine and others who do not belong to the Mazatec church use in speaking of the mushrooms, such as, "We are going to stay up tonight" or "We're going to take the little things."

As a result of these pragmatic and discursive differences, Mazatec church members appear to other locals to use the mushrooms in ways that resemble the practices of hippies rather than shamans. What Mazatec church members cast as a faithful, ethnically correct return to authentically Mazatec ways and a celebration of a distinctly Mazatec patrimony bestowed on Mazatecs by God, others critique as a betrayal of some of the most deeply held, culturally salient codes of behavior. To them, Mazatec church members appear to employ practices that look far less "traditional" than "foreign," thereby violating basic understandings of what it means to use the mushrooms properly, to be from Nda Xo. In this sense, Heriberto and his followers live even farther "beyond the pale" than do most Protestants. By virtue of his mushroom use, Heriberto is transformed from being the consummate insider, a revered representative of the entire community, to one who increasingly resembles an outsider and who, along with his followers, violates basic understandings of what it means to behave like an "authentic Mazatec."

Meeting in the Graveyard: A Vision for the Future in a Visit with the Dead

Complaints about how Mazatec church members use mushrooms are at the core of many arguments against the church. They also cut to the heart of why so many people in the Sierra find this particular revival project objectionable. The disagreement derives from conflicting ideas about what an "authentic indigenous identity" consists of, what relation it bears to modern practice and traditions from the past, and how indigenous identities are tied to the creation—or revival—of indigenous communities. Furthermore, these disputes raise some of the most central and divisive concerns for marginalized and minority communities in Mexico and beyond.

The broader salience of these critiques comes sharply into focus when we view them, and the project they attack, alongside the Sierra's other recent revival initiative, the Day of the Dead Song Contest. While the song contest demonstrates some of the opportunities made possible through a politics of indigenous identity, the Mazatec Indigenous Church points out the shortcomings of identity politics as a vehicle for social change. Viewed against each other, these two revival projects make visible persistent tensions that identity politics force people to confront as they navigate conflicts between modernity and tradition, between an idealized past and a selectively licensed present. The questions raised here about how these two forms of indigenous revival are related to conceptions of community are similar in some ways to debates that happen periodically in the United States about the separation of church and state, or in countries around the globe struggling to balance secular inclusion and religious freedom against deep-seated religiously affiliated ethnic identities whose demands for recognition trouble easy pretensions to liberal uniformity.

In the case of these two revival movements, there is certainly a contingent nature to how they were received; both projects unfolded through specifics of family and local histories. Heriberto's "defection" came to be seen by Alberto and others as a fundamental betrayal not only of deeply held community values but also of his own, considerable efforts to heighten and strengthen

FIGURE 5.2. Eating *mole* during the Day of the Dead fiesta.

them. Certainly, he did not invent the extent to which the Day of the Dead is idealized—and ideologized—as a time of explicit and implicit unity. Muertos is the one time of the year that people are most likely to come home to visit their families; for two days a year, people spend hours cheek to jowl at the graveyard, communing with the dead and the living, even those from whom they are, for whatever reasons, alienated. Reciprocal invitations to share mole are issued from across various fissures of quotidian difference (see fig. 5.2). All of these practices of inclusion aim to transcend factionalism as an existential default, and they long preceded Nda Xo's revival projects. But by doing so much to "revitalize" Day of the Dead as the Ur-Mazatec event, Heriberto became both a highly salient representative of that inclusive ideology and a victim of its critique when he failed to uphold it. Thus, to many people in Nda Xo, Heriberto in a sense became the antithesis of the prodigal son. Rather than returning home full of contrition after a delinquent absence, he was the dutiful son who betrayed years of good deeds by turning his back on the family and the community at large.

Nevertheless, for all of its specificity, in this particular biographical landscape we also see the outlines of more general and pervasive tensions and paradoxes. As we will see in the next chapter, the broad characteristics of the story of Alberto and Heriberto, the song contest, and the Mazatec church, are repeated at a higher level in the differences among kinds of indigenous intellectuals and the projects they promote. Their ultimate goals—at least, in the abstract—are similar in that both aim to valorize Mazatec culture and tradition. Yet they have different ideas about who can do this important work, about the kind of community such a person belongs to and can help bring about. One sees the same problematic tensions at the national level, in which the assumptions on which identity politics are based intersect with views of authenticity, with notions of insider and outsider. When do beliefs and practices adopted outside a community—Catholicism, for example, or particular constructions of indigenous belonging—become part of that community's central vision of itself? When are those ideas no longer a "loan" on par with words like *café* and *hostia*, no longer "ideological borrowing" but seen as "authentic" in their own right? Who is "defending my people and their culture"? Heriberto and his group? Alberto and the other songwriters of Nda Xo? Both? Neither?

The slippage and, alternatively, the congruence between the subjectivities proposed in each of these projects and those accepted by their audiences shed light on why revival projects may meet with divergent popular fates. But this split at the local level is also linked to a related bifurcation at the national level, to which I turn next. Throughout the Americas, globalized discourses about ethnic plurality and indigenous rights have touched ground through local forms of cultural assertion, social movements led in many cases by indigenous authors. In Mexico, given the linkage between linguistic affiliation and ethnic identity, indigenous authors often advance their political agendas by promoting indigenous languages—through indigenous literacy, writing, and, in this case, song composition. But this approach places indigenous authors in a paradoxical position. By using a local, ethnically marked language intimately tied to indigeneity to address concerns of national political importance, such authors must address a double audience. Their interlocutors—local speakers of native languages and national speakers of Spanish— often have mutually exclusive expectations. Thus, while many indigenous authors have been successful in addressing national political goals, relatively few have had the kind of local success seen in Nda Xo—most obviously, the popular success gained by the song contest, but even, in its way, the popular appeal of the Mazatec Indigenous Church. Although the number of people who have embraced the Mazatec church has been modest, the new church's impact on the lives of those it affects has been profound.

The aggressively local focus of the two revival projects in Nda Xo thus are something of a departure from the national norm. Yet here also the pressures of the dual audience at the national level are refracted through the fates of these two projects and the essentialized identities on which they depend—and, ultimately, through the social subjectivities attached to the authors themselves. While the Mazatec Indigenous Church presents ideas about Mazatec personhood that many local people reject, these ideas are heavily influenced by and quite consistent with postcolonial national and international discourses about indigenous rights and indigenous resistance, notions that often locate "authentic" indigenous identity in a pre-Western past and an antimodern present. Meanwhile, promoters of the Day of the Dead Song Contest have the opposite problem. The ideas about indigenous identity they espouse are embraced locally, but through the lens of postcolonial discourses to which many indigenous intellectuals adhere, the visions of indigenous identity that the contest embraces smack of co-option, of willingness to accept a licensed arena for protest—the realm of folklore—in exchange for not demanding more-profound change.

Seen in comparison with a more politically activist and resolutely ethnicized project such as the Mazatec church, the song contest appears humble in its demands. At the same time, the popular success that the song contest has achieved remains a distant dream for proponents of the Mazatec church. Why has the Mazatec church failed to achieve popular appeal while the song contest has thrived? It appears that the church went too far in bucking not only the hegemonic discourses issuing from regional and national institutions, but also their echoes in the speech of local people. In throwing off the external yoke so radically and completely, Heriberto and his group lost their internal audience. In contrast, the song contest is very popular locally partly because at a higher level, it reinforces some of the very discourses it aspires to subvert. In other words, it does what folklore often does: presents an alternative message, but in a realm that is circumscribed, defined, and approved by hegemonic powers and discourses. The participants in the contest thereby implicitly accept the limits of its reach while exercising within those limits the right to dissent.

These two projects and the different fates they have met illuminate the delicate dance of resistance and the multiple constraints placed on change brought about by minority groups in pursuing their interests. It is especially revealing to take the two revival projects in Nda Xo as a symbiotic and mutually supportive pair. Such a reading is, in fact, suggested by an event that happens every year in that self-proclaimed bedrock of collective identity, the locus of so-called Mazatec-ness: the celebration of Day of the Dead. Every year in the Sierra, when Day of the Dead exercises its inclusive allure, Heriberto, Alberto, and other members of the family meet at the grave of their father (see fig. 5.3). It is the one time of the year that, like other families

FIGURE 5.3. The grave of the Prado patriarch during the family vigil held during the Day of the Dead fiesta.

throughout the Sierra, the Prados—those of both mothers, those who are Catholic and those no longer with the church—meet at the graveside of the patriarch and, if only for a moment, reconcile their differences.

This annual moment of local solidarity and family unity suggests a possible reading of the Sierra's revival projects and their disparate fates. These projects can be read, despite their points of specific conflict, as part of a broader agenda of revival—one that embraces not only the ostensibly conflicting projects local to the Sierra but also the national projects I discuss in the next chapter, which, although they have had little impact in local indigenous communities, have become a powerful national force. These national revival projects and the local ones, such as those in Nda Xo, in many ways do appear contrasting. However, if they are taken as part of a broader collective movement, they appear less like opposites and more like mirror images, reciprocal efforts rather than opposed approaches. Taking a broader view both acknowledges the constraints that individual revival projects face in bringing about social change and places them in a more holistic collaborative context that builds a new reading of collective effort out of the various, apparently opposing planes of revival. In viewing the revival projects in Nda Xo alongside each other, this analytical strategy makes visible at the local level the extent to which the two, in contradiction to explicit talk by people in town, actually reinforce each other. The differences between them not only throw into relief essential characteristics of each project that previously were less salient to participants. They also strengthen those beliefs and practices by eliciting their collective reaffirmation in the face of a contrasting model.

SEEING DOUBLE

Indigenous Authors, Readers, and the Paradox of Revival

Xiñee gui'chi',
paraa biree gui'chi',
gasti' cá lu,
gutaguna' diidxa' riree ruaanu,
diidxa' biruba ca bixhozególanu lu guie,
ni bí'ndcabe lu geela'
ra biyaacabe,
ni bitieecabe guriá lídxicabe,
ndaani' xhiu' stícabe,
ra yoo la'hui' stícabe

Why write on paper?
Where was paper born,
that it was born white
and imprisons our words:
those our ancestors carved among flowers,
those they sang in the night
as they danced,
those they used to adorn their houses,
the inside of their temples,
their royal palaces?

—Victor de la Cruz, Zapotec poet and indigenous intellectual, from
the poem "Tu laanu, tu lanu," ("Who are we? What is our name?")
in *La flor de la palabra*

The poem excerpted in the epigraph, "Tu laanu, tu lanu" ("Who Are We? What Is Our Name?"), is from a widely anthologized work by Victor de la Cruz, one of Mexico's most prominent indigenous writers.[1] While his history is unique in many ways, it is also representative of the indigenous intellectuals who drive "the continent-wide rise in . . . literatures in the indigenous languages of Latin America" (Franco 2005: 455). One practice above all unifies them: they publish their work in bilingual editions with the indigenous-language version facing the Spanish-language version. There are departures from this norm, in which texts appear in indigenous languages only: Heriberto Prado Pereda's recent work as part of the Mazatec Indigenous Church, for example, or the set of three Zapotec-language poems that conclude a thirty-poem volume by the Zapotec poet Javier Castellanos (1999 [1986]). But these exceptions are rare, and the convention of bilingual publication is so thoroughly established that publishing monolingual indigenous-language texts is politically charged, a gesture that makes a statement. The vast majority of modern literary works in indigenous languages appear in editions in which the indigenous-language version—the "original" or "true" text—is presented on the left, and the Spanish version—the "translation"—appears on the right.[2]

Thus, the very nature of this literature anticipates a double audience. How readers of indigenous literature *literally* read such texts—beginning with the basics of whether they examine one version or the other, or both—aligns with other tendencies and assumptions. While indigenous writers are at least ostensibly always addressing two (or more) audiences simultaneously, they are also required to "see" double, as well: to pay attention to the different assumptions that go along with writing for different audiences. The ability of a given author to sustain such double vision has implications for the impact and influence authors can have.

The doubleness of these texts also has implications for readers. Most indigenous readers encounter texts written in their native languages in bilingual form, with the two versions on facing pages. Like authors, readers of indigenous texts participate in a peculiar form of double vision: they use two languages at once, or they treat one as largely irrelevant. In the latter case, the text in the indigenous language becomes an emblem representing something about the author's identity, thus framing the work in certain ways, but they do not interact with it beyond reading it as a symbol. Readers of indigenous-language texts also engage in a more pervasive kind of double reading, however, as the bilingual nature of the text is linked, in ways that shift for different types of readers, to different discourses about indigenous identity, national belonging, modernity, and tradition.

What, then, are indigenous-language texts? What are the implications of developing a bilingual literature based on "double texts" and, perhaps, a deeper level of double orientation? Local context is obviously critical to the meaning people make of texts. The Sierra has witnessed at least two cases that demonstrate this: largely unsuccessful attempts by the Summer Institute of Linguistics (SIL) in the mid-twentieth century to promote certain kinds of indigenous language texts (Gudschinsky 1951–52; Pike 1960; Pike and Cowan 1959), and the differential responses by people in the Sierra to the ideas about texts that undergird the Sierra's revival projects. Because indigenous-language literature is explicitly tied to notions of indigeneity, similar perils attend assumptions about how indigenous identity and community are conceived.

The differences among the revival projects in Nda Xo mirror differences among revival projects viewed in the national context. The different approaches that Heriberto Prado Pereda and Alberto Prado Pineda take toward indigenous revival are reflected in the differences among strategies and projects adopted by indigenous intellectuals across the nation—differences that, as in Nda Xo, ultimately are symbiotic. Here, too, the problematic assumptions on which identity politics are based intersect with views of authenticity, with notions of insider and outsider. However, although Heriberto and Alberto are authors with quite different ideas and agendas about indigenous belonging and linguistic rights, when seen from a national perspective, they are more alike than not. The differences between them pale in comparison with the disparity between the kind of locally oriented intellectuals they represent and intellectuals such as Victor de la Cruz and Juan Gregorio Regino, who are more intimately involved in national cultural politics.

This chapter locates the Sierra's two revival movements in national context. In so doing, it sets the stage for the conclusion, in which I consider how indigenous authors' competing audiences produce different kinds of indigenous authors who are collectively transforming Mexico's cultural politics. In this chapter, I focus first on indigenous authors who are well known in Mexico and, to some extent, abroad. These authors and their work—primarily poems and short prose in indigenous languages, as well as essays in Spanish—have had a substantial impact on national discussions about indigenous languages and the people who speak them. The literary movements driven by these authors have an explicit political goal linked to an implicit aesthetic one: raising the status of indigenous languages (and, of course, their speakers) by demonstrating their poetic richness and their ability to serve alongside majority languages as media for great works of art. However, these nationally prominent authors have been less effective than locally oriented intellectuals at stimulating grassroots interest in their work and in promoting popular indigenous-language literacy. I argue that this is largely tied to the implications and repercussions of the convention, widely followed in Mexico and elsewhere in the Americas, of publishing indigenous-language works in bilingual editions, alongside versions in the national language. Songs are the one notable exception to this convention in that they are often printed only in the indigenous language. However, indigenous Mexican authors outside the Sierra rarely use this genre, a situation that contributes to the fairly unusual status of the Sierra Mazateca as a place where revival has had significant popular appeal.

I then turn from profiling nationally known indigenous authors to a consideration of how their audiences read indigenous writers' work. I discuss why the reliance on bilingual editions turns indigenous writing, when cycled through the practical act of reading, into a double entity whose meaning is housed in neither language alone but, rather, in both languages at once as well as in the spaces between them. This leaves indigenous literature semantically open—yet also, arguably, dynamic and interactive—in ways that majority literature is not. These qualities have significant practical implications. Reading bilingual texts is inherently difficult for all but well-educated elites with specialized literary skills. The difficulty this poses for indigenous authors mirrors a higher-level structural paradox indigenous authors are forced to confront in simultaneously addressing multiple audiences—local and national, indigenous-language speaking and Spanish speaking, formally schooled and variously educated—whose expectations and needs are often mutually exclusive. I close by suggesting that this dilemma is a general one faced by various kinds of people who represent minority groups.

The Flowering Word: A Comparative Overview of Modern Indigenous-Language Literary and Literacy Movements

MODERN MEXICO: THE REVOLUTION AND ITS LEGACIES

Most modern indigenous-language literary and literacy movements date from the last two or three decades of the twentieth century.[3] Their birth is directly related to the emergence of the modern Mexican nation. The Mexican Revolution of 1910 dramatically altered national policy by making full integration of indigenous people into the nation a priority as it never had been in the past. Whatever the other effect of these changes, they furthered the demise of indigenous literature and literacy that had begun under colonialism while simultaneously setting the stage for indigenous revival.

The post-Revolutionary era of inclusion was double-edged, for it arrived through state programs that actively promoted acculturation. With the rise of the post-Revolutionary state, *indigenismo*, through *mestizaje*, became an institutionalized discourse realized through state policies. Under indigenismo, Indians' distinctive cultural inheritances were acknowledged but only as the target of mestizaje, or "mestizification," through which Indians would shed the distinct markers of indigeneity and thereby become citizens who participated fully in national life. The use of indigenous languages was an especially salient ethnic marker and hence particularly vulnerable to policies that promoted assimilation, such as the expansion of the national school system into rural and indigenous areas under the bilingual school program of the Instituto Nacional Indigenista (INI). Such schools are officially bilingual—in theory, children are taught in Spanish and the indigenous language until fifth grade, at which point they are "mainstreamed" into Spanish-only instruction. In practice, though, they often operate entirely in Spanish (an issue I return to later). The increased presence of schools in indigenous communities had a negative effect on the use of indigenous languages that began with outright language loss. The school system also actively promoted ideologies and practices that privileged Spanish-language competency. Indigenous parents—themselves nominally bilingual, thanks to the national school system—increasingly were able to socialize their children entirely in Spanish. Thus they began to participate in processes of language shift that are present today in nearly every indigenous community in Mexico. Formal schooling also involved dense interaction with written texts—*Spanish-language* texts, for the most part, that coupled reading and writing to the Spanish language, and hence to mestizaje and assimilation. This conferred on written texts an inherently ambivalent status for indigenous peoples that persists, in different form, into the present. De la Cruz's poem in the epigraph presents the decision to "write on paper" as precisely such a reminder of this ambivalence.

These threats to the vitality of indigenous languages, coupled with the emergence in the late twentieth century of multiculturalism and indigenous-rights movements, laid the groundwork for indigenous-language literary and literacy projects to emerge. Ironically, the people who would wield such a weapon were equipped to do so as a direct result of the expansion of the national school system, which played such an instrumental role in creating the very trends that indigenous intellectuals oppose. The educated, literate, bilingual women and men who lead modern revival movements are among the first generation of indigenous students to have completed their education in the INI's bilingual schools. Most of them, having been "mainstreamed" in elementary school, went on to study further in Spanish-only schools, either in their own communities or, more commonly, in neighboring towns or cities. Secondary schools in rural areas are mostly recent. In Nda Xo, for example, the secondary schools date from the past ten years, and only a couple of communities have them. In addition, they are *telesecundarias* (televised secondary schools), which feature taped instructional sessions in Spanish broadcast nationally from Mexico City. Aside from being an educational disaster—"a Band-Aid that won't even stay on," as one disgruntled parent once told me—such schools have had the paradoxical effect of promoting the nationalization of rural areas while also fostering rural insularity. Young people now no longer leave their communities for schooling, as they once did, and coming from telesecundarias, they are less qualified for work or further education outside their communities. Whether students attend schools of this sort or leave their communities for schooling in cities, their exposure to national (and international) discourses and textual practices, as much as fluency and literacy in Spanish itself, has played a critical role in forming the people at the forefront of Mexico's indigenous revival movements.

RENAISSANCE: A COMPARATIVE SKETCH OF MEXICO'S MODERN LANGUAGE REVIVAL MOVEMENTS

It is useful to view indigenous revival in Mexico comparatively, alongside that of its southern neighbor, Guatemala. Both countries have sizable indigenous populations, but in Mexico there is no formal, institutionalized, truly national organization of indigenous writers and educators. In contrast, the Academia de las Lenguas Mayas de Guatemala (Academy of Mayan Languages of Guatemala; ALMG) is a monumental, even monolithic, presence in Guatemala's national language politics.[4] It is highly institutionalized, with participant members representing each of Guatemala's twenty-one Mayan languages. It has developed a standardized orthography across all language varieties and publishes in each a standard set of grammars, dictionaries, neologism vocabularies, pedagogical materials, and other texts, in addition to various literary works.

Perhaps the closest equivalent in Mexico is the organization Escritores en Lenguas Indígenas (Writers in Indigenous Languages; ELIAC), which is based in Mexico City.[5] The genesis of the organization was in a series of meetings of indigenous writers and activists held between 1990 and 1993 under government sponsorship.[6] Sixty-four indigenous writers from many of Mexico's indigenous groups participated in ELIAC's founding in 1993. The founders also included the renowned nonindigenous Mexican author, critic, and public intellectual Carlos Montemayor, who later became an honorary member. I return later to his involvement in modern indigenous literatures in Mexico.

The mission of ELIAC is to support literary creation, language activism, and linguistic research in Mexico's indigenous languages. Originally, the organization functioned largely as a resource for its sixty-odd members, disproportionately from the indigenous groups closest to the capital. Aside from those who hold one of the organization's rotating official positions, none of ELIAC's members receive direct financial support. As an *asociación civil* (roughly equivalent to a nonprofit organization in the United States), ELIAC has a chronic need to raise funds, which come from federal and private sources, both domestic and international. This alone makes ELIAC quite different from the ALMG, which is sponsored by the Guatemalan government (Warren 1998: xii). Today, ELIAC houses a library and bookstore of indigenous-language texts (particularly those written by its member authors), offers translation services and language instruction in some indigenous languages, and hosts literary and other cultural events pertaining to indigenous-language writing. Although ELIAC still has members from only about a half of Mexico's states (fourteen out of thirty-one) and a third of its officially recognized indigenous groups (twenty-three out of sixty-two), its membership is now more representative. While it still lacks the truly national character of Guatemala's academy, ELIAC and its members have achieved steady media recognition within Mexico and have had a substantial impact on national discourses about the present and future of the country's indigenous languages. However, although some members are involved in the issue, for the most part ELIAC has not been directly involved in indigenous-language literacy.

Aside from the relative weakness of Guatemala's central government compared with Mexico's, two other differences stand in the way of a similar level of institutionalization in Mexico. One is the sheer size (and population) difference: the entire country of Guatemala is only slightly larger than Oaxaca State. More important, Guatemala is far less diverse linguistically than Mexico. It has far fewer total variants, and nearly all of its indigenous languages are Mayan and thus share many basic characteristics. Mexico, on the other hand, has languages from at least eight distinct groupings, in addition to several linguistic isolates. As a result, indigenous-language literary and literacy projects in Mexico have strong local and regional characteristics. The uniformity across such projects nationally stems from the fact that the individuals who lead them have strikingly similar backgrounds and often participate in regional and national networks through a variety of organizations and more informal contacts.

Most modern indigenous literary movements in Mexico date from the late 1970s and early 1980s. Around that time, the Pan-Indian Movement emerged, which, alongside other international indigenous-rights movements, heavily influenced Mexico, a country with one of the largest indigenous populations in the Western Hemisphere. On the domestic front, assimilationist models of indigenismo were coming under attack. Left-leaning intellectuals were espousing new models of nationhood in which indigenous peoples would participate directly in formulating policies that affected them. The SIL, which more than any other entity had influenced the fate of Mexico's indigenous-language speakers, had been effectively evicted from the country, and the new generation of anthropologists and other scholars who headed organizations such as the INI aimed to break from the "imperialist" tendencies of the SIL and the old indigenista establishment. The following passage, written by Carlos Montemayor, one of Mexico's leading figures to champion indigenous literatures, indicates the significance of this cultural shift; it also suggests the political ethos of Mexican intellectuals who have sought to open the nation to distinctly indigenous perspectives:[7]

> The resurgence of Indigenous intellectuals and of writing in Indigenous languages represents one of the most profoundly important cultural events in Mexico at the end of the twentieth century. . . . These writers may be said to represent a dual process: a national one, corresponding to ethnic development and empowerment; and a personal one, consisting of their commitment to their bloody histories of oppression, to their individual cultures, and to their own languages that describe our territory in a fresher and more natural way . . .
>
> During the last five hundred years, non-Indigenous national and foreign researchers have defined Indigenous groups and explained what they think, how they behave, and in what they believe. With these new writers we have the possibility for the first time of discovering, through the Indigenous groups' own representatives, the natural, intimate, and profound face of a Mexico that is still unknown to us. (Montemayor and Frischmann 2004: 1:14)

In the 1970s and 1980s, many regional organizations emerged, aimed at securing indigenous rights and demanding that indigenous people be given larger influence over national affairs. The indigenous intellectuals and activists who led these organizations were not only writers. Many were bilingual schoolteachers, members of Mexico's powerful teachers' union. In indigenous areas such as Oaxaca, teachers who work in the bilingual school program completed their early education in the INI's schools for indigenous children. Ironically, that very educational system, which under indigenista policies had aimed so aggressively to assimilate Mexico's indigenous peoples, produced the indigenous individuals who used their education and status in the educational system to force changes in indigenous language and educational policy.[8]

Another group of indigenous intellectuals has had a significant impact on national discourses and policies about indigenous peoples and their languages: ethnolinguists. Salomón Nahmad, who in 1982 became the general director of the INI after holding various other important regional and national positions, was a leading figure in pushing indigenous policy in this new "postindigenista" direction. He would later write, "Starting in 1976, we looked for ways to open new spaces to the indigenous people, not only within bilingual education as schoolteachers, but rather through grants and opportunities to study in universities, above all in order to raise their participation in the destiny of their own people" (Nahmad Sittón 1990: 19). The first national program through which many of these ethnolinguists were trained was called the Professional Training Program for Ethnolinguists. It began in 1979—the same year the SIL's contract was revoked—under the joint initiative of the INI (under Nahmad's leadership) and Centro de Investigaciones y Estudios Superiores en Antropología Social (Center for Research and Advanced Study in Social Anthropology; CIESAS) (under the leadership of Guillermo Bonfil Batalla). Two generations (or cohorts) of ethnolinguists were produced under this program, the first based in Pátzcuaro (1979–82) and the second in Tlaxcala (1983–86). The program's graduates went on to influence another generation of young indigenous men and women through the training programs they initiated, such as CIESAS's Maestría en Lingüística Indoamericana, founded in 1990, and individual language-specific academies.

One of these academies is Ve'e Tu'un Savi (Academy of the Mixtec Language; lit., House of the Voices of the Rain). In an introduction to a volume of collected essays by the Mixtec writers who founded Ve'e Tu'un Savi, Angeles Romero writes about the history out of which Mixtec linguists and, through them, the modern Mixtec writing movement has emerged. It is a context very similar to the one encountered by Mazatec writers and intellectuals, as well as by indigenous leaders from other indigenous groups. The difficult work of developing alphabetic writing in Mixtec, she writes, began at the end of the 1970s when Bonfil, Nahmad, and others were intimately involved in promoting new, antiassimilationist models of development through which indigenous groups would actively shape their own development.[9] This led to the founding of professionalization programs aimed at training young indigenous people to become promoters of regional indigenous activist work in their regions:

> The work accomplished in support of writing in Mixtec and other Amerindian languages, in the Academy of the Mixtec Language [and similar organizations] . . . can be considered fruit of that experience, because the founders of these academies are ethnolinguists, and their training bequeathed the ideal of forming new generations who have respect for cultural diversity. The eagerness of Mixtecs and other indigenous people of Mexico and Latin America to write their languages is also an important part of the fight for their rights. It has overtaken the simple concern for infrastructural works in their communities and claims the right to their culture and forms of life. (Romero Frizzi 2003a: ix–x)

Institutions in Oaxaca took the lead in carrying on the work begun by the initial ethnolinguistics program. The Oaxaca branch of CIESAS, which in the late 1980s and early 1990s was headed by Nahmad, was particularly instrumental. Through collaboration with other government agencies and with the University of Florida, Gainesville (especially through the involvement of H. Russell Bernard, a professor of cultural anthropology there), CIESAS-Oaxaca began a new project aimed at furthering the model of *auto-investigación* and self-determination by indigenous intellectuals.[10] The project had two agendas: the creation of the Centros de Investigación de las Culturas Indígenas (Research Centers for Indigenous Cultures) and the creation of the Talleres de Escritura de las Lenguas Indígenas (Workshops for Indigenous Language Writing).[11] The centers were located within indigenous areas; were directed and run by indigenous intellectuals, particularly by ethnolinguists trained by the CIESAS program; and were aimed at cultural research, with an emphasis on revitalizing the language, recovering oral tradition, and supporting indigenous artists and writers. The workshops were primarily directed at—and later, staffed by—bilingual schoolteachers. The workshops aimed to use computers to produce indigenous-language texts as a spur to literacy so that indigenous people (especially children) who were newly literate in their languages would have texts to read (Bernard 1996).

This, then, is the milieu from which modern indigenous-language writers have emerged. Although they come from different parts of the country and a variety of indigenous groups, they share a striking number of characteristics. Indigenous writers and educators are overwhelmingly male. They tend to be from indigenous communities that for various reasons (size, geographical location, trade history) are relatively well connected to urban centers that are hubs of cultural activities. Although they speak an indigenous language as a first language, they are fluent in Spanish, if not truly bilingual. They are for the most part highly educated, having finished the equivalent of a college degree (and sometimes higher). In addition, most have trained for careers that place some importance on fluency, though rarely literacy, in an indigenous language. Many indigenous writers, particularly those with ethnolinguistic training, work as bilingual specialists in government offices. There they have some influence on national educational and cultural programs, but rarely in any meaningful way on the promotion of indigenous-language literacy. While such agencies promote linguistic and cultural diversity, they rarely have demonstrated sustained commitment to indigenous-language literacy.

The work that is done in that arena is left to the nation's bilingual schools. Indeed, the vast majority of indigenous authors work, or once worked, as bilingual schoolteachers. They have gone through the national training program that was previously administered by the INI and now, following its replacement, by the Comisión Nacional para el Desarrollo de los Pueblos Indígenas (CDI), which operates in conjunction with the Secretaría de Educación Pública (Secretariat for Public Education; SEP), Mexico's national agency for public education. The training for bilingual schoolteachers prepares them to teach in the country's bilingual elementary schools, a prerequisite of which is fluency in at least one indigenous language. In theory, this means fluency in the language spoken where one will teach. The practical reality, however, is often quite different, especially in places with great linguistic diversity. In Oaxaca, this leads to the absurdly common situation that a bilingual schoolteacher will be assigned to a community that speaks an indigenous language he or she does not.

The Sierra Mazateca, however, seems to be anomalous in this regard: upward of 90 percent of its bilingual schoolteachers speak Mazatec as a first language. This exception means that, to find work as a teacher in the Sierra, one must have at least basic Mazatec skills. The irony is that the children of many schoolteachers, precisely because their parents are relatively well educated and place importance on Spanish fluency, are among those who are most likely to be on the leading edge of language shift. If they learn Mazatec at all, they will do so in early adulthood. In the Sierra, many such children hope to follow in their parents' careers—the profession offers a rare opportunity for steady skilled work in rural communities. Although it is technically prohibited, as is the case in much of Mexico, teachers in the Sierra routinely pass their posts on to their children when they retire. Yet in the Sierra, teachers' children can sometimes be disqualified from taking these positions because they do not speak Mazatec. In one case I know of personally, a young woman in Nda Xo who wanted to take over her mother's position but spoke no Mazatec was sent off to "the rancho" where the compadres she lived with were told to speak to her only in Mazatec.

There is another reason, though, that children of bilingual schoolteachers often do not speak Mazatec well (or at all): many bilingual schoolteachers in the Sierra view indigenous-language instruction as a tool rather than an end, or even as an evil to be engaged in only when one cannot avoid it. This attitude is widespread among bilingual schoolteachers, at least in Oaxaca. As will become clear later in the chapter, when I examine local resistance to Mazatec literacy, local schoolteachers often strongly oppose indigenous-language literacy. Bilingual schoolteachers who become writers in and promoters of indigenous languages are in the minority, meeting some of their greatest criticism from fellow teachers. Ironically, and despite explicit rhetoric to the contrary, the bilingual school system often does not promote indigenous-language literacy.

However, bilingual schoolteachers and other indigenous intellectuals who promote indigenous literatures and literacy are quite unified in their aims. Their similar life trajectories and participation in the same regional and national organizations bring them into contact with one another and with national and international discourses about language politics and indigenous rights. For these reasons, Mexico's language-revival projects have a measure of national cohesiveness. Despite variations, the leaders of indigenous revival movements have comparable political agendas and use markedly similar arguments to forward them, including the strategic use of the past. Their most general aims are to reverse the erosion of indigenous-language use that resulted from the imposition of Spanish and thereby push back against five hundred years of cultural, linguistic, and political oppression.

WRITING FROM "DEEP MEXICO":
INDIGENOUS WRITERS AND ETHNIC REVIVAL

Indigenous writers are united not only by common backgrounds and aims but also the problems they face. First and foremost is the perennial problem of funding: how to make a living in a way that also provides the time, energy, and resources to write or to promote indigenous-language literacy. Montemayor writes, "The development of these Indigenous writers and the individual nature of their texts vary widely throughout the country" (Montemayor and Frischmann 2004: 1:4–5). I would argue, however, that underneath the fairly superficial differences in their histories and work, they actually have much in common, above all because relatively few professions are available to indigenous intellectuals. They occupy similar positions in the available institutional infrastructure. The revival work carried out by ethnolinguists and bilingual schoolteachers is heavily influenced by state agencies and non-indigenous Mexican intellectuals. Because there are no indigenous writers or intellectuals who have access to trust funds or "family money" (none that I know of, anyway), their work is tied to the vicissitudes of "soft money," or external and often fleeting funding.[12] The training that indigenous writers receive generally stems from government institutions and programs, many of which (e.g., CIESAS's initial ethnolinguistics project) are funded for circumscribed periods. Indigenous writers and educators who are leading figures in their respective languages usually have received one (sometimes more) of the national grants offered annually for indigenous writers. In addition, nongovernment entities often fund the work of indigenous writers. Montemayor discusses some of these different vectors of institutional and funding support:

> The support of retired military personnel and Juchitec artists was an integral part of the growth of Zapotec literature in the Isthmus; the Harvard University project directed by Evon Z. Vogt, the persistence and goodwill of Robert Laughlin, and the consulting of North American theatre director Ralph Lee were essential in the evolution of the Tzeltal and Tzotzil literature of Chiapas; the University of Florida at Gainesville and Professor H. Russell Bernard provided support to Jesús Salinas Pedraza and his wife, Josefa Leonarda González Ventura; and in the case of Yucatán, my own participation facilitated the formation of an important group of writers. To these four evolutionary processes we must add one more, which predated all the rest: the one promoted by Miguel León-Portilla from the National Autonomous University of Mexico, which has been of importance for the pre-Hispanic, colonial, and contemporary history of literature in the Nahuatl language.

I have worked with Mayas from Yucatán and Campeche; with Tzotzil and Tzeltal groups from Chiapas; with Zapotec poets from the Isthmus of Tehuantepec; with Zapotecs, Mixes, and Chinantecs from the Sierra de

Oaxaca; with Mixtecs in Guerrero and Purepechas in Michoacán. I have dealt personally with other writers from the Huasteca regions and from the Sierra Tarahumara and collaborated in the organization of the First and Second National Congress of Writers in Indigenous Languages, as well as in the creation of the Association of Indigenous-Language Writers. (Montemayor and Frischmann 2004: 1:4)

This passage is telling in several ways. The first is the most obvious: with the possible exception of the genesis of Zapotec writers in the isthmus, the groups of writers Montemayor mentions have been heavily supported and influenced by nonindigenous scholars and intellectuals. Furthermore, this support is fundamentally material: "outsiders" are essential to the process of securing funding by applying for grants and soliciting donations, not only in Mexico, but also in the United States and elsewhere.

There are other concerns, though, lurking in the shadows of Montemayor's statement. Although this requires reading between the lines, the passage hints at an issue with deeper implications: the matter of *where* the transactions between indigenous writers and their supporters take place. The literary movements Montemayor describes are all based in urban centers, such as Mexico City, San Cristóbal de las Casas, Mérida, Calkini, Oaxaca City, and Juchitán. Most indigenous intellectuals live and work in regional urban cities rather than in the predominantly rural communities from which they originally come, primarily because work opportunities are greater in urban centers than in pueblos. In this they are not unusual, of course. Mexicans across the country migrate to urban centers and the United States in search of work that is not available in rural communities. But because indigenous writers tend overwhelmingly to live in urban centers, taking them away from daily contact with their communities (and hence, with indigenous-language speakers), they are also more likely to be plugged into the concerns and social networks of those urban environments.[13] In a codetermining process, indigenous writers who live in cities are more likely to be oriented toward regional and national networks of indigenous intellectuals and their supporters, while indigenous writers who live in cities are more likely to be recruited to participate in such networks.

The importance of these networks among indigenous writers and their supporters is another issue that hovers in the margins of Montemayor's passage. Throughout it, and throughout much of his other work, Montemayor stresses his personal connections to the writers he works with and the closeness of his collaboration with them. *Encuentros en Oaxaca, México* (1998) is, essentially, a book-long testament to his relationships with indigenous writers from Oaxaca State.[14] Such an emphasis is, of course, part of his own credentialing process; inasmuch as he functions as a kind of "literary ethnographer," an interpreter and intermediary, the close yet professional nature of his relationship with these authors is critical to the authority on which his claims rest—such as, in the case of anthologies, his decision to include particular writers and works but not others. From the perspective of indigenous authors, this signals that relationships with Montemayor and other patrons of indigenous writing are critical to success—ranging from access to funding to publication opportunities to other benefits that accrue from being allied with powerful intellectuals and scholars. As in all relationships, those that indigenous authors build with their supporters come with strings attached.

One such string on which almost all relationships between indigenous intellectuals and their promoters and collaborators depend is use of the Spanish language. Most nonindigenous supporters of indigenous-language literature speak one indigenous language, at the most, and often do not do even that. In addition, the centers where most indigenous writers are based are mestizo-dominated towns and cities where life takes place in Spanish (again with the notable exception of Juchitán). The difficulties caused by relying so heavily on Spanish are obvious, at the least on a symbolic level: Spanish has been the language of oppression, of acculturation, of discrimination, of disempowerment—in short, the language of empire. It is the very mechanism through which indigenous people have long been excluded from arenas of power and from the nation.

But there is a deeper irony behind the utterly pervasive use that indigenous intellectuals make of the Spanish language. Spanish is also, for indigenous people, a lingua franca: relationships *among* indigenous intellectuals, most of which cross ethnic and, hence, linguistic boundaries, also require Spanish. For practical reasons, relationships among indigenous intellectuals are often cross-ethnic: most indigenous groups have, at most, a handful of individuals involved in indigenous writing and activism. There are ideological reasons, as well. The promotion of indigenous writing is often tied to a broader agenda of multicultural inclusion and the celebration of diversity. On the most pedestrian level, programs and organizations that support indigenous writers stress the need for representatives from as many different indigenous groups as possible. When such individuals communicate with each other, they do so in Spanish; in a place such as Oaxaca, with high levels of linguistic variation, even members of the same indigenous group—for example, Mazatec intellectuals from the highlands and lowlands—would use

Spanish, as well. Thus, ironically, the characteristic that all indigenous authors share—that their first language (at least, officially) is an indigenous language—means that the only language they share is Spanish, the very language against whose hegemony their work is directed.

This brings us back to the tendency for indigenous-language writing to appear in bilingual editions. Here is another facet of the important role Spanish plays in the work of indigenous writers. The writers must be proficient in Spanish for all of the structural and institutional reasons I have mentioned; further, writing in Spanish is intimately involved in the very work they produce. Spanish versions take up half of the work in a bilingual edition, requiring authors to give careful thought to how their language, ideas, and images are presented in Spanish. Furthermore, some of the most engaged readers of their work, and almost all of the most powerful members of their audiences, speak Spanish as a first language and hence will be much better equipped to form opinions about the Spanish version. Indigenous authors are thus frequently, and paradoxically, in the position of paying greater attention to the Spanish version than to the indigenous-language version. In addition, some of the most visible and public work they do—essays, talks, lectures, editorials, interviews—will generally be done entirely in Spanish.[15]

These realities are indexed in the following commentary Montemayor offers of his work with indigenous writers:

> In regard to the Spanish texts, I have left almost intact the versions of [several authors]. . . . In the other cases I have participated in varying degrees and circumstances in the editing of the material, whether in the actual writing in the Indigenous languages or in the first or final versions in Spanish. During the editing stage of the publication of the *Colección Letras Mayas Contemporáneas*, I translated or revised the final versions of translations for almost all the works. For the present book I have newly revised the texts of the chosen works both in their original languages and in their translations to Spanish to such a degree that readers familiar with both books will find numerous changes. (Montemayor and Frischmann 2004: 1:6–7)

I rely here on Montemayor's discussion because he has been such an important figure in promoting indigenous authors. In addition, this unusually specific account of how he works with indigenous authors is representative of his own approach as well as those of others doing similar work. The passage reflects issues discussed earlier: the centrality of the Spanish language and the extent to which the Spanish translation becomes the focus of editorial efforts. In the same essay, Montemayor mentions that for one of Castellanos's texts, the author "did not accept my revisions willingly, as he considered the final version 'too Spanish'" (Montemayor and Frischmann 2004: 1:7). That quote does more than foreground the power discrepancy between Castellanos and Montemayor that, while indeed a reality, is similar to the relationship that many authors, indigenous and not, have to their editors or translators. It also indicates the ambivalent position indigenous authors inhabit when they engage in the enterprise itself.

Whatever poetic assumptions might be imported alongside these other assumptions are impossible for me to judge, being neither a native speaker of an indigenous Mexican language nor knowledgeable about the vast majority of those languages. Discursive biases are clearly involved, however, in the promotion of indigenous writing. One particularly salient discursive convention involves emphasizing the links between indigenous authors and the past. As I showed in earlier chapters, Miguel León-Portilla routinely emphasizes the continuity between contemporary writers and Mesoamerica's ancient "high civilizations."[16] For him, this is a fundamentally ennobling gesture that allows an indigenous writer to be a poet rather than a mere animator of folkloric scraps. But such attitudes go far beyond León-Portilla. As Donald Frischmann writes, he has been "guided by the desire to inspire other people, Indigenous and non-Indigenous, to pay due attention, both critical and human, to the contemporary voices that address us from the depths of time" (Montemayor and Frischmann 2004: 1:27). Montemayor adds a novel twist to the paradigm, elevating modern indigenous writers by linking them not to the ancient past of the New World but to the ancient peoples of the Old World: "I have stated on other occasions that the Indigenous peoples of Mexico still conserve an ancient knowledge which was shared by the Greeks and Romans of old: the knowledge that the world is not something inert or inanimate but a living being. Because of this, their relationship to the earth, the mountains, and the rivers is different" (Montemayor and Frischmann 2005: 2:5). The following comment by de la Cruz is but one example that demonstrates how indigenous authors might find such views confining. The comment—made during a meeting of Mazatec intellectuals who aimed to establish a Mazatec research center—directly contradicts the sentiments expressed by León-Portilla and Montemayor:

> All cultures change; if they don't, they don't survive. Those that survive will be those that adapt. Today it is much cheaper to use objects made of plastic rather than clay. Moreover, it is not only a matter of recovering but rather

of creating anew with new technologies and of developing the capacity for creativity. I think this is more important than cultural restoration. You can't close your eyes to the environment around you. It is important to take into account that everything changes, that everything is in the process of being transformed. (de la Cruz, quoted in Dalton 1990: 83)

I do not wish to call into question the history of oppression and the widespread prejudice against indigenous languages—the "far-reaching . . . artistic discrediting of these languages" (Montemayor and Frischmann 2004: 1:1)—that scholars such as Montemayor and León-Portilla are critiquing. They champion and valorize indigenous writers and their languages precisely because ideas about their inferior status stubbornly survive. Despite the undeniable fact that indigenous difference is embraced far more fully than it once was, nation-states and other powerful entities continue to attack cultural difference, albeit through different means. León-Portilla and Montemayor—along with others, such as Russell Bernard and Robert Laughlin, who have been heavily involved with particular indigenous writers—are renowned scholars and intellectuals who have done a great deal to promote the work of indigenous writers, to get their work published, and to allow them to have lives as writers and indigenous intellectuals.[17] I also do not mean to suggest that indigenous writers are entirely beholden to such figures or that their careers as prominent indigenous authors are due primarily to their contacts with powerful people and organizations. Rather, my point is that the system in which these authors work is riddled with invisible biases. Discursive paradigms that cast indigenous intellectuals in certain ways—as living bearers of the grand past, for example—are profoundly limiting, even as they license particular individuals to participate. Despite their immense goodwill, people who have worked, often thanklessly and at personal cost, in the service of promoting indigenous-language authors have been unable to change certain sociological realities that place serious limits on the opportunities available to indigenous writers.

In other words, indigenous writers are essentially called on to become representatives of "deep Mexico." *México profundo*, by the Mexican anthropologist Guillermo Bonfil Batalla—who, as mentioned earlier, has played an instrumental role in "opening a national space" for indigenous intellectuals—has profoundly shaped discourses in Mexico about indigenous identity and the place of indigenous people in the nation. The book posits a tension in Mexican culture between a "deep" or authentic Mexico, "a subordinated civilization that stems from the millenarian agrarian culture of Mesoamerica" (Lomnitz 2001: 263), and an "artificial" Mexico, Western and capitalist, created by the marginalizing engines of globalization and multinational capital. Many scholars have criticized this model—not least, Claudio Lomnitz, who points out that "there is a sense in which Bonfil's civilizational approach is merely a refashioned inversion of the modernist trope of tradition versus modernity" and that "'deep' and 'artificial' are images that re-create an obsolete and unpromising form of nationalism, while at the same time they are at least successful in indicating and denouncing profound rifts in Mexican society" (Lomnitz 2001: 264). Nevertheless, as Lomnitz himself recognizes, the image of a deep Mexico continues to hold immense allure, not least to indigenous intellectuals and their supporters; this is represented, for example, in Heriberto's dedication to "those writers who promote the literature of *México profundo*" (Prado Pereda 1997: ii). Bonfil was not only expressing an interpretation of fissures in Mexican nationalism; he was also voicing a solution to them. His immensely popular book became the mouthpiece for a new vision of Mexican nationalism seeking to overturn the assimilationist indigenismo of old and replace it with activist celebration of that Mexico of indígenas and campesinos submerged by the great wave of neoliberal restructuring.

Bonfil's deep Mexico characterizes indigenous people as members of a vast, oppressed underclass whose character is fundamentally opposed to Western, capitalist civilization. This has, indeed, become the dominant paradigm under which identity politics in Mexico operates, casting indigenous people in the role of living bearers of the "millenarian agrarian culture of Mesoamerica" (Lomnitz 2001: 263). This view also applies to indigenous authors and intellectuals, whose authority turns in part on their purported representativeness with respect to other members of the community. Of course, for authors and other artists, competing forces are pushing in the opposite direction, stressing their unique, nonrepresentative talent and abilities. Nevertheless, presenting a persona in keeping with the paradigm of ethnic representativeness is one of the rules by which the "game" of identity politics is played. For all of the rhetoric about empowering and "giving voice" to indigenous people that has become so prevalent in Mexico, indigenous writers are *structurally* in precisely the same position Mexican indigenous leaders have been in for years—certainly since the Revolution. They are subject to the whims of a patronage system that ties their power to certain kinds of alliances and the presentation of certain kinds of personae.

The paradoxical position this system forces on indigenous authors could be demonstrated by any number of cases. I discuss three cases from Oaxaca here that, because they pertain to different periods in the recent past, illustrate the history that has shaped indigenous intellectuals working in the present. The first concerns the Centro Editorial de Literatura Indígena, Asociación Civil (Center for Native Language Publishing; CELIAC), an organization in Oaxaca City; the second is the Centro Mazateco de Investigaciones (Mazatec Research Center); and the third is Uken Ke Uken, Yalálag's cultural center. They illustrate the general trends discussed earlier, such as the importance of urban settings, Spanish competence, and alliance with powerful patrons. Many of the people participating in these cases buy heavily into the notion of a "deep Mexico," promoting indigenous writers precisely because doing so represents the chance to undo Mexico's domination of indigenous people as the "real" nation.

The most influential Workshop for Indigenous Language Writing produced under the auspices of CIESAS-Oaxaca came to be called CELIAC. Located in Oaxaca City, CELIAC has as its charter "to promote the preservation of native languages and cultures in Mexico through the publishing of books in those languages" (Bernard 1996). The people directly involved in the center's operations are mostly bilingual schoolteachers and native indigenous-language speakers from various parts of Oaxaca and Mexico. The organization dates from 1987, and until 1993, it was supported by the government and attached to CIESAS-Oaxaca. In 1993, CELIAC became an independent nonprofit organization and began to be funded by the University of Florida, which continues to support its activities. Not coincidentally, Russell Bernard, a professor at the University of Florida, has been heavily involved in CELIAC from its founding; part of his university website is dedicated to CELIAC, where he points out the precarious financial situation of the organization and calls on readers to support it.[18]

The financial situation is more insecure for organizations not located in large urban centers. This has been the case with the Mazatec Research Center, one of the indigenous research centers CIESAS-Oaxaca set up in the late 1980s. Four Mazatec intellectuals participated, two from the highlands and two from the lowlands; all studied in Tlaxcala in the second cohort of indigenous people trained in CIESAS's ethnolinguistics program. I have already introduced two of them: Florencio Carrera González and Juan Gregorio Regino (1992, 1999, 2001). The others were Juan Casimiro Nava, a Huauteco author who regularly serves as a judge for Nda Xo's Day of the Dead Song Contest (Casimiro Nava and García 1992; Toledo 2006), and Vicente Aguilar Mata, who comes from Soyaltepec in the lowlands. The ethnolinguistics program aimed for its graduates to become, in essence, "ethnic missionaries" who would return to their communities to promote ethnic self-knowledge and the valorization of indigenous values and practices tied to indigenous languages. Founding the center was seen as the next step toward accomplishing that goal in the Mazatec region. In 1989–90, the four Mazatec intellectuals held several meetings—in Spanish—with the assistance of various researchers from CIESAS, particularly Nahmad and the prominent Mexican researcher Margarita Dalton.[19] Also present for at least one of these meetings were other Oaxacan indigenous intellectuals, including de la Cruz; a couple of Chinantec bilingual schoolteachers; and various Mazatec bilingual schoolteachers, including Apolonio Bartolo Ronquillo, who is also a published poet (see Bartolo Ronquillo 1998). At a meeting in 1990, Jesus Salinas of CELIAC offered a workshop on using computers to produce written texts and to standardize a Mazatec alphabet. Later that year, the core participants—the four Mazatec ethnolinguists and the CIESAS researchers helping them—began the ultimately successful process of founding the center as an asociación civil.

However, the Mazatec intellectuals involved in the center also encountered problems. Obviously, the center's founding depended on external support, financial and otherwise; and doubtless, the CIESAS researchers involved in this project and related initiatives were keenly aware of the paradoxical situation posed by their involvement. As Nahmad (quoted in Dalton 1990: 80–81) said, "Anthropology should be in the service of the pueblos and not the government. What is the Mazatec project—what the Mazatec people want for their culture? We know that the project of the Mexican State was to finish off the pueblos and ethnicities and to integrate them. But you all, what do you want? You are the organic intellectuals of the Mazatec community and you should know what it is that you want, you are the experts in this area, you are the ones who are shaping the future generations of Mazatecs."

Dalton herself takes pains to point out that during the planning stages, the Mazatec intellectuals often met by themselves, without the CIESAS researchers. Certainly, it was an enormous improvement over earlier eras that the Mazatecs involved made all of the decisions about the center and took on responsibility for its daily operations. As discussed at one of the meetings, the politics of the INI's local presence represented but one of many cases of "neocolonialism" in which misguided policies from the past persisted in the present. At that time, the INI's regional office in Temascal had been in existence for forty years, yet it had never had a Mazatec director. Nevertheless, the difficulties of making the Mazatec Research Center self-sufficient and independent were immense and have meant that outsiders such as the CIESAS researchers continue to play a vital role in preserving the viability of such projects.

The Mazatec intellectuals involved faced not only the problem of securing funding beyond the initial funds CIESAS provided but also the related concern about where to house the center—or, actually, the *centers*, as they decided to open one office in the highlands (Huautla) and another in the lowlands (Temascal). Ultimately, both were located in formerly abandoned buildings the owners had agreed to donate, a testament to the organization's shoestring budget. In addition, those working in the center struggled with how to earn a living. As several of the participants noted, the Sierra Mazateca offered almost no related employment opportunities outside work as bilingual schoolteachers or local school administrators. Those involved ultimately petitioned the SEP for relief from regular responsibilities to work at the center. In a pattern common among Mexican indigenous intellectuals, those associated with the center were able to work for it only part time, limiting their ability to enact many of their plans, particularly the labor- and time-intensive goal of teaching and fostering indigenous-language literacy.

Finally, one of the greatest problems faced by the center's Mazatec intellectuals was local resistance to their revival efforts. Many of the center's projects were aimed at bilingual schoolteachers. In particular, the center aspired to teach schoolteachers a standardized Mazatec alphabet and encourage them to use it in promoting Mazatec literacy among their students. However, many teachers were opposed to indigenous-language literacy. In addition to ideological opposition, the teachers were motivated by skepticism about the intellectuals' motives because of their ties to outside people and organizations.[20] As Florencio Carrera (quoted in Dalton 1990, 75) said, while the center was still in the planning stages, "The problems we have had in the region since we came back [after completing the ethnolinguistics program in Tlaxcala] are jealousy and selfishness on the part of some people. Others have the impression that we have come to take something away from them. Still others think that we're not going to do anything to help our people."

A similar set of problems emerging from internal divisions stymied Uken Ke Uken, the cultural center that housed Yalálag's cultural and language workshop and communitarian radio station. Although Yalálag's intellectuals intended their cultural center to be seen as "neutral territory," many other members of the community did not see the project that way. As Juan Gregorio said during one of the meetings for the Mazatec center, "We want this work to be by Indians and for Indians" (quoted in Dalton 1990: 82). Instead, many local people in both areas—the Mazatec region and Yalálag—viewed their cultural centers with skepticism or even outright hostility, assessing them through the prism of longstanding and ongoing factionalism. Many indigenous communities are likewise deeply divided by civil disputes, posing great difficulties for indigenous intellectuals and the projects they pursue. Their status as well-educated, bilingual cosmopolitans is the very quality that implicates them in the community's internal divisions.

This certainly was true of Heriberto Prado in his attempts to use the Mazatec Indigenous Church to revitalize Mazatec language and culture. However, compared with that of other indigenous intellectuals, Heriberto's story is also atypical—and its unusual qualities are precisely what have allowed his work to have the grassroots relevance so many indigenous writers lack. An external institution supported him, too. However, he is one of the few indigenous intellectuals in Mexico whose credentials and support came through the Catholic Church rather than the government. For some of the historical reasons discussed earlier, in the Sierra Mazateca—and, perhaps, in other indigenous communities, particularly those where Catholicism remains the default religion—people rarely discuss the church as an institution of domination. Heriberto's and Alberto's alliance with an "external" entity and "outside" individuals thus did not have the disqualifying baggage attached to it that Huautla's intellectuals encountered. The nature of the work Heriberto did on behalf of the Catholic Church required his focus to be far more local than is possible for most indigenous intellectuals: he had the kind of steady "funding" most indigenous intellectuals find only in jobs located in urban centers such as Oaxaca City and Mexico City. Furthermore, his literary work and the work he did to promote it were complementary to, if not the very substance of, his pastoral duties. The popular success of his earlier projects—the promotion of Mazatec songs for the church, the Day of the Dead Song Contest, and the level of Mazatec literacy that both made possible—are directly tied to this local orientation. It allowed Heriberto to do the labor-intensive work required to teach his orthography and disseminate Mazatec texts to his own "army" of "bilingual schoolteachers"—the catechists—who then did the community-wide work that intellectuals from the Mazatec Research Center never found possible. And although Heriberto has now lost the institutional backing of the Catholic Church, his new profession—shopkeeper—allows him to maintain a resolutely local focus, as do Alberto and other songwriters from Nda Xo.

The flip side of Heriberto's local orientation, however, is that he has had little or no impact outside the Sierra—precisely the arena in which most indigenous intellectuals achieve their greatest success. In the one anthology of indigenous writing in which his work has appeared (Montemayor and Frischmann 2005: 2:124–51), he is arguably the least well known of the nearly thirty authors. Because he has not yet published with one of the prominent national presses that produce works of indigenous literature, he is one of the least published, as well. Although he has twice received grants (1992–93 and 1996–97) from the Fondo Nacional para la Cultura y las Artes (National Fund for Culture and Arts; FONCA), as have most indigenous writers, he is not a member of ELIAC and did not help found the Mazatec Research Center (though he is senior to many who did). Much of his work is unpublished, and most of his published work is available only in the Sierra. Although his low national profile is partly intentional, a product of his reticence to subject himself to the constraints attached to being a "professional Indian," his influence outside the Sierra remains limited. This means that he would be in no position, for example, to bring about serious changes in how the Catholic Church operates—even regionally and even if his current revival work garnered more local support than it has so far.

What made it possible for Heriberto and the people with whom he has worked to succeed in promoting Mazatec literacy and writing—namely, their fundamentally, even aggressively, local orientation—is precisely what other indigenous intellectuals struggle so mightily to achieve, often with little success. Indigenous writers have, indeed, had enormous impact nationally in Mexico. In addition to hundreds of books written by indigenous authors and numerous anthologies of their work, several national literary and cultural magazines—including regular inserts in national newspapers such as *La Jornada*—publish indigenous-language writing. Almost every state has one or more magazines that publish regional indigenous authors. Bilingual textbooks in indigenous languages are available throughout the country, and indigenous intellectuals now occupy powerful positions in the government agencies that oversee indigenous education and language policy. However, they have on the whole found it far more difficult to have similar success in creating local, literate publics for indigenous-language works.

This mixed legacy comes sharply into focus when we consider Heriberto's life and career as a writer alongside the life and career of Gregorio Regino, today the best-known author writing in Mazatec (see fig. 6. 1). Gregorio Regino lives in Mexico City, rather than in his hometown in the Mazateca Baja, and is a prominent member of the national literary scene, having won two FONCA grants and the Nezahualcóyotl Prize for Literature in Indigenous Languages, Mexico's highest prize for indigenous-language writing. A founding member and past president of ELIAC, Gregorio Regino currently serves as the director of intercultural development at the National Office of Popular

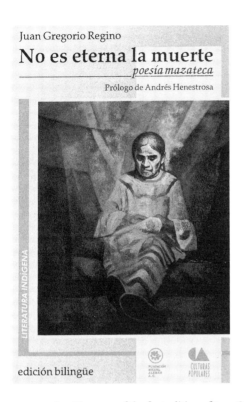

Juan Gregorio Regino

No es eterna la muerte
poesía mazateca

Prólogo de Andrés Henestrosa

LITERATURA INDÍGENA

edición bilingüe

FIGURE 6.1. The cover of the first edition of Juan Gregorio
Regino's first book of poems (1992), featuring a portrait of
María Sabina, to whom one of the volume's poems is dedicated.

and Indigenous Cultures, a division of the National Council for Culture and
Arts (CONACULTA).

In an interview about his experiences with Ines Hernández Avila, a well-
known Native North American author and scholar, Gregorio Regino says that
in his earlier career as a bilingual teacher, he

> learned to be an agent of acculturation . . . who would take Spanish to the
> community [and] displace everything Indigenous. . . . What the govern-
> ment wanted at that time was to homogenize the Mexican people, and we
> were molded that way. We were supposed to end this difference, no more
> Indigenous language. . . . But [then] I pursued a degree in ethnolinguistics
> [and] I began to see that there was a colonizer and a colonized. In a way
> what I had done in school was a reflection of this. . . . So that's what made
> me wake up and in a way stop feeling ashamed of my own [background]

but instead [I felt] more anger or impotence about all that had occurred while we'd been doing nothing, that even we ourselves were agents of the government [helping] to erase our peoples. . . .

This is when I broke with my training, because from that time to now I'm another person. Now I write in my language, I think in my language, I instill in the children and my people our identity, our culture, our language. In spite of the fact that I don't live there [in Oaxaca] and that I'm not with Indigenous people [here in Mexico City], I try, from here, to show that an Indigenous person is also capable of being in front of a computer. An indigenous person is capable of directing a national office, an institution, of writing a newspaper, of creating a book. To me that is important, that those who are not Indigenous realize what Indigenous people are capable of and that they not continue reproducing the idea that the Indigenous person is ignorant, illiterate, one who is always in a marginalized situation. (Quoted in Hernández Avila 2004: 125–27)[21]

Seeing Double: Bilingual Texts and the Practice of Reading

THE READING LESSON: THE DOUBLE VISION
OF INDIGENOUS LANGUAGE WRITING

Perhaps no "native writer" in anthropological literature has achieved quite so iconic a status as the chief of the Nambikwara from "The Writing Lesson" (Lévi-Strauss 1992 [1955]). Claude Lévi-Strauss distributes paper and pencils to the Nambikwara, who "have no written language," and watches as they imitate him. But the chief has "further ambitions":

No doubt he was the only one who had grasped the purpose of writing. So he asked me for a writing-pad. . . . [As we worked together,] if I asked for information. . . . [H]e did not supply it verbally but drew wavy lines on his paper and presented them to me, as if I could read his reply. He was half taken in by his own make-believe; each time he completed a line, he examined it anxiously as if expecting the meaning to leap from the page, and the same look of disappointment came over his face. But he never admitted this, and there was a tacit understanding between us to the effect that his unintelligible scribbling had a meaning I pretended to decipher. . . . Was he perhaps hoping to delude himself? More probably he wanted to astonish his companions, to convince them . . . he was in alliance with the white man and shared his secrets. . . . [Writing] had been borrowed as a symbol, and for a sociological rather than an intellectual purpose, while its reality remained unknown. . . . A native still living in the Stone Age had guessed that this great means towards understanding, even if he was unable to understand it, could be made to serve other purposes. (Lévi-Strauss 1992 [1955]: 296–98)

As Lévi-Strauss presents him, the chief is a deeply ambivalent figure, a wily native who alone among "his tribe" recognizes the power latent in writing. Yet as he scratches out the ciphers that so confound Lévi-Strauss, who sees in them the dark fate of a man oppressing his own people, the chief himself remains a cipher whose motives and perspectives — on the meaning, if you will, of writing — are no more transparent than the unintelligible script he produces. At its heart, though, Lévi-Strauss's story offers a powerful lesson: his "writing lesson" is an episode of double instruction in which learning operates from both directions. While it may begin with the native mimicking the anthropologist, the anthropologist learns, from watching himself mirrored, about the dangers of his own contaminating presence. The geminate character of the lesson — and, hence, the multiplication of meaning — suggests the tendency for cross-cultural encounters to spawn semantic gulfs across which widely divergent interpretations become not only possible but routine.

However, the lesson that Lévi-Strauss takes away from the encounter is not, as Jacques Derrida (1998 [1976]) claims, the one he should have embraced, for he mistakes one form of ethnocentrism for another. Derrida's critique illustrates how Lévi-Strauss's distrust of native writing — and, though Derrida makes less of it, the man deploying it — is the story of a man who misapprehends the image in the mirror the chief held up to him. The corruption the anthropologist saw in the chief's scribblings, Derrida says, was the ghost of Western "logocentrism," the habitual European distrust of writing, the debased stepsister of speech. Yet Derrida's deconstruction of the encounter preserves the idea that the moment is fundamentally revealing: what "the native" does tells us a great deal — not, as it turns out, about him but about us, those who study him.

But another form of ethnocentrism is at work in Lévi-Strauss's "reading" of the chief's so-called make-believe, for while writing may be seen as a poor substitute for speech, it also has a noble purpose degraded by the use the chief makes of it. To Lévi-Strauss, writing is designed to be an instrument of the scientific project, a skill obtained "as a result of a long and laborious training," to be used for "acquiring knowledge" (Lévi-Strauss 1992 [1955]: 296, 298). Writing, then, when used "properly" — independently of political calculation and the exercise of power — can be not only corrupting but also elevating, raising human beings above factionalism and recruiting them to participation in knowledge gathering as a universal enterprise.

This is, of course, an attitude many would reject, not least the "native writers" of Mexico. De la Cruz's poem certainly suggests how thoroughly political the act of writing is. Ultimately, that is at least part of Derrida's point: ostensibly neutral categories, and the supposedly fixed relations among them, are shot through with ethnocentric assumptions. Even so, how much closer does Derrida's critique bring us to understanding what the Nambikwara chief was up to when he filled the blank page with loops and lines? Would the chief share any of the queasiness about the act of writing that Lévi-Strauss suggests he should and that de la Cruz's poem alludes to: the notion of writing as enslavement, a form of colonial exploitation either visited on him or that he visits on others? Or would he see things differently, through precisely the kind of modernistic, individualistic "getting ahead" mentality that Lévi-Strauss—and so many indigenous intellectuals—reject?

The problem, of course, is that what the natives say and do is no more transparent nor direct a reflection of reality than, say, the texts they leave behind. One man's corruption by the evils of development is another man's liberation by the advances of modernity. While intellectuals, not least indigenous ones, may worry, as de la Cruz suggests they do, about the purity of Indian villages being spoiled by the proliferation of plastic, de la Cruz himself sees the matter differently, as a form of resilience and adaptation. On the matter closer at hand of indigenous-language literacy, as demonstrated by the differences even among bilingual schoolteachers, "the natives" are by no means united on the subject. That lack of unity is tied not only to differences among writers but also to differences among audiences—including differences in how audiences make sense of what indigenous authors write. If we return to the question animated by Lévi-Strauss's story, understanding the meaning of "native writing" goes beyond understanding the motives of the chief, the writer. Making sense of the work of Mexico's indigenous authors requires looking not just at authors' motives, the choices they make in addressing different audiences, but also at how people in those audiences respond: how readers interact with indigenous-language texts.

ALPHABET SOUK: HAWKING MAZATEC ORTHOGRAPHIES TO THE
MASSES (OR, WHY X DOESN'T ALWAYS MARK THE SPOT)

For many indigenous writers, answering the question about which audience they will address begins with the script itself: the alphabet, colonizing weapon or tool of liberation, whose capricious relationship to the human voice plagues writers and readers alike. If writing is a fundamentally political act, then the script chosen likewise becomes a vehicle through which power is exercised. This lesson certainly is not lost on indigenous Mexican writers, for whom colonization has been a history of domination through linguistic subordination. The imposition of prescribed orthographies has played a major role in this process, from the Spanish friars to the SIL to those bilingual schoolteachers who are Gregorio Regino's "co-opted" form of organic intellectual, complicit in the dissemination of hegemonic rather than counterhegemonic discourses. It is thus precisely with the letters of the alphabet—humble building blocks, amino acids in the mighty protein chain of literacy—that most indigenous intellectuals begin in their quest to revitalize their language by constructing a reading public.

Creating a "practical alphabet" is deemed so important to many indigenous intellectuals because, in contrast to Spanish, few indigenous languages have standardized orthographies. Those that do (e.g., Yucatec Maya) generally have very low internal variation, which in much of Mexico is the exception rather than the rule. In some cases (e.g., Zapotec), no standardized alphabet exists even within the same broad language variant. For example, in Sierra Norte Zapotec—itself but one of the four main variants of Zapotec—at least seven different orthographies are in use. The situation for Mazatec is similar. In the Sierra alone, there are at least four orthographies that I know of, in addition to the assorted idiosyncratic systems used by individual songwriters. As a result of the anxiety engendered by orthographic inconsistency—underpinned and licensed, of course, by the use of a standardized language such as Spanish as a model—often one of the first goals indigenous writers and educators tackle is the development of a practical, cross-dialect alphabet. This is one of several ways that revival projects in Nda Xo diverge from the national norm. As we have seen, the Day of the Dead Song Contest embraces orthographic heterodoxy, a feature of that revival project that, I argue, has been crucial to its ability to attract widespread participation. Nonetheless, it differs from the approach taken by many organizations, whose first item of business is often to agree on an alphabet, viewing that as a foundation on which to build—and, for better or worse, institutionalize responses to—further language-revival issues.

Such a project, however, often involves years of contentious debate. Such was the case with the Academia de la Lengua Mixteca (Ve'e Tu'un Savi), which followed the model of Guatemala's ALMG. Ve'e Tu'un Savi's trajectory is one that other Mexican indigenous groups, including Zapotecs and Mazatecs, are trying to follow, beginning with the long process of devising a standard orthography.²² The Zapotec case is particularly interesting for how it harks back to "classic" indigenous-language literatures and literacy. Its efforts to create a Pan-Zapotec orthography have relied heavily on the colonial orthography of Fray Juan de Cordoba (1578) and to some extent on Zapotec glyphs. Mixtec is another language spoken primarily in Oaxaca that, like Zapotec and Mazatec, has many variants. Ve'e Tu'un Savi began as a collection of Mixtec writers, activists, and bilingual schoolteachers interested in language revitalization. Its first goal was a Pan-Mixtec alphabet, which it agreed to in 1997 after seven years of discussion and at which point it became the Academia de la Lengua Mixteca, now widely recognized as the "voice" of Mixtec intellectuals. This gives the organization and individuals associated with it a level of prominence and authority that "less-organized" indigenous groups do not share. It does so, though, at the expense of marginalizing other Mixtec-language projects and the individuals associated with them. Mixtecs affiliated with the SIL, for example, strongly disagree with Ve'e Tu'un Savi precisely on the issue of a Pan-Mixtec alphabet, which the SIL's linguists, who are experts on Mixtec, claim is impossible to achieve in a practical orthography. Mixtecs affiliated with the SIL generally are not represented, as is Ve'e Tu'un Savi, in regional and national debates in which Mixtec intellectuals are participants.

In the meantime, other goals, such as indigenous-language literacy itself, must be held in abeyance until agreement can be reached. Montemayor offers the following commentary on the importance to indigenous authors of orthographic decisions:

> The development of the Indigenous writer is a more laborious and delayed process than that of the Mexican authors who write in Spanish. Not only is it an individual vocation; it is also a project with collective consequences, influenced by many aspects of an educational and social nature and by the choice of which alphabet to use. Up to now, the definition of these alphabets for Indigenous languages has been done solely by official institutions, based on the opinions of Indigenous specialists who no longer form an integral part of their communities or those of non-native linguists and specialists. The agreements about unifying the use of different alphabets in diverse official publications have doubtless been somewhat useful, but they are not comparable to the real, productive literary use of those alphabets by authors who are neither "official" nor subject to the guidelines laid down by government programs.
>
> Because of these factors, the Indigenous writers are confronted by a cultural commitment that obliges them to rethink almost everything having

to do with their language from the very moment that they decide which alphabet to use. Other challenges, such as their formal literary training, come later. (Montemayor and Frischmann 2004: 1:5)

One issue that makes debates about orthography so contentious is the wide variety of attitudes, based on both practical and ideological concerns, that indigenous intellectuals take toward previously devised alphabets. Many intellectuals, for example, state as an explicit goal for their literary and literacy efforts the correction of all externally derived alphabets, which they see as tainted through connection to larger projects of domination and oppression. A not uncommon argument among indigenous intellectuals—especially in Oaxaca, with its overwhelming linguistic diversity—is that the Spanish promoted dialectal variation to foster isolation and division within indigenous groups (see, e.g., Castellanos 1994). Although this view is not supported by historical linguistic research (which places such divisions much earlier), written texts can bridge variations in spoken language with relative facility. Indigenous intellectuals frequently stress this in claiming the importance of literary and literacy projects for promoting internal unity within a language group. Such arguments also feature prominently in efforts by indigenous intellectuals to devise universal, cross-dialect alphabets. Many such debates, for example, center on the ever controversial use of the letter X to represent the phoneme that in English is written sh (see Suslak 2004). Used by Spanish priests, X also appears in modern orthographies by the SIL, the INI, and the SEP—a history that at once taints the character through association with colonialism while making it widely used across a range of readers and writers. And so the simple letter X can mark the locus of an impasse, with those arguing for keeping it on practical grounds duking it out with those who claim it is a representative of colonial and neocolonial domination.

Once a practical alphabet has been agreed to, more problems await. Factionalism, particularly among bilingual schoolteachers, directly impedes the promotion of a given alphabet. Furthermore, few speakers of indigenous languages will be "virgin" readers: most will have some experience, however nominal, of the existing alphabets the intellectuals seek to displace. As a result, even when readers or teachers do not resist the new orthography for ideological reasons, they often do so for practical ones, out of habit.

Only after the obstacles linked to promoting the practical alphabet are largely eliminated can indigenous intellectuals begin to tackle the even more daunting problem of how to mount successful literacy programs. Because there are no national or state level programs beyond those used in bilingual schools—whose promotion of indigenous-language literacy is nominal—most such literacy programs are ad hoc, run by individual writers, teachers, or local organizations. The same practical problems—funding, factionalism, and so on—that indigenous intellectuals commonly face apply here, too, and as a result, there are few systematic attempts at indigenous-language literacy, either across a language or variant or even within a given community. The writers who head literacy workshops are by necessity almost always originally members of the indigenous community where the workshop is held and are thus situated along assorted social fault lines. As a result, attendance at such workshops is often exclusionary in practice, if not in theory, as participation (and nonparticipation) is linked to a complex system of social identities.

Reception not only of literacy programs but also of the literature itself is likewise highly inflected by local norms and values. Almost all indigenous language groups have some individuals involved in language revival. Yet in many cases, these activities have nominal local impact even if they have regional and national visibility. The literature that is produced goes largely unread and plays no ongoing, active role in the social life of the community.

Finally, although it is an obvious point, indigenous authors face none of these challenges when they address audiences, indigenous or not, in Spanish. That language is fully standardized; the production of literacy in Spanish is thoroughly institutionalized; the publication and dissemination of Spanish-language texts is widely supported; and the creation of an audience in the more profound sense of the word—through imparting not only reading skills but also the ability to interpret and appreciate texts in Spanish—is heavily promoted through a variety of public and private venues. While in any given text, the indigenous-language version and the Spanish one may face each other across the page in an iconic representation of parity, centuries and worlds of difference and inequality surround the two sides.

OF DIALECTS AND ARMIES: WEIGHTED BILINGUALISM
AND THE READER OF INDIGENOUS-LANGUAGE TEXTS

In contradistinction to readers of Spanish and other standardized languages with institutionalized scripts, most readers come to indigenous-language texts with no clear expectation of how speech will be represented graphically. Unless they are comfortable with the orthography in question, uncovering the relationship between phoneme and grapheme is largely a process of trial and error. In this exercise in experimentation, the reader tests the written symbols against guesses at which spoken words are being represented. Indigenous authors are an exception. Especially if they are working in their own orthography (i.e., the one they use and often helped devise), they can read indigenous-language texts fluently and silently, without reference to a Spanish version. Note, though, that they are often reading texts that they wrote, so that fluency is tied to familiarity. Furthermore, once indigenous authors stray outside their own orthographies or texts written in linguistic variants closest to their own, they read written texts the same way those less comfortable with them do: through reference to a double text. They, too, compare the Spanish version with the indigenous one and measure the written indigenous text against the language when spoken.

This process of deciphering is one reason indigenous writers hesitate to publish their work exclusively in indigenous languages. Bilingual editions allow indigenous authors to piggyback on the enormous head start Spanish has in orthographic predictability and habits of literacy. Most people who are interested in learning to read and write in indigenous languages are already literate (if marginally) in Spanish—or, as with children, they are in the process of becoming so inside a wider social system in which Spanish has a massive institutional advantage. Even those who do not speak Spanish and are illiterate in both languages—such as inhabitants of small communities in the Sierra Mazateca—are nevertheless far more familiar with Spanish-language texts. Regardless of how predominant the indigenous language is otherwise, in daily life the vast majority of written texts—newspapers, calendars (the single most common wall decoration in the Sierra), labels on packages, political posters, graphics on television—are in Spanish. Note, however, that for some authors, bilingual texts may serve other purposes. Placing the Spanish and indigenous versions side by side can highlight the sophistication of the indigenous-language version when the Spanish appears impoverished, lacking richness that is present in the indigenous-language text.

Song texts in Nda Xo constitute a special case in which authors rarely produce work in a bilingual format. These texts are somewhat unusual, however, in how the written texts intersect with oral performance. There are a few other cases in which authors present their work entirely in an indigenous language (see, e.g., R. Molina Cruz 1991). Such a choice often carries an additional political message of being "just for us." It may also intimate to speakers of indigenous languages that they should try, as much as possible, to expunge Spanish from their lives—or, at least, learn to read without depending on that language. Promoting social solidarity—and at the same time taking advantage of the ability of written texts to cross dialectal boundaries more easily than the spoken word—is an agenda explicitly expressed by Javier Castellanos (1994) in the preface to his book of poems. Furthermore, the final poems in the volume appear in Zapotec only, and each is dedicated to the speakers of one of the four main variants of Zapotec. However, the decision to present a text solely in an indigenous language may purchase a political and social statement at the cost of limiting the text's audience, for speakers and non-speakers of indigenous languages alike.

The disparity between the indigenous language and Spanish is reflected in the process native speakers use to read indigenous-language texts, which in turn strengthens the impetus to produce work in bilingual editions. With the exception of the tiny number of speakers in any given indigenous language who read and write in it regularly, for most speakers, the process of reading a text in the native language is essentially one of slow and arduous deciphering, even for people who are well educated. The ability to speak an indigenous language and the ability to read in it are separate skills—perhaps more so than is the case with highly institutionalized and standardized languages such as Spanish. Even in the very early stages of learning Mazatec (and Zapotec), I could read and transcribe the languages more easily than almost all of the native speakers, even though I was unable to produce, or even understand, speech in the language that many two-year-olds could handle.

The method I most commonly observed speakers use to decode texts is to tack back and forth between the indigenous-language version and the Spanish one. Consulting first the Spanish to get a sense of what the indigenous language is trying to say, the reader then compares the written version of the indigenous language with his or her guesses about how one might gloss the Spanish version in the indigenous one. When the indigenous version is understood, finally, it is as a flash or an epiphany, the sudden recognition of something that moments ago was strange but has suddenly become familiar and yet glimpsed anew through the process of alienation. In more than one hundred instances of watching indigenous people read texts in their own languages, I never saw anyone read a text silently or read without reference to the Spanish text. In both cases, reading required seeing double—that is, comparing the written text to the spoken text and often relying on the written Spanish text to decode the indigenous-language version.

When only an indigenous language version was available—such as with Mazatec songs—the "double vision" persisted, although the source of the second text shifted. If the text had been in circulation for some time, the second text was the speaker's or singer's memory, and the written text served as a mnemonic. If the text was a new one, the second text in some cases was the spoken version—often presented by the author when teaching the song. More commonly, though, the new song was learned in pragmatic contexts—

a religious event or a night dancing as *chajma* (ancestors, the dead)—in which singers read the text in mixed company with other singers who were variably familiar with it. In such cases, other singers near the reader produced the second text, and the reader compared their singing with the written text. In fact, if I happened to be standing near someone who did not know a song text well, I often was asked to read it, since even before I learned much Mazatec I could be counted on to "translate" the text into speech. In many cases, though, people have no immediate reference to a written version at all. Most singers learn a song by sheer repetition. In particular, new songs introduced during the Day of the Dead fiesta might be repeated thirty times or more across a given evening, and for practical reasons, if for no others, it would be unusual for written song sheets to be used.

Because these reading practices rely on various forms of textual coupling, the text itself becomes fundamentally hybrid and doubled. It consists not of one language's version or the other as primary but, rather, of both as they interact within the same integrated, diglossic entity. The meaning of the text lies not in one version or the other but rather in both as they work in concert. One of the great contributions of belletrists such as León-Portilla is that they work within native languages and from a deep understanding of their semantic and grammatical resources, in contradistinction to many scholars before them who relied largely or exclusively on Spanish translations of the indigenous-language original. But here, a belletristic approach would produce a deep misapprehension about how indigenous-language literacy operates and how indigenous-language literature is received. The textual practices of readers and authors fundamentally problematize the notion of what the text itself is, replacing the simple model of the single-language "original" on which so many ideologies of translation are based with one that is more complex, integrated, and bilingual. Furthermore, accessing the text itself becomes dependent on context, as the text becomes not just the two languages' versions in tandem but also how they interact through the medium of a bilingual reader or writer.

Belletristic approaches would generate analogous misunderstandings about how and why indigenous-language literature is produced. Text authorship takes place in a thoroughly diglossic context that fundamentally shapes the nature of indigenous-language writing. Most indigenous writers—with some exceptions, such as Mazatec songwriters—aim from the beginning to produce work that will appear in bilingual editions. The national grants for writers in indigenous languages require as much and judge a work's value— with the possible exception of widely spoken indigenous languages, such as

Nahuatl or Yucatec Maya—based on the perceived quality of the Spanish version. At the same time, the indigenous-language text is the key to the author's legitimacy and authority, for speakers from the same language community as the author, as well as for those from outside of it.

Every indigenous author I interviewed from across Mexico presented the indigenous-language version as the primary, "authentic" text, in keeping with larger national and international discourses and ideologies of indigenous identity politics. This, in turn, is tied to their insistence that the indigenous language is their first language. To a person, they all claim—at least, officially—to write the indigenous-language version first and then to produce the Spanish translation from it. At the same time, some readers of the indigenous languages who are themselves highly bilingual in Spanish comment that the Spanish versions sometimes "read better" than the indigenous-language texts, which have idiomatic "echoes" of the Spanish. They furthermore suggest either that the Spanish version was written first or that the two were written within a more fully bilingual process than the explicitly ideologized model of indigenous-language texts would suggest.

Given the influence of nonindigenous intellectuals, as both readers and supporters, it should not be surprising that the Spanish-language version is given more attention than the indigenous-language version, however much that might contradict normative metacultural notions of indigenous language texts. In light of the characteristics of indigenous authorship in Mexico that I have laid out here, it would not be surprising if some authors wrote in Spanish first. Nor would doing so necessarily indicate that the author is not truly "indigenous" or not truly an indigenous-language author. Only within a particular ideology of indigenous authorship—in which the indigenous-language version is considered the "original" and the Spanish version the "translation"—does writing in Spanish first constitute a violation. An articulation of this view was raised recently in a scathing editorial by the renowned Zapotec author Victor Terán (2010a; see also Terán 1995, 2010b). He stated that many recipients of grants for national indigenous authors merely pretend that their "language of inspiration"—their first language—is indigenous. In reality, he claimed, they write in Spanish and subsequently translate their work into the indigenous language.

Privately and "off the record," many indigenous authors I spoke to confessed that this practice was indeed widespread and that they do sometimes write in Spanish first. One well-known author who recently won the Nezahualcóyotl Prize confessed that he had barely made the deadline the prize committee gave him to finish the indigenous-language version of his winning manuscript, which he wrote in Spanish first. However, precisely because the vast majority of indigenous texts are "translated" into Spanish by their authors, the practice of indigenous literary production is more complicated than the explicit discourse suggests. Furthermore, the fact that indigenous authors must be thoroughly bilingual calls the alleged primacy of the indigenous language more deeply into question. In this respect, Juan Gregorio Regino is rather unusual in insisting—both in print and in my interviews with him—that he is fully bilingual. His *lengua materna* is not one language or the other, he says, because he learned both from his mother as he grew up. However, while this attitude is unusual among established indigenous authors, my new research suggests that embracing bilingualism, and publicly acknowledging the importance of Spanish to indigenous authorship, is increasingly common among young indigenous-language authors and activists. Thus, a generational shift may be under way, and both indigenous authors and their audiences may be evolving in new directions that depend more fully and more openly on the importance of bilingualism.[23]

Nevertheless, Gregorio Regino's stand on bilingualism is at odds with prevailing discourses about indigenous authorship in Mexico. It is Terán who gives the dominant ideology eloquent, if inflamed, voice. Within such an ideology it would be anathema to claim, for example, that for indigenous authors—à la Samuel Beckett, whose translations into English of his original French texts have made the translated versions the authoritative ones—translation becomes the instrument of perfection. Yet subverting the dominant discourses about indigenous authors would allow not only a more accurate understanding of the work indigenous authors do but also a greater appreciation for their artistry as they selectively and skillfully draw on the resources of two radically different linguistic systems. Nonetheless, taking such a position, for now, remains politically impossible. At least in explicit discourse—what indigenous authors and those who support them are willing to say in public and in print—the indigenous-language text remains the privileged "original." Any suggestion that it is subordinated to the Spanish version—that it is the expendable medium within which the Spanish version thrives—is rejected: the word flowering on the wrong language.

The Singing Lesson: A New Approach to Revival

What does all of this have to say about the songwriters in Nda Xo? What does it signify that the most prominent Mazatec writers, even when they are writing in explicitly literary genres such as poetry, label many of their works "songs"?[24] What difference does it make that, in the Sierra Mazateca, the reading public is also a *listening* public? What kind of thing does an indigenous-language text become if it was meant not so much to be read as to be sung?

In discussing the poststructural critique of "The Writing Lesson," Gary Tomlinson (2007) points out that most scholars have tended to ignore how Derrida's deconstruction of entrenched logocentrism, though aimed at Lévi-Strauss, was also directed at Jean-Jacques Rousseau, whose *Essai sur l'origine des langues* was as concerned with singing as with speech. Taking that insight as a point of departure, Tomlinson uses a Derridean unsettling of relationships among speech, writing, and song—specifically, the subordination of writing and song to speech—to examine centuries of misapprehension by Europeans of Amerindian singing. He then turns that strategy on a specific text to open a new space for understanding New World singing: the *Cantares mexicanos*, part of the corpus of ancestral Mesoamerican writing that living indigenous writers hold up as their patrimony, the so-called golden age of Mesoamerican literature whose greatness they seek to revive in the present. But, of course, part of Tomlinson's point is that the *Cantares mexicanos* are not written texts in any straightforward sense and that we make assumptions about their textuality at our peril. This returns us briefly to the question of what the chief of the Nambikwara, the "native writer" in Lévi-Strauss's parable masquerading as ethnographic objectivity, was doing when he put pencil to paper. Although I cannot answer that question for the chief, that "native still living in the Stone Age," the question bears asking for Mexico's contemporary indigenous writers: what are *they* doing when they put pen to paper?

If we take seriously their own words on the subject, we might revive Lévi-Strauss's anxieties about the corrupting, colonizing power of writing. Victor de la Cruz's poem suggests that writing is a form of enslavement, of consigning the language of the ancestors to paper, which "was born white / and imprisons our words." Yet this is also a view that most indigenous authors explicitly reject and that most indigenous writings, including de la Cruz's poem, implicitly contradict. As Gregorio Regino says, he conceives of his writing not as an instrument of colonization but as a tool for reversing it. Within such a vision, the chief of the Nambikwara is not, in fact, "mimicking" the anthropologist—if such a label even applies, if the chief was not, in fact, as the title suggests, participating in a lesson—to use writing as a weapon against his own people. Rather, he is perhaps practicing the art, learning it, perfecting it, to use it for other ends—among them, perhaps, some form of indigenous revival.

The question then becomes how he—and other indigenous writers, such as Juan Gregorio Regino and Heriberto Prado Pereda—use writing to serve particular ends. If we take into account what these indigenous writers have to say, it matters a great deal how they answer the question about what they are doing with their writing. To Gregorio Regino, for example, how one answers marks the difference between being "agents of the government [helping] to erase our peoples" and writers who can say, "I write in my language, I think in my language, I instill in the children and my people our identity, our culture, our language." But is that, then, the measure of success—that an author writes in his (or her) native language? Most indigenous intellectuals I interviewed say that is not enough; that it matters who is reading and who is listening; that reaching an audience is as critical to an indigenous author's work as creating poems or composing songs. But just as the text for indigenous authors and readers is double, so, too, is the audience. The authors discussed in this chapter demonstrate just how hard it is to reach both audiences, to write for two very different sets of readers-listeners, at once. Hence, indigenous writers themselves become double, divided into two broad types: those whose focus and impact is national or regional but who struggle in creating local readerships, and those whose center of attention and arena of influence is local but who have had a more limited effect on regional and national discourses or policies about indigenous peoples.

If we return for a moment to the Prado brothers as they light candles at their father's grave, one way to interpret the division between them is as a story in miniature of the national scene, in which indigenous writers tend to fall into two groups. For a variety of reasons—financial, ideological, social— the two Prados made choices that divided them, just as indigenous intellectuals, in choosing one kind of career over another, one audience over another, make choices that render the other kind of work difficult if not practically impossible. But if we look further back, to the genesis of the song contest, we see a time when the two brothers worked together harmoniously, when they were able to strike a balance between creating texts and creating audiences. That part of the story offers a more hopeful reading of the meaning of revival. I take up that reading in the conclusion as I discuss how different kinds of cultural work and divergent—even competing—models of authorship collectively shape new possibilities for the future.

SINGING FOR THE DEAD AND THE LIVING

Revival, Indigenous Publics, and the National Afterlife

Tojo k'ausakji, tojok'uasachon,
tojesa manguine jin. . . .

li to basa mana, kitjobison na jin
i naxinanda jña

ali nibatjinguina,
i tijnakole ñano tsa naina si k'uatso.

Our world continues on
and now we say goodbye. . . .

It makes us sad, but at least we walked here
for our pueblo

Don't be sad,
next year, God willing, we will see each other again.

—Crescencio García, Mazatec songwriter, from "Tojesa manguine jin"
("Now We Say Goodbye")

Just before I left for Mexico to begin research for this book, I attended a conference required by one of the granting agencies that generously funded my research. The program was interdisciplinary, and I was one of the few anthropologists participating. Most of the other attendees were social scientists from other disciplines. The keynote address, for example, was given by a sociologist; it was an exegesis on the pitfalls of "selecting on the dependent variable." During the conference, we attended sessions during which other participants critiqued our research proposals; my workshop happened to be run by the same scholar who had given the keynote address. All I can remember now of the event was a question he asked: are these language-revival movements you want to study really just a hothouse phenomenon? I found the comment offensive, though at the time I could not articulate why.

Nevertheless, I have been asked versions of that question many times since. The "hothouse" criticism takes many forms, but at bottom it questions the legitimacy and viability of revival movements. Such sentiments are not uncommon even from people I regard as knowledgeable outsiders — that is, people who know a lot about Mexico (in many cases, more than I do), even if they do not know much about indigenous-language writing. They include anthropologists, historians, academics from other disciplines, people who work for nongovernmental organizations, and employees of government organizations such as the CDI, whose work involves interfacing with indigenous communities. One day not long after I had arrived in Oaxaca, the same attitude was expressed during a conversation I had with a priest over a cup of hot chocolate on the Zócalo (the main plaza in Mexico City). "Oh, that's all fake," he said, referring to the many literary books published nationally in indigenous languages. Unlike the comment by the sociologist at the conference, this version of the "hothouse" criticism was voiced by someone whose opinion was informed by far more experience than I had. The priest had spent many years living in a remote town in the mountains of Oaxaca. For the previous few years, he had been collaborating with people from the town on a vocabulary of the local variant of Zapotec that was spoken there.

I think the priest was suggesting that programs to support indigenous writers are little more than window dressing. He was implying that the government was merely paying lip service to the value of linguistic diversity: by publishing a few books each year in indigenous languages, the government was getting good public relations on the cheap. But while such interpretations of the government's motives are understandable — perhaps even warranted — it struck me as unfair to the authors who participate in the programs. Such comments seemed to imply that those authors are cynics or dupes, pawns in the state's plan to dress up the nation in multicultural drag or professional Indians playing the "race card" and trading on accidents of birth and timing to win a kind of ethnic lottery. In any case, the comments left no space for indigenous writers to act as agents, as people who create social realities rather than merely react to those put in place by others. Furthermore, such criticisms implied that the whole enterprise of indigenous authorship was somehow tainted because it was propped up by the government and other nonindigenous, nonlocal forms of support. But how is such support any different from the external funding received by other kinds of authors, artists, and intellectuals? Did the Medicis create a hothouse, too?

Are artist colonies like Yaddo and MacDowell "fake"? What about funding scholars receive from the National Science Foundation or from the National Endowment for the Humanities; from the Wenner-Gren Foundation or the Social Science Research Council; from the Institute for Advanced Study or the National Humanities Center?

In other words, quiet bigotry is embedded in the very question about the artificiality of indigenous authors. To ask whether indigenous authorship is the product of artificial intervention—whether its survival is dependent on economic life support—is to assume that cultural authenticity is violated by participation in national and global networks, particularly when they involve money. If the analogous question were asked of authors or intellectuals in the United States, it would seem uninformed, and if it were asked of an individual who also belongs to a minority group, it would appear racist (or sexist, homophobic, or ageist). Yet it appears to be a perfectly reasonable question to ask of indigenous authors. And, indeed, it is one that indigenous intellectuals openly invite at times by insisting on the right to self-sufficiency and autonomy—or, as Heriberto Prado Pereda prefers to call it, autochthony.

Furthermore, knowledgeable outsiders are not the only ones who make such critiques. Indigenous intellectuals are regarded with ambivalence not only by observers of indigenous communities but also by people who live in those communities. As I showed in chapter 6, local people sometimes treat indigenous intellectuals with suspicion, particularly if they have open ties to patronage networks and connections to government funding agencies. Almost all indigenous intellectuals I interviewed spoke about being targets of open criticism by people in the towns they were from, particularly from *maestros bilingües* (bilingual teachers)—"The maestros are my strongest critics" was a sentence I heard often—but also from others. As one author put it, "People claim I'm getting rich by selling our culture." This is a charge that echoes Claude Lévi-Strauss's indictment of the Nambikwara chief who ostensibly used writing skills at the expense of others in the tribe (1992 [1955]). The prevalence of such denunciations adds another dimension to the paradoxes indigenous authors face: even when they specifically target local audiences, people may oppose their efforts on ideological grounds.

The hothouse criticism is further problematic because it is profoundly shortsighted. Revival movements, like all social movements, unfold alongside other events and even other social movements. They arise out of particular historical contexts and take shape over years, if not decades. Focusing on revival movements in relative isolation, rather than examining how they might relate to broader social and historical contexts, makes it easy to cast doubt on the financial links that support such movements from outside. But doing so provides an incomplete and distorted picture. The relevant context for revival movements is much broader than the movements themselves. At minimum, revival movements, like social movements in general, are in dialogue with one another, as well as with other events and trends that emerge over long periods that may extend years into the future. These connections among local, regional, and national movements are contextually specific and may even be closely tied—as we saw with key figures in the Sierra Mazateca's revival movements—to the life histories of particular individuals. These particularities in the Sierra's revival movements are exposed when viewed against nationally oriented writers such as Juan Gregorio Regino. But their distinctive features become clearer still when compared with other revival movements that likewise have arisen locally.

I conclude the book by briefly comparing other homegrown social movements in Oaxaca with revival movements in the Sierra Mazateca. These movements throw into relief some of the distinctive characteristics of the Sierra's revival movements that have allowed them to achieve popular traction; above all, the movements from the Sierra stand apart from many others for how they are harnessed to singing. But comparing the Sierra's revival movements with others in the state does more than illuminate the unique qualities of each. By considering these other movements in aggregate, we gain a better sense of the myriad ways in which different revival movements that focus on language are mutually influencing and jointly constructing. This, in turn, makes visible how understanding indigenous revival in Mexico requires attention to the complex ways that the work of different kinds of authors, with different kinds of audiences, is necessary and interrelated. Viewing these different movements and the interactions among them in a holistic, historicized framework—taking both a long and a wide view—offers the most complete picture of the social work accomplished by indigenous revival. In turn, this perspective suggests the unique opportunities that indigenous revival movements may offer in the future as they continue to critique the nation while creating new possibilities for national belonging.

Comparative Cases: Viewing Indigenous Revival in the Sierra Mazateca alongside Other Revival Movements

The Juchitán Renaissance is an obvious comparative case.[1] Indeed, a central figure is Victor de la Cruz, a poet, historian, and indigenous intellectual who appeared earlier in the book. A native of the small Oaxacan city of Juchitán, de la Cruz was an important figure in the rise of the political organization Coalición Obrera Campesina Estudiantil del Istmo (Coalition of Workers, Peasants, and Students of the Isthmus; COCEI) that has received so much attention from researchers and the popular press. Howard Campbell is one of the movement's most extensive chroniclers. Writing during the coalition's heyday, Campbell stated, "COCEI is one of the most successful peasant organizations in contemporary Mexico and Juchitán, Oaxaca is the center of the country's most active indigenous cultural movement" (1990: 47). Juchitán has a long history of indigenous resistance, artistic ferment, and "organic, indigenous intellectualism"—a history that has lent itself to what the historian Colby Nolan Ristow (2008: 42) calls "Juchiteco exceptionalism." Although the emergence of COCEI was a pivotal event, even decades before that, Juchitán was an important cultural center. Juchitecos were active in the cultural life of Mexico City, founding the Juchiteco Students Association in 1923 and sponsoring cultural and literary activities in Isthmus Zapotec (Campbell 1990; Rubin 1997).

The rise of COCEI to power after winning the municipal elections in the early 1980s ushered in a shift toward strongly leftist politics in the region that lasted through the 1990s. The political success of COCEI also inaugurated a commitment to broad ethnic and cultural revival, with the Zapotec language taking a central place in both (Rubin 1997). In a well-cited quote, Victor de la Cruz claimed, of the movement, that "up in City Hall, they yell, tell jokes, collect taxes, and administer justice in Zapotec" (Campbell 1990: 356; Rubin 1997: 228). Art, culture, and language were intimately bound to politics during the Juchitán Renaissance. Furthermore, writers like de la Cruz were involved in projects that bridged cultural and political domains. In his case, this meant not only producing his own creative works in Zapotec and editing the work of other Zapotec authors in anthologies (see de la Cruz 1999 [1983]) and in the Juchiteco cultural magazine *Guchachi' reza* (*Iguana Rajada*; Sliced iguana). This also meant that "he gave himself and his students the task of rewriting the history of Mexico from a Zapotec perspective" (de la Peña 1997: 127–28). As Campbell (2001) vividly describes the era, Juchitán's numerous writers, political figures, visual artists, and other intellectuals were engaged in a long-term collaborative effort to join the region's political and artistic forces behind the celebration of Zapotec language and culture.

We find another interesting point of comparison in returning to Yalálag, the town in Oaxaca's Sierra Norte with which this book began.[2] The indigenous language spoken by the majority of people in the town is likewise Zapotec (with roughly 20 percent speaking Mixe), though the Zapotec that is spoken there is a markedly different variant from the one spoken in Juchitán. Unlike Juchitán's movement, the revival activities in Yalálag have received little scholarly or popular attention.[3] The movement in Yalálag I had originally gone to study centered on Uken Ke Uken, the Center for the Study and Development of the Zapotec Language and Tradition. The Zapotec phrase from which the center takes its name is difficult to translate but is used in colloquial speech to prompt action, to encourage people to face even what appears impossible. The organization was founded in 1995 by the municipal authorities, though it had antecedents in work that the Mexican linguist Juan José Rendón did in the 1980s with Yalalteco children, resulting in the publication of several booklets of stories in Zapotec.

The year after Uken Ke Uken was founded, the recently deceased Yalalteco poet Mario Molina Cruz (1996, 2001), who by then had been living for years in Oaxaca where he held a governmental position, was invited to hold workshops with children. The aim was to teach Zapotec literacy and to "vindicate and defend the language, art, and tradition that nourish the Zapotec root of communitarian life" (Molina Cruz 1998: 9). The collaboration resulted in two small books, one featuring bilingual versions of stories by the children (Molina Cruz 1997) and another that discussed the workshop's methods (Molina Cruz 1998). A further collaboration was planned for the following year, but disputes over its financing put an end to it; eventually, the language workshop and the center's other activities resumed, only to be shut down again by the events recounted in the introduction. Uken Ke Uken finally reopened in 2004 in a new building and with computer equipment provided by the philanthropic organization Fundación Alfredo Harp Helú. Since then, the center has made active use of its space—a beautiful building designed by an award-winning Oaxacan architect—which holds a library, houses the town band, offers computer access to young people, and provides a venue for meetings and small events. But the center has struggled to find financing to support its activities, especially those focused on the language—that is, the writing workshop and the community radio station. It has also struggled with "personnel issues." In 2011, for example, the center's most active leaders held civic posts that prevented them from keeping the center active, exacerbating a broader generational problem in which young people are not taking on leadership roles in the organization.

Obviously, one of the most striking things about these movements when read against those from the Sierra Mazateca is how different all three are from each other. Juchitán, as an urban center, presents a setting for revival that is very different from Yalálag or Nda Xo, a difference that carries a host of other entailments. Juchitán's movement has critical mass, in terms of the sheer number of indigenous intellectuals who participate in it, in a way that Yalálag and Nda Xo do not. And Juchitecos have access to economic and educational resources that are not available to people from Nda Xo and Yalálag. While a leading patron of Juchitán's revival is the famous (and wealthy) Juchiteco painter Francisco Toledo, he is not bankrolling the entire movement because he does not need to. Many other Juchiteco artists and writers also live from their art, work as professionals (de la Cruz, for example, is an investigator at Centro de Investigaciones y Estudios Superiores en Antropología Social [Center for Research and Advanced Study in Social Anthropology; CIESAS]), or exploit other economic possibilities that even a small city has in greater abundance than do rural towns such as Yalálag and Nda Xo. The differences in educational access are equally stark, not only in the quality of the education available in the different settings, but also in terms of the legacies—or lack thereof—of having generations of indigenous intellectuals in Juchitán's case and nothing comparable in the other two locations. And the infrastructure that exists between urban centers such as Oaxaca and Juchitán means that someone like de la Cruz can move between the two places much more easily and regularly than indigenous intellectuals could in either of the rural locales—a difference that, in turn, has profound implications for how a given indigenous author orients himself or herself toward social networks and reading audiences.

Finally, these cases of revival differ radically in how they engage with formal politics. In Juchitán, the connection between the revival movement and politics is direct, and the intertwining of political and cultural activities is deep and overt. In Yalálag, cultural activities are always, if often accidentally, coupled to political concerns, making it difficult to carve out a neutral space for ostensibly communitarian projects such as indigenous revival. The Mazatec Indigenous Church, like Juchitán's revival movement, has an explicit political orientation, but its target is not the political realm of governance. Instead, its political battles are against the Catholic Church and its often unchallenged prominence in the politics of daily life in Nda Xo. The Day of the Dead Song Contest, on the other hand, cultivates an indirect engagement with local politics, a strategy that allows the revival project's purported neutrality to produce striking political results.

What this constellation of cases highlights even more strongly, however, is the symbiotic relationship among these various revival movements. Juchitán, while certainly an outlier compared with most indigenous communities, is in other ways an intermediate setting that spans the difference between revival projects unfolding in cosmopolitan contexts such as Oaxaca and Mexico City and those taking place in small, rural towns. Indeed, de la Cruz himself has functioned in just such a mediating capacity. He worked with Mazatec intellectuals—in his capacity as a CIESAS investigator—to create a Mazatec research center; he also has been active in promoting the work of Mario Molina Cruz and other Zapotec writers from outside the isthmus alongside the Juchiteco authors at the center of the Zapotec literary scene (de la Cruz 1999 [1983]). More broadly, the Juchitán Renaissance and many other axes of cultural activity in Oaxaca have collectively defined Oaxaca as a space where indigenous intellectuals are at the center of social life and are deeply involved in cultural production. These sites include the previously mentioned activities in Yalálag; strong cultural institutions and community museums in Teotitlán del Valle, Santa Ana, and other towns in Oaxaca; and the vibrant community of artists and artisans in those towns and others, such as Ocotlán. Such cultural activities are shot through with internal contradictions and have ambivalent relationships to insiders and outsiders, to different audiences and markets. As discussed earlier in the book, celebrations of "indigenous culture" are almost always related in complex ways to marketing for tourists and other cultural consumers. Nonetheless, the broader context of indigenous cultural and linguistic activities in Oaxaca State contributes to the social matrix that has allowed indigenous revival in the Sierra Mazateca to thrive. The host of social movements occurring across the state and beyond help define the revival movements taking place in the Sierra, making visible the ways they are mutually supportive.

The Mazatec Indigenous Church is in many ways reacting against the popular success of the song contest and the myriad forms of cultural and linguistic heterodoxy it licenses. The supporters of the song contest and of Catholic Church–related singing are, in turn, reacting against the ongoing challenge to their ranks and religious practices posed by the Mazatec church. While the two movements are contrasting in many ways—and, as we have seen, people in the Sierra position them as opposing in how they talk about them—they are nevertheless symbiotic. Each movement defines itself in part against the other, even as the two movements share a host of assumptions that go unremarked. This is particularly true where the language is concerned: both movements place speaking, writing, and, above all, singing in Mazatec at the center of their revival efforts. The cultural distinctiveness of singing in these movements is brought out especially clearly in the comparison with the movements in Juchitán and Yalálag. Although both Zapotec movements draw on other expressive channels and traditions to bolster indigenous-language writing, the lateral support in each case is different—visual art in Juchitán's case and the town band in Yalálag's. This lends further credence to the notion that tying revival projects in the Sierra to singing was strategically productive, a choice that engendered new forms of ethnically marked expression rooted in the deep cultural embedding singing has in the Sierra Mazateca.

All of these movements highlight the importance of taking a long view, historically, when assessing revival projects. In Yalálag in particular, the danger of focusing too narrowly is obvious: while in any given year revival might appear dormant, when viewed over decades, it is clear that in Yalálag the movement continues to advance, though unevenly. In the Sierra Mazateca, knowing that the two newer revival movements share origins in the Liberation Theology of the Catholic Church—and in local, church-supported efforts to promote singing in Mazatec—clarifies the reciprocal relationship between the two and gives their explicit opposition greater nuance. At the same time, foregrounding this history helps makes visible the emotional stakes in the disputes among the supporters of each, revealing why the differences have at times been so passionately argued.

This, then, brings us back to one of the points with which I began: that of the enduring tension between different kinds of indigenous intellectuals.[4] This is a contrast Heriberto Prado Pereda laid out early in the book—however, as I did with the work of Mikhail Bakhtin, I want to make an important amendment. Of those who are interested in "redeeming indigenous culture," Heriberto says, there are two types: those who do so from within and those who do so from the outside. Although for him, only those in the first category are effective and to be commended, I suggest—as with my earlier modification of Bakhtin's ideas—that neutralizing the negative valence around the second category would allow us to read the linked pair more productively. I think it is more helpful to take that second category to mean the kinds of indigenous intellectuals discussed in chapter 6—nationally oriented indigenous intellectuals who may be physically distant from their communities, thus approaching them from "outside," but who are nevertheless deeply involved in valorizing indigenous culture.

Becoming this kind of indigenous author does indeed entail some of the risks to which Heriberto alludes. National visibility may be purchased at the cost of participation in hegemonic projects that jeopardize local revival movements—or, more starkly, may threaten the survival of indigenous-language writing and even of indigenous languages themselves. Yet becoming the kind of indigenous intellectual Heriberto praises is likewise a fraught path. By refusing to participate in webs of institutional patronage and dialogue, such authors risk national and international obscurity and irrelevance—which likewise can threaten the survival of indigenous writing and indigenous languages. On the other hand, the cases from the Sierra Mazateca presented here represent a way to circumvent such dilemmas and illustrate why we need to place revival movements in broad context. While the paradoxes faced by individual authors and particular revival movements are real and often structurally determined, it is also possible, in some measure, to transcend them through the symbiotic relations among them and the collaborative work they perform in aggregate.

The Future of Indigenous Publics: An Afternote on Hothouse Blooms

[A] person can be the author of much more than a book. . . . [W]e might call them "initiators of discursive practices."

—Michel Foucault, "What Is an Author?"

What matter who's speaking, someone said, what matter who's speaking.

—Samuel Beckett, *Texts for Nothing*

In taking the longer, wider view of revival in the Sierra Mazateca, it is helpful briefly to revisit Foucault's "initiators of discursive practices." Foucault begins his essay "What Is an Author?" with Beckett's quote, "what matter who's speaking." Beckett issues the thought as a statement; it is already decided that the author does not matter, and the texts he has written will go on to live whatever life they will without him. Foucault, on the other hand, ends his essay by recasting the quote as a question, "What matter who's speaking?" Although the question is rhetorical, by presenting the issue in the interrogative, Foucault is assuming the presence of an interlocutor, an audience. And this leads me to ask the questions, What matter who's listening? What matters who's reading? For as I have shown, understanding who is speaking or writing also requires asking questions about who is listening and who is reading.

Foucault uses Beckett's quote to examine different kinds of authors. For him, a "typical" author is one "whose function is to characterize the existence, circulation, and operation of certain discourses in society" (Foucault 1977: 124), suggesting that authors have a special role to play in the sedimentation and crystallization of discourses, in the promotion of the status quo. In contrast, "initiators of discursive practices" do something different. Like Antonio Gramsci's subversive type of "organic intellectuals," they undermine rather than reinforce hegemonic powers, disseminating counterhegemonic discourses instead. But how do we tell the two classes of authors apart? In this book I have discussed indigenous intellectuals who could comfortably be classified as organic intellectuals. Their explicit ties to particular groups (i.e., indigenous people) are precisely what license them to speak as (ethnic) authorities. In fact, one of the only studies from the past couple of decades on the Mazatec region focused on individuals similar to those discussed here (even, in some cases, the same individuals). The author described them as follows: "many Mazateco linguists and schoolteachers . . . rather self-consciously refer to themselves as *intelectuales orgánicos* (organic intellectuals)" (Duke 1995: 2).

But what kind of "organic intellectuals" are they? Are they aligned with the dominant classes or with the dominated? Is their work counterhegemonic? Or is their work, despite explicit discourses espousing counterhegemonic agendas, complicit with hegemonic discourses and structures of domination? Does their work do what "folklore" often does: accept a circumscribed realm for asserting difference in exchange for not otherwise questioning the existing structures of inequity? To put the question somewhat differently, are indigenous authors merely human window dressing, merely hothouse blooms?

This book offers a resounding no, but providing convincing evidence for that answer requires looking beyond the authors themselves, beyond their texts, to their audiences and effects. This is why it is so critical to examine both production and reception, the lives of indigenous authors as well as those of their readers, and the revival movements that indigenous intellectuals lead and yet that also exist independent of them. That is why it does indeed matter not just who is speaking and writing but also who is reading, who is listening. But even this approach has its limits. Many important questions about indigenous revival in Mexico cannot yet be answered. The responses are still taking shape and will be for many years to come. We cannot yet distinguish between the two classes of authors as Foucault could, because we do not have history or hindsight to rely on; we do not yet have in front of us a wealth of other texts that a given author's work has made possible. In Michael Warner's terms, the authors here are "writing to a public that does not yet exist" (Warner 2005: 130). It is thus impossible to know whether a given author's work is ultimately "world-making" (Warner 2005: 149) or merely world reinforcing.

Theorists from Karl Marx to Theodor Adorno to Pierre Bourdieu and beyond have found art to be complicit in drugging the public. They argue that, despite its potential to be a crucible for social warfare, culture is also the premiere venue in which social inequality is reinscribed. How, then, do we know whether an author's work is redressing domination or abetting it? Or more profoundly, is that even the right question to ask? Engaging with the matter of whether revival movements subvert hegemonic structures would require choosing among competing measures for effectiveness. And yet the existence of such competing measures, and the conflicting values they represent, is built into the very nature of the projects pursued by indigenous intellectuals and, by extrapolation, other cultural producers. Is success linked to the influence of the author in question? To the influence of his or her texts? Does influence consist of a wide readership? Of a particular type of readership? Does it consist of disseminating foundational types of skills, such as the ability to read in indigenous languages—thus providing the conditions of possibility for indigenous literatures rather than creating the literature itself? Or does the value of revival movements rest in their capacity for social reproduction—to produce not just new readers but new writers, as well? As we have seen, if we take the broader view of indigenous-revival movements, their meaning and value may reside in all of these, though in practice it is almost never possible for a given movement to achieve all at once. This situation in turn brings us back to the importance of taking a long and wide view toward revival movements. Doing so makes it possible to see how different kinds of "success" can work together, forming part of a broader collaborative effort to advance social goals even as particular projects aimed at them fall short.

The authors I discuss in this volume have a double agenda: that of creating indigenous literatures and of promoting indigenous literacy. In practice, succeeding at both is a nearly impossible feat for a given individual to achieve. These indigenous authors also have double audiences—national and local, Spanish speaking and indigenous-language speaking, fully literate and variously literate, and so on. Furthermore, both audiences are moving targets, changing shape and focus as a direct result of indigenous authors' own efforts and of the ongoing impact of their work to promote contemporary readership in indigenous languages. As we saw in chapter 6, current debates around the role of bilingualism in indigenous authorship speak to how the ground is shifting beneath indigenous authors' feet, even as some lament what those changes mean. The meaning of success, therefore, is deeply heterogeneous.

And yet indigenous authors continue to reinscribe a boundary between hegemonic and counterhegemonic discourses, as Juan Gregorio Regino did when he asserted the difference between indigenous intellectuals who support oppression and those who combat it. What light, then, do these revival projects shed on hegemony and its limits? If success is measured by the ability to unite people behind a cause that would subvert hegemonic discourses, how do they move beyond the pressure those very discourses exert on their audiences? I have argued here that contradictions in identity politics often place indigenous authors in paradoxical positions where some ideas can be promoted only at the expense of alienating either the national audience that allows such authors the space to participate in national debates or the local audience on which their national legitimacy rests. Yet when taken in concert, the work of these authors, with their different orientations to the double audience and double agenda, offer a more hopeful picture. There may be no "initiators of discursive practices" among them, but in the aggregate, might they offer new discursive possibilities, new potential for social transformation?

At this point, it is impossible to say. But if I could give any single piece of evidence in support of why I think the entire complex of indigenous revival is promising in this broader sense it would be crystallized in an event that occurred during one of my stays in the Sierra. It took place in Nda Xo's cemetery on the last day of the Day of the Dead fiesta (see fig. C.1). The sun was setting, blanketing the mountains, the tombstones, and all of us in a vibrant but fragile orange glow, a brilliant color close to that of the marigolds covering the graves. The chajma had already broken the piñatas, and various groups of them were playing their last songs in the cemetery. They were still in disguise, their bodies still surrendered to the ancestors, though once they had finished singing they would take off their masks and go back to their silent homes. Crescencio García's "Tojesa manguine jin" (Now we say goodbye) was one of the songs they sang; it was written especially for this part of the fiesta, the last day, when everyone says goodbye to the dead until the coming year.

Alberto Prado Pineda and I were sitting next to each other on a slab of concrete covering a tomb. The group of chajma near us began to play a song I had heard a few times before. It was a sad song, in the minor mode. I liked it from the first time I heard it, in part because somber music is in keeping with my musical taste, but also because it is different in character from many of the other chajma songs: celebratory and ebullient songs, music to encourage people to stay up all night and dance, songs that people will welcome into their homes as a kjuanda, blessing. This song was slower and more deliberate than most, inclined to foster—at least in me—a moment of reflection on the easily forgotten truth that we will all die someday.

FIGURE C.1. *Huehuentones* (including one wearing a Vicente Fox mask) at the graveyard as the Day of the Dead fiesta draws to a close. The huehuentones or chajma are dancing, singing, and making music to say goodbye to the ancestors until the year to come.

FIGURE C.2. In Nda Xo's cemetery during the Day of the
Dead fiesta.

After the chajma finished the song, I told Alberto how much I liked it. He
smiled.

"I wrote that song," he said.

We sat a little longer in silence.

And then he said, "They'll play that for me, too, someday."

Notes

Introduction: *Leaving the Pueblo*

1. The majority of residents in Villa Hidalgo (Yalálag) speak Sierra Norte Zapotec, although roughly 20 percent speak the unrelated but neighboring indigenous language Mixe. I use Limeta Mestas's real name because he was frequently mentioned in press coverage of his death. Throughout this book, I use the real name of anyone who might be considered a public figure—published authors, for example—and pseudonyms for all others. This choice is not unproblematic. For example, it is sometimes difficult to know where to draw the dividing line between the public and private lives of authors I know personally. My hope is that even if the result is flawed, the spirit behind the convention is clear. I want to protect the identity of most people I discuss while openly acknowledging the achievements of, and challenges faced by, those to whom I refer by their true names.

2. The anthropological literature on community factionalism and political violence in Mexican indigenous communities is vast, as is the subset of this literature concerning Oaxaca specifically. Some of the most important examples in the latter category are classic texts in anthropology: de la Fuente 1949; Greenberg 1989; Kearney 1972; Nader 1964, 1990; Parsons 1936.

3. The radio station is programmed and managed locally, unlike most radio stations broadcasting in indigenous areas, which were initiated under the Instituto Nacional Indigenista, now known as the Comisión Nacional para el Desarrollo de los Pueblos Indígenas, the government agency designed to interface with Mexico's indigenous populations.

4. See the Oaxaca government's website at http://www.oaxaca.gob.mx (accessed October 25, 2012). Note that Oaxaca also has a sizable population of afro-mestizos as well as smaller groups of speakers of other indigenous languages, including political and economic refugees from Chiapas and Guatemala.

5. Indeed, the only other language grouping that comes close is the country's most widely spoken variety, Nahuatl. It has only thirty variants, less than half the number of variants of either Mixtec or Zapotec, although those languages have a third the number of speakers that Nahuatl does (INALI 2008a, 2008b).

6. Nda Xo is the Mazatec name for both the county seat (*cabecera*) and its surround-

ing county (*municipio*); the official name is Santa María Magdalena Chilchotla. As with many administrative units in Mexico (e.g., Oaxaca State and its capital), the larger entity and its central population center bear the same name.

7. Oaxaca is in an ongoing race to the bottom with Chiapas for this distinction.

8. The Mazatec region is anomalous in this regard: while its domestic migration rates are near those of other regions of Oaxaca, it has seen relatively little migration to the United States.

9. Laurie Goering, "In Mexico, a Quest for Autonomy: Indigenous Groups Seek Greater Say in Local Affairs," *Chicago Tribune*, June 15, 2001, 1.4.

10. I am indebted to many recent books on the politics of nationhood and ethnicity, particularly in Latin America and the Caribbean, including Colloredo-Mansfield 2009; Gregory 2006; Paley 2001; Starn 1999; Thomas 2004; Turino 2008. There is a particularly rich literature on Mexican nationalism, including Bartra 2002; Gutmann 2002; Joseph and Nugent 1994; Jung 2008; Lomnitz 2001; Mallon 1995; Speed 2007; Stephen 2002.

11. Recently, some theorists have argued that these seemingly opposing trends are in fact intimately, systemically linked: see, e.g., Appadurai 2006; Comaroff and Comaroff 2009; Geschiere 2009; Hale 2006; Ong 2006.

12. Other authors have likewise theorized the political tensions inherent in globalization, nationalism, and transnationalism but through a sideways glance, examining aspects of social life—such as language, performance, and music—that are less obviously implicated in political projects: see, e.g., Eisenlohr 2007; Fox 2004; Goldstein 2004; Goodman 2005; Hirschkind 2006; Inoue 2006; Lemon 2000; Samuels 2004; Wedeen 2008; Weidman 2006. Earlier texts on similar themes include Caton 1990; Graham 1986, 1995; Herzfeld 1997; Irvine 1989; Keane 1997; Kulick 1992.

13. As the name suggests, the PRI arose following the Revolution in 1910 and had a political monopoly for most of the twentieth century. Its hold on power has steadily weakened; Mexico's first non-PRI president, Vicente Fox, was elected in 2000.

14. The canonical article—and almost the only study to date—on Mazatec whistle speech is Cowan 1948.

15. The vast literature on the invention of tradition runs from the seminal volume of that name (Hobsbawm and Ranger 1983) to its subsequent critiques and augmentations (e.g., Appadurai 1996; Briggs 1996; Clifford 2000; Gustafson 2009; Orta 1998; Rappaport 2005).

16. For example, there are four main, mutually unintelligible variants of Zapotec—what linguists and native speakers alike refer to as "the Zapotecs"—and each has numerous mutually unintelligible subvariants. Until recently, Mexico's official indigenous language count was sixty-two; following the creation of INALI in 2003, that number was revised to sixty-eight *agrupaciones lingüísticas* (linguistic groupings) and 364 *variantes lingüísticas* (linguistic variants) (INALI 2008a). As a point of comparison, the Summer Institute of Linguistics—the field arm of the Wycliffe Bible Translators, which has been responsible for the majority of descriptive linguistic research in Mexico (and worldwide)—claims 283 indigenous languages are currently spoken in Mexico. I take

no single figure as the truth, given that all of the institutions involved have political interests in categorizing linguistic difference. Yet while these competing figures indicate the political nature of linguistic categorization, they also reflect Mexico's—and especially Oaxaca's—fundamental linguistic diversity.

17. In Guatemala, other factors—dress, religious practices, parentage—often trump language use. Some leading Mayan intellectuals from Guatemala do not speak any native language. In my experience, indigenous Mexicans greet this scenario with confusion and disbelief, finding an indigenous person who does not speak an indigenous language to be a contradiction in terms.

18. See Roman Jakobson's seminal essay on the poetic function of language, in which, to paraphrase, *how* something is said is as important as *what* is said (Jakobson (1964 [1960]).

19. As I discuss later, Nahuatl and Yucatec Maya are somewhat exceptional.

20. Oaxaca's Zapotec-speaking isthmus region is a notable exception. Modern Zapotec literature has been written there since at least the turn of the century (de la Cruz 1999 [1983]).

21. Jack Goody (1977) and Walter Ong (1982) are most widely associated with this position. A variant of this view is Benedict Anderson's seminal work on the role that print capitalism and reading played in the rise of nationalism (Anderson 1995 [1983]).

22. For this argument in Latin American and Spanish colonial contexts, see Boone and Mignolo 1994; Collins and Blot 2003; Houston 2004; Mignolo 1995; Rafael 1988; Rappaport and Cummins 2011; Salomon 1982.

23. Derrida (1998 [1976]) is, of course, well known for the latter view. For a recent work using Derrida's theories to critique centuries of thought on Amerindian song, see Tomlinson 2007. Ethnographies of literacy in social context include Besnier 1995; Heath 1972; Messick 1993.

24. On the social life of texts, see Bauman and Briggs 1990; Silverstein and Urban 1996; Urban 2001. On intertextuality and interdiscursivity, see Bauman 2004; Hill 2005; Silverstein 2003, 2004, 2005.

25. Here Derrida does not transcend structuralist binaries but, rather, inverts and unsettles them, deconstructing the relationship of the parts but not introducing new ones. This is one reason Charles Sanders Peirce (1932) has enduring appeal across the social sciences, as the tripartite nature of his semiotic system poses a thorough departure from the entrenched dualities of structuralism.

26. I owe my general recognition of the importance of song to Gary Tomlinson.

27. Steven Feld and Aaron Fox (1994) give a thorough review through that date; research since then is covered in Faudree 2012b.

28. There are numerous poet-songwriters closer to home, including Bob Dylan, Leonard Cohen, and Patti Smith. But note that labeling such artists "poets" operates within the aforementioned paradigm: the artists are held up as a special class of poet who put their words to music.

29. I am in dialogue with a footnote in Anderson (1995 [1983]: 43): "We still have no giant multinationals in the world of publishing."

30. Despite being somewhat misleading, I use the term "Aztec" because it is the most widely used for the pre-Columbian empire of central Mexico.

31. For critiques, see Tomlinson 2007, from which I borrow the term, as well as Hanks 2010.

32. Miguel León-Portilla is widely considered the leading figure: see, e.g., León-Portilla 1992 [1962]; León-Portilla and Shorris 2001.

33. Indeed, the privileging of ancient societies and their present survivals has been the most problematic legacy of the term "Mesoamerica." Here, too, León-Portilla has had monumental influence. A television program that aired in 2006 illustrates the absurd but typical extremes of this view. The program featured commentary by León-Portilla and his readings of texts in Classical Nahuatl (the Aztecs' language) that describe indigenous responses to the conquest. Interspliced was footage of the miserable living conditions of indigenous people today, primarily from Chiapas—allusions that, following the Zapatista Rebellion, symbolize Mexico's oppression of its indigenous populations. The general message was not simply that Indians have been persecuted for five hundred years, but that their present complaints are ennobled by reference to a glorious, pre-Columbian past from which they were ruthlessly torn by colonial and national oppression.

34. The leading figure is Carlos Montemayor, who wrote extensively about modern indigenous authors and edited several anthologies of their work: see, e.g., Montemayor 1993, 1998, 2001, 2004; Montemayor and Frischmann 2004, 2005, 2007.

35. However, see the study of an early colonial document in Scholes and Roys (1968 [1948]), an early exception in the scholarship that nevertheless partakes of the ancientist bias.

36. These include the radical difference of indigenous languages from Spanish and other Indo-European languages and, with a few exceptions, the lack of pedagogical materials and opportunities for formal instruction in indigenous languages.

37. Attitudes about the relative (lack of) sophistication of minority languages are more widespread and tenacious than corresponding views about cultural or racial complexity. Indeed, many indigenous people themselves hold such views. During visits to the Sierra, people I do not know well frequently ask some version of the question, "But why would you want to study [our language]? It's just a dialect, not a real language." As with Great Divide theorists, scholarly assumptions about the relative complexity of languages may be more sophisticated but equally problematic.

38. I treat the rich literature on the introduction of alphabetic literacy in the Americas in chapter 1.

39. There is also a large literature on bilingual, indigenous, and rural education in Mexico: see, e.g., Kowalewski and Saindon 1992; Vaughan 1997.

40. On the Pan-Mayan Movement, see Warren 1998. On language revitalization in the Yukon, see Meek 2010. On education and ethnic plurality in Peru, see García 2005. And on the politics of bilingual education in Bolivia, see Gustafson 2009. See also Blommaert 2008 on literacy in central Africa.

41. The explicit ideology of indigenous authorship holds the version in the indige-

nous language to be the original and the version in Spanish to be the translation. However, the vast majority of indigenous texts are translated into Spanish by their authors, making the practice of indigenous literary production more complicated than the explicit discourse suggests, an issue I explore in chapter 6.

Chapter 1: From Revolution to Renaissance

1. The chapter epigraph is only one version of a story that circulates widely in the Sierra: see Boege 1988: 106–7; Martínez Gracida 1883; Neiburg 1988: 13–14; Starr 1908: 231–32. Chikon Tokoxo is the lord (chikon) of Nindo Tokoxo, the Cerro de Adoración (Mountain of Adoration) located outside Huautla de Jiménez. At least one early historical account (the Relación de Teutitlán of 1581) claims that Quetzalcoatl (the plumed serpent, a major ancient Mesoamerican deity) was worshipped throughout the region and was known in the Sierra as Chikon Tokoxo. A mecapal is a tumpline made of ixtle fiber used to carry heavy loads on one's back. Renato García Dorantes was a Huauteco businessman and intellectual who wrote frequently for La Faena. Ben Feinberg (2003: 221, 225) discusses him as Huautla's "most visible [and] ambitious culture broker and one of the wealthiest men in town," a position that makes him an ambivalent figure in the view of other locals.

2. Stone translated brujo using the exoticizing term warlock. Although Stone shows respect for the wide cultural differences between his team and indigenous people they encounter, articles about the cave expeditions in the popular press — including Outside, Wired Magazine, and National Geographic — are shot through with "Orientalizing" references, portraying Mazatecs as "machete-wielding locals convinced the gringos are devil worshippers who come to steal ancient Mayan [!] gold": Dave Philipps, "Back to the Dark: A Mile under Mexico, the Search Grinds on for the World's Deepest Cave," Colorado Springs Gazette, April 14, 2006, http://www.gazette.com (accessed July 10, 2010).

I have never heard Serranos talk about devils and caves, although they frequently claim that each unique geographical feature, such as a cave, has its own chikon (earth spirit or earth lord). Respect and sometimes payment must be made to these spirits to avert harm. I heard many stories about the dangerous power of caves. Most communities in greater Nda Xo are within walking distance of caves, but probably not coincidentally, they are not immediately next to them. I heard various permutations of the idea that caves offer great treasure but at the cost of great loss: the discoverer would never marry or would lose loved ones. On cavers and local ideas about caves, see Feinberg 2003. Historically, caves had other associations, serving as burial places for "kings and nobles of the Mazatec nation"; mention is made of caves as royal cemeteries specifically for Chilchotla's nobility (Martínez Gracida 1883: 560–61). For archaeological work examining caves as elite cemeteries in the Sierra, see Steele 1987.

3. On another expedition, AT&T donated twenty-two kilometers of fiber-optic cable for communications from underground. "But the might of AT&T's fiber optics, as it turned out, was no match for a machete-equipped Mazatec Indian community. . . . [W]hole kilometers of fiber-optic cable were slashed by locals. A black wire strung

through the jungle might anger the spirits of the cave, the peaceful Mazatecs thought. A few hacks with the machete was all it took to disconnect elaborate plans": J. Carl Ganter, "Deep, Dark, and Disconnected," *Wired*, vol. 2, no. 10, 1994, http://www.wired.com (accessed July 10, 2010).

4. See Juan García Carrera's interview with Renato García Dorantes in the inaugural issue of *La Faena* (2000: 5–9).

5. All direct quotes are from *National Geographic*'s interview of Bill Stone. "Field Dispatch: Race to the Center of the Earth" concerned the expedition Stone led in February–April 2004 aimed at establishing Cheve Cave as the world's deepest cave: see "The Politics of Caving," video, available online at http://ngm.nationalgeographic.com/ngm/caverace/week1/index.html (accessed October 25, 2012). That trip, which ultimately was inconclusive, was followed by another in spring 2005 and a third in spring 2006 that cost the lives of two cavers. As of this writing, expeditions to the cave still have not reached the bottom.

6. Systems for recording information existed in other parts of the New World, especially Andean khipus and Moche pictographies (Boone and Urton 2011; Salomon 2004).

7. Stephen Houston, personal communication, December 2011. See also Monaghan 1990. This is not, of course, to say that performance is not important to traditions that rely on alphabetic literacy—witness the animation of the Bible in Catholic Mass. It is, rather, to say that, as John Monaghan and others have suggested, pre-Columbian texts are perhaps better thought of as scripts for public performances rather than texts to be read silently and individually.

8. On texts in various languages, mostly Oaxacan, see also López Cruz and Swanton 2008; Schroeder 2010; Van Doesburg 2008.

9. Of particular note is Susan Schroeder's work on the Nahua annalist Chimalpahim (Lockhart et al. 2006; Schroeder 1991, 2010). Schroeder not only produced a large corpus of work on Chimalpahin but also (in a move other New Philologists, beginning with Lockhart himself, have followed) has made Chimalpahin's work available to wider audiences by initiating the publication of the six-volume *Codex Chimalpahin*. Other important work on similar sources includes Rolena Adorno's research positioning Mexican and Peruvian indigenous and mestizo chroniclers—among them, Fernando Alva de Ixtlilxochitl, Felipe Guaman Poma de Ayala, and El Inca Garcilaso de la Vega—as "indigenous ethnographers": see Adorno 1982, 1989. Finally, on Peruvian indigenous historians, see Salomon 1982.

10. The *Florentine Codex* (Anderson and Dibble 1970–82), a twelve-book work compiled by the Franciscan priest Fray Bernardino de Sahagún, is "the largest and most impressive native-language work of the early period" (Restall et al. 2005: 14).

11. Among the most important are Nahuatl texts such as the *Cantares Mexicanos* (Bierhorst 1985) and the dramatic texts analyzed in Burkhart (1989, 1996).

12. The New Philology is also known as the Lockhart School, after its foundational figure, James Lockhart (see Lockhart 1991, 1992, 1993). Other New Philologists include Robert S. Haskett (1991), Matthew Restall (1997a, 1997b), Susan Schroeder (1991),

Kevin Terraciano (2004), and Stephanie Wood (2003). For the evolution of New Philology, see Restall 2003.

13. The Quechua-speaking population is estimated at 8 million to 10 million (Durston 2008: 41). The Nahuatl-speaking population is estimated at 1.38 million (INALI 2008b).

14. Languages vary widely in terms of when initial descriptive linguistic work about the languages appears—and, of course, as recent work by Errington (2008) reminds us, linguistic work has long been tied to the exercise of power, particularly in colonial settings. In Mexico, Zapotec was one of the earliest languages described: an exhaustive, multivariant vocabulary appeared just fifty years after the fall of the Aztec capital (Cordoba 1578). Yet liturgical texts in Mazatec, spoken in an adjacent but more remote area, did not appear until more than two centuries later; humble vocabularies, nowhere near the scope of Cordoba's, did not appear until about 1830. The first extensive treatises of the language appear in the late nineteenth century (Belmar 1978 [1892]; Brinton 1892a, 1892b), roughly three hundred years after similar work first appeared in Zapotec.

15. Remaining gaps were filled beginning in the mid-twentieth century by the SIL as part of its (Protestant) evangelizing project. Unlike the orthographies of the Spanish priests, the SIL's alphabets often include diacritics for phonetic properties that are not present in Spanish. However, this has prevented such orthographies from being widely used by indigenous writers and intellectuals, who prefer practical alphabets without special characters.

16. It might be more accurate to speak of golden ages (plural) of indigenous-language literacy, as historical trajectories of indigenous text production vary by language and region. Nahuatl literacy began in the 1540s, peaked in 1580–1610, and was eclipsed after 1770 by writing in Spanish. Literacy in Yucatec Maya did not gain traction until 1640, steadily increasing thereafter to climax in the same period Nahuatl literacy declined (1770–1820). Mixtec literacy began in the 1570s but did not peak until the 1670–1720 period and declined steadily after 1770 (Restall et al. 2005: 15–17).

17. Yasnaya Aguilar, personal communication, January 2012.

18. For a comprehensive study of Mexico's history of language policies, see Heath 1972.

19. Matthew O'Hara (2009) argues that this move was less about the church's interest in promoting indigenous education and literacy in Spanish than about the church's internal tensions, serving to secularize its missions and hence weaken the power of religious orders.

20. Eric Van Young (2001: 479) claims that even by 1800, the "proportion of monolingual indigenous language speakers was still quite high" (see also Guardino 2005: 76). Yanna Yannakakis (2008: 161–91) offers further evidence, showing that election disputes following the new laws demonstrated the elusive state of enforcement on the indigenous-language ban as local authorities selectively forced compliance, thus exerting continued power over municipal elections.

21. Indeed, language use and linguistic difference have been the intervention point

for many authors cited here. Additional authors worth mentioning for their focus on language or communication—if on very different theoretical and methodological terms from the New Philologists—are Serge Gruzinski (1993), Susan Kellogg (1995), and Tzvetan Todorov (1984 [1982]).

22. Others have made a different but related argument. Rather than identifying a general trend to submerge modern indigenous reality while elevating indigenous pasts, they stress how *representations* of the nation marginalize contemporary indigenous people while valorizing ancient Mesoamerican societies, forming a dominant discursive and symbolic trope in Mexican national self-representation (Craib 2004; Lomnitz 1992, 2005).

23. The history of indigenous writing and literacy in Oaxaca is the subject of new collaborative work I am pursuing with ethnohistorians and linguists. We aim to rethink received ideas about indigenous-language writing in the independence and early national periods by using Mazatec as a case study.

24. Although the very first Mazatec texts date from the late colonial period (Arrona 1796, 1797), a few more texts were published after independence (e.g., Quintero 1838; Rio 1820). With one exception (Pimentel 1865), this was followed by a lapse of several decades until the century's end (Belmar 1978 [1892]); Brinton 1892a, 1892b).

25. Personal communication, Sebastian Van Doesburg, November 2011.

26. Central works in the vast scholarly literature on the Mexican Revolution include Dawson 2004; Katz 1981; Knight 1990; Vaughan 1997; Vaughan and Lewis 2006.

27. Vasconcelos also meant for Mexican nationalism to challenge American imperialism. This theme resonated with the emerging postmodern sensibility of the U.S. Hispanic rights movement, whose leaders reinterpreted "la Raza" to articulate their *exclusion* from the nation-state.

28. An exception is Smith's work on indigenous-language use in the army in the 1930s, suggesting that Zapotec speakers from Juchitán developed a military register of Zapotec: Benjamin Smith, personal communication, December 2011.

29. The SIL's role in national educational policy is fascinating, particularly its influence in the Mazateca. Kenneth Pike (1948), one of the organization's leading intellectual figures, did groundbreaking research there; his sister Eunice also conducted extensive fieldwork in and around Huautla. Although I leave this subject for another study, briefly, the SIL began work in Mexico in 1936 and aligned itself fully and enthusiastically with the Mexican state and indigenismo. This meant promoting literacy in the native language both as crucial for receiving the Gospel and as a stepping stone to literacy and facility in Spanish, thus speeding indigenous people's integration into national life (Stoll 1982: 63–68). Until 1979, the SIL was heavily involved in indigenous literacy and education. During the institute's forty years of active work in Mexico, almost all indigenous people who learned to read and write in native languages did so, directly or indirectly, through its linguist-missionaries, with support and encouragement from the federal government (King 1994: 116). During the political shift that began in the late 1960s, when assimilationist indigenismo came increasingly under attack, the SIL was likewise targeted. In 1979, the Secretariat of Public Education canceled its contract

with the SIL. Although the SIL continues to operate in Mexico, it is far less active and influential today than it once was.

30. While elsewhere in Mexico, guasmole refers to a particular mole (sauce), here it denotes a bright yellow-orange fruit from the lowlands (to³jndi³), a festive and coveted food whose short season coincides with Day of the Dead. July 22 is the feast (saint) day for Mary Magdalene. In the original text, the phrase used for in Mazatec is *el dialecto Mazateco*, just one of many examples illustrating how frequently even indigenous intellectuals—here, both the author and the magazine's editor—have internalized dominant discursive conventions about the inferiority of indigenous languages. Also in the original, the phrase used for "mushrooms" is the diminutive *los honguitos*, an expression that conveys affection and intimacy. This is one way speakers indicate that these mushrooms are "special" (i.e., hallucinogenic—rather than merely edible).

31. Nda Xo 'Foaming Water' (*nda* [water] plus *xo* [foam, froth]) is named for this spring.

32. The official figure is 206,559 (INEGI 2005), although following a well-documented trend of rising figures for indigenous populations in Mexico—even as the percentage of speakers is often dropping—the actual total may be higher. The figure for Mazatec speakers in 1970 was 101,541, or less than half the 2000 figure, and in 1990, it was 168,374, or roughly three-quarters of the 2000 figure. Mazatecs are the ninth largest ethnic group in Mexico (INEGI 2005).

33. Nda Xo's municipal population is roughly 20,000; approximately 1,500 people live in the cabecera, while the remaining 18,500 live in more than a hundred smaller communities (INEGI 2010).

34. In 2005, a landslide in Nda Xo killed nine people, an event covered by national and international media. In 2006, after years of infighting, Nda Xo finally delivered on longstanding promises to pave the road into town. Just after the first couple of kilometers were paved, a landslide dumped several boulders—one as big as a house—in the middle of the road, destroying it. There is also a particular kind of hallucinogenic mushroom, the "landslide" variety, that appears at the site of fresh mudslides—in Spanish, *derrumbe*, and in Mazatec, ndi¹xi³tjo³ ki³xo³ ("little things who spring forth" plus "landslide") or ndi¹tso³jmi² na³ngui³ ("little things" plus "land").

35. In Nda Xo, 94.9 percent of the population speaks Mazatec; 29.7 percent are monolingual (INEGI 2010).

36. The Sierra town of San Juan Coatzospan is a linguistic island, a municipio that since the colonial era has been inhabited by Mixtec speakers.

37. This exoticization of the Mazatec region is not uncommon, either. The first account of a mushroom ritual refers to the shaman overseeing it as a brujo, retaining that term throughout the English account (J. Johnson 1939a).

38. Encomienda was a colonial labor system through which tribute was extracted.

39. Including the family of María Sabina.

40. For descriptive articles on Mazatec society generally, see Bauer 1968 (1908); F. Cowan 1946; Johnson 1939b; Starr 1902, 1908; Weitlaner and Hoppe 1969. For analytical articles on specific aspects of Mazatec society, see Carrera González 2000b;

F. Cowan 1947; G. Cowan 1946, 1952, 1954; Johnson 1939a; Kirk 1966; E. Pike 1949; Stavenhagen 1960; Weitlaner and Weitlaner 1946. Compilations and analyses of Mazatec tales and myths include Inchaustegui 1977, 1983, 1994; Portal 1986; Ríos Nolasco 1992. A recent study using present calendrical practices partly to illuminate past ones is Van Doesburg and Carrera González 1997. All Mazatec intellectuals and many others are familiar with the calendar, which, my ethnographic research (December 2011) confirms, continues to be used in agriculture.

41. Major changes included the rise of coffee caciques, whose status was based less on rank than class and whose power ultimately eclipsed the Ch^{4}ota^4 Jchi^{1}nga^3 (Consejo de Ancianos [Council of Elders]), men who rose to power through the cargo system, an older system of indigenous self-rule widely discussed in scholarly literature.

42. Vanilla has been a successful if socially divisive cash crop elsewhere in Mexico (Kourí 2004), but in the Sierra it seems to be used mostly by women to scent their hair. Passion fruit is not widely eaten in Mexico; in the Sierra, people use it mostly for juice or to flavor *aguardiente* (cane liquor). The result is a locally popular beverage sold by shopkeepers, including one who runs a "little hospital for drinkers," where passion-fruit liquor is purportedly a bestseller (*La Faena* 1: 20). Feinberg claims Huautla has turned to another substitute for coffee: schoolteachers. As told by a former employee of Inmecafe, "Huautla lived on coffee. Now it lives on teachers" (quoted in Feinberg 2003: 93).

43. XEOJN, "La Voz de la Chinantla," is located in San Lucas Ojitlán, a Chinantec-speaking town. Its signal cannot be picked up in most of the Sierra.

44. Although others discuss the event—Feinberg (2003: 49) dates the road's completion to 1959—I use the date in Pearlman 1981, because she focuses directly on its role in changing gender relations and because hers concurs with the date in Van Doesburg and Carrera González 1997. The road project was initiated by the INI's Centro Coordinador Indígenista, established in Huautla in 1959 (Van Doesburg and Carrera González 1997: 165–66). Although the founding of INI's center in Huautla is hardly discussed in scholarly literature, the presence of a local INI office undoubtedly had important social repercussions.

45. Like many Oaxacan municipios, communities in the Sierra routinely have contested elections, sometimes resulting in violence (Feinberg 2003: 53–55). Oaxaca's Usos y Costumbres Law of 1994 was meant to allow indigenous communities to elect municipal officials through traditional means rather than political parties. Though in the Sierra it has often operated as such in name only, the legislation was groundbreaking, the result of years of struggle by indigenous groups. Although it is only one of Mexico's thirty-two federal entities, Oaxaca has a whopping 570 municipios, nearly a fourth of the national total and nearly twice the number of Puebla, the state that follows (INEGI 2010). Thus, the law directly affected a large number of municipios nationwide and has become the model for indigenous rights legislation across the country.

Chapter 2: "Land of the Magic Mushroom"

1. The term most often used for outsiders is cho⁴ta⁴xi¹n (people who are different): *chota* (person) plus *xi¹n* (apart, separate); cf. *chotaxi⁴n* (hunter). Note that Mazatec nouns are not usually marked for number (i.e., a distinction between singular and plural is rarely made). *Chotayo⁴ma⁴* (poor people)—*chota* plus *yo⁴ma⁴* (poor, humble); cf. *yo³ma¹* (avocado)—is a common autodesignator used by Mazatec speakers. Another is *chota e¹n i⁴ma⁴ na¹* (people who speak our language, the language of the poor)—*chota* plus *en* (language) plus *ima* (poor) plus *-na¹* (first person plural possessive [inclusive]); cf. *-na⁴* (first person singular possessive). In my experience, people in the Sierra, including Mazatec writers, often talk about Mazatecs being "poor people" who speak a "little language." On intellectuals' largely unsuccessful attempts to "rehabilitate" the term *chotayoma* by substituting words without the negative connotations, see Duke 1996: 240–41.

2. *Cho⁴ta⁴* (person) plus *chji⁴ne⁴* (master, knower [of]).

3. This ritual is extremely common in Mexico. In the Sierra, it involves purification by smoke from copal incense while prayers (usually in Mazatec) are uttered. The most critical element requires passing a natural object over the person in a brushing, wiping motion. Many people use eggs, but that day the shaman used a cluster of flowers and branches with leaves; these must be either freshly cut or taken from an altar.

4. There are clear differences between lowland and highland veladas. Edward Abse (2007) gives a detailed analysis of how veladas have changed over the past century—changes with generational dimensions that are linked to historical events I discuss in this chapter and the previous one. My discussion of veladas is taken from my ethnographic experience and from numerous other sources, including Abse 2007; Bauer 1968 (1908); Boege 1988; Duke 1996, 2001; Estrada 1989 (1977), 1981, 1996; Feinberg 1997, 2003; García Carrera 1986; Huber and Sandstrom 2001; Incháustegui 1977, 1983, 1994; Johnson 1939a, 1939b; Miranda 1997; Munn 1973, 2003; Pérez Quijada 1996; Pike and Cowan 1959; Tibón 1983; Van Doesburg and Carrera González 1997; Wasson 1957; Wasson et al 1974; Weitlaner 1952.

5. The first is morning glory seeds, found across Mexico and known as *olloliuhqui* or *piule* (Nahuatl terms for the white and blue varieties, respectively) or, in Mazatec, as *to³ tjo³n* (treasured seed): *to* (fruit, seed) plus *tjon* (treasure, money, coin). The second is *Salvia divinorum*, a sage-like herb known in Mazatec as *xka⁴ Pastora* (Leaf of the Shepherdess—i.e., Mary, *xka⁴* [leaf]). Salvia was originally found only in the Sierra but recently has been "advertised" through thousands of videos of users' experiences on the Internet and has become widely available around the world (see Faudree 2012a). The third plant is *na³xo² la¹mba¹* or *datura*, known elsewhere in Mexico as *floripondio*, *toloatzin*, or *toloache*.

6. Altars also feature flowers and cut greenery, often used in limpias. Other plants used in veladas include San Pedro, or *piciate*, a paste of ground green tobacco mixed with lime and water or cane liquor that is placed in crosses on participants' foreheads and inner wrists to protect against malign spirits; ground cacao seeds mixed with

water, which is useful in combating nausea; and copal incense, a tree resin widely used in Mesoamerican rituals.

7. The participant structure of veladas seems to vary greatly. Abse (2007) claims that some of the variation stems from new religious practices, in dialogue with historical shifts, that cause people to treat shamans with increased skepticism and hence to embrace "Protestant-style" veladas free of shamans. He argues that these changes are linked to different ideologies about veladas' purpose, as people have recast them from healing rituals to rituals that shed light on the future and "life paths." My experiences with veladas held among Mazatec Indigenous Church members (see chapter 5) reflect similar tendencies. Members' explicit talk about *veladas* suggests that their practice is closely tied to an increasingly political reading of "traditional" shamanism: shamans are viewed as closely allied with the church and, hence, with a more hierarchical, rather than broadly "communitarian," knowledge structure.

8. A few examples suggest the rich semantic field that surrounds the term *chikon*. In isolation, *chikon* can mean owner, boss, or superior; a sacred being or deity; something large or powerful; a foreigner; a blond or light-skinned person. I often heard people who were relatively light-skinned called chikon and lighter-skinned children described with pride as being chikon. *Chikon* is used in various contexts that clearly mark it as sacred or religious, such as na chikon (godmother [na^4 (woman)]), kjua chikon (prayer group, religious matter [kjua^4 (thing, substantive marker)]), nda kjua chikon (holy water [nda^1 (water)]). Words less obviously tied to the sacred realm are nevertheless suggestive: chikon ts'oa (stomach gas [ts'oa^4 (stomach)]); chikon ni (macaw [ni^2 (red)]); chje chikon (anaconda [*mazacuate*] or other large snake [chje^4 (snake)]); chikon xa (authority [such as municipal president] [xa^2 (work)]), nda chikon (ocean [or other large body of water, such as the Miguel Alemán reservoir on the edge of the Sierra] [nda^1 (water)]).

9. Such spirits are sometimes called la'a, translated locally as *duende* (imp, goblin), a term with a more malevolent connotation. I understand such spirits to be attached to less important, nondescript locations.

10. Many sabios use the trope of the book as a symbol for knowledge imparted during veladas (see, e.g., Feinberg 1997; Munn 1973). María Sabina spoke of her curing knowledge as "my Book" (Wasson et al. 1974: 84, 86, 108, 134, 136, 156). The *Libro de la Sabiduría* (Book of wisdom) or *Libro de la Lenguaje* (Book of language) was the accumulated sacred wisdom she had received during veladas and used to heal people (Estrada 1989 [1977]). Note that she uses the Spanish loan word *libro* (book). Only recently derived neologisms exist in Mazatec, and they are not widely used. Xo^{4}n (paper) is probably the closest word in common usage, but I have never heard it used to refer to an entire book; nor have I seen it used that way in written texts.

11. When quoting from Estrada's work, I rely on the Spanish version (Estrada 1989 [1977]) rather than its subsequent English translation (Estrada 1981). Estrada, a Huauteco and native Mazatec speaker, ostensibly provided the first attempt to "give voice" to the woman behind the mystique. Nevertheless, his account does not provide a Mazatec version of his interviews with María Sabina, and some locals have questioned his ac-

count, including Juan García Carrera, who is also a native of Huautla and the editor of *La Faena* and who wrote his own book in response (García Carrera 1986).

12. Michael Duke (2001) claims that although this is the most important form of ritual sexual abstinence, similar sexual taboos pertain to hunting, ritual praying (especially during mourning), and key agricultural practices. Federico Neiburg (1988) makes the interesting claim that agricultural sexual taboos pertain to subsistence crops—foods for local consumption, thus part of local social relations—but not to cash crops such as coffee.

13. On Mazatec "food witchcraft," see Gudschinsky 1959; Pike 1949.

14. Purity is an important value to all major rituals in the Sierra and is well documented in scholarly literature (see, e.g., Abse 2007; Boege 1988; Duke 2001; Incháustegui 1977, 1994).

15. In the latter case, the diminutive particle *-ito*, on par with its use in other contexts to convey affection and intimacy, is how speakers indicate that the mushrooms are the hallucinogenic kind rather than tjain³, Mazatec for nonhallucinogenic edible mushrooms.

16. This observation stems from probing Mazatec speakers about other "noneuphemistic" ways to refer to such entities. The few vocabularies and dictionaries for Mazatec are inconclusive. Most were produced by the SIL and are strikingly devoid of any mention of the mushrooms or veladas—or, indeed, of any reference to things one could classify as "pagan." The only exception I could find was an entry in a small vocabulary book: xi³tjo³, glossed simply as "a certain type of mushroom" (Pike 1952).

17. The Tina and R. Gordon Wasson Ethnomycological Collection Archives, Botany Libraries, Harvard University Herbaria, available online at http://www.huh.harvard.edu/libraries/wasson.htm (accessed March 1, 2012).

18. The later veladas involved the chemist James A. Moore, the anthropologist Guy Stresser-Péan, and the mycologist Roger Heim. Duke (1996: 107) notes that although Wasson was unaware of it, Moore was actually a CIA operative acting on the agency's interest in hallucinogenic drugs.

19. The monthly magazine *La Faena*, subtitled *Herencia Cultural de los Mazatecos* (Cultural Heritage of the Mazatecs), is published mostly in Spanish, with some Mazatec and, occasionally, a little (broken) English. Unless noted otherwise, texts quoted from the magazine originally appeared in Spanish. *La Faena* takes its name from the Spanish word used in the Sierra for communal labor, called *tequio* elsewhere in Mexico, and in Mazatec xa¹va³sen³: xa¹ (work) plus va³sen³ (half); cf. nd'ia³ va³sen³ (*ayuntamiento* [town hall]): nd'ia³ (house, building) plus va³sen³ (half). The magazine's logo features stylized conch shells, used to summon men for communitarian labor.

20. Although marijuana and hallucinogenic mushrooms are often grouped together as psychotropic plants, in the Sierra they belong to distinct categories. Unlike marijuana, ndi xitjo are medicinal, not "recreational" drugs.

21. For a small selection of what "María Sabina studies" has to offer, see Ceraso 2008; Estrada 1989 (1977), 1981; García Carrera 1986; Rothenberg 2003; Rubio Montoya 1992; Tedlock 2005; Tibón 1983; Wasson and Wasson 1957; Wasson et al. 1974.

See also Valentina P. and R. Gordon Wasson, *Mushroom Ceremony of the Mazatec Indians of Mexico*, audio recording Folkways FR 8975 (New York: Folkways Records and Service Corporation, 1957).

22. Based on research in Huautla, Duke (1996) and Feinberg (1996) make this point in different ways. Duke argues that Wasson's vision has profoundly affected "Mazatec subjectivity." Feinberg claims that outsiders construct Mazatec identity by creating contexts in which locals highlight cultural boundaries and mediators cross them. Although Feinberg presents this as general trait of Mazatec identity, I think it may apply to a particular category: shamans and other culture brokers. Both arguments are essentially stronger versions of the one I make, doubtless tied to the inescapability of discourses about Wasson, María Sabina, and the mushrooms in the "metropole."

23. The development of a Mazatec professional or middle class only indirectly tied to agriculture is relatively recent. It dates from the second half of the twentieth century, when coffee brought a new level of wealth and increased insertion into the market economy. The Prado family is not atypical. The father was a prosperous campesino, and all of his fourteen children are professionals or married to professionals (teachers mostly, but also government employees and merchants, as well as a house builder and a mariachi musician). The one exception was married to a campesino who won the Day of the Dead Song Contest in 2001; one of Nda Xo's most notorious drunks, he died in 2011 from a head injury after a fall.

24. Polygamy was widespread in the Sierra even a generation ago, and most middle-aged people I know there are products of polygamous marriages. Such marriages involved two or three wives and occasionally more. One man reportedly had thirty to forty wives, more than eighty children, and countless grandchildren. Now, polygamous marriages are rare. With the possible exception of a case discussed later, I knew about only one man younger than fifty who had more than one wife—a composer who won the song contest in 2002 and ran for municipal president in 2004. However, his second marriage was semisecret; his second wife, the younger sister of the first wife, rarely left the house. Several people I mentioned this to were surprised to hear that she, too, was married to the man known as her sister's husband.

25. Achieving this office when he did was a different index of social standing in the Sierra than it is now, as he did so under the old system that relies on being named to the post by the Council of Elders. As Neiburg (1988) writes about the nearby *municipio* (county) of Tenango, whose situation mirrors Nda Xo's, the town council or Consejo de Ancianos fell into sharp decline after the rise of political parties in the last decades of the twentieth century. Now, achieving such posts is seen as a reflection of personal wealth or status within a political party. Several people remarked, with some disgust, that the president serving a three-year term in 2000–2003—a merchant in his mid-thirties, a civic profile far different from that of many previous presidents— "doesn't even speak well," meaning he was uncomfortable speaking in public, especially in Mazatec. This image is very much at odds with that presented by at midcentury by George Cowan (1952), in which the president's weekly public addresses played a critical social role.

26. The Prelature of Huautla was founded in October 1972 by the Congregación de Misioneros Josefinos, as part of the centennial celebration of the order's existence. The Josefinos order of the Catholic Church was founded in Mexico by José María Vilaseca in 1872. Beyond the dedication of its priests to Saint Joseph, the order's mission is to evangelize to the indigenous and poor. Although the Josefinos are now involved in many countries (El Salvador especially, but also Chile, Venezuela, Costa Rica, Guatemala, and Angola), they have been most active in Mexico, working primarily in indigenous areas. The choice to establish in their centennial year a new prelature in the poorest, most indigenous state in the country was thus an explicit extension of their founding legacy. Monsignor Ramírez Sánchez, who was born in Mexico City, arrived the following year and served as Huautla's bishop until he retired. Administratively, the prelature is subordinate to the Archdiocese of Antequera, Oaxaca, and oversees seven parishes spread across nineteen municipios. Chilchotla (Nda Xo) is one of these parishes; another is San José Tenango, the parish where Heriberto Prado served as a priest.

27. Secundaria is the equivalent in the U.S. system to middle school or junior high school. Particularly in Heriberto Prado's generation, completing secundaria was an achievement in and of itself. Although the standards have since changed, it was not uncommon at that time—and in some isolated Sierra communities it remains so—for primaria (grade school) teachers themselves to have finished only primaria. Such teachers, though, were at least functionally bilingual, a skill by no means commonly held today by students who finish primaria.

28. This means, of course, that more than 70 percent are bilingual. The rise in recent decades of bilingualism among indigenous speakers—both in the Sierra and in Mexico as a whole—has deep implications for indigenous authors, readers, and revival projects. I take this theme up in chapter 6.

29. During his first presidency in 1963—the same year, significantly, that the Coffee Fair was founded—construction began on the only road into Nda Xo. It was overseen by a committee headed by an uncle of Alberto and Heriberto Prado. Though the road was winding and rocky, and periodically was made impassable by landslides and falling boulders, its completion three years later was a momentous date in the history of Nda Xo.

30. Fernando Palacios Cházares, "Heriberto Prado sacerdote retirado por tener esposa," Las Noticias (Oaxaca), 1999.

31. This includes de la Cadena 2000; García 2005; Green 2009; Gustafson 2009; Hale 2006; Niezen 2003; Postero 2007; Povinelli 2002; Ramos 1998; Starn 1999; Tsing 2004.

32. Note that this category is used by many researchers, most of whom highlight its constructed nature even as they rely on it. Notable examples include Feierman 1990; Jackson and Warren 2005; Rappaport 2005; Stavenhagen 2002; Warren 1998; Warren and Jackson 2002.

1. I follow common usage in referring to the holiday in the singular (*día*), although it is more accurately labeled "Days of the Dead" (Childs and Altman 1982; Lomnitz 2005).

2. For a discussion of the symbolic competition between Halloween and Day of the Dead as a reflection of geopolitical tension between the United States and Mexico, see Brandes 1998.

3. Although Day of the Dead has become a booming business in parts of Mexico, the sites featured in this ethnography receive very few tourists.

4. Scholars writing on Day of the Dead include Brandes 1997, 1998; Carmichael and Sayer 1992; Childs and Altman 1982; Norget 1996; Nutini 1988. For visual art, the most famous example is the satirical work of José Guadalupe Posada, although artists such as Frida Kahlo, José Clemente Orozco, and especially Diego Rivera featured Muertos themes in their work.

5. Many scholars, including Claudio Lomnitz (2001), have critiqued the museum.

6. For a brilliant analysis of the role Day of the Dead has played in the ongoing and contested construction of Mexican nationalism in the Mexican—and international—public sphere, see Lomnitz 2005.

7. Ronald Niezen (2003) discusses such tensions as "paradoxes" of indigenous movements.

8. Carrera is discussed in Abse 2007; Dalton 1990; Feinberg 2003. I thank Edward Abse for initially putting me in contact with Maestro Carrera.

9. This is reflected in several linguistic indices, including the percentage of the population who are monolingual, the percentage whose *lengua materna* is Mazatec, the prevalence of Mazatec in daily life, and the relative "purity" of the Mazatec spoken. This final issue, which I discuss later, is a favorite point of intervention by indigenous intellectuals and drives the generation of neologistic replacements for Spanish loan words and other "purification" practices. The other three are reflected in figures from the most recent national census (INEGI 2010), which indicate that Chilchotla tends to be more conservative linguistically than the rest of the region (which, in turn, appears to be linguistically conservative compared with the rest of the state and country).

10. *Cha^{1}jma^2* (*cha^1* "man, person" plus *jma^2* "black"), or *los negritos* (the black men). The name calls to mind *negritos* who take on the role of quintessential Others in folk festivals throughout Mexico and Latin America; some scholars link them to colonial "imports"—that is, African slaves or the history of the Christian-Moor conflicts, both brought to the New World by the Spanish (Bricker 1981). However, in the Sierra, people never translate the word literally. Instead, they use *viejitos* (old people), *antepasados* (forefathers), and so on. Chajma are always represented as old people or ancestors and are never represented in blackface (or with black animal faces), as is often done in the "Danza de los Negritos" of other folk customs from elsewhere in Mexico. Thus, the Othering invoked by the name *chajma* is more ambivalent, marking not political or cultural but, rather, existential difference—the dead set apart from the living.

11. *Naxo* (flower) plus *ngojo* (grave, hole). This flower, the golden marigold, is known in Mexico by the Nahuatl word *zempoalxochitl* (*zempazuchitl*). In the Sierra, once the candles are lit, they become tied directly to the dead. If a candle burns all the way down, the dead person will be burned, as well. Thus, candles must be snuffed out with care, using a flower. Wasson mentions María Sabina doing this in a velada, a gesture casting the room into darkness, after which "the proceedings take place, pagan-fashion, on the floor, the habitual practice of the American Indian" (Wasson 1980: xxii).

12. The fiesta is highly gendered. Almost all of the musicians are adult men, male youths, or boys and often are members of an extended family. The dancers, too, are almost always men. Some women try to pass as men, although this is considered risky, because the fiesta's disguises, heavy drinking, and nocturnal setting contribute to the sense that huehuentones are not subject to normal social propriety. Women dancing as chajma usually go with male relatives or compadres who "watch over" them.

13. Some families—particularly Protestants—do not admit the chajma, although most groups simply avoid their houses. Protestants do participate in other parts of the fiesta, including the breaking of the piñatas.

14. Atole agrio is a slightly fermented corn gruel served with a topping of black beans and special ground chili and sesame-seed sauce. It is a labor-intensive and locally marked ritual food that is served on special occasions (e.g., weddings) and always during the Day of the Dead fiesta.

15. During the fiesta, the social boundaries around the graveyard are somewhat fluid, but during the rest of the year, people in Nda Xo are careful to delimit the liminal space cemeteries occupy. Graveyards are ambivalent spaces: the resting place of loved ones, they are also fields of danger where the living expose themselves to the power of "bad air" and harmful spirits. Everyone I met in Nda Xo held some version of these beliefs, whose outward expression takes the form of a practice people routinely use when returning from the cemetery of lighting copal incense or redolent leaves such as laurel and bathing themselves in the purifying smoke.

16. The "traditional" part of the fiesta ends when the ancestors remove their disguises. On that evening, the musicians do not play, and the night is eerily quiet. As one woman said during my first Muertos in the Sierra, "That night, you won't hear a sound. It's very sad." Recently, Nda Xo and other Sierra towns have started to bring rock bands from Oaxaca and other nearby cities to play on the final evening—concerts that stand in stark contrast to the rest of the fiesta. The music is amplified through loudspeakers, and people dance as couples in front of the band. This innovation has received a mixed response. Some find the events irrelevant or offensive, a violation of the fiesta's traditionalistic spirit, while young people have greeted them with enthusiasm.

17. There may be one musical precedent in the Sierra for the contest. I could find no other mention in scholarly literature, but Robert Weitlaner and Walter Hoppe (1969: 521) claim that an "aesthetic manifestation" of Mazatec culture is the "love of music, and almost all towns have at least one band. In the principal fiestas bands from neighboring towns get together to compete." Frederick Starr (1908) also mentions the importance of the town band in discussing his visit to Huautla.

18. Although most catechists are men, some are women, and at least one female catechist has written Mazatec songs for the church. However, because of the fiesta's highly gendered nature—women participate openly in the evening chajma visits only as hostesses—almost no women are involved in composing songs for the contest or, consequently, for wider circulation of the songs on CDs.

19. This program, which is sponsored by the Centro de Investigaciones y Estudios Superiores en Antropología Social (Center for Research and Advanced Study in Social Anthropology; CIESAS), awards licenciaturas (bachelor's degrees), through which indigenous-language speakers learn linguistic analysis of their native languages. CIESAS is one of Mexico's premiere institutions for social-science research.

20. The teponaxtle is a Mesoamerican log drum that is hollowed out from the bottom, with an H-shape slit cut in the top. One sounds the drum by striking the two resulting tongues with mallets.

21. Ben Feinberg (2003: 110) claims that huehuentones "must not wear a stitch of their own clothing—all the clothes are borrowed from someone else." In my experience, people spend the entire fiesta swapping clothes (the better to disguise oneself) but do not observe such prohibitions.

22. Among the chaxo'o who danced from house to house that year there were a number of "Osama bin Ladens" who, because I was the only non-Mexican at the fiesta and an American, to boot, enjoyed taking occasional jesting potshots at me with plastic guns, to great general amusement.

23. E. Gabino García Carrera, "Celebran sexto encuentro cultural de huehuentones y ritual de Muertos," Las Noticias (Oaxaca), November 2, 2005. I would spell the group's name "Chaxo'o Najnča," whose meaning is closer to "the Huehuentones of the center [of town]" (najnča, "center of the pueblo"). The spelling in Carrera's article is idiosyncratic and, I assume, was provided by the locals he interviewed, because Carrera, who is based in Oaxaca, is not a Serrano. Such discrepancies in how speech is represented in writing are ubiquitous, and many indigenous intellectuals cite them as a reason that orthographic standardization is necessary.

24. On a related argument about the indio permitido (authorized Indian), see Hale 2006.

Chapter 4: Scenes from a Nativist Reformation

1. The text in this chapter's epigraph appears in the orthography Heriberto devised; nasalization is indicated by the capital letters M, N, and Ñ.

2. Kjua⁴chi³kon³: kjua⁴ (thing [substantive marker]) plus chi³kon³ (white, or light-skinned, person; something sacred; sacred spirit). These prayer groups function much like cofradías (religious brotherhoods, widely discussed in anthropological literature on Latin America). The Sierra's kjuachikones lack the deep history of traditional cofradías and demonstrate much greater participation by women. Each one is associated with a locally important saint, and collectively they conduct the essential religious activities of the community, from cleaning and maintaining the church grounds to sponsoring

religious fiestas. In other ways, they are similar to Christian Base Communities, a key local organizational unit of the Catholic Church under Liberation Theology, although they are pointedly lacking in the politicized character motivating the initial foundation of base communities.

3. The use of the term *compañera* reveals the ambivalent feelings that many people in Nda Xo, including Alberto, have about Ana.

4. Of course, religious difference and emergent religious forms have been of special interest to anthropologists as well; and even if only some of them deal with religious violence, most grapple in some measure with religious conflict. Important recent texts in this vein include Bowen 2010; Keane 2007; Robbins 2004.

5. See, e.g., de la Fuente 1949; Friedrich 1986; Greenberg 1989; Kearney 1972; Nader 1964, 1990; Nash 1970.

6. Tim Weiner, "Sixteen Arrested in Killings of 26 over Land Disputes in Mexico," *New York Times*, June 3, 2002, A1.

7. Hermann Bellinghausen, "La comunidad recobrada," *Ojarasca*, August 1999, 9.

8. Matilde Pérez U., "En Mazatlan, Oaxaca, crece el terror paramilitar," *La Jornada*, September 14, 1998, A23.

9. Kui⁴Nndja¹le⁴: Kui⁴Nndja¹ (we sing [imperative; inclusive]) plus -le⁴ ([to] him); nai³na¹ (God); nga³ ([definitive]); en¹ (word, language); na¹ (our [inclusive])

10. The bass violin is the one instrument Muertos musicians never use because it is not portable for house-to-house visits.

11. A few were not written by Heriberto and are in the public domain. Among them is "Naxo Loxa" (Orange Blossom), the unofficial national anthem of the sierra Mazateca, played at weddings and other special occasions. The Mazatec-language lyrics were written in the early twentieth century by the author, politician, and wealthy coffee plantation owner José Guadalupe García Parra. While an important antecedent to the new tradition of Mazatec song authorship discussed in this book, it seems to be an isolated, anomalous case. And although the song does have lyrics, it is routinely performed without them, using only instrumental music—a factor limiting its resonance as a precedent for living Mazatec songwriters.

12. The Sanctus and Benedictus appear in the same song. Some of these Masses do not contain settings of either the Credo or the Lord's Prayer.

13. Kyrie, Gloria, Credo, Sanctus and Benedictus, Agnus Dei.

14. Nda³ (good) is not to be confused with nda¹ (water, river).

15. The Spanish translations for these excerpts are, respectively, *lo mejor*, *el favor*, *gloria*, *reino*, *gracias*, Buena (Nueva), *voluntad*, *gusto por platicar*, and *soluciones*.

16. This is an evocative word: naxin (rock) plus nanda (water). It (like the Spanish term *pueblo*) signifies both a town and the people who live in it, a community. Such "water-hill" calques are well attested in Mesoamerica (Smith-Stark 1994), and in general, such lexical calques have been a privileged site for defining Mesoamerica as a cultural-linguistic area.

17. The core members performed as Grupo Claridad, later renamed Jt-Tin Nda Xo (Grupo Aqua Espuma, *agua espuma* being the literal Spanish translation of Chilcho-

tla's Mazatec name, Nda Xo). Under this name, the group made its first (eponymous) recording, of Heriberto's sixth Mass.

18. Then, as now, couples often "pair off" first. The formal wedding occurs several years later, often at the same time as their children's baptisms.

19. Reaction to *El crimen de Padre Amaro* (The crime of Father Amaro, 2002), the highest-grossing Mexican film in history, epitomizes this attitude. The film concerns a young priest's illicit relationship with a woman. The Catholic Church, outraged by the film, led protests against it, but "its viewers haven't considered it so offensive and have seen it as a valid approach to an unconcealable reality": see Nelson Carro, "El crimen del Padre Amaro," *El Ojo Que Piensa*, August 2003; J. Hoberman, "It's a Sin," *Village Voice*, November 13–19, 2002.

20. The church's ongoing sex-abuse scandal in the United States has periodically made news in the Sierra. In my experience, people react with horror when they hear that priests are molesting boys rather than women. "Oh, that's much worse," is a typical response.

21. I rely on newspaper articles, accounts written by local residents, and oral histories. Although I did not witness these precipitating events, I have seen similar conflicts between priests and communities. The parish priest at a tiny rancho where I lived was run out of town shortly after I arrived. According to one account, when he finally drove off in his truck—which was church property—people were so mad they pelted it with rocks, cracking the windshield. Similar problems surfaced with his successor.

22. The PRD is the most left leaning of Mexico's major parties.

23. Weddings and baptisms are among the most important, and thus expensive, events in the Sierra. Given the area's relative poverty, some families must save for years to raise the money required. Without a priest to perform the rituals at their center, these events are deeply "infelicitous."

24. E. Gabino García Carrera, "Por déspota y prepotente, rechazan a sacerdote en San Miguel Huautepec," *Las Noticias* (Oaxaca), 1999. In the original, the priest was quoted as using the second person familiar, further emphasizing his purported lack of respect. If the priest did say this or something like it, it would indeed represent an offensive attitude that is strikingly ignorant or dismissive of the emotional, logistical, and financial difficulties required to heed his words.

25. Fernando Palacios Cházares, "Heriberto Prado sacerdote retirado por tener esposa," *Las Noticias* (Oaxaca), 1999, 2.

26. Ibid.

27. In submunicipal communities—agencias and congregaciones—new authorities are elected annually. These are unpaid positions and may constitute a hardship for those who fill them. In the cabecera of Nda Xo, the authorities occupy paid positions and are elected every three years.

28. Hermengildo Ramírez Sánchez, pastoral letter, February 18, 1999. Copies in the collections of Heriberto Prado Pereda and Paja Faudree.

29. Palacios Cházares, "Heriberto Prado sacerdote retirado por tener esposa."

30. Comunidad de Misioneras Indígenas de Nuestra Señora de Guadalupe, program

bulletin, November 11, 1998, Santa María Magdalena Chilchotla, Oaxaca. Copy in the collection of Paja Faudree.

31. In this respect—as well as in the publicness with which his libido was expressed—Heriberto is perhaps more like England's King Henry VIII. Both Henry's and Heriberto's rifts with the Catholic Church share a (quasi)nationalistic flavor and are as much political as religious, entailing a different attitude toward reform and toward breaking with church tradition than Luther took. Another relevant religious figure is Joseph Smith, founder of the Church of Jesus Christ of Latter-day Saints. Both Joseph Smith and Heriberto Prado saw their foundational missions as restorationist and holistic, in both cases producing insular movements. Like Smith, Heriberto resembles a prophet, gaining access to divine knowledge through texts and visions, and both held the view that the original inhabitants of the Americas had prior knowledge of Jesus Christ. I thank Gary Tomlinson and Paul Kockelman for suggesting these analogies.

32. Many people in Nda Xo see Heriberto and his group as Protestants, referring to them in both languages by the terms commonly used for Protestants.

33. My discussion here and in chapter 5 concerning the divergence between ideology and practice owes much to foundational social scientific theories of language (e.g., Bakhtin 1981; Bourdieu 1991; Voloshinov 1986) as well as to the extensive research in linguistic anthropology on linguistic ideology (e.g., Bauman and Briggs 2003; Irvine and Gal 2000; Kroskrity 2000; Makihara and Schieffelin 2007; Schieffelin et al. 1998).

34. Mexican indigenous intellectuals often adopt linguistic purism. Like Heriberto, they are vigilant about identifying Spanish loan words and replacing them with neologisms.

35. Kissing the earth is certainly not foreign to canonical church practice: no less a symbol of Catholic orthodoxy than Pope John Paul II kissed the earth every time he arrived in a new country, for example. My point, though, is that such a gesture has become a routine part of religious practice for the Mazatec Indigenous Church. This gives the gesture a different meaning from the one it had for the late pope, who kissed not so much the earth itself as the particular nation and the people to whom it belonged.

36. María Sabina also used this imagery: "the niños son la sangre de Cristo" (Estrada 1989 [1977]: 74). Eunice Pike and Florence Cowan (1959: 145) claimed that Mazatecs believe mushrooms spring up where Christ spat on the ground during his life, a more negative claim I have not encountered elsewhere. Although this interpretation distances the mushrooms from the act of salvation represented by the Crucifixion (which might appeal to evangelicals like Pike and Cowan), it also echoes the claim Heriberto makes that Christ came to the Americas during his life.

37. Although the word *sabio* is Spanish, I do not think it is widely used elsewhere in the way it is here—that is, to refer to a shaman. It some ways, it echoes the Mazatec word for shaman: *cho⁴ta⁴ chji⁴ne⁴* (*chota* [person] plus *chjine* [master in/of, artisan]). *Chjine* is also used to refer to the broad class of experts: *chjinenajni* (musician), *chjinečhjoa* (tanner), *chjinekicha* (blacksmith), *chjinexjao* (mason), *chjineya* (carpenter), *cjine'en* (interpreter), *chjinexki* (doctor), *chjinexkixi ni'ño* (dentist). A free translation of chota chjine, then, might be something like "master of masters" or "chief expert."

38. In the original, Heriberto refers to this table as "la mesa celestial" and "la mesa sagrada." The former is the Spanish version he uses in referring to *ya misa xkon* (*ya* [tree (made of wood)]) plus *misa* (table) plus *xkon* (sacred, heavenly). This is one of the thirteen tables of "Mazatec cosmovision," which, as Alberto wrote in an article on the topic, features "thirteen heavens and in every heaven there is a door beyond which are the respective tables, where one has to place the corresponding offerings" (Prado Pineda 2004: 5). Heriberto has written several poems about these tables, which figure prominently in drawings on the covers of his books and other booklets, such as the one produced for the consecration of the Misioneras (Comunidad de Misioneras Indígenas de Nuestra Señora de Guadalupe, program bulletin).

Chapter 5: Meeting at the Family Crypt

1. Fernando Palacios Cházares, "Heriberto Prado sacerdote retirado por tener esposa," *Las Noticias* (Oaxaca), 1999.

2. As in many Mexican communities, this figurative expression of leadership finds literal expression in the "staffs of office" awarded to community officials. Heriberto owns one of these from serving on the municipal education committee. He occasionally uses the staff in veladas, to great dramatic effect. The most notable occasion I witnessed was a velada during which Jesus spoke through Heriberto during the ceremony, wielding the staff in the process.

3. He made the same argument about another death that occurred around that time. When he returned to Nda Xo from the bank in Tehuacán, one of the town's wealthiest residents was killed by someone who turned out to be his own cousin; the cousin also killed the man's servant, who was very poor. Heriberto's comment was particularly revealing because it came on the heels of a discussion of how tragic the situation was: the rich man's wife had never borne children, and the poor man left behind four young children and a wife pregnant with the fifth. "If they had prayed more, they'd be alive today," Heriberto said.

4. I think Alberto meant not only that his brother fully opposed the Catholic Church but that Heriberto had adopted the same sort of absolutism that U.S. President George W. Bush had in opposing his enemy, expressed in the oft-repeated phrase from his post-9/11 address (delivered a few weeks before Alberto's comment), "Either you are with us, or you are with the terrorists" ("Address to a Joint Session of Congress and the American People," September 20, 2011, http://georgewbush-whitehouse .archives.gov/news/releases/2001/09/20010920–8.html [accessed October 20, 2012]).

5. When speakers say this in the context of a Spanish utterance, they will actually say "e-ska-le." In other words, they will treat it like a foreign word, on par with loan words from English that start with the letter *s*, such as smoking, sprite, sky, and Spiderman (spelled *Espaider-men* on many bootlegged Spiderman items available in shops around town).

6. When I was first getting to know them, Ana referred to Heriberto as "like a sabio" and "almost a sabio," or someone who knows as much about mushrooms as shamans

do. On my first day in Nda Xo, when the sabio offered to do a velada with me, both insisted later that I should do a velada with Heriberto instead, since he knew how to do the ceremonies just as well.

7. Especially in some of Heriberto's speech and writing, discourses about alternative medicine blend with invocations to "reclaim . . . the values of our Mazatec indigenous people." For example, he writes about promoting the "recovery of the sick, medicinal herbs, [and] urine therapy [*urinoterapia*]" (Prado Pereda, n.d.: 20).

8. As noted earlier, the one aspect of Mazatec society that is relatively well documented ethnographically is mushroom use. My understanding of the discrepancy between how Mazatec church members and other people use mushrooms thus derives not only from my experience with Mazatec church members and others but also from scholarship on the subject.

Chapter 6: Seeing Double

1. Victor de la Cruz is a widely known poet, essayist, editor, and historian from Juchitán, Oaxaca. He writes in both Zapotec (Isthmus variant) and Spanish. He holds bachelor's, master's, and doctoral degrees from the National Autonomous University of Mexico (UNAM) and is a researcher at CIESAS-Oaxaca.

2. Arguably, indigenous authors from Spanish-speaking Latin American countries—especially from Ecuador, Guatemala, Mexico, and Peru, which have large indigenous populations—are at the forefront of the production of indigenous-language literature. Native authors from the United States and Canada have been critical to the emergence of modern indigenous literatures, but most leading authors write in English rather than in indigenous languages (however, see Webster 2009). Here I refer to the "Spanish version" because in Mexico it is the national-language half of indigenous texts.

3. There are some exceptions. Literature in Isthmus Zapotec, for example, dates from the early twentieth century. However, that movement arose in an indigenous area that is primarily urban, in contradistinction to the vast majority of indigenous communities in Mexico. This section's title is taken from *La Palabra Florida*, a national literary magazine for bilingual Spanish and indigenous-language literature published in Mexico City by ELIAC. *La flor de la palabra* is also the title of an influential anthology of Zapotec writing edited by Victor de la Cruz (1999 [1983]). Both titles refer to a complex set of associations in ancient Mesoamerican writing and representation—and other allusions to them in modern contexts—among elites, speech, and flowers: see Hill 1992; Houston 2000; Taube 2004.

4. *Indigenous Movements and Their Critics* (Warren 1998) is the authoritative text on the Pan-Mayan Movement. See also Cuxil 2002; England 2003; Fischer and Brown 1996; French 2010; Nelson 1999; Richards and Richards 1997.

5. It is also known as the Asociación Nacional de Escritores en Lenguas Indígenas (National Association of Writers in Indigenous Languages). It was known initially as Casa de los Escritores in Lenguas Indígenas and is still occasionally called by that name.

6. The direct sponsor was the Indigenous Language and Literature Program of the

National Office of Popular Cultures, which has since been renamed the Dirección General de Culturas Populares e Indígenas and is a subsidiary of CONACULTA.

7. Montemayor, one of Mexico's most prolific and acclaimed public intellectuals, was a poet, novelist, essayist, critic, translator, and editor/anthologist of contemporary indigenous literature. More than any other figures, he and Miguel León-Portilla (who also is nonindigenous) have led the promotion of Mexico's indigenous literature. León-Portilla has worked almost exclusively on literature in Nahuatl from the colonial and precolonial eras; Montemayor focused almost entirely on modern indigenous writing in Yucatán and, later, elsewhere. León-Portilla, speaking from the same celebratory impulse, has expressed a similar sentiment: "Something unexpected and quite wonderful happened during the last quarter of the twentieth century: a growing number of Mesoamericans took up pen, typewriter, or computer and produced widely varied literary works. At first they were influenced, perhaps overly so, by what they had read of their own ancient literature. They went back again and again in poetry and narrative to describe the sufferings of their people, and to denounce, with good reason I might add, the injustices that had been committed against them. . . . Through many ups and downs, Mesoamerican literature has not only survived for more than 2000 years but now flourishes once again" (León-Portilla and Shorris 2001: 14).

8. The power of the union is indicated by its nearly annual strikes, which shutter schools for weeks or even months but have often led to larger disruptions. The power of the Oaxaca section of the union came into focus particularly clearly in 2006, when the strike in Oaxaca kicked off a broad—and ultimately violent—social movement that dramatically affected the entire state, turning the city into a police state for several months.

9. *Etnodesarrollo*, or *desarrollo con identidad* (development with identity), refers to the idea that development must address local priorities, including ethnic identity.

10. That project is the Dirección General de Education Indígena (National Office of Indigenous Education) of the SEP and the Instituto Indigenista Interamericano (Interamerican Indigenist Institute; III), a subsidiary of the Organization of American States, which is based in Mexico City and encompasses sixteen member countries. Its director at the time, the Peruvian anthropologist José Matos Mar, has written about the use of computers to "preserve indigenous languages" (Matos Mar 1992).

11. The special "Oaxaca y el CIESAS" issue of *América Indígena* was dedicated entirely to articles on this project. In addition to articles by well-known Mexican scholars such as Nahmad, who edited the issue, it featured articles by prominent Oaxacan indigenous intellectuals such as Juan Julián Caballero and Victor de la Cruz. My discussion is drawn from the articles in that special issue.

12. One exception might be the Zapotec writer Natalia Toledo, daughter of the renowned painter Francisco Toledo of Juchitán and an esteemed writer and artist in her own right. As I discuss in the conclusion, in this and other respects, the isthmus region of Oaxaca is somewhat exceptional.

13. This is one of the reasons that the literary and artistic scene in Juchitán is so distinct. Of course, the distances, physical and otherwise, between rural and urban locales could be reduced substantially if Mexico had better infrastructure—roads and

telephone service, in particular. This is one of the ways that Guatemala has superseded Mexico, a difference that has had implications for literary movements in each country.

14. To my knowledge, no indigenous author has produced a reciprocal account of encounters with Montemayor (or other nonindigenous supporters), a disparity that indexes in complex ways some of the political-economic issues discussed in this chapter.

15. However, indigenous intellectuals will often use these contexts to begin with a few token words of introduction in a native language before shifting into Spanish for the remainder of the talk. Arguably, this disrupts the hegemony of Spanish even while acquiescing to it and benefiting from the opportunities that doing both provides.

16. Popular and scholarly interest in modern indigenous writing in recent decades is doubtless in complex dialogue with the concomitant interest in rediscovering ancient and colonial indigenous texts and publishing them in the two-column bilingual format standard for modern authors. This trend dates from León-Portilla's seminal volume *The Broken Spears* (1992 [1962]) and extends to more recent attempts to "recover" lost native voices, a vast body of work discussed in chapter 1.

17. Robert Laughlin has been instrumental in the founding and ongoing work of Sna Jtz'ibajom (House of the Writer), a collective of indigenous writers and artists from the Chiapas highlands. The existence of Sna Jtz'ibajom reflects issues raised in this chapter about pressures from different audiences; the political implications of language use; and the urban, educational, and bilingual backgrounds required of indigenous authors. Sna Jtz'ibajom has been heavily supported by nonindigenous outsiders. They include Laughlin and other members of the Harvard Chiapas Project, the Bread and Puppet Theater Company, Ralph Lee (whose theatre company produces the annual Greenwich Village Halloween Parade), and the Mexican poet and artist Francisco Alvarez Quiñones. It has been funded by the Ford Foundation, the Smithsonian Institution, the W. K. Kellogg Foundation, Cultural Survival, the Merck Family Fund, and the Inter-American Foundation. Such support complicates any straightforward notion that the creation of Sna Jtz'ibajom "carefully let the Indians speak for themselves" (Laughlin 1995: 542). I do not elaborate on this case here, despite its suitability to illustrating trends I discuss, because so many other people have already written about this group (see, e.g., Frischmann 1994; Laughlin 1995).

18. See Bernard's website at http://nersp.osg.ufl.edu/~ufruss/CELIAC.htm (accessed October 25, 2012).

19. While some of the information about the center's genesis is available elsewhere, my discussion relies heavily on Dalton 1990. Eckert Boege, another prominent researcher who wrote an important ethnography of the lowlands Mazatec area (see Boege 1988), also attended one of the meetings.

20. This echoes my experience with Mazatec church members: the skepticism with which some came to view me was, I believe, tied to similar concerns. Their doubts came to a head shortly after I had gone for a walk with one of the members, the woman who treated me with the most suspicion. During the walk, she asked what my family did that allowed them to support me. I had no idea that she or any of the others thought my family supported me; eager to set her straight, I explained that I supported myself

through grants I had earned. After the velada that resulted in the group's decision that I should move out of Heriberto's house, he mentioned the grants in passing, with disdain, implying it was evidence that my agenda competed with theirs.

21. Although the interview was conducted in Spanish, it was published only in English translation, and my excerpt is taken from that version.

22. Publications resulting from or documenting earlier efforts include Castellanos 1994; Gregorio Regino 1993; and Molina Cruz 1995, 1998. More-recent efforts are ongoing, and my knowledge of them is based primarily on interviews with individuals involved.

23. Such a shift is doubtless tied to broader demographic shifts, such as that bilingualism may be on the rise nationally, particularly among speakers age thirty-five or younger.

24. See Bartolo Ronquillo 1998; Gregorio Regino 1992, 1999; Prado Pereda 1997. All of these works are made up in whole or in part of texts labeled "cantos."

Conclusion: Singing for the Dead and the Living

1. Of all of the social movements in Mexico, the Juchitán Renaissance has been one of the mostly richly documented (Campbell 1990, 1994, 2001; de la Cruz 1999 [1983]; de la Peña 1995; Ristow 2008; Rubin 1997). My observations about this movement are based on this literature, as well as on my visits to Juchitán and interviews with some of the indigenous intellectuals who have participated in the movement.

2. My observations about Yalálag are based on repeated visits there over the past decade and on interviews with key figures in Uken Ke Uken at various points over that period—especially Juana Vázquez Vázquez and Joel Aquino Maldonado—and on interviews with others who have supported the organization in various ways, including Juan José Rendón, Mario Molina Cruz, and Angeles Romero Frizzi.

3. See, however, Gutiérrez Najera 2007; M. Molina Cruz 1997, 1998.

4. As discussed earlier, Oaxaca is strongly identified with its ferment of cultural activities, led by indigenous intellectuals, artists, and specialists working in a range of media. The complex relationship laid out here between different kinds of authors and their audiences is related to similarly complex relationships between indigenous artists, healers, and ritual specialists and the consumers for their products—rituals, arts, crafts, ceremonies, and so on. Like indigenous literature, these cultural products marked as indigenous are shared by local audiences or markets and also by national and international ones, particularly those involving tourists. As has been the subject of many anthropological studies, such cultural products often sit at the intersection of divergent systems of significance, where local and tourist meanings diverge partly because of linguistic boundaries: locally circulating meanings are differentially accessible to tourists, who do not speak the indigenous language. While it is beyond the scope of this book to explore how these dynamics affect those between indigenous authors and their audiences, complex interactions clearly are at play that tie indigenous authors and their audiences into a broader arena of contestations and transactions surrounding "indigenous culture."

References

Abse, Edward. 2007. "Towards Where the Sun Hides: The Rise of Sorcery and Transformations of Mazatec Religious Life." PhD diss., University of Virginia, Charlottesville.

Adorno, Rolena, ed. 1982. *From Oral to Written Expression: Native Andean Chronicles of the Early Colonial Period*. Syracuse: Syracuse University Press.

———. 1989. "Arms, Letters and the Native Historian in the Chronicles of the New World." *1492–1992: Re/Discovering Colonial Writing*, ed. René Jara and Nicholas Spadaccini, 9–50. Minneapolis: Prisma Institute.

Agha, Asif. 2007. *Language and Social Relations*. Cambridge: Cambridge University Press.

Aguirre Beltrán, Gonzalo. 1973. *Regiones de refugio: El desarrollo de la comunidad y el proceso dominical en mestizo América*. Mexico City: Instituto National Indigenista.

Anderson, Arthur J. O., and Charles Dibble, ed. and trans. 1970–82. *Florentine Codex: General History of the Things of New Spain*. Santa Fe: School of American Research Press.

Anderson, Benedict. 1995 (1983). *Imagined Communities: Reflections on the Origin and Spread of Nationalism*. New York: Verso.

Appadurai, Arjun. 1996. *Modernity at Large: Cultural Dimensions of Globalization*. Minneapolis: University of Minnesota Press.

———. 2006. *Fear of Small Numbers: An Essay on the Geography of Anger*. Durham: Duke University Press.

Arrona, Ignacio. 1796. *Cuaderno de idioma mazateco*. Chicago: Edward E. Ayer Manuscript Collection, Newberry Library.

———. 1797. *Confesionario en idioma mazateco*. Chicago: Edward E. Ayer Manuscript Collection, Newberry Library.

Babb, Florence E. 2011. *The Tourism Encounter: Fashioning Latin American Nations and Histories*. Stanford: Stanford University Press.

Bakhtin, Mikhail M. 1981. *The Dialogic Imagination: Four Essays*, ed. Michael Holquist, trans. Caryl Emerson and Michael Holquist. Austin: University of Texas Press.

Barabas, Alicia M., and Miguel A. Bartolomé. 1973. *Hydraulic Development and Ethnocide: The Mazatec and Chinantec People of Oaxaca, Mexico*. Copenhagen: International Workgroup for Indigenous Affairs.

———. 1983. "Apostles of Ethnocide: Reply to Partridge and Brown." *Culture and Agriculture* 24: 5–9.

Bartolo Ronquillo, Apolonio. 1998. *Alas de viento: Tjiunga'e tjao.* Mexico City: Dirección General de Culturas Populares.

Bartra, Roger. 2002. *Blood, Ink, and Culture: Miseries and Splendors of the Post-Mexican Condition.* Durham: Duke University Press.

Baud, Michiel, and Johanna Louisa Ypeij, eds. 2009. *Cultural Tourism in Latin America: The Politics of Space and Imagery.* Leiden: Brill.

Bauer, Wilhelm P. 1968 (1908). "Paganismo y superstición entre los Indios Mazatecas." *Traducciones mesoamericanistas* 2: 247–57.

Bauman, Richard. 2004. *A World of Others' Words: Cross-Cultural Perspectives on Intertextuality.* New York: Wiley-Blackwell.

Bauman, Richard, and Charles L. Briggs. 1990. "Poetics and Performance as Critical Perspectives on Language and Social Life." *Annual Review of Anthropology* 19: 59–88.

———. 2003. *Voices of Modernity: Language Ideologies and the Politics of Inequality.* Cambridge: Cambridge University Press.

Beckett, Samuel. 1974. *Texts for Nothing.* London: Calder and Boyars.

Belmar, Francisco. 1978 (1892). *Ligero estudio sobre la lengua mazateca.* Mexico City: Colegio de México.

Benítez, Fernando. 1970. *Los indios de México.* Mexico City: Biblioteca Era.

Bernard, H. Russell. 1996. "Language Preservation and Publishing." *Indigenous Literacies in the Americas: Language Planning from the Bottom Up,* ed. Nancy H. Hornberger, 139–56. New York: Mouton de Gruyter.

Besnier, Niko. 1995. *Literacy, Emotion, and Authority: Reading and Writing on a Polynesian Atoll.* Cambridge: Cambridge University Press.

Bierhorst, John, ed. and trans. 1985. *Cantares Mexicanos: Songs of the Aztecs.* Stanford: Stanford University Press.

Blommaert, Jan. 2008. *Grassroots Literacy: Writing, Identity and Voice in Central Africa.* New York: Routledge.

Boege, Eckhart. 1988. *Mazatecos ante la nación: Contradicciones de la identidad étnica en el México actual.* Mexico City: Siglo Veintiuno.

Bonfil Batalla, Guillermo. 1987. *México profundo: Una civilización megada.* Mexico City: Secretaría de Educación Pública and Centro de Investigación y Estudios Superiores en Antropología Social.

Boone, Elizabeth Hill. 2007. *Cycles of Time and Meaning in the Mexican Books of Fate.* Austin: University of Texas Press.

Boone, Elizabeth Hill, and Walter D. Mignolo, eds. 1994. *Writing without Words: Alternative Literacies in Mesoamerica and the Andes.* Durham: Duke University Press.

Boone, Elizabeth Hill, and Gary Urton, eds. 2011. *Their Way of Writing: Scripts, Signs, and Pictographies in Pre-Columbian America.* Cambridge: Harvard University Press.

Bourdieu, Pierre. 1991. *Language and Symbolic Power,* ed. John B. Thompson, trans. Gino Raymond and Matthew Adamson. Cambridge: Harvard University Press.

Bowen, John R. 2010. *Religions in Practice: An Approach to the Anthropology of Religion.* Needham Heights, Mass.: Allyn & Bacon.

Brading, David A. 1991. *The First America: The Spanish Monarchy, the Creole Patriots, and the Liberal State*. Cambridge: Cambridge University Press.

Brandes, Stanley. 1997. "Sugar, Colonialism, and Death: On the Origins of Mexico's Day of the Dead." *Comparative Study of Society and History* 39 (2): 270–99.

———. 1998. "The Day of the Dead, Halloween, and the Quest for Mexican National Identity." *Journal of American Folklore* 111 (442): 359–80.

Bricker, Victoria R. 1981. *The Indian Christ, the Indian King: The Historical Substrate of Maya Myth and Ritual*. Austin: University of Texas Press.

Briggs, Charles L. 1996. "The Politics of Discursive Authority in Research on the 'Invention of Tradition.' " *Cultural Anthropology* 11 (4): 435–69.

Brinton, Daniel Garrison. 1892a. "Observations on the Chinantec Language of Mexico: And on the Mazatec Language and Its Affinities." *Proceedings of the American Philosophical Society* 30 (137): 22–31.

———. 1892b. "On the Mazatec Language of Mexico and Its Affines." *Proceedings of the American Philosophical Society* 30: 137.

Brown, Michael F. 2004. *Who Owns Native Culture?* Cambridge: Harvard University Press.

Burkhart, Louise. 1989. *The Slippery Earth: Nahua-Christian Moral Dialogue in Sixteenth-Century Mexico*. Tucson: University of Arizona Press.

———. 1996. *Holy Wednesday: A Nahua Drama from Early Colonial Mexico*. Philadelphia: University of Pennsylvania Press.

Campbell, Howard. 1990. "The COCEI: Culture, Class, and Politicized Ethnicity in the Isthmus of Tehuantepec." *Ethnic Groups* 8 (1): 29–56.

———. 1994. *Zapotec Renaissance: Ethnic Politics and Cultural Revivalism in Southern Mexico*. Albuquerque: University of New Mexico Press.

———. 2001. *Mexican Memoir: A Personal Account of Anthropology and Radical Politics in Oaxaca*. Westport, Conn.: Bergin and Garvey.

Cancian, Frank. 1992. *The Decline of Community in Zinacantan: Economy, Public Life, and Social Stratification, 1960–1987*. Stanford: Stanford University Press.

Carmichael, Elizabeth, and Chlöe Sayer. 1992. *The Skeleton at the Feast: The Day of the Dead in Mexico*. Austin: University of Texas Press.

Carrera González, Florencio. 2000a. "Chota Chjine ximale baá xki: Sabios que adivinan con el maíz." *La Faena*, vol. 1, no. 4, 14.

———. 2000b. *La reconstrucción de la boda mazateca en el contexto huautleco*. Huautla de Jiménez, Oaxaca: Consejo Nacional para la Cultura y las Artes.

———. 2000c. "Los sabios que adivinan con el maíz." *La Faena*, vol. 1, no. 7, 18.

Carrera Gonzalez, Florencio, and Sebastian van Doesburg. 2001. "El calendario mazateco actual como fuente para el estudio del calendario antiguo." *Memoria de la Primera Mesa Redonda de Monte Alban; Procesos de cambio y conceptualizacion del tiempo*, ed. Nelly M. Robles Garcia, 255–68. Mexico City: INAH and CONACULTA.

Casimiro Nava, Juan, and Felipe García. 1992. *Don Romulo, el curandero: Relato de niños mazatecos*. Mexico City: Instituto Nacional Indigenista.

Castellanos M., Javier. 1994. *Cantares de los vientos primerizos*. Mexico City: Editorial Diana.

———. 1999 (1986). *Yell chia lhen xtilla/Mi pueblo y mi palabra.* Oaxaca: C. Javier Castellanos M.

Caton, Steven Charles. 1990. *"Peaks of Yemen I Summon": Poetry as Cultural Practice in a North Yemeni Tribe.* Berkeley: University of California Press.

Cela, Camilo José. 1970 (1967). *María Sabina, el carro de heno: O, el inventor de la guillotina.* Madrid: Alfaguara.

Ceraso, Antonio. 2008. "Entheogens and the Public Mystery: The Rhetoric of R. Gordon Wasson." *Configurations* 16 (2): 215–43.

Chance, John K. 2001. *Conquest of the Sierra: Spaniards and Indians in Colonial Oaxaca.* Tulsa: University of Oklahoma Press.

Childs, Robert V., and Patricia B. Altman. 1982. *Vive tu Recuerdo: Living Traditions on the Mexican Days of the Dead.* Los Angeles: Museum of Cultural History.

Chuchiak, John. 2005. "In servitio dei: Fray Diego de Landa, the Franciscan Order, and the Return of Extirpation of Idolatry in the Diocese of Yucatán, 1573–1579." *Americas* 61 (4): 611–46.

———. 2010. "Writing as Resistance: Maya Graphic Pluralism and Indigenous Elite Strategies for Survival in Colonial Yucatan, 1550–1750." *Ethnohistory* 57 (1): 87–116.

Cifuentes, Barbara. 1998. *Letras sobre voces.* Mexico City: Centro de Investigación y Estudios Superiores en Antropología Social.

Clanchy, Michael. 1990. *From Memory to Written Record.* Cambridge: Cambridge University Press.

Clarke, Colin. 2000. *Class, Ethnicity, and Community in Southern Mexico: Oaxaca's Peasantries.* Oxford: Oxford University Press.

Clifford, James. 2000. "Taking Identity Politics Seriously: 'The Contradictory, Stony Ground . . .' " *Without Guarantees: In Honour of Stuart Hall,* ed. Paul Gilroy, Lawrence Grossberg, and Angela McRobbie, 94–112. New York: Verso.

———. 2007. "Varieties of Indigenous Experience: Diasporas, Homelands, Sovereignties." *Indigenous Experience Today,* ed. Marisol de la Cadena and Orin Starn, 197–224. Oxford: Berg.

Cline, Howard F. 1966. "Colonial Mazatec Lienzos and Communities." *Ancient Oaxaca,* ed. John Paddock, 207–97. Stanford: Stanford University Press.

Collins, James, and Richard K. Blot. 2003. *Literacy and Literacies: Texts, Power, and Identity.* Cambridge: Cambridge University Press.

Colloredo-Mansfeld, Rudolf Josef. 1999. *The Native Leisure Class: Consumption and Cultural Creativity in the Andes.* Chicago: University of Chicago Press.

———. 2009. *Fighting like a Community: Andean Civil Society in an Era of Indian Uprisings.* Chicago: University of Chicago Press.

Comaroff, John L., and Jean Comaroff. 2009. *Ethnicity, Inc.* Chicago: University of Chicago Press.

Cordoba, Juan de. 1578. *Vocabulario en lengua zapoteca: Hecho y recopilado por el muy reverendo padre Fray Juan de Córdova de la Orden de los Predicadores que reside en está Nueva España.* Chicago: Edward E. Ayer Manuscript Collection, Newberry Library.

Cowan, Florence H. 1946. "Notas etnográficas sobre los Mazatecos de Oaxaca." *América Indígena* 6 (1): 27–39.

———. 1947. "Linguistic and Ethnological Aspects of Mazateco Kinship." *Southwestern Journal of Anthropology* 3 (3): 247–56.

Cowan, George M. 1946. "Mazateco House Building." *Southwestern Journal of Anthropology* 2 (4): 375–90.

———. 1948. "Mazateco Whistle Speech." *Language* 24: 280–86.

———. 1952. "A Mazateco President Speaks." *América Indígena* 12: 323–41.

———. 1954. "La importancia social y política de la faena mazateca." *América indígena* 14: 67–92.

Craib, Raymond B. 2004. *Cartographic Mexico: A History of State Fixations and Fugitive Landscapes.* Durham: Duke University Press.

Cuxil, Demetrio Cojtí. 2002. "Educational Reform in Guatemala: Lessons from Negotiations between Indigenous Civil Society and the State." *Multiculturalism in Latin America: Indigenous Rights, Diversity and Democracy,* ed. Rachel Sieder. New York: Palgrave Macmillan.

Dalton, Margarita. 1990. "El aqua y las mil formas de nombrarla: El Centro Mazateco de Investigaciones." *America Indígena* 50 (2–3): 62–93.

Dawson, Alexander S. 2004. *Indian and Nation in Revolutionary Mexico.* Tucson: University of Arizona Press.

de la Cadena, Marisol. 2000. *Indigenous Mestizos: The Politics of Race and Culture in Cuzco Peru.* Durham: Duke University Press.

de la Cadena, Marisol, and Orin Starn, eds. 2007. *Indigenous Experience Today.* Oxford: Berg.

de la Cruz, Victor. 1999 (1983). *La flor de la palabra.* Mexico City: Ediciones de la Casa Chata, Centro de Investigación y Estudios Superiores en Antropología Social.

de la Fuente, Julio. 1949. *Yalálag, una villa Zapoteca Serrana.* Mexico City: Museo Nacional de Antropología, Serie Científica.

de la Peña, Guillermo. 1995. "Nationals and Foreigners in the History of Mexican Anthropology." *The Conditions of Reciprocal Understanding,* ed. James W. Fernandez and Milton B. Singer, 276–303. Chicago: Center for International Studies, University of Chicago.

———. 1997. "Anthropology." *Encyclopedia of Mexico: History, Society and Culture,* ed. Michael S. Werner. Chicago: Fitzroy Dearborn Publishers.

Derrida, Jacques. 1998 (1976). *Of Grammatology,* trans. Gayatri Chakravorty Spivak. Baltimore: Johns Hopkins University Press.

Díaz del Castillo, Bernal. 1968. *Historia verdadera de la conquista de la Nueva España.* Madrid: Espasa-Calpe.

Duke, Michael R. 1995. "Writing Mazateco: Linguistic Standardization and Social Power." *Texas Linguistic Forum* 3: 305–14.

———. 1996. "Gordon Wasson's Disembodied Eye: Genre, Representation and the Dialectics of Subjectivity in Huautla de Jiménez, Mexico." PhD diss., University of Texas, Austin.

———. 2001. "Staying Clean: Notes on Mazatec Ritual Celibacy and Sexual Orientation." *Celibacy, Culture, and Society: The Anthropology of Sexual Abstinence*, ed. Elisa J. Sobo and Sandra Bell, 125–36. Madison: University of Wisconsin Press.

Durston, Alan. 2007. *Pastoral Quechua: The History of Christian Translation in Colonial Peru, 1550–1650.* Notre Dame: University of Notre Dame Press.

———. 2008. "Native-Language Literacy in Colonial Peru: The Question of Mundane Quechua Writing Revisited." *Hispanic American Historical Review* 88: 141–70.

Edmonson, Munro S., ed. and trans. 1982. *The Ancient Future of the Itza: The Book of Chilam Balam of Tizimin.* Austin: University of Texas Press.

———. 1986. *Heaven Born Merida and Its Destiny: The Book of Chilam Balam of Chumayel.* Austin: University of Texas Press.

Eisenlohr, Patrick. 2007. *Little India: Diaspora, Time, and Ethnolinguistic Belonging in Hindu Mauritius.* Berkeley: University of California Press.

England, Nora. 2003. "Mayan Language Revival and Revitalization Politics: Linguists and Linguistic Ideologies." *American Anthropologist* 105 (4): 733–43.

Errington, Joseph. 2008. *Linguistics in a Colonial World: A Story of Language, Meaning, and Power.* Malden, Mass.: Blackwell.

Espinosa, Mariano. 1910. *Apuntes históricos de las tribus chinantecas, mazatecas y poplucas.* Mexico City: Imprenta de Vázquez e Hijos.

Estrada, Alvaro. 1981. *María Sabina: Her Life and Chants,* trans. Henry Munn. Santa Barbara: Ross-Erickson.

———. 1989 (1977). *Vida de María Sabina, la sabia de los hongos.* Mexico City: Siglo Veintiuno.

———. 1996. *Huautla en tiempo de hippies.* Mexico City: Grijalbo.

Farriss, Nancy. 1984. *Maya Society under Colonial Rule: The Collective Enterprise of Survival.* Princeton: Princeton University Press.

Faudree, Paja. 2012a. "'Following the Thing' in the Land of the Magic Mushroom: Text, Talk, and the Politics of Ethnic Authorship." Paper presented at the Cogut Center for the Humanities, Providence, R.I., Brown University, April 17.

———. 2012b. "Music, Language, and Texts: Sound and Semiotic Ethnography." *Annual Review of Anthropology* 41: 519–36.

Feierman, Steven. 1990. *Peasant Intellectuals: Anthropology and History in Tanzania.* Madison: University of Wisconsin Press.

Feinberg, Ben. 1996. "A Toyota in Huautla: Metacultural Discourse in the Sierra Mazateca of Oaxaca, Mexico." PhD diss., University of Texas, Austin.

———. 1997. "Three Mazatec Wise Ones and Their Books." *Critique of Anthropology* 17 (4): 411–37.

———. 2003. *The Devil's Book of Culture: History, Mushrooms, and Caves in Southern Mexico.* Austin: University of Texas Press.

Feld, Steven, and Aaron Fox. 1994. "Music and Language." *Annual Review of Anthropology* 23: 25–53.

Finnegan, Ruth. 1988. *Literacy and Orality: Studies in the Technology of Communication.* New York: Blackwell.

Fischer, Edward, and McKenna Brown, eds. 1996. *Maya Cultural Activism.* Austin: University of Texas Press.

Foucault, Michel. 1977. "What Is an Author?" *Language, Counter-Memory, Practice,* ed. Donald F. Bouchard, trans. Sherry Simon, 124–28. Ithaca: Cornell University Press.

Fox, Aaron. 2004. *Real Country: Music and Language in Working-Class Culture.* Durham: Duke University Press.

Franco, Jean. 2005. "Some Reflections on Contemporary Writing in the Indigenous Languages of America." *Comparative American Studies* 3 (4): 455–69.

French, Brigittine M. 2010. *Maya Ethnolinguistic Identity: Violence, Cultural Rights, and Modernity in Highland Guatemala.* Tucson: University of Arizona Press.

Friedrich, Paul. 1986. *The Princes of Naranjá.* Austin: University of Texas Press.

Frischmann, Donald. 1994. "New Mayan Theatre in Chiapas: Anthropology, Literacy, and Social Drama." *Negotiating Performance: Gender, Sexuality, and Theatricality in Latin/o America,* ed. Diana Taylor and Juan Villegas, 213–39. Durham: Duke University Press.

Frye, David L. 1996. *Indians into Mexicans: History and Identity in a Mexican Town.* Austin: University of Texas Press.

García, Crescencio. 1997. "Tojesa manguine jin." "Cantos en torno al tiempo santificador indio," by Heriberto Prado Pereda. Unpublished ms., copy in the collection of Paja Faudree.

García, María Elena. 2005. *Making Indigenous Citizens: Identities, Education, and Multicultural Development in Peru.* Stanford: Stanford University Press.

García Carrera, E. Gabino. 2004. "La oposición no logra consensar para ir en coalición a la alcaldía." *Las Noticias* (Oaxaca), September 8, C4.

García Carrera, Juan. 1986. *La otra vida de María Sabina.* Mexico City: Esfuerzo.

———. 2002. "La limpia en mazateco que reanimó al Papa Juan Pablo II en su visita a la Cd. de México." *La Faena* vol. 2, no. 25, 6.

García Dorantes, Renato. 2001. "Se acaba este año: Je tifeta no jebi." *La Faena,* vol. 2, November–December, 17–19.

Geschiere, Peter. 2009. *The Perils of Belonging: Autochthony, Citizenship, and Exclusion in Africa and Europe.* Chicago: University of Chicago Press.

Goldstein, Daniel. 2004. *The Spectacular City: Violence and Performance in Urban Bolivia.* Durham: Duke University Press.

Goodman, Jane E. 2005. *Berber Culture on the World Stage.* Bloomington: Indiana University Press.

Goody, Jack, ed. 1977. *The Domestication of the Savage Mind.* London: Cambridge University Press.

Graham, Laura. 1986. "Three Modes of Shavante Vocal Expression: Wailing, Collective Singing, and Political Oratory." *Native South American Discourse,* ed. Joel Sherzer and Greg Urban, 83–118. Berlin: Mouton de Gruyter.

———. 1995. *Performing Dreams: The Discourse of Immortality among the Xavante of Central Brazil.* Austin: University of Texas Press.

Gramsci, Antonio. 2000. *The Antonio Gramsci Reader: Selected Writings, 1916–1935*, ed. David Forgacs. New York: New York University Press.

Green, Shane. 2009. *Customizing Indigeneity: Paths to a Visionary Politics in Peru*. Stanford: Stanford University Press.

Greenberg, James B. 1989. *Blood Ties: Life and Violence in Rural Mexico*. Tucson: University of Arizona Press.

Gregorio Regino, Juan. 1992. *Tatsjejín nga kjabuya/No es eterna la muerte* [Death is not eternal]. Mexico City: Dirección General de Culturas Populares.

———. 1993. *Alfabeto Mazateco*. Oaxaca: Instituto Oaxaqueño de las Culturas, Centro de Investigación y Estudios Superiores de Antropología Social, and Organización de Investigadores de la Cultura Mazatec.

———. 1994. *No es eterna la muerte*. Mexico City: Editorial Diana.

———. 1999. *Ngata'ara stsee: Que sigo llovienda*. Mexico City: Escritores en Lenguas Indígenas.

———, ed. 2001. *Hacia una literatura indígena moderna: Nijmi tsi'e nga ndiba isien: Cantares para el amanecer*. Oaxaca: Instituto Estatal Educación Pública Oaxaca, Centro de Estudios y Desarrollo de las Lenguas Indígenas de Oaxaca.

Gregory, Steven. 2006. *The Devil behind the Mirror: Globalization and Politics in the Dominican Republic*. Berkeley: University of California Press.

Gruzinski, Serge. 1993. *The Conquest of Mexico: The Incorporation of Indian Societies into the Western World, 16th–18th Centuries*. Cambridge: Polity.

Guardino, Peter F. 2005. *The Time of Liberty: Popular Political Culture in Oaxaca, 1750–1850*. Durham: Duke University Press.

Gudschinsky, Sarah. 1951–52. "Solving the Mazatec Reading Problem." *Language Learning* 4 (1–2): 61–65.

———. 1958. "Native Reactions to Tones and Words in Mazatec." *Word* 14 (2): 338–45.

———. 1959. "Toneme Representation in Mazatec Orthography." *Word* 15 (3): 446–52.

Gustafson, Bret. 2009. *New Languages of the State: Indigenous Resurgence and the Politics of Knowledge in Bolivia*. Durham: Duke University Press.

Gutiérrez Najera, Lourdes. 2007. "Yalálag Is No Longer Just Yalálag: Circulating Conflict and Contesting Community in a Zapotec Transnational Circuit." PhD diss., University of Michigan, Ann Arbor.

Gutmann, Matthew. 2002. *The Romance of Democracy: Compliant Defiance in Contemporary Mexico*. Berkeley: University of California Press.

Habermas, Jürgen. 1991. *The Structural Transformation of the Public Sphere: An Inquiry into a Category of Bourgeois Society*, trans. Thomas Burger and Frederick Lawrence. Cambridge: MIT Press.

Hale, Charles R. 2006. *Más Que un Indio: Racial Ambivalence and the Paradox of Neoliberal Multiculturalism in Guatemala*. Santa Fe: School of American Research Press.

Halperín Donghi, Tulio. 1993. *The Contemporary History of Latin America*. Durham: Duke University Press.

Hanks, William F. 2010. *Converting Words: Maya in the Age of the Cross*. Berkeley: University of California Press.

Hapka, Roman, and Fabienne Rouvinez. 1997. "La Ruinas Cave, Cerro Rabon, Oaxaca, Mexico: A Mazatec Postclassic Funerary and Ritual Site." *Journal of Cave and Karst Studies* 59 (1): 22–25.

Haskett, Robert S. 1991. *Indigenous Rulers: An Ethnohistory of Town Government in Colonial Cuernavaca.* Albuquerque: University of New Mexico Press.

Heath, Shirley Brice. 1972. *Telling Tongues: Language Policy in Mexico, Colony to Nation.* New York: Teachers College Press.

Hellier-Tinoco, Ruth. 2011. *Embodying Mexico: Tourism, Nationalism and Performance.* Oxford: Oxford University Press.

Hernández Avila, Inés. 2004. "Interview: A Conversation with Juan Gregorio Regino, Mazatec Poet." *American Indian Quarterly* 28 (1–2): 121–29.

Herzfeld, Michael. 1997. *Cultural Intimacy: Social Poetics in the Nation-State.* New York: Routledge.

Hill, Jane. 1992. "The Flower World of Old Uto-Aztecan." *Journal of Anthropological Research* 48 (2): 117–44.

———. 2005. "Finding Culture in Narrative." *Finding Culture in Talk: A Collection of Methods,* ed. Naomi Quinn, 157–202. New York: Palgrave Macmillan.

———. 2008. *The Everyday Language of White Racism.* New York: Wiley-Blackwell.

Hirschkind, Charles. 2006. *The Ethical Soundscape: Cassette Sermons and Islamic Counterpublics.* New York: Columbia University Press.

Hobsbawm, Eric, and Terence Ranger, eds. 1992 (1983). *The Invention of Tradition.* Cambridge: Cambridge University Press.

Hofmann, Albert. 1990. "Ride through the Sierra Mazateca in Search of the Magic Plant 'Ska Maria Pastora." *The Sacred Mushroom Seeker: Essays for R. Gordon Wasson,* ed. Thomas J. Riedlinger, 115–28. Portland, Ore.: Dioscorides.

Houston, Stephen J. 2000. "Into the Minds of Ancients: Advances in Maya Glyph Studies." *Journal of World Prehistory* 14 (2): 121–201.

———, ed. 2004. *The First Writing: Script Invention as History and Process.* Cambridge: Cambridge University Press.

———. 2011. "All Things Must Change: Maya Writing over Time and Space." *Their Way of Writing: Scripts, Signs, and Pictographies in Pre-Columbian America,* ed. Elizabeth Hill Boone and Gary Urton, 21–42. Cambridge: Harvard University Press.

Huber, Brad R., and Alan R. Sandstrom, eds. 2001. *Mesoamerican Healers.* Austin: University of Texas Press.

INALI. 2008a. *Cátalogo de las lenguas indígenas nacionales.* Mexico City: INALI.

———. 2008b. "Estadística General." http://site.inali.gob.mx/pdf/estadistica/GENERAL/ (accessed November 5, 2012). Mexico City: INALI.

Incháustegui, Carlos. 1977. *Relatos del mundo magico mazateco.* Mexico City: Instituto Nacional de Antropología e Historia.

———. 1983. *Figuras en la niebla: relatos y creencias de los mazatecos.* Mexico City: Premia Editora.

———. 1994. *La mesa de plata: Cosmogonía y curanderismo entre los mazatecos de Oaxaca.* Mexico City: Instituto Oaxaqueño de las Culturas.

INEGI. 2005. *II conteo de población y vivienda*. Mexico City: INEGI.

———. 2010. *XIII Censo general de población y vivienda*. Mexico City: INEGI.

Inoue, Miyako. 2006. *Vicarious Language: Gender and Linguistic Modernity in Japan*. Berkeley: University of California Press.

Irvine, Judith. 1989. "When Talk Isn't Cheap: Language and Political Economy." *American Ethnologist* 16 (2): 248–67.

Irvine, Judith, and Susan Gal. 2000. "Language Ideology and Linguistic Differentiation." *Regimes of Language: Ideologies, Polities, and Identities*, ed. Paul Kroskrity, 35–83. Santa Fe: School of American Research Press.

Jackson, Jean E., and Kay B. Warren. 2005. "Indigenous Movements in Latin America, 1992–2004: Controversies, Ironies, New Directions." *Annual Review of Anthropology* 34: 549–73.

Jakobson, Roman. 1964 (1960). "Closing Statement: Linguistics and Poetics." *Style in Language*, ed. T. A. Sebeok, 350–77. Cambridge: Cambridge University Press.

Johnson, Jean Bassett. 1939a. "Elements of Mazatec Witchcraft." *Ethnological Studies* 9: 128–50.

———. 1939b. "Some Notes on the Mazatec." *Revista mexicana de estudios antropológicos* 3: 142–56.

Joseph, Gilbert M., and Daniel Nugent. 1994. *Everyday Forms of State Formation: Revolution and the Negotiation of Rule in Modern Mexico*. Durham: Duke University Press.

Jung, Courtney. 2008. *The Moral Force of Indigenous Politics: Critical Liberalism and the Zapatistas*. Cambridge: Cambridge University Press.

Katz, Friedrich. 1981. *The Secret War in Mexico: Europe, the United States, and the Mexican Revolution*. Chicago: University of Chicago Press.

Keane, Webb. 1997. *Signs of Recognition: Powers and Hazards of Representation in an Indonesian Society*. Berkeley: University of California Press.

———. 2007. *Christian Moderns: Freedom and Fetish in the Mission Encounter*. Berkeley: University of California Press.

Kearney, M. 1972. *The Winds of Ixtepeji: World View and Society in a Zapotec Town*. New York: Holt, Rinehart, & Winston.

Kellogg, Susan. 1995. *Law and the Transformation of Aztec Culture, 1500–1700*. Tulsa: University of Oklahoma Press.

King, Linda. 1994. *Roots of Identity: Language and Literacy in Mexico*. Stanford: Stanford University Press.

Kirk, Paul L. 1966. "Proto-Mazatec Phonology." PhD diss., University of Washington, Seattle.

Knight, Alan. 1990. "Racism, Revolution, and Indigenismo: Mexico, 1910–1940." *The Idea of Race in Latin America, 1870–1940*, ed. Richard Graham, 71–114. Austin: University of Texas Press.

Kouri, Emilio. 2004. *A Pueblo Divided: Business, Property, and Community in Papantla, Mexico*. Palo Alto, CA: Stanford University Press.

Kowalewski, Stephen A., and Jacqueline J. Saindon. 1992. "The Spread of Literacy in a

Latin American Peasant Society: Oaxaca, Mexico, 1890 to 1980." *Journal for the Comparative Study of Society and History* 35 (5): 110–40.

Kroskrity, Paul, ed. 2000. *Regimes of Language: Ideologies, Polities, and Identities.* Santa Fe: School of American Research Press.

Kulick, Don. 1992. *Language Shift and Cultural Reproduction: Socialization, Self, and Syncretism in a Papua New Guinean Village.* New York: Cambridge University Press.

Larsen, Libby. 1994. *I Just Lightning: Vocal Score for SSAA Chorus and Percussion,* trans. Eloina Estrada de Gonzalez and Henry Munn. New York: Oxford University Press.

Laughlin, Robert M. 1995. "From All, for All: A Tzotzil-Tzeltal Tragicomedy." *American Anthropologist* 97: 528–42.

Leary, Timothy. 1964. *The Psychedelic Experience: A Manual Based on the Tibetan Book of the Dead.* New York: Citadel Press.

Lee, Benjamin. 1992. "Textuality, Mediation, and Public Discourse." *Habermas and the Public Sphere,* ed. Craig Calhoun, 402–20. Cambridge: MIT Press.

Lemon, Alaina. 2000. *Between Two Fires: Gypsy Performance and Romani Memory from Pushkin to Post-Socialism.* Durham: Duke University Press.

León-Portilla, Miguel, ed. 1992 (1962). *The Broken Spears: The Aztec Account of the Conquest of Mexico.* Boston: Beacon.

León-Portilla, Miguel, and Earl Shorris, eds. 2001. *In the Language of Kings: An Anthology of Mesoamerican Literature, Pre-Columbian to the Present.* New York: W. W. Norton.

Lévi-Strauss, Claude. 1992 (1955). *Tristes Tropiques,* trans. John and Doreen Weightman. New York: Penguin.

Lockhart, James. 1991. *Nahuas and Spaniards.* Stanford: Stanford University Press.

———. 1992. *The Nahuas after the Conquest.* Stanford: Stanford University Press.

———, ed. and trans. 1993. *We People Here: Nahuatl Accounts of the Conquest of Mexico.* Berkeley: University of California Press.

Lockhart, James, Susan Schroeder, and Doris Namala. 2006. *Annals of His Time: Don Domingo de San Anton Munon Chimalpahin Quauhtlehuanitzin.* Stanford: Stanford University Press.

Loewe, Ronald B., and Helene Hoffman. 2002. "Building the New Zion: Unfinished Conversations between the Jews of Venta Prieta, Mexico, and Their Neighbors to the North." *American Anthropologist* 104 (4): 1135–47.

Lomnitz, Claudio. 1992. *Exits from the Labyrinth: Culture and Ideology in the Mexican National Space.* Berkeley: University of California Press.

———. 2001. *Deep Mexico, Silent Mexico: An Anthropology of Nationalism.* Minneapolis: University of Minnesota Press.

———. 2005. *Death and the Idea of Mexico.* Cambridge: Zone.

López Cruz, Ausencia, and Michael Swanton, coords. 2008. *Memorias del Coloquio Francisco Belmar: Conferencias sobre lenguas otomangues y oaxaqueñas.* Mexico City: Instituto Nacional de Antropología e Historia.

Makihara, Miki, and Bambi B. Schieffelin, eds. 2007. *Consequences of Contact: Language Ideologies and Sociocultural Transformations in Pacific Societies.* New York: Oxford University Press.

Mallon, Florencia. 1995. *Peasant and Nation: The Making of Post-colonial México and Perú.* Los Angeles: University of California Press.

Mannheim, Bruce. 1991. *The Language of the Inka since the European Invasion.* Austin: University of Texas Press.

Mannheim, Bruce, and Krista E. Van Vleet. 1998. "The Dialogics of Southern Quechua Narrative." *American Anthropologist* 100 (2): 326–46.

Martínez Gracida, Manuel. 1883. *Colección de cuadros sinópticos de los pueblos, haciendas, y ranchos del estado libre y soberano de Oaxaca.* Oaxaca: Imprenta del Estado.

Matos Mar, José. 1992. "Keystrokes to Preserve Indigenous Languages," trans. William Daniels. *Américas* 17 (1): 52–53.

Meek, Barbara A. 2010. *We Are Our Language: An Ethnography of Language Revitalization in a Northern Athabascan Community.* Tucson: University of Arizona Press.

Messick, Brinkley Morris. 1993. *The Calligraphic State: Textual Domination and History in a Muslim Society.* Berkeley: University of California Press.

Mignolo, Walter D. 1994. "Signs and Their Transmission: The Question of the Book in the New World." *Writing without Words: Alternative Literacies in Mesoamerica and the Andes,* ed. Elizabeth Hill Boone and Walter D. Mignolo, 351–71. Durham: Duke University Press.

———. 1995. *The Darker Side of the Renaissance: Literacy, Territoriality, and Colonization.* Ann Arbor: University of Michigan Press.

Miranda, Juan. 1997. *Curanderos y chamanes de la sierra mazateca.* Mexico City: Gaturperio.

Molina Cruz, Mario. 1995. *El Arcoiris Atrapado: La literatura indígena en material didáctico.* Oaxaca: Centro de Investigación y Difusión Zapoteca de la Sierra Juárez.

———. 1996. *El Volcan de Petalos.* Mexico City: Consejo Nacional para la Cultura y las Artes.

———. 1997. *Tu Xkúlh Lhén Chíw'dao: La Guajolota y sus pipilos (Fabulas de fin del siglo).* Oaxaca: Cedes-22.

———. 1998. *Yi' kube = Fuego nuevo: Educar sin Exterminar.* Oaxaca: Taller de Lengua y Tradición Zapoteca de Yalálag.

———. 2001. *Ga'bi'yalhan yanhi benhii ke will: Done la luz del sol no se pierda.* Mexico City: ELIAC.

Molina Cruz, René. 1991. *Be'ne gub'yelhe.* Mexico City: Centro de Investigación y Estudios Superiores en Antropología Social–Oaxaca, Gobierno del Estado de Oaxaca.

Monaghan, John. 1990. "Performance and the Structure of the Mixtec Codices." *Ancient Mesoamerica* 1: 133–40.

———. 2002. "The Indigenous Nobility and the Reinscription of Mesoamerican Codices." Electronic document, Foundation for the Advancement of Mesoamerican Studies, Inc. Available online at www.famsi.org/zapotecwriting (accessed October 21, 2011).

Montemayor, Carlos. 1993. *Situación actual y perspectivas de la literatura en lenguas indígenas.* Mexico City: Consejo Nacional para la Cultura y las Artes, Dirección General de Publicaciones.

———. 1998. *Encuentros en Oaxaca, México.* Mexico City: Editorial Aldus.

———. 2001. *La literatura actual en las lenguas indígenas de México*. Mexico City: Universidad Iberoamericana.

———, ed. and trans. 2004. *La voz profunda: Antología de la literatura mexicana contemporánea en lenguas indígenas*. Mexico City: Joaquín Mortiz.

Montemayor, Carlos, and Donald Frischmann, eds. 2004. *Words of the True Peoples: Anthology of Contemporary Mexican Indigenous-Language Writers/Palabras de los seres verdaderos: Antología de escritores actuales en lenguas indígenas de México*, vol. 1, prose/prosa. Austin: University of Texas Press.

———. 2005. *Words of the True Peoples: Anthology of Contemporary Mexican Indigenous-Language Writers/Palabras de los seres verdaderos: Antología de escritores actuales en lenguas indígenas de México*, vol. 2, poetry/poesía. Austin: University of Texas Press.

———. 2007. *Words of the True Peoples: Anthology of Contemporary Mexican Indigenous-Language Writers/Palabras de los seres verdaderos: Antología de escritores actuales en lenguas indígenas de México*, vol. 3, theater/teatro. Austin: University of Texas Press.

Munn, Henry. 1973. "The Mushrooms of Language." *Hallucinogens and Shamanism*, ed. Michael J. Harner, 86–122. London: Oxford University Press.

———. 2003. "The Uniqueness of Maria Sabina." *María Sabina: Selections*, ed. Jerome Rothenberg, 140–63. Berkeley: University of California Press.

Nader, Laura. 1964. "An Analysis of Zapotec Law Cases." *Ethnology* 3: 404–19.

———. 1990. *Harmony Ideology: Justice and Control in a Zapotec Mountain Village*. Stanford: Stanford University Press.

Nahmad Sittón, Salomón, ed. 1990. "Oaxaca y el CIESAS: Una experiencia hacia una nueva antropología." Special issue of *América Indígena* 50 (2–3).

Nash, June. 1970. *In the Eyes of the Ancestors: Belief and Behavior in a Mayan Community*. New Haven: Yale University Press.

Navarrete, Carlos. 1982. *San Pascualito Rey y el Culto a la Muerte en Chiapas*. Mexico City: Universidad Nacional Autónoma de México, Instituto de Investigaciones Antropológicas.

Neiburg, Federico G. 1988. *Identidad y conflicto en la sierra mazateca: El caso del Consejo de Ancianos de San José Tenango*. Mexico City: Instituto Nacional de Antropología e Historia, Escuela Nacional de Antropología e Historia.

Nelson, Diane M. 1999. *Finger in the Wound: Body Politics in Quincentennial Guatemala*. Berkeley: University of California Press.

Niezen, Ronald. 2003. *Origins of Indigenism: Human Rights and the Politics of Identity*. Berkeley: University of California Press.

Norget, Kristin. 1996. "Beauty and the Feast: Aesthetics and Performance of Meaning in the Day of the Dead, Oaxaca, Mexico." *Journal of Latin American Lore* 19: 53–64.

———. 1997. " 'The Politics of Liberation': The Popular Church, Indigenous Theology and Grassroots Mobilization in Oaxaca, Mexico." *Latin American Perspectives* 24 (5): 96–127.

Nutini, Hugo G. 1988. *Todos Santos in Rural Tlaxcala: A Syncretic, Expressive, and Symbolic Analysis of the Cult of the Dead*. Princeton: Princeton University Press.

O'Hara, Matthew D. 2009. *A Flock Divided: Race, Religion, and Politics in Mexico, 1749–1857.* Durham: Duke University Press.

Ong, Aihwa. 2006. *Neoliberalism as Exception: Mutations in Citizenship and Sovereignty.* Durham: Duke University Press.

Ong, Walter. 1982. *Orality and Literacy: The Technologizing of the Word.* New York: Methuen.

Orta, Andrew. 1998. "Converting Difference: Metaculture, Missionaries, and the Politics of Locality." *Ethnology* 37 (2): 165–85.

Paley, Julia. 2001. *Marketing Democracy: Power and Social Movements in Post-dictatorship Chile.* Berkeley: University of California Press.

Parsons, Elsie C. 1936. *Mitla: Town of the Souls, and Other Zapotec-Speaking Pueblos of Oaxaca, Mexico.* Chicago: Chicago University Press.

Partridge, William L., and Antoinette B. Brown. 1983. "Desarrollo agricola entre los Mazatecos reacomodados." *America Indígena* 153: 343–62.

———. 1984. "Etnodesarollo en la Mazateca." *América Indígena* 44 (2): 405–8.

Paz, Octavio. 1959 (1950). *El laberinto de soledad*, 2d ed. Mexico City: Fondo de Cultura Económica.

Pearlman, Cynthia L. 1981. "Women and Men in Transition: Gender and Change in the Mazatec Sierra, Oaxaca, Mexico." PhD diss., Indiana University, Bloomington.

Pedro Castañeda, Alejandrina. 2001. *Riqueza ancestral de la cultural mazateca.* Mexico City: Carteles Editores.

Peirce, Charles Sanders. 1932. *Collected Papers of Charles Sanders Peirce*, ed. C. Hartshorne and P. Weiss. Cambridge: Harvard University Press.

Pérez Quijada, Juan. 1996. "Tradiciones de chamanismo en la mazateca baja." *Alteridades* 6 (12): 49–59.

Pike, Eunice V. 1949. "Texts on Mazatec Food Witchcraft." *México Antiguo* 7: 287–94.

———. 1952. *Vocabulario mazateco.* Mexico City: Instituto Lingüístico de Verano.

———. 1960. "Mushroom Ritual versus Christianity." *Practical Anthropology* 7 (2): 49–52.

———. 1971. *An Uttermost Part.* Chicago: Moody.

Pike, Eunice V., and Florence Cowan. 1959. "Mazatec Sexual Impurity and Bible Reading." *Practical Anthropology* 6 (4): 145–50.

Pike, Kenneth L. 1948. *Tone Languages: A Technique for Determining the Number and Type of Pitch Contrasts in a Language, with Studies in Tonemic Substitution and Fusion.* Ann Arbor: University of Michigan Press.

Pimentel, Francisco. 1865. "El cuicateco, el mazateco y el chuchon." *Cuadro descriptivo y comparativo de las lenguas indígenas de Mexico*, vol. 2, 257–62. Mexico City: Imprenta de Andrade y Escalante.

Portal, Ana M. 1986. *Cuentos y mitos en una zona mazateca.* Mexico City: Instituto Nacional de Antropología e Historia.

Postero, Nancy Grey. 2007. *Now We Are Citizens: Indigenous Politics in Postmulticultural Bolivia.* Stanford: Stanford University Press.

Povinelli, Elizabeth. 2002. *The Cunning of Recognition: Indigenous Alterities and the Making of Australian Multiculturalism.* Durham: Duke University Press.

Prado Pineda, Alberto. 2000. "La historia de 'María Magdalena,' la santa que se apareció en Chilchotla." *La Faena*, vol. 1, no. 8, 19–20.

———. 2004. "El acro y su significado . . . Ya nas'o tsitjin kua josin t'oyani." *La Faena*, vol. 4, no. 35, 5.

Prado Pereda, Heriberto. 1986. *Kui⁴Nndja¹le⁴ nai³na¹ nga³ en¹ na¹: Cantemos a dios en nuestra lengua (Mazateca)*. Mexico City: Ideal.

———. 1991. *Sitsayako naśinanda ko naina, kuiNndjale*. Huautla de Jiménez: Prelatura de Huautla.

———. 1993. "Kjuale ndi ik'ien itsan." Unpublished ms., copy in the collection of Paja Faudree.

———. 1994. *Kjuachikonle chita jch-chinga*. Huautla de Jiménez: Prelatura de Huautla.

———. 1997. *Cantos en torno al tiempo santificador indio*. Unpublished ms., copy in the collection of Paja Faudree.

———. 2001. "Una síntesis de la cultura mazateca en su conjunto." *La Faena*, vol. 2, no. 13, 13–15.

———. n.d. "CIPREPACMA: Consejo Indígena Pro-Rescate del Patrimonio Cultural Mazateco." Unpublished ms., copy in the collection of Paja Faudree.

Quintero, Francisco. 1838. *Quaderno de mazateco, para el uso de Francisco de Paula Quintero, borrador en que se va asentado el confesionario*. Charlottesville: Special Collections Department, Alderman Memorial Library, University of Virginia.

Rafael, Vicente L. 1988. *Contracting Colonialism: Translation and Christian Conversion in Tagalog Society under Early Spanish Rule*. Ithaca: Cornell University Press.

Ramos, Alcida Rita. 1998. *Indigenism: Ethnic Politics in Brazil*. Madison: University of Wisconsin Press.

Rappaport, Joanne. 2005. *Intercultural Utopias: Public Intellectuals, Cultural Experimentation, and Ethnic Pluralism in Colombia*. Durham: Duke University Press.

Rappaport, Joanne, and Thomas B. F. Cummins. 2011. *Beyond the Lettered City: Indigenous Literacies in the Andes*. Durham: Duke University Press.

Redfield, Robert, and Alfonso Villa Rojas. 1934. *Chan Kom: A Maya Village*. Chicago: University of Chicago Press.

Restall, Matthew. 1997a. "Heirs to the Hieroglyphs: Indigenous Writing in Colonial Mesoamerica." *Americas* 54 (2): 239–67.

———. 1997b. *The Maya World: Yucatec Culture and Society, 1550–1850*. Stanford: Stanford University Press.

———. 2003. "A History of the New Philology and the New Philology in History." *Latin American Research Review* 38 (1): 113–34.

Restall, Matthew, Lisa Sousa, and Kevin Terraciano, eds. and trans. 2005. *Mesoamerican Voices: Native-Language Writings from Colonial Mexico, Oaxaca, Yucatan, and Guatemala*. Cambridge: Cambridge University Press.

Richards, Julia Becker, and Michael Richards. 1997. "Mayan Language Literacy in Guatemala: A Socio-historical Overview." *Indigenous Literacies in the Americas: Language Planning from the Bottom Up*, ed. Nancy Hornerger, 189–211. Berlin: Mouton de Gruyter.

Rincón Mautner, Carlos. 1996. "The Notes and Sketch of Lienzo Seler I or Mapa de Santa Maria Ixcatlan, Oaxaca, Mexico: Description and Commentary." *Latin American Indian Literatures Journal* 12 (Fall): 146–77.

Rio, Mariano del. 1820. *Vocabulario y frases en lengua mazateca, pueblo de Huehuetlán.* Charlottesville: Special Collections Department, Alderman Memorial Library, University of Virginia.

Ríos Nolasco, Miguel. 1992. *Costumbres, tradiciones, cuentos y leyendas de Huautla de Jiménez, Oaxaca.* Oaxaca: M. Ríos Nolasco.

Ristow, Colby Nolan. 2008. "From Repression to Incorporation in Revolutionary Mexico: Identity Politics, Cultural Mediation, and Popular Revolution in Juchitan, Oaxaca, 1910–1920." PhD diss., University of Chicago.

Robbins, Joel. 2004. *Becoming Sinners: Christianity and Moral Torment in a Papua New Guinea Society.* Berkeley: University of California Press.

Romero Frizzi, María de los Angeles. 2003a. *Escribir para dos mundos: Testimonios y experiencias de los escritores mixtecos.* Oaxaca: Fondo Editorial, Instituto Estatal Educación Pública Oaxaca.

———. 2003b. *Escritura Zapoteca: 2500 Años de Historia.* Mexico City: Centro de Investigación y Estudios Superiores en Antropología Social, Consejo Nacional para la Cultura y las Artes, Instituto Nacional de Antropología e Historia.

Ros Romero, Consuelo. 1992. *La imagen del indio en el discurso del Instituto Nacional Indigenista.* Mexico City: Centro de Investigaciones y Estudios Superiores en Antropología Social.

Rothenberg, Jerome, ed. 2003. *María Sabina: Selections.* Berkeley: University of California Press.

Rubin, Jeffrey W. 1997. *Decentering the Regime: Ethnicity, Radicalism, and Democracy in Juchitán, Mexico.* Durham: Duke University Press.

Rubio Montoya, Enrique Gonzalez. 1992. *Conversaciones con María Sabina y otros curanderos: Hongos sagrados.* Mexico City: Publicaciones Cruz O.

Rugeley, Terry. 2009. *Rebellion Now and Forever: Mayas, Hispanics, and Caste War Violence in Yucatán, 1800–1880.* Stanford: Stanford University Press.

Salomon, Frank. 1982. "Chronicles of the Impossible: Notes on Three Peruvian Indigenous Historians." *From Oral to Written Expression: Native Andean Chronicles of the Colonial Period,* 9–39. Syracuse, N.Y.: Maxwell School of Citizenship and Public Affairs, Syracuse University.

———. 2004. *The Cord Keepers: Khipus and Cultural Life in a Peruvian Village.* Durham: Duke University Press.

Salomon, Frank, and Jorge Urioste. 1991. *The Huarochirí Manuscript: A Testament of Ancient and Colonial Andean Religion.* Austin: University of Texas Press.

Samuels, David. 2004. *Putting a Song on Top of It: Expression and Identity on the San Carlos Apache Reservation.* Tucson: University of Arizona Press.

Schieffelin, Bambi B., Kathryn A. Woolard, and Paul V. Kroskrity, eds. 1998. *Language Ideologies: Practice and Theory.* New York: Oxford University Press.

Scholes, France V., and Ralph L. Roys. 1968 (1948). *The Maya Chontal Indians of Acalan-*

Tixchel: A Contribution to the History and Ethnography of the Yucatan Peninsula. Norman: University of Oklahoma Press.

Schroeder, Susan. 1991. *Chimalpahin and the Kingdoms of Chalco*. Tucson: University of Arizona Press.

———, ed. 2010. *The Conquest All Over Again: Nahuas and Zapotecs Thinking, Writing, and Painting Spanish Colonialism*. Sussex: Sussex Academic Press.

Sherman, Amy L. 1997. *The Soul of Development: Economic Transformation in Guatemala*. Oxford: Oxford University Press.

Silverstein, Michael. 1985. "Language and the Culture of Gender: At the Intersection of Structure, Usage, and Ideology." *Semiotic Mediation: Sociocultural and Psychological Perspectives*, ed. Elizabeth Mertz and Richard A. Parmentier, 219–59. Orlando, Fla.: Academic Press.

———. 2003. "Indexical Order and the Dialectics of Sociolinguistic Life." *Language and Communication* 23 (3–4): 193–229.

———. 2004. " 'Cultural' Concepts and the Language–Culture Nexus." *Current Anthropology* 45 (5): 621–52.

———. 2005. "Axes of Evals: Token versus Type Interdiscursivity." *Journal of Linguistic Anthropology* 15 (1): 6–22.

Silverstein, Michael, and Greg Urban, eds. 1996. *Natural Histories of Discourse*. Chicago: University of Chicago Press.

Smith, Benjamin T. 2007. "Defending 'Our Beautiful Freedom': State Formation and Local Autonomy in Oaxaca, 1930–1940." *Mexican Studies/Estudios Mexicanos* 23 (1): 125–53.

———. 2012. *Provincial Conservatism in Mexico: Religion, Society, and Politics in the Mixteca Baja, 1750–1962*. Albuquerque: University of New Mexico Press.

Smith-Stark, Thomas C. 1994. "Mesoamerican calques." *Investigaciones lingüísticas en Mesoamerica: Estudios sobre lenguas americanas*, ed. Carolyn J. MacKay and Verónica Vásquez. Mexico City: Instituto de Investigaciones Filológicas, Seminario de Lenguas Indígenas, UNAM.

Soto Laveaga, Gabriela. 2009. *Jungle Laboratories: Mexican Peasants, National Projects, and the Making of the Pill*. Durham: Duke University Press.

Speed, Shannon. 2007. *Rights in Rebellion: Indigenous Struggle and Human Rights in Chiapas*. Stanford: Stanford University Press.

Starn, Orin. 1999. *Nightwatch: The Politics of Protest in the Andes*. Durham: Duke University Press.

Starr, Frederick. 1902. *The Physical Character of the Indians of Southern Mexico*. Chicago: University of Chicago Press.

———. 1908. *In Indian Mexico: A Narrative of Travel and Labor*. Chicago: Forbes.

Stavenhagen, Rodolfo. 1960. "Descendencia y nombres entre los Mazatecos." *Revista mexicana de estudios antropológicos* 16: 231–32.

———. 2002. "Indigenous Peoples and the State in Latin America: An Ongoing Debate." *Multiculturalism in Latin America: Indigenous Rights, Diversity and Democracy*, ed. Rachel Sieder, 24–44. New York: Palgrave Macmillan.

Steele, Janet Fitzsimmons. 1987. "Blade Cave: An Archaeological Preservation Study in the Mazatec Region, Oaxaca, Mexico." Master's thesis, University of Texas, San Antonio.

Stephen, Lynn. 1991. "Culture as a Resource: Four Cases of Self-Managed Indigenous Craft Production in Latin America." *Economic Development and Cultural Change* 40 (1): 101–30.

———. 2002. *Zapata Lives! Histories and Cultural Politics in Southern Mexico.* Berkeley: University of California Press.

———. 2005. *Zapotec Women: Gender, Class, and Ethnicity in Globalized Oaxaca.* Durham: Duke University Press.

Stoll, David. 1982. *Fishers of Men or Founders of Empire? The Wycliffe Bible Translators in Latin America.* Cambridge, Mass.: Cultural Survival.

Street, Brian, ed. 1993. *Cross-Cultural Approaches to Literacy.* Cambridge: Cambridge University Press.

———. 2003. "Autonomous and Ideological Models of Literacy: Approaches from the New Literary Studies." *Current Issues in Comparative Education* 5 (2): 1–15.

Suslak, Daniel. 2004. "The Story of Ö: Orthography and Cultural Politics in the Mixe Highlands." *Pragmatics* 13 (4): 551–63.

Tanck de Estrada, Dorothy. 1999. *Pueblos de indios y educación en el México colonial, 1750–1821.* Mexico City: Centro de Estudios Históricos, El Colegio de México.

Taube, Karl A. 2004. "Flower Mountain: Concepts of Life, Beauty, and Paradise among the Classic Maya." *Anthropology and Aesthetics* 45 (Spring): 69–98.

Távarez, David. 2010. "Zapotec Time, Alphabetic Writing, and the Public Sphere." *Ethnohistory* 57 (1): 73–85.

Tedlock, Barbara. 2005. *The Woman in the Shaman's Body: Reclaiming the Feminine in Religion and Medicine.* New York: Bantam Books.

Tedlock, Dennis, ed. and trans. 1985. *Popol Vuh: The Mayan Book of the Dawn of Life.* New York: Simon and Schuster.

Terán, Víctor. 1995. *Yuuba' xtí' guendarusaana: El dolor del abandono.* Mexico City: Fundación Guie' Xhuuba' and Editorial Praxis.

———. 2010a. "Escritores indígenas: En qué lengua se piensa cuando se escribe." *Las Noticias* (Oaxaca), July 19.

———. 2010b. *Poems,* trans. David Shook. New York: The Poetry Translation Center.

Terraciano, Kevin. 2004. *The Mixtecs of Colonial Oaxaca: Ñudzahui History, Sixteenth through Eighteenth Centuries.* Stanford: Stanford University Press.

Thomas, Deborah. 2004. *Modern Blackness: Nationalism, Globalization, and the Politics of Culture in Jamaica.* Durham: Duke University Press.

Thomson, Guy P. C., and David G. LaFrance. 2002. *Patriotism, Politics, and Popular Liberalism in Nineteenth Century Mexico: Juan Francisco Lucas and the Puebla Sierra.* Wilmington, Del.: Scholarly Resources.

Tibón, Gutierre. 1983. *La ciudad de los hongos alucinantes.* Mexico City: Panorama Editorial México.

Todorov, Tzvetan. 1984 (1982). *The Conquest of America: The Question of the Other*. New York: Harper and Row.

Toledo, Natalia. 2006. *Kjoabiya ndsoko tjayao/La Muerte pies ligeros*, illus. Francisco Toledo and trans. Juan Casimiro Nava. Mexico, D.F: Fondo de Cultura Económica.

Tomlinson, Gary. 2007. *The Singing of the New World: Indigenous Voice in the Era of European Contact*. Cambridge: Cambridge University Press.

Tsing, Anna. 2004. *Friction: An Ethnography of Global Connection*. Princeton: Princeton University Press.

Turino, Thomas. 2008. *Music in the Andes: Experiencing Music, Expressing Culture*. Oxford: Oxford University Press.

Urban, Greg. 2001. *Metaculture: How Culture Moves through the World*. Minneapolis: University of Minnesota Press.

Urcid, Javier. 2005. "The Zapotec Scribal Tradition: Knowledge, Memory and Society in Ancient Oaxaca." Electronic document, Foundation for the Advancement of Mesoamerican Studies, Inc. Available online at www.famsi.org/zapotecwriting (accessed October 21, 2011).

Van Doesburg, Sebastián, coord. 2008. *Pictografía y escritura alfabética en Oaxaca*. Oaxaca: Instituto Estatal Educación Pública Oaxaca.

Van Doesburg, Sebastián, and Florencio Carrera González. 1997. *Códice Ixtlilxochitl: Apuntaciones y pinturas de un historiador (segunda parte)*. Mexico City: Akademische Druck- und Verlagsanstalt, Graz, and Fondo de Cultura Económica.

Van Young, Eric. 2001. *The Other Rebellion: Popular Violence, Ideology, and the Mexican Struggle for Independence, 1810–1821*. Stanford: Stanford University Press.

Vasconcelos, José. 1997 (1925). *The Cosmic Race: A Bilingual Edition*, trans. Didier T. Jaén. Baltimore: Johns Hopkins University Press.

Vaughan, Mary K. 1997. *Cultural Politics in Revolution: Teachers, Peasants, and Schools in Mexico, 1930–1940*. Tucson: University of Arizona Press.

Vaughan, Mary K., and Stephen E. Lewis, eds. 2006. *The Eagle and the Virgin: Nation and Cultural Revolution in Mexico*. Durham: Duke University Press.

Villa Rojas, Alfonso. 1955. *Los mazatecos y el problema indígena de la cuenca de Papaloapan*. Memorias del Instituto Nacional Indigenista, vol. 7. Mexico City: Ediciones del Instituto Nacional Indigenista.

Voloshinov, Valentin N. 1986. *Marxism and the Philosophy of Language*, trans. Ladislav Matejka and I. R. Titunik. Cambridge: Harvard University Press.

Walker, Alice. 2003. *Absolute Trust in the Goodness of the Earth: New Poems*. New York: Random House.

Warman, Arturo, Guillermo Bonfil Batalla, Margarita Nolasco, Mercedes Olivera, and Enrique Valencia, eds. 1970. *De eso que llaman antropología mexicana*. Mexico City: Editorial Nuestro Tiempo.

Warner, Michael. 2005. *Publics and Counterpublics*. Cambridge, Mass.: Zone.

Warren, Kay B. 1998. *Indigenous Movements and Their Critics: Pan-Maya Activism in Guatemala*. Princeton: Princeton University Press.

Warren, Kay B., and Jean E. Jackson. 2002. *Indigenous Movements, Self-Representation, and the State in Latin America.* Austin: University of Texas Press.

Wasson, R. Gordon. 1957. "Seeking the Magic Mushroom." *Life,* May 13, 100–120.

———. 1968. *Soma: Divine Mushroom of Immortality.* New York: Harcourt Brace Jovanovich.

———. 1980. *The Wondrous Mushroom: Mycolatry in Mesoamerica.* New York: McGraw-Hill.

———. 1981. "Retrospective Essay." *Maria Sabina: Her Life and Chants,* ed. Álvaro Estrada. New York: Ross-Erikson.

Wasson, R. Gordon, George Cowan, Florence Cowan, and Willard Rhodes. 1974. *Maria Sabina and Her Mazatec Mushroom Velada.* New York: Harcourt Brace Jovanovich.

Wasson, Valentina P., and R. Gordon Wasson. 1957. *Mushrooms, Russia, and History.* New York: Pantheon.

Webster, Anthony K. 2009. *Explorations in Navajo Poetry and Poetics.* Albuquerque: University of New Mexico Press.

Wedeen, Lisa. 2008. *Peripheral Visions: Publics, Power, and Performance in Yemen.* Chicago: University of Chicago Press.

Weidman, Amanda. 2006. *Singing the Classical, Voicing the Modern: The Postcolonial Politics of Music in South India.* Durham: Duke University Press.

Weitlaner, Robert J. 1952. "Curaciones Mazatecas." *Anales del Instituto Nacional de Antropología e Historia* 4: 279–85.

Weitlaner, Robert J., and Walter A. Hoppe. 1969. "The Mazatec." *Handbook of Middle American Indians,* vol. 7, part 1, ed. Robert Wauchope, 516–22. Austin: University of Texas Press.

Weitlaner, Robert J., and Irmgard Weitlaner. 1946. "Mazatec Calendar." *American Antiquity* 11 (3): 194–97.

Winter, Marcus. 1984. "La cueva de Tenango: Descubrimientos arqueológicos en la Sierra Mazateca de Oaxaca." Paper presented at the Simposio Oaxaca en Jalisco, Guadalajara.

Wood, Stephanie. 2003. *Transcending Conquest: Nahua Views of Spanish Colonial Mexico.* Tulsa: University of Oklahoma Press.

Wright-Rios, Edward N. 2009. *Revolutions in Mexican Catholicism: Reform and Revelation in Oaxaca, 1887–1934.* Durham: Duke University Press.

Yannakakis, Yanna. 2008. *The Art of Being In-between: Native Intermediaries, Indian Identity, and Local Rule in Colonial Oaxaca.* Durham: Duke University Press.

belletristic approach to indigenous literature, 18–22, 36, 231

bilingual education: effects of, 55–56, 77–78, 205; indigenous languages and, 20–21, 52, 55, 201–2; linguistic diversity and, 207; revival movements and, 56, 201–2; state policies and programs on, 20–21, 52, 55–56, 201–2, 205, 207. See also education

bilingualism: in Catholic services, 168; in emerging indigenous middle class, 58, 77–78; growth of, 265n28, 276n23; role of, 247

bilingual teachers: attitudes toward bilingual education, 208, 218, 224–25, 227; attitudes toward indigenous intellectuals, 218, 238; children of, 207–8; effects of being, 55–56, 205, 221–22; as organic intellectuals, 225

bilingual texts: advantages and use of, 228–30, 233, 247; availability of, 220; implications of, 28, 198–200; literacy in indigenous languages and, 200; and publishing historical indigenous-language texts, 275n16; reading, 198–200, 222–24, 230–31; writing in, by indigenous authors, 28–29, 119, 149, 198–200, 212–13, 220, 229, 231–33, 241

Bonfil Batalla, Guillermo. See Deep Mexico

brujos (witches), 32, 69, 252n2, 259n37

Carrera González, Florencio, 218; disagreement with Heriberto Prado Pereda, 144

catechists, 125, 161–62; Heriberto Prado Pereda and, 100, 163, 219; roles and duties of, 125, 161–62, 168, 268n18; singing and promoting church songs, 100, 125, 135, 143

Catholic Church: Alberto Prado Pineda's involvement in, 96, 98–99, 123, 156;

autochthonous church and, 178, 179; conflict with Heriberto Prado Pereda, 158–62, 177–80, 185, 188, 272n4; criticisms of, by Heriberto Prado Pereda, 163–64, 169–70, 177–80, 184–85, 188, 189, 270–71n31, 272n4; Day of the Dead fiesta and, 98, 107; Day of the Dead Song Contest and, 125, 140, 185, 219; defections from, 158–60, 163, 178–79; effect of, on revival movements, 56–57, 92; enculturation and, 41, 96–97, 178; goals of, 42, 178; Heriberto Prado Pereda's activities in, 93–96, 99–100, 123, 148, 156, 161–62, 169, 177, 219; indigenismo and, 122–23, 167, 179; and indigenous culture, support of, 55, 178–79; indigenous education and, 56–57, 257n19; indigenous identity and, 187; and indigenous intellectuals, effect on, 56–57, 92; indigenous languages and, 35–36, 38, 41, 47–48, 56–57; and indigenous people, relationship with (see under indigenous people and populations); John Paul II, Pope, 97, 99, 130, 180; Josefino missionaries, 93, 95, 264–65n26; languages used in services, 168; liberationist period, and retreat from, 95–97, 179–80; linguistic work of priests, 35, 37–38, 40, 47, 227, 257n14; literacy and, 35–37, 41, 56–57, 125–26, 257n19; Mazatec identity and, 187; and Mazatec Indigenous Church, criticism by and opposition of, 160–74, 178, 184, 186, 187, 242, 270n31; Mazatec language services and prayers in, 100, 123–26, 149, 151–52, 168; prominence in the Sierra Mazateca, 25, 70, 76–77, 93, 94 (fig. 2.3); song initiative, 96–98, 106, 123–26, 136, 141–43, 148–51, 219; songs by Heriberto Prado Pereda for, 124, 148–58. See also John Paul II; Lib-

eration Theology; Misioneras Indígenas de Nuestra Señora de Guadalupe;
Prelature of Huautla; Vatican II
Catholic Mass, 62 (fig. 1.2); autochthonous, 98; Day of the Dead fiesta and,
98, 107; limpias during, 99–100, 170;
music for, 98, 124–25, 150–51, 153–
56, 170, 269n17; performed by Heriberto Prado Pereda, 161
caves in the Sierra Mazateca, exploration
of, 32, 255–56nn2–3, 256n5
cemeteries: Day of the Dead fiesta and,
107, 109 (fig. 3.2), 118–20, 175, 192,
248, 249 (fig. C.1), 250 (fig. C.2);
meaning of, 267n15
Center for the Study and Development of
the Zapotec Language and Tradition.
See Uken Ke Uken; Zapotec language
Centro de Investigación y Estudios Superiores en Antropología Social (Center
for Research and Advanced Study in
Social Anthropology; CIESAS), 205–6,
209, 216–18, 242, 268n19, 274n11
Centro Editorial de Literatura Indígena,
Asociación Civil (CELIAC; Center for
Native Language Publishing), 216–17
Centro Mazateco de Investigaciones
(Mazatec Research Center), 213,
216–19, 243
Centros de Investigación de las Culturas
Indígenas (Research Centers for Indigenous Cultures), 206
chajma (ancestors, the dead), 82, 117,
188, 267nn12–13; meaning of term,
266n10; during Day of the Dead festival, 82, 119–20, 120 (fig. 3.4), 122, 128
(fig. 3.6), 188, 230–31, 248, 249 (fig.
C.1); perceptions of, 188–89; during
Song Contest, 126, 127–30, 136
chaxo'o (umbilical-cord men), 117–18,
119, 268n22. See also chajma
chikon (earth spirit), 81, 145, 166,
255n2, 262nn8–9

Chilchotla. See Nda Xo
chota chjine (sabios, shamans), 81, 145;
meaning of word, 271n37; as active
Catholics, 187; critical of Heriberto
Prado Pereda, 190; local views of, 187–
88, 262n7; mushroom use, 80–81,
190; performing a limpia, 77, 261n3;
politics and, 262n7; sexual abstinence
of, 82, 188, 263n12; as symbols of
Mazatec society, 91, 129; and veladas,
81. See also María Sabina Magdalena
García; veladas
Christian Base Communities, 98, 268–
69n2
Coalición Obrera Campesina Estudiantil
del Istmo (Coalition of Workers, Peasants, and Students of the Isthmus;
COCEI), 240
coffee, rise and fall of, 67, 70, 72–73, 93,
260n41, 264n23
Comisión Nacional para el Desarrollo de
los Pueblos Indígenas (National Commission for the Development on Indigenous Peoples), 207, 251n3
commercialization: of celebrations, 243;
of mushrooms, 90–91; of Song Contest, 131
Committee for the Revival of Mazatec
Culture (CIPRECMA), 156
community: building, 9–10, 134–35,
156; communion with dead and, 9,
138; division, in Nda Xo, 135, 157–58,
187–88, 191–92; fragility of, 174;
images of, 136–37; leaders' representativeness, 10, 12, 73; and Mazatec
Indigenous Church, 180–85; modernization and, 73; mushroom use and,
172, 191; nature and meaning of, 138,
174–77, 180, 185–86, 191–92; singing in shared indigenous language
and, 10; symbol of, for Nda Xo, 61–63,
185–91. See also factions and factionalism

concientización (consciousness raising), and Liberation Theology, 96, 98

conflict: communal, 172; and complementarity between Song Contest and Mazatec Indigenous Church, 142–43, 174, 194–96, 243–44; diversity and, 29; ethnic, 3, 14, 44–45, 49, 57, 73, 101, 191; between evangelical and economic projects of Spanish, 42; between Heriberto Prado Pereda and Alberto Prado Pineda, 146, 163, 185–86, 235; between Heriberto Prado Pereda and the Catholic Church, 163–64, 270–71n31; involving Mazatec Indigenous Church (*see* Iglesia Indígena Mazateca); modernization and, 73; political, 1–9, 12, 29, 57, 73, 146–48; regarding hippie mycotourists, 73; regarding veladas, 79; religious, 79, 89, 143, 146–48, 161, 162, 175–77, 269n4, 270n21; revival movements and, 6, 29; social, 12, 73, 139; in Yalálag, 1–4, 6–8. *See also* factions and factionalism; violence

Congregación de Misioneros Josefinos (Josefino missionaries), 93, 95, 264–65n26. *See also* Catholic Church

cultural diversity, 137, 206. *See also* diversity; ethnic diversity; linguistic diversity

cultural revival movements: with language focus, 106, 240; political success of COCEI and, 240; role of Catholic Church in, 57; in Yalálag, 3–4. *See also* Day of the Dead Song Contest; Iglesia Indígena Mazateca; indigenous-language literary and literacy movements; indigenous revival movements; revival movements

culture. *See* indigenous culture; Mazatec people and culture

dam (Presa Miguel Alemán), 64, 66 (fig. 1.3), 72

Day of the Dead fiesta (Día de los Muertos): activities during: in Mexico, 107, 109; in the Sierra Mazateca, 26, 117–20, 192 (fig. 5.2); antiquity of, 108–10; gendered nature of, 118–19, 267n12; graveyard visits during, 107, 109 (fig. 3.2), 118–20, 175, 192, 248, 249 (fig. c.1), 250 (fig. c.2); huehuentones and, 25, 76, 85 (fig. 2.1), 93, 96, 110, 160, 168, 264–65n26; illustrated, 108 (fig. 3.1), 115 (fig. 3.3), 120 (fig. 3.4), 128 (fig. 3.6), 192 (fig. 5.2), 195 (fig. 5.3), 249 (fig. c.1); indigenous identity and, 98; innovation and, 122, 267; Masses during, 98, 107; Mazatec identity and, 98; Mexican view of death and, 107–8; migrants' visits during, 130, 192; music, role of, in activities, 80, 112, 119–20, 122, 124, 136, 267n6; outside influences on, 122; past and tradition, importance of, 78–79, 120; piñatas at, 119–20, 120 fig 3.4; reconciliations during, 27, 192, 194–96; tradition and innovation, tension between, 113–14, 122. *See also* chajma; Day of the Dead Song Contest; huehuentones

Day of the Dead Song Contest: described and pictured, 113–17, 126–35, 129 (fig. 3.7), 132 (fig 3.8); altar contest, 118; apolitical character of, 9–10, 26–27; appeal of, national and local, 194–96, 199; authenticity of, 27; Catholic Church and, 140; commercialization of, 131; complementarity of, with Mazatec Indigenous Church, 28, 142–43, 174, 191–92, 194–96, 243–44; conflict over, between Alberto Prado Pineda and Heriberto Prado Pereda, 185; discourses about indigenous rights and resistance and, 194; funding for, 139–40; goals of, 123–26; heterodoxy of, orthographic and linguistic, xiii, 126–27, 225, 243; history of, 123–26; illustrated, 129 (fig. 3.7), 132 (fig. 3.8); impacts and importance of, 9–10, 26–27, 106–7, 122–23, 135–37, 140; and indigenismo, 122; innovation and, 26–27, 78–79, 106, 113, 118, 122–23, 126, 138–39, 140; instruments used, 127, 150, 268n20, 269n10; judging criteria, 127–28, 130–31; literacy in indigenous languages and, 9–10, 26–27, 106, 123–26, 136, 138–39; local focus of, 193–94; masks worn, 130, 268n22; and Mazatec identity and culture, 122–23, 128, 129, 131, 137–39, 140; modernity and tradition, balancing, 26, 110, 130; music and, 26–27, 78–79, 106, 127, 129 (fig. 3.7); negotiating social conflict and, 139; politics and, 9–10, 26–27, 106, 138, 174–75, 242; popular success of, xiii, 9–10, 24, 26–27, 78–79, 114, 133, 135–39, 141, 174, 193–94, 219, 243; precedents for, 122, 124, 267n17, 269n11; tradition and innovation, tension between, 26, 78–79, 106–7, 113–14, 118, 123, 130–31, 140, 143; uniqueness of, 24

dead, the: altars for, 108 (fig. 3.1), 118, 119; interaction with, 9–10, 113, 117, 119, 192; presence of, 105; singing and dancing for, 78–79, 113, 137–38. See also chajma, huehuentones

death, Mexican view of, 105, 107–8, 138, 148–49

Deep Mexico, 33, 44, 97–98, 214–16

de la Cruz, Victor, 242–43, 273n1, 273n3; on cultural change, 213–14; Juchitán Renaissance and, 239–40; national orientation of, 199; poem by, 197–98, 201, 224, 234

Democratic Revolution Party (Partido de la Revolución Democrática; PRD), religious conflict and, 160–61, 162, 270n22

Derrida, Jacques, 17, 223–24, 234, 253n23, 253n25

desarrollo con identidad (development with identity), 274n9

development: antiassimilationist, 206; economic, 52–53, 72; ethnic, 55, 204, 274n9

Día de los Muertos festival. See Day of the Dead fiesta

diversity: ambivalence by state regarding, 57–58; indigenous literature and, 211; marginalization and, 58; national commitment to, 20; national programs and, 207; pre-Columbian and current, 13–14; promotion of indigenous writing and, 211. See also cultural diversity; ethnic diversity; linguistic diversity

education: access to, 242; as agent of change, 77–78; bilingual (see bilingual education); church involvement in, 56–57, 257n19; Indian problem and, 48–49; indigenous identity and, 78; in INI schools, 55–56, 201–2, 205; language and assimilation and, 48–49, 51–52; level of, among indigenous readers, 21–22; politics of, 52; school system, 265n27; SIL programs in, 258–59n29; state policies on (see state policies on education and language)

Ejército Zapatista de Liberación Nacional (EZLN; Zapatista Army of National Liberation), 13, 95

elections, 270n27; in Nda Xo, 147; in Oaxaca, 8–9; violence, 146–47, 260n45; in Yalálag, 1–3

enculturation (enculturación): Catholic Church and, 41, 96–97, 178

Escritores en Lenguas Indígenas (ELIAC; Writers in Indigenous Languages), 202–3

ethnic cartographies, 31, 45, 73–75

ethnic diversity: as challenge for state, 13; ethnic revival and, 29; managing, 50, 58; and national unity, 13; in Oaxaca, 4; support of, 50–51. *See also* cultural diversity; diversity; linguistic diversity

ethnic politics, 8–9, 14, 15, 24, 25, 33, 102

ethnic revival movements. *See* indigenous revival movements

ethnolinguists, 207, 209, 221; indigenous language revival and, 205–6; training program for, 56, 126, 144, 205–6, 209, 216–17, 268n19. *See also* Summer Institute of Linguistics

etnodesarrollo (ethnic development), 55, 204, 274n9

factions and factionalism: literacy programs and, 227–28; in Nda Xo, 5, 135, 142–43, 146–47, 175–77, 192; religious, 17, 27–28, 141–43, 146–48, 162, 175, 177, 185, 187; transcending, 10, 134–35, 192, 223–24; in Yalálag, 1–8, 218–19. *See also* community; conflict; violence

Faudree, Paja: and conflict between Alberto Prado Pineda and Heriberto Prado Pereda, 185–87, 275–76n20; relationship with Heriberto Prado Pereda, 144–46; skepticism about, 275–76n20

Fiesta de Todos Santos. *See* Day of the Dead fiesta

Florencio Carrera González. *See* Carrera González

folklore, function of, 180, 194, 246

Foucault, Michel, on authorship, 101, 245–46

funding: for Day of the Dead Song Contest, 139–40; for Heriberto Prado Pereda, 219–20; implications of, 238–

39; for indigenous intellectuals, 209–10; for revival movements, 238–39

globalization: as a cause of ethnic violence, 3; ethnic revival movements and, 8, 12, 76, 92; negative effects of, 5, 25, 79, 214–15

graveyards. *See* cemeteries

Gregorio Regino, Juan, 149–50, 247–48; book of poems by, 221 (fig. 6.1); CIESAS ethnolinguistics program and, 216–17; national orientation of, 199; poem by, 105; on using indigenous languages, 220–22, 233–35

Guatemala: compared to Mexico, 202–4, 274–75n13; indigenous languages in, 13–14, 202–4, 253n17

hallucinogens. *See* mushrooms; psychotropic plants

hegemony: compromising with and opposing, 11, 29, 112, 143, 177, 184, 194, 212, 225, 244, 245–48, 246

Heriberto Prado. *See* Prado Pereda, Heriberto

hippie mycotourism, 25, 32, 73, 76–79, 85–87, 89. *See also* mycotourism; tourism

House of the Writer (Sna Jtz'ibajom), 275n17

Huautla, 66 (map 1.1), 84, 118 (map 3.1); importance of, 113–14; linguistic data on, 116 (table 1.3); mycotourists and, 84–85, 87, 90–91; political violence in, 146; Prelature of (*see* Prelature of Huautla); road to, 72–73, 145; song contest in, 131, 133

huehuentones (old men, ancestors, the dead), 110, 131; during Day of the Dead fiesta, 112, 119–20, 120 (fig. 3.4), 249 (fig. c.1), 267n12, 268n21. *See also* chajma huipil (native dress), 83–84, 86 (fig. 2.2), 99, 129–30

identity: among criollos, 43–44; Indian, 43–44; national, 13, 51, 63, 108, 110; social, 38, 43. *See also* indigenous identity; Mazatec identity

identity politics, 24, 76; authenticity and, 193, 199; Deep Mexico and, 215; image of Mazatecs and, 33; language and, 232, 248; revival and, 11; social change and, 191

iglesia autóctona (autochthonous church), 98, 125–26, 167–68, 178

Iglesia Indígena Mazateca (Mazatec Indigenous Church), 27, 140, 166, 168, 193–94; appeal of, national and local, 194–96, 199; as autochthonous church, 167–68; complementarity of, with song contest, 28, 142–43, 174, 191–92, 194–96, 243–44; criticisms of, 27, 142, 166, 173, 175–79, 184, 187–88, 190–91; criticisms of Catholic Church by, 164–74, 178, 184, 186, 187, 242, 270n31; death, dealing with, 182–85; effects of, on local practices, 142–43; founding of, 160–64; gap between ideology and practice, 168, 172–73, 176, 271n33; goals and ideology, 27, 142, 167–72, 176, 242–43; Heriberto Prado Pereda's role in, 160–65, 167–69, 181–84, 219; image of Mazatec identity and, 142, 173, 175–77, 187, 194; innovation and, 183, 187–88, 190–91; Liberation Theology and, 167, 180; membership, 164; mushroom use in, 27, 171–72, 188–91, 273n8; nature of community and, 180–85; politics of, 140, 142, 165–67, 194, 242; practices and rules, 142, 165–73, 271n35; Protestantism and Protestants, compared with, 166;

separatist image, 178–79; singing in Mazatec, 170, 179; social distance of members, 164–67, 181–85; success, lack of, 194; tradition and innovation, tension between, 177, 187–88; veladas, use of, 172, 181–82, 184–85, 189, 262n7

INALI (Instituto Nacional de Lenguas Indígenas; National Institute of Indigenous Languages), 4, 252–53n16

Indian problem, 42–43, 48–49; ambivalence of state, 57–58, 110–11, 113, 122–23. *See also* indigenismo

indigeneity: meaning of, and indigenous, compared, 101–4, 265n32; modernity and, 63; revival and, 101–4; understandings of, 75–77

indigenismo: Catholic Church and, 167, 179; criticisms of, 55, 167, 179–80, 204, 215, 258–59n29; Day of the Dead Song Contest and, 122; indigenismo de participación, 55; indigenous-language literacy and, 201; influences on, 78, 110; initial formulations of, 42–43; in mid-twentieth century, 52–57; modernization and, 53–54; during national period, 48–49, 50; nuevo, 54–56; Revolutionary, 49–51, 201; Summer Institute of Linguistics and, 258–59n29; use of radio to spread, 72. *See also* Indian problem; mestizaje; state policies and attitudes toward indigenous people

indigenous, meaning of, and indigeneity, compared, 101–4, 265n32

indigenous authors and writers: agendas and goals of, 28, 37, 39, 199–200, 204, 229–30, 234–35, 247–48; bilingual texts, writing, 28–29, 119, 149, 198–200, 212–13, 220, 229, 231–33, 241; characteristics of, 207; distrust and criticisms of, 218–19, 238;

indigenous authors and writers (*cont.*) double audiences for, 21–23, 28–29, 193, 198, 200, 235, 247–48, 276n4; founding of indigenous organizations and, 202–5, 226; functions of, 101, 245–46; impacts of, 220, 247; importance of colonial indigenous-language texts to, 38–39; and indigenous languages, rise of, 198; links with past, 213; monolingual texts, use of, 198, 229–30; and mushrooms, topic of, 79; networks among, 210–11; as organic intellectuals, 103–4, 245–46; orientation of, local vs. national, 22–23, 199, 244–45; problems faced, 208–10, 215–19, 238; as representative of Deep Mexico, 214–15; social context of texts and, 19, 22–23; Spanish use by, 207, 211–13, 216–17, 228, 232–33, 254–55n41, 275n15; success of, reasons for, 247; support for, 206, 208–10, 215–19, 237–38, 274nn10–11; types of, 23, 244–46; urban residency of, 5–6, 210, 216, 220, 274–75n13. *See also* indigenous intellectuals; indigenous-language literary and literacy movements; indigenous languages; indigenous literature; political activism; political activists

indigenous culture: activities in Oaxaca, 240, 243, 276n4; celebrations of, and commercialization, 243; government support of, dangers in, 139; mycotourists in search of, 78, 90, 243; National Council for Culture and Arts (Consejo Nacional para la Cultura y las Artes; CONACULTA), 220–21; redeeming, attitudes toward, 23, 244; Research Center for Indigenous Cultures, 206; support of, 55, 178–79. *See also* Mazatec people and culture

indigenous identity: authenticity and, 74, 92, 177–80, 191, 194; diffusion of ideas about, 78; discourses about, 22–23, 25, 101, 198–99, 214; displays of, 111–12, 140; language as marker of, 13–14, 201, 253n17; linguistic affiliation and, 139, 193, 199; modernity and, 63; state policies regarding, 58. *See also* identity; Mazatec identity

indigenous intellectuals: agendas and goals of, 192–93, 205, 208; alphabet creation and, 225, 227; ambivalence and skepticism toward, 6, 10, 12, 16, 218–19, 238, 275n17, 281; and Deep Mexico, 214–15; differences among, 144, 199, 244–49; double audiences for, 21–23, 28–29, 193, 198, 200, 235, 247, 276n4; employment and support of, 209, 219; ethnic identification and, 31; ethnolinguists, 205–6; factors shaping, 49, 56–57, 92, 216–19; funding and employment, 209–10; importance of, 204, 219–20; in Juchitán, 241–43; as link to tradition, 11; literacy and, 227–28; local orientation of, 219–20; and mushrooms, debates about, 79, 89, 91–92; national policy and, 42, 44, 56, 144; Spanish use by, 12, 211–13, 216–17, 228, 232–33, 254–55n41, 275n15; urban residency of, 5, 210, 216, 274–75n13; validity and meaning of term, 103–4. *See also* bilingual teachers; indigenous authors and writers; political activism; political activists; Prado Pereda, Heriberto; Prado Pineda, Alberto

indigenous-language literary and literacy movements, 4–5, 14, 43, 200–222, 225, 240; comparison between Mexico and Guatemala, 202–4; criticisms of, 236–39; goals of, 28, 106, 199–200, 208, 227; "hothouse" character of, 236–40, 246; impacts of, 228; local nature of, 203–4; modern, birth and growth of, 204–8; renaissance in,

202–8; state programs fostering, 227–28; success of, reasons for, 136; tensions within, 20; ubiquity of, 228; urban focus of, 6. *See also* cultural revival movements; Day of the Dead Song Contest; Iglesia Indígena Mazateca; indigenous revival movements; literacy in indigenous languages; revival movements

indigenous languages, 13–14, 21; attitudes toward, 38–39, 52; bilingual education and, 20–21, 52, 55, 201–202; Catholic Church and, 35–36, 38, 41, 47, 56–57; data on, 7 (table 1.1), 65 (table 1.1), 116–17 (table 3.1); documents in, 21, 35–37, 198; education and assimilation and, 48–49, 51; in Guatemala, 202–3; history of, 36–39, 40–42, 46–48, 51–52; as markers of ethnic indigeneity, 13–14, 201, 253n17; Mixtec language, 4, 205–6, 226; orthographies for, 124, 126–27, 225; and politics, 5, 13, 38, 193, 198, 202; research centers, support for and ambivalence toward, 215–19; sophistication of, 19, 254n37; state's attitude toward, 47–48; in Western alphabetic script, 18–19, 35. *See also* indigenous-language literary and literacy movements; linguistic diversity; literacy in indigenous languages; Mazatec language; Nahuatl language; Zapotec language

indigenous literature: approaches to research on, 18–23; belletristic approach to, 18–20, 22, 36, 231; context-text relationship and, 15–16, 19–22; double audience for, 21–23, 28–29, 193, 198, 200, 235, 247, 276n4; effects on, of Mexican Revolution, 200–201; history of, 8–15, 36–37, 43, 46–49; impacts of, 220, 247; increase in, 198, 204; monolingual, use and im-

plications of, 198, 228–31; Nahuatl dominance of, 39–40; nationally and internationally, 28; reading, 230–31; relevance of, 22–23, 37–38, 43; sociological approach to, 20; support programs for, 20–21, 208–10, 215–19, 237–38; unequal emphasis on, by scholars, 58–59. *See also* indigenous authors and writers; indigenous languages

Indigenous Missionaries of our Lady of Guadalupe (Misioneras Indígenas de Nuestra Señora de Guadalupe), 163–65, 169, 189

indigenous people and populations: colonial policies toward, 42–43; effect of liberalism on, 44–45, 48; marginality and marginalization of, 13, 44, 50, 58–60, 133, 214–15, 222, 258n22; in National Museum of Anthropology, 110–11, 180; participation of: in independence movement, 44–45; in Mexican Revolution, 49–50; state policies toward, 54–55, 57–58, 63, 110, 113, 122–23, 180, 217

indigenous people and populations, Catholic Church relationship with: concientización and enculturación, 96, 98; Heriberto Prado Pereda, according to, 178–80; Liberation Theology and greater outreach, 56, 125–26; Mazatec identity and, 187; songs in Mazatec and, 151

indigenous revival movements: aims and focus of, 14, 104, 106, 208; antecedents of, 24; and birth of Mazatec Indigenous Church, 141–43; Catholic Church's effect on, 56–57; comparisons of, 4–5, 239–44; criticism of leaders, 58; debt of, to bilingual education, 55, 201–2; different approaches to, 191, 199; double audiences and, 28, 92; effect of Mexican indigenous revival movements (*cont.*) Revolution on, 200–201; effects of secondary schooling on, 202; globalization and, 8, 12, 76, 92; impacts of, 10–11, 20–21, 247; language focus of, 106; in Mazatec Sierra, 88–92; in Mexico and Guatemala compared, 202; politics of, 6, 10, 14–15, 16, 27, 29, 79, 174, 242; roles of authors and activists in, 23; tension between local and national and, 33; unanswered questions about, 246. *See also* cultural revival movements; Day of the Dead Song Contest; Iglesia Indígena Mazateca; indigenous-language literary and literacy movements; revival movements

inequality, 13, 48, 247

INI. *See* Instituto Nacional Indigenista

innovation: connection between singing and writing, 9–10; Day of the Dead fiesta and, 122, 267; Day of the Dead Song Contest and, 26–27, 78–79, 106, 113, 118, 122–23, 126, 138–39, 140; Mazatec Indigenous Church and, 183, 187–88, 190–91; poetic use of language, 14–15; revival movements and, 24, 26, 76–77; tradition and, tension between (*see* tradition and innovation, tension between)

Institutional Revolutionary Party (Partido Revolucionario Institucional; PRI), 8–9, 146, 160–62, 252n13

Instituto Nacional de Lenguas Indígenas (National Institute of Indigenous Languages; INALI), 4, 252–53n16

Instituto Nacional Indigenista (National Indigenist Institute; INI), 53–55, 207, 251n3, 260n44; bilingual school program, 55, 201–2, 205; neocolonial aspects of, 217; new view of indigenista programs, 54–55, 204–5; radio station program, 72, 78

John Paul II, Pope, 97, 99, 130, 180. *See also* Catholic Church

Josefino missionaries. *See* Congregación de Misioneros Josefinos

Juchitán Renaissance, 239–44, 276n1

language: politics and, 5, 9–10, 19, 22, 24, 28, 38, 39, 102–3, 127, 193, 198, 202, 208. *See also* agendas and goals *under* indigenous authors and writers *and under* indigenous intellectuals; indigenous-language literary and literacy movements; indigenous languages; Mazatec language; Nahuatl language; Zapotec language

León-Portilla, Miguel (supporter and scholar of Nahuatl literature), 21, 46, 209, 213–14, 231, 254nn32–33, 274n7, 275n16

Lévi-Strauss, Claude, 222–24, 234, 238

Liberation Theology, 2, 5, 76, 95–98, 163; birth of a Mazatec literature and, 92–100; concientización and enculturación and, 96–97; effects of, 25, 56–57; goals of, 106, 125–26, 148, 154; in Heriberto Prado Pereda's songs, 97–98, 154, 156; indigenista policy and, 123; influence of, on Heriberto Prado Pereda, 97–98, 154, 156; Nda Xo revival movements and, 167, 180, 244

limpia (ritual cleansing), 77, 99, 100, 261n3

linguistic and orthographic conventions used in this volume, xii–xv

linguistic diversity, 13–14, 20, 40, 203, 237; bilingual programs and, 207; challenges posed by, for state, 13, 41–43, 58; data on, 4, 13, 252–53n16; indigenismo and, 43, 51; indigenous texts and, 39, 41; in Mixtec language, 4, 81; in Oaxaca, 4, 39, 56, 227, 251n4; Spanish-language dominance and,

40–41, 57–58, 229; Summer Institute of Linguistics on, 252–53n16; textual analysis and, 19, 254n36; in Zapotec language, 4, 252–53n16. *See also* cultural diversity; diversity; ethnic diversity

literacy: autonomous and ideological models of, 16; linguistic anthropology and, 16–17; politics and, 9–10, 28; and singing, 9–10, 17–18, 33, 124–25, 139; sociological approach to, 20; in Spanish language, 4, 14, 68 (table 1.2), 116–17 (table 3.1), 136, 202, 228–29

literacy in indigenous languages: alphabet and orthography development and, xiii, 224–27; alphabetic, 35–36; bilingual texts and, 200; church's efforts regarding, 35–37, 41, 56–57, 125–26, 257n19; dominance of one at expense of others, 39–40; history of, 14, 34–35, 37, 39–41, 43, 46–47, 57–58, 69, 200–201, 257n16; individuals promoting: Heriberto Prado Pereda, 101, 124, 144, 219–20; indigenous authors and intellectuals, 20, 22, 37–39, 193, 199–200, 207, 208–9, 218, 227–28, 247; institutions promoting (Catholic Church, 35–36, 41, 56, 124–25, 257n19; state, 15, 20–21, 56–58, 208, 227–28); pictorial basis of, in Mesoamerican writing, 34, 256n7; politics and, 9–10; programs promoting (ambivalence toward, 58; Day of the Dead Song Contest, 26–27, 106, 124, 219; funding issues, 20; impacts of, 16–17; Summer Institute of Linguistics, 258n29; Uken Ke Uken, 3, 241); resistance to, 208, 218, 224; and revival movements, focus of, 9–10, 14; singing and, 9–10, 17–18, 33, 124–25, 139; success of programs, reasons for, 136–38; Summer Institute of Linguistics and, 258–59n29. *See*

also alphabets; education; indigenous-language literary and literacy movements; orthographies

marginality and marginalization: of indigenous populations, 13, 44, 50, 58–60, 133, 214–15, 222, 258n22; of shamans, 188–89; of the Sierra Mazateca, 33, 40, 59–60, 63, 70

María Sabina Magdalena García (shaman), 18, 81, 82, 135; fame of, 87–90; *Life* magazine article about Wasson and, 83–84; María Sabina studies, 89–90; membership in Catholic Church, 187; recording of, in National Museum of Anthropology, 90, 111; wearing of huipil and, 129–30

marriage, 158–59, 264n24, 269n18. *See also* polygamy

Mary Magdalene (patron saint of Nda Xo), story of, 60–63, 62 (fig. 1.2), 166

masks, during Day of the Dead activities, 112, 129–30, 248, 249 (fig. C.1), 268n22

Mazateca Baja, 64–68, 66 (map 1.1)

Mazatec culture. *See* Mazatec people and culture

Mazatec identity: authenticity and, 63, 74–75, 89, 92, 101, 137, 138–39, 173, 176–77, 186–87, 194; Catholic Church and, 187; conflicts about, 28, 89, 191; Day of the Dead and, 124; Day of the Dead fiesta and, 98, 194–95; Day of the Dead Song Contest and, 137; Heriberto Prado Pereda and, 74, 101–2, 120; Mazatec Indigenous Church and, 142, 173, 175–77, 187, 191, 194; Mazatec language and, 139; Mazatec tradition and, 133; mycotourism and, 76, 78; songs dealing with, 133–34; suspicion of, 218–19, 238; symbols and images of, 24–25, 31, 89, 91–92, 98, 138–39, 176–80, 264n22 (*see also* sym-

Mazatec identity (cont.)
bols under Mazatec people and culture); veladas and, 79; who defines, 57. See also identity; indigenous identity; Mazatec people and culture

Mazatec Indigenous Church. See Iglesia Indígena Mazateca

Mazatec language, 261n1; alphabet as used in this book, xiv (table N.1), xv (table N.2); alphabet development, 217–18; Catholic services and prayers in, 100, 123–26, 149, 151–52, 168; characteristics of, 9–10, 151–54; constructed nature of, 102–3; data on, 4, 64, 65 (table 1.1), 68, 68 (table 1.2), 96, 116–17 (table 3.1), 259n32, 265n28; literacy in, 101, 124–25 (see also literacy in indigenous languages); Mazatec identity and, 42, 139; orthographies for, 124, 126–27, 225; relative scarcity of texts in, 40, 257n14; song initiative of Catholic Church and, 96–98, 106, 123–26, 136, 141–43, 148, 219; songs in (see under songs); tonal and musical character of, xiv–xv, 9, 38, 139; use of, as marker of indigeneity, 42. See also singing in Mazatec language

Mazatec people and culture: as Christians before conquest, 171, 177–78, 270–71n31, 271n36; Committee for the Revival of Mazatec Culture (CIPRECMA) and, 156; Day of Dead Song Contest and, 122–23, 128, 129, 131, 140; depictions of, 30–33, 69, 71–72, 101, 255n2; ethnographic studies on, 71–73; history of, 68–73; impacts of modernization on, 71–73, 133; legendary origins of, 30–31, 255n1; middle class, 264n23; in National Museum of Anthropology, 110–11, 180; in preconquest past, 177–78; symbols of, 25, 91–92, 106, 114,

129–30, 139, 267n17 (see also symbols and images of under Mazatec identity); writings on, 71, 73. See also indigenous people and populations; Mazatec identity; Mazatec people and culture; Sierra Mazateca

Mazatec Research Center (Centro Mazateco de Investigaciones), 213, 216–19, 243

Mesoamerica: diversity of, 34; documents in indigenous languages from, 19, 36–40; Indian problem in, 42–43; languages and writing systems, 34–43, 58–59; literacy in, 39–40, 69; millenarian agrarian culture of, 214–15; orthographies for, 38; preconquest, 13, 34; religions of, 108; valorization of, 108, 258n22

mestizaje, 50, 201. See also Indian problem; indigenismo; state policies and attitudes toward indigenous people

Mexican anthropology: literature of, on political violence in Mexico, 3, 251n2; state policies and, 53–54, 204, 217; and studies of the Sierra Mazateca, 60

Mexican Revolution, 12, 49–51; policies toward indigenous people, 200–201

Mexican War of Independence, 44

Mexico, 6 (map I.1); compared to Guatemala, 202–4; diversity in, 13–14, 42 (see also cultural diversity; diversity; ethnic diversity; linguistic diversity); history of language and literacy in, 34–60; indigenous languages in, 7 (table 1.1), 65 (table 1.1), 252n16, 259n32 (see also indigenous languages); interaction between indigenous people and state (see indigenismo; mestizaje; state policies and attitudes toward indigenous people). See also Deep Mexico; state policies and attitudes

middle class, 77–78, 264n23

migration. *See* out-migration

La misa autóctona (The autochthonous Mass), 98

miscegenation, 50. *See also* mestizaje

Misioneras Indígenas de Nuestra Señora de Guadalupe (Indigenous Missionaries of our Lady of Guadalupe), 163–65, 169, 189

missionaries, 42, 172. *See also* Catholic Church; Misioneras Indígenas; priests; Summer Institute of Linguistics

Mixtec language: development of alphabet for, 205–6, 225–26; diversity within, 4, 81; early writing system, 34–35; literacy in, 257n16 (*see also* literacy in indigenous languages). *See also* indigenous languages

modernity, 63, 73, 79; Day of Dead Song activities and, 26, 110, 130; indigeneity and, 63, 191; tradition and (*see* tradition and modernity); the young and, 130, 133

modernization: anthropology and, 53; conflicts regarding, 73; impacts of, on Mazatec communities, 71–73; Indians as objects of, 40, 52–53; indigenismo and, 53–54; resistance to, 71–72; revival as, 73–74

Molina Cruz, Mario, 1, 241

Montemayor, Carlos (supporter of indigenous writers and literature), 21, 203–4, 209–14, 219, 226–27, 254n34, 274n7, 275n14

Muertos (Día de los Muertos). *See* Day of the Dead fiesta

multiculturalism, 31, 201, 211, 237

Museo Nacional de Antropología (National Museum of Anthropology): Maria Sabina recording at, 90, 111; treatment of indigenous people by, 110–12, 180

mushroom ceremonies. *See* veladas

mushrooms, psychedelic, 83, 263nn15–16; commercialization of, 90–91; debates about, 79, 89, 91–92; and indigeneity and ethnic identity, 89, 91–92, 264n22; influx of outsiders and, 25, 73, 76; in Mazatec Indigenous Church, 27, 171–72, 188–91, 273n8; sense of community and, 172; sexual abstinence and, 82, 188, 263n12; shamans' purposes in using, 190; as symbols of Mazatec society and identity, 25, 89–90. *See also* hippie mycotourism; mycotourism; tourism

music: for Catholic Church, 150–51, 157, 157 (fig. 4.2); in Day of the Dead activities, 80, 112, 119–20, 122, 124, 136, 267n6; Day of the Dead Song Contest and, 26–27, 78–79, 106, 127, 129 (fig. 3.7); ethnic belonging and, 139; importance and ubiquity of, 122; inspired by María Sabina, 90; for Masses, 98–99, 150; Mazatec language and, 9, 18, 139, 149; notation for, 126; recordings of, 26, 106, 122, 135, 156–57, 157 (fig. 4.2), 269n17; superiority of, in Nda Xo, 114; during veladas, 139; in Yalálag and Nda Xo revival movements, 3–5. *See also* Day of the Dead Song Contest; singing; songs

musicians: activities of, during Day of the Dead fiesta, 26, 80, 113, 115 (fig. 3.3), 119, 126, 127, 129 (fig. 3.7); gender of, 267n12; quality of, in Nda Xo, 114

mycotourism: commercialization and, 90; Mazatec identity and, 76, 78–79; in Nda Xo, 190; posthippie, 88–92, 123. *See also* hippie mycotourism; tourism

NAFTA (North American Free Trade Agreement), 5, 9

education and training of, 55–56, 206; founding of indigenous organizations and, 202–5, 226; urban residence of, 5

political agendas of writers and intellectuals, 28, 37, 39, 192–93, 199–200, 204–5, 208, 229–30, 234–35, 247–48

political parties, 8, 72, 73, 147, 162, 260n45, 264n25

politics: conflict and (*see* political *under* conflict); cultural, 199; of education, 52; ethnic, 8–9, 14, 15, 24, 25, 33, 102; of indigeneity, 102–3; Juchitán Renaissance and, 239–42; language and, 5, 9–10, 19, 22, 24, 28, 38, 39, 102–3, 127, 193, 198, 202, 208 (*see also* agendas and goals *under* indigenous authors and writers *and under* indigenous intellectuals); of liberalism, 48; literacy and, 9–10, 28; Mazatec Indigenous Church and, 140, 141–42, 166–67, 174–75, 191–94, 242, 262n7; in Nda Xo, 146–48; in Oaxaca, 8–9, 45, 56; shamanism and, 262n7; songs and, 18, 133–35, 155–56, 229–30; violence and (*see* political *under* violence); writing and, 34–35, 198, 224–25, 234–35. *See also* identity politics; Liberation Theology

politics and revival movements, 14–16, 29, 79; Day of the Dead Song Contest, 9–10, 26–27, 106, 138, 174–75, 242; Juchitán Renaissance, 240, 242; Mazatec Indigenous Church, 27, 174–75, 242; in Yalálag, 6, 242

polygamy, 71, 92–93, 96, 145, 264n24

Prado, Plutarco, 92–93, 195 (fig. 5.3)

Prado Pereda, Heriberto, 92–103; and Alberto Prado Pineda, conflict with, 143, 146, 163, 185–86, 194–96, 235; and Ana, relationship with, 98, 158–60; approach to ethnic revival, 199; and author of this volume, relationship with, 144–46, 275–76n20; autochthonous Mass and, 98; Catholic Church: authority within, 161–62, 169, 177; criticisms of and opposition to, 163–64, 169–70, 177–80, 184–85, 188, 270–71n31, 272n4; involvement with, 93–96, 99–100, 123, 148, 156, 219; Catholic Church and Bishop Ramírez Sánchez, feuds with, 160–62, 177–80; Catholic Church song initiative and, 96–98, 106, 123–26, 136, 141–43, 148–51, 219; criticisms of, 158–60, 174, 187–92, 194, 271n32 (*see also* Iglesia Indígena Mazateca, criticisms of); Day of the Dead Song Contest and, 123–26, 185–86, 192; and Florencio Carrera, disagreement with, 144; funding and support for, 219–20; goals of, 156, 192–93, 235; impacts of, 61, 99–101, 144, 219–20; on indigenous culture, redeeming, 23, 244; indigenous identity and, 74, 101–2, 120; influence of, local vs. national, 23, 199, 219–20, 244; inspiration for others, 101; Liberation Theology's influence on, 97–98, 154, 156; literacy, promoting, 101, 124–25, 144, 219–20; Mary Magdalene legend, recounting of, 60–61; Mazatec Indigenous Church and, 160–65, 167–69, 181–85, 189, 219; mushroom use by, 91–92, 188–91; as organic intellectual, 184; orthography by, 124, 126–27, 144; priesthood, leaving, 158–62, 270n21; songs and writing by, 75, 97–98, 100, 133, 141, 148–58, 149 (fig. 4.1), 198; songs by, for the church, 98, 124–25, 148–58, 269n17; veladas, conducting, 185–86, 189, 272n2. *See also* Iglesia Indígena Mazateca

Prado Pineda, Alberto, 93–96, 143–44, 192–93; approach to ethnic revival,

Prado Pineda, Alberto (*cont.*)
199; and Catholic Church, involvement with, 93, 95–96, 98–99, 143;
Day of the Dead Song Contest and,
123, 126; and Heriberto Prado Pereda,
conflict with, 143, 146, 163, 185–86,
191–96, 235, 272n4; and Heriberto
Prado Pereda, reconciliation with,
194–96; importance of, 61; telling of
Mary Magdalene legend, 61
Prelature of Huautla, 85 (fig. 2.1);
founding of, 96, 264–65n26; and rise
of Catholic Church in the Sierra Mazateca, 25, 76. *See also* Ramírez Sánchez
Presa Miguel Alemán dam, 64, 66 (fig.
1.3), 72
PRI. *See* Partido Revolucionario Institucional
priests: liberationist theology and, 95;
limitations, 100, 125; sexual relationships of, 158–60, 270nn19–20; working with indigenous languages and
peoples, 35–38, 40, 47, 227. *See also*
Catholic Church; Congregación de
Misioneros Josefinos
Protestantism and Protestants: compared with Mazatec Indigenous
Church, 166, 191; evangelization by,
148; literacy and, 16; in Nda Xo, 14;
violence against, 163. *See also* Summer
Institute of Linguistics
psychotropic plants, 9, 80, 83, 262n5,
263n20. *See also* mushrooms
public works. *See* Presa Miguel Alemán
dam; roads in the Sierra Mazateca

radio stations, 72, 78; in Yalálag, 3, 218,
241, 251n3
Ramírez Sánchez, Monsignor Hermenegildo (bishop of Huautla), 93, 97; disputes with Heriberto Prado Pereda,
160–62, 177–80. *See also* Prelature of
Huautla

religion: death and, 107–9; indigenous
texts, 36–37, 47; mushroom use and,
9, 27, 80, 88, 90, 171; song and, 98,
151–53, 156, 230–31. *See also* Catholic
Church; chota chjine; conflict; factions and factionalism; Iglesia Indígena Mazateca; violence
revival movements: assessing, 12, 16,
33, 244; bilingual education and,
56, 201–2; in broad context, 238–39,
243–47; Catholic Church and, 56–57,
92; Committee for the Revival of
Mazatec Culture (CIPRECMA), 156;
comparisons among, 26, 199, 202–3,
225–26, 239–47; criticisms of, 236–
38; elite dominance of, 5; goals of,
11, 199–200; "hothouse" character of,
236–37; indigenous-language documents, importance of, 37–38, 43; and
innovation, 24, 26, 73–74, 76–77;
leaders, criticisms of, 10–12, 58; literacy and, 9–10, 14, 33; local, regional,
and national, tensions among, 28,
175, 220–21, 244–45; as modernization, 73–74; and politics (*see* politics
and revival movements); popular success of, 5, 73–74, 174, 193–94; questions raised by, 177, 246–48; recency
of, 43, 200–201; singing, importance
of, 33, 244; social change, potential
for creating, 174, 191, 196; tradition
and innovation, tension between, 11,
14; urban-centeredness of, 6; varieties of, 14; viability of, 237; in Yalálag, 3–4, 6, 241, 242. *See also* Day of
the Dead Song Contest; Iglesia Indígena Mazateca; indigenous-language
literary and literacy movements;
Juchitán Renaissance; Prado Pereda,
Heriberto
Revolution. *See* Mexican Revolution
roads in the Sierra Mazateca, 72–73,
260n44, 265n29

rosary groups (kjuachikon), 99, 144, 163, 268–69n2

sabio: meaning of word, 271n37. *See also* chota chjine
Seminario Regional del Sureste (SERESURE; Regional Seminary of the Southeast), 95–98
sexual abstinence and taboos, 263n12; mushroom use and, 82, 188, 263n12
shamans. *See* chota chjine
Sierra Mazateca: caves in, exploration of, 32, 255–56nn2–3, 255n5; crops, 72, 260n42; ethnographic research on, 71–73; history of, 68–73; languages in, 64, 68 (table 1.2), 116–17 (table 3.1); marginality of, 33, 40, 59–60, 63, 70; overview of, 64–68; view of, 59 (fig. 1.1). *See also* Huautla; Mazatec identity; Mazatec language; Mazatec people and culture; Nda Xo
SIL. *See* Summer Institute of Linguistics
singing, communication modes and, 17–18
singing in Mazatec language, 150–51; Catholic Church's song initiative and, 25, 76, 123, 126, 136; church support of, 244; Day of the Dead fiesta and, 113, 119, 124; Day of the Dead Song Contest and, 26, 78; to and for the dead, 26, 78, 113, 137, 138; and literacy, 9–10, 17–18, 33, 124–25, 139; in Mazatec Indigenous Church, 170, 179; revival movements and, 4–5, 24, 78–79, 123–24, 233–35, 239, 243–44; tension between tradition and modernity and, 10, 71, 133; in veladas, 1, 25, 79, 81, 139; without a written text, 230–31. *See also* Day of the Dead Song Contest; Mazatec language; music; songs
singing in Mazatec language, importance of, 233–34; to circulation of texts, 17–18; in community building,

9–10; to ethnic belonging, 139; in the lyrics, 148–49; to Mazatec language, 4–5; in mushroom ceremony, 25; to revival efforts, 243–44
Sna Jtz'ibajom (House of the Writer), 275n17
songs: audience for, 235; composition rules, 126–27; Day of the Dead fiesta and, 120; Day of the Dead Song Contest and, 27, 114, 118, 122, 126, 131–32, 135, 136–37; excerpts and titles of, 132–34, 152–56; importance of, 18, 78–79, 135–37; indigenous identity and, 133–34; in indigenous texts, 14, 36; learning, without texts, 230–31; liberationist content of, 97–98; and literacy, 9–10, 17–18, 33, 124–25, 139, 193; in Mazatec language, 28, 78, 96, 106, 122–24, 135–36, 141–42, 200; in Mazatec language, by Heriberto Prado Pereda, 75, 92, 97–98, 99–100, 124–25, 133, 141, 148–58, 149 (fig. 4.1), 168, 182–83, 198, 269n17; monolingual texts of, 229, 230; and politics, 133–35, 155–56, 229–30; promotion of, 156–57; song initiative of Catholic Church, 96–98, 106, 123–26, 141–43; teaching, 125; use of in Mazatec Indigenous Church, 168, 170. *See also* Day of the Dead Song Contest; music; singing
Spanish language: and acculturation, 211; association of, with state and state attitudes, 57–58; institutionalization of, 48; literacy in, 4, 14, 68 (table 1.2), 116–17 (table 3.1), 136, 202, 228–29; predominance of, 14, 21–22, 40–42, 51–52, 57–58, 229, 257n19; as a superior language, 28, 51–52; use of, by indigenous intellectuals and writers, 211–13, 216–17, 228, 232–33, 254–55n41, 275n15. *See also* bilingual *headings*

state policies and attitudes: commitment to ethnic plurality and diversity, 15, 20; on literacy in and use of indigenous languages, 16–17, 20–21, 40–41, 52, 57–58, 216–17, 228–29, 237–38; Mexican anthropology and, 53–54; role of indigenous intellectuals in formulation of, 56

state policies and attitudes toward indigenous people, 12–14, 110, 122–23, 180, 217; ambivalent nature of, 50, 63, 110–11, 113; on assimilation, 13–14, 42, 201, 205; ethnic identity, 58; history of, 42, 48–49, 50–52; integration and acculturation, 200–201; in National Museum of Anthropology, 110–12; reactions to, 43; telesecundarias (televised secondary schools), 202. See also acculturation; assimilation; Indian problem; indigenismo; mestizaje

state policies on education and language: ambivalence in, 57–58; bilingual schools, 20–21, 52, 55–56, 201–2, 205, 207; funding and programs, 20–21; during independence, 51–53; language used, 52; school system expansion, 77–78; shifts in, 33

Summer Institute of Linguistics (SIL): bilingual education and, 55–57; bilingual text development by, 199; on linguistic diversity, 252–53n16; and Mixtec alphabet, 226, 263; orthographies of, xiv, 225, 227, 257n15; Protestant evangelization and, 148; role in national educational policy, 204, 258–59n29

teachers' union, 56, 205, 274n8
telesecundarias (televised secondary schools), 202
Teotitlán-Huautla road, 72–73, 265n29
tourism: cultural products and, 276n4;

Day of the Dead and, 107, 122–23, 266n3; ethnic, 79, 90, 107, 122–23, 266n3; tourism economies and, 77, 243. See also hippie mycotourism; mycotourism

tradition and innovation, tension between: Day of the Dead fiesta and, 113–14, 122; Day of the Dead Song Contest and, 26, 78–79, 106–7, 113–14, 118, 123, 130–31, 140, 143; in Huautla's song contest, 131; Mazatec Indigenous Church and, 177, 187–88; Nda Xo's religious factions and, 143; in revival movements, 11, 14; song, importance of, 18, 78–79; in writing, 14–15

tradition and modernity, tension between, 71, 74–75, 89, 215; authenticity and, 11–12, 176, 191, 193; balanced, through singing in Mazatec, 10, 27, 71, 133–34; difficulty of separating, 92, 112–13; factionalism and, 143; Mazatec strategies for dealing with, 63; in mushroom ceremony, 79; revival and, 73–74

Uken Ke Uken (Center for the Study and Development of the Zapotec Language and Tradition), 216, 218–19; cultural revival in Yalálag and, 3–4, 240–41. See also Zapotec language
umbilical-cord men (chaxo'o), 117–18

Vatican II, 179; effects of, 76, 95, 148; Indian problem and, 56. See also Liberation Theology
Ve'e Tu'un Savi (lit., "House of the Voices of the Rain"; Academy of the Mixtec Language), 205, 225–26
veladas (mushroom ceremonies): described, 80–82; altar used in, 261–62n6; conflicts regarding, 79; different forms of, 261n4; importance of,

79; language use and euphemisms, 81–82; Mazatec culture and, 139; modernizing forces and, 79; mycotourism and, 89; participants in, 262n7; singing in, 1, 25, 78, 79, 81, 124, 139; spirits invoked, 81; taboos, 82, 87, 263n12; use of, by Heriberto Prado Pereda and Mazatec Indigenous Church, 172, 181–82, 184–85, 189, 262n7. *See also* mushrooms

violence: cultural, 29; depictions of, in region, 3, 251n2; drugs and, 8–9; election, 146–47, 260n45; ethnic, 29; political, 1–4, 13, 24, 35, 56, 58, 135, 146–47, 251n2, 260n45; religious, 146, 148, 269n4; and teachers' union strike, 56; in Yalálag, 1–4, 6–8, 23–24, 146; Zapatista uprising, 13. *See also* conflict; factions and factionalism

War of Independence, 44
Wasson, R. Gordon, 80–89
writing: alphabet, importance of, 127, 206; church's interest in, 47; by illiterate Nambikwara, 222–23, 234, 238; impacts of, 16, 253n16; Mesoamerican, 34–38, 40, 58–59, 257n16,

268n23; and oral vs. written communication, 16–17; political nature and power of, 34–35, 223–25, 234–35; revival movements and, 14, 243; singing and songs and, 9–10, 17–18, 123–24, 127. *See also* alphabets; indigenous authors and writers; indigenous literature; literacy; orthography

Yalálag: depictions of, 2, 3; language revival in, 3–5, 240–42, 244; outmigration from, 6; political violence in, 1–4, 6–8, 24, 146; radio station in, 3, 218, 240–41, 251n3; research center in (Uken Ke Uken), 3–4, 216, 218–19, 241

Zapatista Army of National Liberation (Ejército Zapatista de Liberación Nacional; EZLN), 13, 95
Zapotec language: data on, 65 (table 1.1); development of standard orthography and, 225–26; diversity of, 4, 252–53n16; Juchitán Renaissance and, 240; revival in Yalálag and, 3, 240–41; vocabulary in, 257n14; writing system, 34. *See also* Uken Ke Uken

DATE DUE

ANTh 2800	

UPI   PRINTED IN U.S.A.